# Management Development Programme 3

We work with leading authors to develop the strongest educational materials bringing cutting-edge thinking and best learning practice to a global market.

Under a range of well-known imprints, including Financial Times/Prentice Hall, Addison Wesley and Longman, we craft high quality print and electronic publications which help readers to understand and apply their content, whether studying or at work.

Pearson Custom Publishing enables our customers to access a wide and expanding range of market-leading content from world-renowned authors and develop their own tailor-made book. You choose the content that meets your needs and Pearson Custom Publishing produces a high-quality printed book.

To find out more about custom publishing, visit www.pearsoncustom.co.uk

# Management Development Programme 3

Compiled from:

*Developing Essential Study Skills*
Second Edition

by Elaine Payne and Lesley Whittaker

*Research Methods for Business Students*
Fourth Edition

by Mark Saunders, Philip Lewis and
Adrian Thornhill

*Business Ehics and Values:*
*Individual, Corporate and International*
*Perspectives* Second Edition

by Colin Fisher and Alan Lovell

*The Business Student's Handbook:*
*Learning Skills for Study and Employment*
Third Edition

by Sheila Cameron

PEARSON
Custom
Publishing

Pearson Education Limited
Edinburgh Gate
Harlow
Essex CM20 2JE

And associated companies throughout the world

*Visit us on the World Wide Web at:*
www.pearsoned.co.uk

First published 2008

Taken from:

*Developing Essential Study Skills* Second Edition by Elaine Payne and Lesley Whittaker
ISBN 978 0 273 68804 4
Copyright © Prentice Hall Europe 1999
Copyright © Pearson Education Limited 2006

*Research Methods for Business Students* Fourth Edition by Mark Saunders, Philip Lewis and Adrian Thornhill
ISBN 978 0 273 70148 4
Copyright © Pearson Professional Limited 1997
Copyright © Pearson Education Limited 2000, 2003, 2007

*Business Ehics and Values: Individual, Corporate and International Perspectives* Second Edition by Colin Fisher and Alan Lovell
ISBN 978 0 273 69478 6
Copyright © Pearson Education Limited 2003, 2006

*The Business Student's Handbook: Learning Skills for Study and Employment* Third Edition by Sheila Cameron
ISBN 978 0 273 68883 9
Copyright © Sheila Cameron 1999, 2005

ISBN 978 1 84658 811 2

Printed and bound by in Great Britain by Henry Ling Limited at the Dorset Press, Dorchester, DT1 1HD.

# Contents

**Visit the Companion Websites for valuable learning material.**

*Research Methods for Business Students, Fourth edition.*

www.pearsoned.co.uk/saunders

- Multiple choice questions to test your learning.
- Tutoials on Excel, NVivo and SPSS
- Updated research datasets to practice with.
- Updated additional case studies with accompanying questions.
- Smarter Online Searching Guide – how to make the most of the Internet in your research.
- Real life examples of good and bad research.

*The Business Students Handbook, Third Edition.*

www.pearsoned.co.uk/cameron

- Questionnaires such as 'How effective is your time management?'
- Checklists on essay planning, project planning, job application and interviews.
- Advice on topics such as 'How to deconstruct essay and exam questions' and 'How to check your written communication.'

*Business Ethics and Values: Individual, Corporate and International Perspectives, Second Editon.*

www.pearsoned.co.uk/fisherlovell

- Links to relevant sites on the web.
- New case material and discussion and commentary on case studies contained within the book.
- Commentaries on suggested assignment briefs contained within the book.
- Answers to the quick revision tests.
- Updates including group work exercises and postings concerning contemporary issues and how the ethical arguments and theories discussed in the book relate to current 'hot topics'.

# Introduction

Following discussions with students and staff we have decided to compile a text book to support the Management Development Programme in year 3 (MDP3) which will also be a valuable resource for students in their Honours year.

The topics which are covered this year include Social, ethical and sustainability issues in Business and Management, Research Methods and Project Planning/Management.

Social, ethical and sustainability issues are becoming increasingly important in organisations in the twenty first century. At Strathclyde Business School all MDP3 students will have an opportunity to research and evaluate how organisations manage these issues and how their approaches impact on the organisation/market and their employees. Additionally you will be encouraged to reflect on how organisational responses/strategies may significantly affect your career decision making and planning. Where do you want to work when you graduate? The values and culture of an organisation will affect the employee relationship and how you may be expected to be treated.

Research and project planning are important skills to be utilised both in University especially in your Honours year and in employment.

This book will provide you with an accessible resource as an introduction to the relevant literature and research in these areas. It will also provide very useful practical examples and short case studies. This is a compulsory text for MDP3 and will also be a very useful reference for your dissertation completion in Honours year.

**We would like to acknowledge sponsorship of the text by Procter and Gamble and BAE Systems.**

## The Management Development Programme (MDP) Key Skills and Employability

The relationship between higher education and employment is a key topic internationally. The policy context agenda of knowledge economy, global competitiveness and technological change have all impacted on how Universities can best equip their students for employment in the graduate labour market and lifelong learning. The 'key skills' agenda driven by the Dearing Report, 1997 identified the importance in higher education of the following:

- Numeracy

- Information technology

- Communication

- Team working

Additionally the report highlighted how to engage students to 'reflect upon their own learning performance and /or achievements to plan for their personal, educational and career development'. More recently the term employability defined as 'a set of achievements, understandings and personal attributes that make individuals more likely to gain employment and be successful in their chosen occupations' Knight and Yorke (2003, p.5) has been adopted by government, higher education and employers.

Knight and Yorke (2003) describe **Employability** in the curriculum as:

**U** subject understanding

**S** skills, including 'key skill'

**E** efficacy, beliefs, personal qualities

**M**-metacognition, encompassing self awareness

Hawkridge(2005) identifies employability in business education as preparation for continuing professional development (CPD) and lifelong learning rather than first destinations. In the contemporary graduate labour market career progression frequently involves movement from one organisation to another rather than traditional notions of a career with one organisation. Accurate assessment of individual knowledge, skills, personal qualities and self awareness are essential. Additionally students will frequently require to complete CPD in the professions as a compulsory element of learning and development e.g. Chartered Institute of Personnel and Development (CIPD), many Strathclyde students will follow this route on graduation.

The Management Development Programme has reflexively developed by adopting a research informed approach and engaging in action research. Innovation and review is central and we aim to have clear messages linked to the importance of reflection skills, personal development, self assessment and employability.

### Why is the Management Development Programme important?

The Management Development Programme (MDP) has been introduced to develop your business, management and personal skills. In consultation with employers, the programme focuses on those skills which are recognised as important for your personal development in preparation for your future career in a professional or management role working in the public, private or voluntary sector.

Increasingly, organisations are seeking flexible employees who can adapt to change, are effective in operating in multi- disciplinary teams, have confidence in presenting and have well-developed interpersonal skills. The MDP develops these skills across three years, enhances your employability and integrates with your knowledge of business acquired through your selected academic subjects.

The MDP is an integral part of the undergraduate programmes in the Strathclyde Business School. It is a compulsory class which runs in Years 1-3 and students must successfully complete all three years in order to graduate or to progress to study at Honours degree level. The approach to learning is problem-based and students work in project teams.

The programme is one of the largest interdisciplinary programmes within Business Schools in the UK involving all Business School Departments and has been recognised internationally. Students from Harbin University in China have participated in the programme completing MDP2 and 3 in 2006/7 and we welcome this international partnership where students have the opportunity to work together to develop the skills required in the global economy in the 21st century.

## External Recognition

MDP has led the way in developing skills for employability. It is regularly reviewed by external examiners, and contributed to the achievement of both EQUIS and AACSB accreditation for the Strathclyde Business School. We also have partnership arrangements with Edith Cowan University, Perth, Western Australia.

## Programme Details

The **first year** of the Programme developed the breadth of your business knowledge, introduced you to working in teams, presentation skills, project management and planning, analysing and presenting information and statistics.

In **MDP2** you developed knowledge and skills in key areas of management and your interpersonal skills focussing on entrepreneurial and leadership behavioural skills, innovation and creativity approaches, skills for decision-making (including stakeholder analysis and power interest matrix) and negotiation in practice.

In **MDP3** you will be further developing your information and research skills by critically evaluating information sources. You will develop an understanding of the increased significance of the role of social, ethical and sustainability issues and will develop your understanding and skills by working on a team project.

• Social, ethical and sustainability issues in Business and Management

• Business Research Methods

• Project Planning/Management

The latter two  skills will be particularly helpful in preparation for completion of your dissertation in Honours year.

## Teaching and Learning

As in previous years the emphasis is on:

- Active problem based learning

- Students having responsibility for developing their own understanding

- Lecturer/tutor as the facilitator of learning

The course is continuously assessed through group and individual written assignments and presentations.

The class is taught by a cross-departmental team from Strathclyde Business School (SBS) There are usually eight teams in each group, supported by a member of academic staff and a graduate teaching assistant.

## Student Personal Development Planning

The University is committed to enabling all students to develop Student Personal Development Planning. As in previous years you will be expected to reflect on your learning and experiences and will be required to complete a reflective assessment focussing on your skills and specific behaviours developed.

Throughout the year you will be encouraged to record your skills, develop your personal profile and curriculum vitae in preparation for company internships on completion of year 3 and graduate employment.

## Employers and MDP

We work with major employers in all sectors and prizes for the best team projects have been sponsored by Deloitte for MDP1, Procter and Gamble MDP2 and Ernst Young have sponsored prizes for MDP3 .The selected top three teams require to present to the organisations and their senior staff. At a practical level personnel, frequently Strathclyde Graduates participate in MDP group sessions, observe business presentations and give feedback to students. They all value the skills which the students are acquiring as being essential for prospective employees.

## Graduates and MDP

The following statements reflect the views of two recent graduates:

"In modern business graduate employers are looking for far more than graduates with a degree. They are looking for graduates with negotiation and decision making skills, with experience of working in and leading teams on a variety of projects and with excellent IT and presentation skills. The Management Development Programme is what enables business students at Strathclyde to obtain these skills and gain an advantage in the graduate job market. Through a combination of individual and team based assignments MDP students graduate with much more than just a degree."

Kevin Feehan – BA (Hons) Management Science 2007 obtained employment at Procter & Gamble, Information Decision Solutions.

"Having participated in the Management Development Programme for three years, I can look back and reflect on how it has benefited me in numerous occasions. The frequent number of presentations that were compulsory within the course, increased my confidence and also prepared me for job interviews during my final year of study. As the content of the course includes a wide variety of resources, it gives students the ability to develop a wide range of skills that I have found very beneficial in my final year of study and I can predict that these skills will continue to be useful when furthering my career at the end of University."

Larah Henderson BA (Hons) Accounting and Finance 2007 obtained employment at Ernst Young, Graduate Accountant.

## References

Knight, P and Yorke, M (2003). Assessment, Learning and Employability in Higher Education. Maidenhead:Open University Press

Hawkridge, D. (2005) Enhancing Student's Employability: The national scene in Business, Management and Accountancy (Prepared for the higher Education Academy by the Subject Centre for Business, management and Accountancy.(http:// www.business.heacademy.ac.uk/ resources/landt/employ/bmaemployability.pdf

Dearing Report (1997) The National Committee of Inquiry into Higher education http://www.leeds.ac.uk/educol/ncihe/ accessed 21/June/2007

# Semester 1

## Social, Ethical and Sustainability Issues in Organisations

## Introduction to Semester 1:
## Social, Ethical and Sustainability Issues in Organisations

The first semester's goal is to integrate preceding MDP topics by looking at the limits to acceptable business (including enterprises and organisations) behaviour. Rather than evaluating performance just by the bottom line we seek to evaluate Social, Ethical and Sustainability issues in organisations. There is extensive learning and research involved, so group work makes most sense to allow a systematic and thorough evaluation of businesses/ organisations. The organisations you will be assigned will include those from the public and private sectors – in your groups you can compare whether the same criteria are appropriate.

The first session of this semester introduces the range of options for extending business evaluation beyond financial criteria. Business Ethics has a long academic and practical tradition in evaluating the social and ethical issues associated with commercial practice. Learn to distinguish a particular issue (e.g. child labour in football sourcing) from the criteria with which to evaluate (UN rights of the child, responsibility for all supplier sourcing).

The second session of this semester introduces tools to evaluate systematically the range of sources of information which you will encounter on your project. You need to be able to assess the independence and reliability of any information source you may use. Do not simply be persuaded by good argument or spin, examine the source and their agenda.

The third session revisits **Stakeholders** previously covered in MDP2. Stakeholder analysis is one of the key methods of Business Ethics analysis and is introduced in detail in this session. The Fourth session addresses **Organisational Response** enabling each team to make recommendations for the organisation that are in tune with its processes and objectives. In the final session presentations of the team projects from all the organisations studied In the group sessions will be given. This provides an opportunity to learn best practice and to analyse problem solving from your peers.

For this team project there is a weblog provided on the VLE. This enables members of your team to communicate asynchronously (generating all the benefits of social computing) and to share material. You are encouraged to use this as weblogs and social media are increasingly used in organisations.It will be a further skill which you can include in your CV and most importantly it will support effective team working, project management skills as well as allowing more flexible use of your time.

# Topic 1
## Social, Ethical and Sustainability Issues

# Introduction: Social, Ethical and Sustainability Issues in Organisations

## Business Regulation and Ethical Issues

What is ethical? Intuitively obvious, this is not an easy question to answer.

Are ethical issues about the law or do they raise concerns about right and wrong behaviour which whilst perhaps not illegal is still in some sense unacceptable? This is quite an important distinction since what is legal is not necessarily the same as what you might consider as ethically correct. The law reflects social norms and values and regulates our behaviour and that of organisations, including business. Legal regulations cover all areas of business activity- how goods and services are marketed and advertised; how people are employed and treated in the workplace; how financial accounts should be kept; the environmental impact of business activities, the sustainability impact of the organisation's activities and where businesses can operate. The degree to which the law regulates business - what areas it regulates and how much it regulates - is subject to different views and to change over time and across different countries.

So, what regulations apply now may be significantly different from what applied several years ago. Businesses conducting their activities across different countries may find significant differences in regulations.

But whilst the law may be some guide to what a society at a particular point in time regards as acceptable or unacceptable behaviour, it does not cover the whole range of actions. Sometimes the law is quite general and perhaps establishes basic rules and standards of behaviour however frequently these rules are not implemented.

This still leaves a lot to individual and corporate discretion and judgement. There is nothing to prevent organisations from going well beyond what is legally required. Should the basic principle of business operations be to minimise the harmful effects of those operations, or to positively seek to promote good outcomes? As long as businesses operate within the prevailing laws is it's only responsibility to satisfy the interests of its owners? Do we judge good business performance only by reference to profits and economic efficiency, or do we expect other outcomes too? Auditing is growing from a financial audit to a social and environmental audit.

Whilst some of these questions raise fairly general issues about what are the purposes of business activities in our society, we can begin thinking about these issues from our own personal experiences, values and reflections. What do you think is correct behaviour and actions in business situations? Sometimes there may be no obvious right or wrong answer, sometimes it is clearer.

Your team will be assigned an organisation: you should read the following chapter and divide up the task of reading and researching material on the organisation so you can focus on being able to advise the organisation what to do about the highlighted ethical, social or sustainability issue.

Fisher and Lovell's Chapter 1 gives clear definitions of corporate social, ethical and environmental performance. The stakeholder theory section is valuable but you will come back to this in session 3. Fisher & Lovell's Chapter 9 expands information on sustainability and will give you a good basis to a systematic approach to their cases. It has an important section on the **triple bottom line**: make sure you read understand and use the concept.

# Perspectives on business ethics and values

## Learning outcomes

Having read this chapter and completed its associated activities, readers should be able to:

- Identify the good, tragic, comic, satirical and farcical elements in the way in which people and organisations deal with matters of ethics and morality.

- Explain the basic features of stakeholder theory.

- Evaluate the business case for business ethics and the validity of its claims.

- Give an account of the various arguments about the moral status of business, organisations and management.

## Stories and business ethics

The study of business ethics begins with stories. Families and societies have always used stories to illustrate and reinforce their sense of values, justice and fairness. And so it is in business and organisations. There are the stories often found in organisational glossy newsletters of good deeds done by staff volunteering to work among disadvantaged groups and the benefits that the organisation has brought to the communities it works within. Then there are the more gossipy stories that are told, and half told, as episodes are interrupted by work or authority figures, that tell of jealousies and spites, corruption and abuse, lying and distortion.

Czarniawska (2004: 21) pointed out that there are four types of dramatic story in the European classical tradition – romances, tragedies, comedies and satires, each of which has its characteristic figure of speech. Each of them can represent different kinds of business ethics issues.

## Figures of speech

DEFINITIONS

### Metaphor

Makes comparisons by referring to one thing as a different thing. So calling all the employees in an organisation 'assets' is a metaphor. If you said of a chief executive officer 'she is a Branson among business leaders', this would be a use of metaphor and a means of making a hero of her. It could also be a kind of paralipsis in which attention is drawn to something – that the CEO is a woman and Branson a man – while pretending to pass over it. As a form of irony this paralipsis could be taken as a criticism of the CEO.

### Metonymy

Uses an attribute of something to represent the thing itself. Chairpersons sit in a chair when they hold a board meeting. The chair is their attribute, so they become known as chairs. In tragedy a single attribute can undermine a person's integrity; a good person is often brought low because of a part of their behaviour or character.

### Synecdoche

Uses a part of something to represent the whole. Business people wear suits and so that particular aspect of them comes to represent them and their role. Others refer to them as suits, as in 'are the suits arriving today to check us out?'. Suits are also a means by which business people present a good image of themselves. In comedy synecdoche points out the comic pretensions between ambition and reality. The smartness of the clothes can emphasise the vacuity of the wearer.

### Irony

Speaking or writing in such a way as to imply the opposite of what is being said. Often used to imply mockery or jest. It is therefore the basis of much satire.

Romances are based on the quest of a single individual to achieve some noble goal that is only achievable because human beings have an innate, if sometimes well disguised, goodness. The Quaker heroes of the past such as Joseph Rowntree who built model factories and villages for model workers, or more modern heroes such as Anita Roddick who sought, against the odds, to make selling beauty products a beautiful process, are good examples. Such heroes become metaphors for their particular brand of ethical management.

Tragedies tell of people who try to behave well but who, by challenging fate, come to personal grief. The stories of whistleblowers who reveal corporate wrong-doing but in so doing lose their families, their homes and their livelihoods are a good example. Tragedy is based on metonymy, as in the film *The China Syndrome* (Bridges, 1979) in which Jack Lemmon plays an engineer in a malfunctioning nuclear power station who is the only person to be troubled by a vibration felt as a test procedure was conducted. The vibration is a metonym for the potential cataclysm that is waiting to happen.

Comedies are stories about how human imperfections and weaknesses make the achievement of a happy ending difficult. The ways in which companies that are foreign to a new country they have begun to operate in often get their attempts to integrate wrong are a strong source of comedy. The western business-men, for it is mostly men who would do this, who ignorantly offend their Arab business partners by putting their feet up on their desk after concluding a deal in an attempt to show that the formal business is over and everyone can relax, and so revealing the soles of their shoes, have a degree of comic potential. The dirty soles of the shoes act as a synecdoche, a part of the businessman, which stands for the unwholesomeness of the whole man.

Satires work ironically. By contrasting people's behaviour with their words, or by defining the context in which the words are said, it is made clear that people meant the opposite of what they said. When corporations are accused of not taking care of

- customers, by not closing the doors on the *Herald of Free Enterprise* (*see* p. 328), or

- employees, as in the Bhopal incident in which 20,000 people were killed or harmed by a chemical leak from an American owned chemical works in the city (*see* p. 469) (the leak could have been prevented if procedures, management and maintenance had been rigorous), or

- the environment when the oil companies are accused of despoiling the Niger Delta (*see* p. 475),

organisations often reply by saying that the objects and subjects they have damaged are in fact their top priority. They thereby make themselves the object of satire. People then take such claims as ironies. In the film *Super Size Me*, Morgan Spurlock (2004) tested McDonald's claim that its food is not intrinsically unhealthy by living for a month on its products. Of course such a diet made him an unhealthier person (that is irony).

> **Connexion point**
>
> The ethical issues raised by the film *Super Size Me* are discussed in Case study 2.23 (pp. 91–2).

There is, in business ethics as in life generally, a narrow point of balance

- between romance and satire

- and between tragedy and comedy.

These tensions are the narrative dynamic behind business ethics issues. The heroes of romances can easily become the subject of satirists' scorn. In the struggles between heroes and villains the heroes can overreach themselves and believe they really do have magical powers, in some cases literally. In 1999 in the oil producing delta region of Nigeria members of a cult known as the *Egbesu* began a violent campaign against, as they saw it, the despoliation of their homeland by the oil companies (Ibeanu, 2000: 28). It was believed that the charms they wore made them impervious to bullets. The heroes may then become ridiculous and the villains begin to look more benign. Tragedy can, uncomfortably, have comic elements. As Marx (1963: 1) pointed out, history repeats itself, 'first time as tragedy, second time as farce'. Just as commonly comedy can descend into tragedy. The difference between an organisational comedy of incompetence and a tragedy may be no more than the operation of chance. If luck remains with the organisation then we can all laugh at its bumbling, but if luck runs out the story can become tragic, for some. In December 2004 (Harding, 2004) a Delhi school-boy from one of the elite schools, doubtless anxious to show off his new mobile phone with built-in camera, used it to take a video clip of his girlfriend providing him with oral sex. Unfortunately for him within a few days the video clip was on sale on Bazee.com, the Indian version of eBay, and indeed owned by eBay. The company took the item off the website as soon as they became aware of it but nevertheless an uproar ensued in India and a mildly, if in poor taste, comic event turned serious. The boy was taken to juvenile court and expelled from school. Avnish Bajaj, the CEO of Bazee.com and a US citizen, was arrested and thrown into the notoriously overcrowded Tihar gaol. For three people at least tragedy was a tale of prosperity, for a time, that ended in wretchedness. The matter was debated in the Indian parliament and the BJP party denounced the incident as the result of American 'interference'. The American government in its turn was taking a serious interest in Mr Bajaj's imprisonment. Condoleeza Rice, the soon to be American Secretary of State, was reported to be furious at the humiliating treatment meted out to an American citizen. The Indian software industry association called for Bajaj's immediate release.

It would appear that the issues and problems that form the subject of business ethics can appear in different forms, sometimes as romances, sometimes as tragedies, sometimes as comedies and sometimes as satires. It follows that stories are a good mechanism through which business issues can be studied and understood. If we can understand how the plots of these stories can lead to either good or bad outcomes we can develop an intuitive knowledge of how to encourage more happy endings than bad ones. Or at least the stories might palliate, or help us come to terms with, the dilemmas we face (Kirk, 1974: 83).

| Case study 1.1 | **The *Hindustan Times*, Monday 29 November 2004** |
| --- | --- |

I am writing this part of the chapter in a hotel room in New Delhi, India. A copy of the newspaper has been slid under the door to my room. A number of its stories show the range of business ethics issues. The lead story is a *romance*: a hero entrepreneur and philanthropist, in this case Sir Richard Branson, is reported to have attended a party in New Delhi at which 4.5 crore (a crore is ten million) rupees had been raised for a children's educational charity. 'The creation of wealth is fine. But businesses need to pay back to the society in a number of ways', said Branson. The next day it was also reported that the Government of India might allow Branson to buy a personal stakeholding in a domestic airline, even though the rules on foreign direct investment would not allow Virgin Atlantic, his own airline, to buy such a stake.

*Tragedy* was represented by a story that a former High Court judge was likely to be charged with receiving bribes and manipulating judgments to favour the person who had paid the bribes. It is a tragedy because a judge appointed to uphold the law, and who no doubt originally intended to do so, allowed himself to give way to external pressures and so destroyed his reputation.

A story that *satirises* itself is that twenty years after the Bhopal incident American scientists are proposing to recreate the gas leak under controlled experimental conditions. In particular they want to discover whether deadly chemicals such as carbon monoxide and hydrogen cyanide were released as well as other chemicals in the original leak. The irony is that it seems that, when only Indian citizens had been harmed and killed by such a leak, the Americans had been content to ignore the possibility that these two gases were involved. But, by 2004, when it was possible that American citizens might be subject to such a chemical attack by terrorists, then it was suddenly important to know the truth. The *Hindustan Times* reported that Indian scientists already know the truth, from their clinical studies of the victims, that these gases had been released. The report was also *ironic* (in the technically incorrect meaning of its being an unhappy coincidence) in that on the same day *BBC World* reported that an Amnesty International report had condemned both Union Carbide and the Government of India for not ensuring that past and continuing victims of the incident were properly compensated.

*Comedy* was represented by a report on how fog was, as in the past, causing airline passengers at Delhi's airport to become unhappy because it delayed their flights. This should not have been the case, but the proposed anti-fog landing system had not been implemented as planned. The *Hindustan Times* poked gentle fun at the airport's management who had proposed to avert passengers' displeasure by providing a gallery of pictures of Delhi's ancient monuments to entertain and inform them. This apparent dedication to customer service when their solution was comically inadequate ('but what if, after viewing all the sketches, the foreign tourist still has time to kill before he could catch his flight?') indicates a bureaucratic disdain for customers. (When I arrived at the airport the sketches were found to be few in number, unexceptionable and unviewed by anyone but me.)

There is one other story in the paper that suggests a fifth dramaturgical genre is needed – *farce*. The characteristic figure of speech of farce is hyperbole or excessive exaggeration to the point of silliness. Laloo Prasad Yadav is a notorious figure in Indian politics (Dalrymple, 1999: 10–25). When he was imprisoned for corruption, while Chief Minister of the State of Bihar, he was replaced in the post by his wife. When the new national government was formed in 2004, Laloo was made Minister for Railways. The paper reported he was in a bitter spat with a ministerial colleague, Ram Vilas Paswan, who had been railway minister in the 1990s. Both wanted the railway job: allegedly it is a rich source of kickbacks. In a speech to a political rally in Patna, the capital of Bihar, Laloo said 'Lots of money was made in that time [when Paswan had the portfolio]. I will make all those files that show corruption public. He is now in deep trouble.' The farcical elements are that the pot is calling the kettle black; that a government department has had files proving alleged corruption for ten years but has not taken any action; and that a politician has claimed the moral high ground by the unethical practice of revealing confidential official papers in an attempt to gain a political advantage over a rival.

## Activity 1.1

Choose a daily newspaper or weekly magazine and identify as many stories in it as you can that deal with an aspect of business ethics. Read each story in turn and decide whether it has elements of romance, tragedy, comedy, satire or farce within it.

One of the long running business ethics stories concerns a moral decision that faces profit seeking organisations. It is a conflict between public duty and self-interest. Should they only exercise their social and environmental duty if it coincides with the financial interests of their owners? In this case they will be heroes in the stories of the owners but villains in the tales of everyone else. Or should they prevent the organisation harming society and the environment, beyond the demands of the law if necessary, even if it will hurt the owners' immediate interests? In this case their ascription to the roles of hero and villain in the stories will be reversed.

Following the Asian tsunami in 2004 many Australian companies made donations to the appeal fund. Stephen Matthews, a spokesman for the Australian Shareholders' Association, criticised the companies, saying that they had no approval for their philanthropy. He implied that companies should not make such donations without expecting something in return.

Boards of directors don't have a mandate from their shareholders to spend money in this way. [ ] There is a role for business to make a contribution in relation to the tsunami, particularly those businesses who have activities up in South Asia. [ ] Where their businesses are dependent on those sorts of markets there could possibly be a benefit for shareholders in them making donations to relief.

(ABC News Online, 2005a)

Later the Association's chief executive tried to limit the damage of the ensuing public disdain by clarifying the statement. The ASA was not opposed to companies making donations because 'it is in everyone's interests that the affected communities and economies recover as soon as possible'. Companies should however disclose to the shareholders the extent of their giving (ABC News Online, 2005b). Some commentators thought, uncharitably, that the rapid donations of cash and goods to the affected regions by some large companies was an attempt to have their brands associated with humanitarian good works (Simpson, 2005).

The story illustrates the question of whether a business case should be proven for acting in a socially and environmentally responsible way before it is necessary for an organisation to adopt the role. This is dealt with in the next section.

## The business case for business ethics

Should private, profit seeking organisations behave in a socially responsible and moral way, beyond the requirement of the law, because it is the right thing to do or because it pays them to do so? This might be seen as a moral dilemma; indeed in many ways it is the central issue in business ethics. If it is true that corporations that behave in a responsible and ethical manner do in fact make better returns for their owners than do those organisations that cut corners or behave badly, then the philosophical question of whether organisations ought to behave well is redundant. Do the well-behaved hero companies actually achieve their reward and despite their tribulations win through and enter into a successful long-term relationship with their investors and reach the top of the corporate financial performance league tables, or, in folk story terms, marry the princess and ascend the throne (Czarniawska, 2004: 78)? Several people have sought to answer this question.

There are sensible arguments that can be used to suggest that corporate bad behaviour can be bad for business. It would be logical to assume that a business that was seen to behave badly would lose the esteem and respect of its customers and so lose sales and profitability. A poor image would counteract the large sums that companies spend on developing their brands. Conversely if a company is associated with good behaviour, using renewable resources, not employing child labour in its factories in developing countries and providing good training and development opportunities for its staff, it should be good for sales. This is one of the motivations behind the fair trade movement.

## The fair trade labels

The fair trade (or alternative trade) movement began in the late 1960s as an attempt to give small and independent farmers and artisans in the third world a better return on their efforts. As such, small-scale producers did not have access to first world markets and as they were many and the purchasers were relatively few they received only a small percentage of the price that their products eventually sold for in the developed countries. This situation was made worse because much of the processing and packaging of the basic products, which adds much of the value to a product, was done in the developed countries and not in the countries of origin. At this stage large NGOs such as Oxfam started selling third world products in their shops at terms that were beneficial to the producers. They also encouraged the setting up of cooperatives and credit unions and local processing plants that all added value to the producers.

In the 1980s a Dutch priest who worked, with the support of a church-based NGO, alongside small-scale Mexican coffee producers realised that there could be a marketing advantage in selling the coffee under a 'fair trade' label. The development of such labels meant that fair trade products were not just available in charity and ethnic shops but in mainstream supermarkets and retailers (IRC, 1998). Some research conducted in Belgium (de Pelsmacker *et al.*, 2003) distinguished four groups of coffee buyers:

- Fair trade lovers – 10% of sample who are willing to, and sometimes do, pay the premium price for fair trade coffee.
- Fair trade likers – 40% of the sample who were well disposed to fair trade products and could be encouraged to buy them by effective marketing.
- The flavour lovers (24%) and the brand lovers (25%) were not influenced at all by the fair trade label.

As the range of fair trade label goods increased to include tea, honey, chocolate and clothes, the researchers concluded a large potential and profitable market would open up for such products.

In 2002, the Co-op in the UK announced that it would make all its own brand chocolate products fair trade. This was seen as a major change that would enable it to charge a premium for its products and achieve a good level of sales. Cadbury Schweppes (2004) take a different view and point out that only 0.1 per cent of worldwide cocoa sales goes through the fair trade system which pays the producers a social premium on top of the going market price. One reason why this is so is that fair trade works best through producer cooperatives and there are still very few of these in the producing countries. They also argue that if most producers were paid a social premium this would result in a cocoa glut that would eventually lead to a collapse in cocoa prices. Their approach is to work directly with producers and provide programmes that can improve the farmers' efficiency and the value they can add to their crops.

However, these benefits of good behaviour are not guaranteed. A brand untarnished by a poor reputation is most likely to affect the buying decisions of consumers, but less likely to influence business purchasers, who will rate a good deal before a sense of social responsibility. Bad corporate behaviour will only diminish reputation, and good behaviour boost it, if it becomes known. Many companies of course have public relations departments and corporate communications departments that are designed to prevent harm being done to their brands and reputation. Making bad behaviour known requires that wrongdoing is seen and made public and that there are ways of measuring good behaviour so that credit can be given to those corporations that score well on some kind of ethics scale. There are measures of social, ethical and environmental performance, but these are mostly designed to meet the needs of the ethical investment community rather than consumers and purchasers.

## Measures of corporate social, ethical and environmental performance    **DEFINITIONS**

There are a number of standard measures, or more properly indices, that are available for assessing the social and environmental performance of corporations.

**FTSE4Good:** This index is calculated from a number of factors that cover the three areas of:

- working towards environmental sustainability
- developing positive relationships with stakeholders
- upholding and supporting Universal Human Rights.

The factors are sometimes but not always measurable things. Judgements about whether a company is complying with international ethical standards are also included. A panel of experts meets to decide whether companies' performance entitles them to be included in the index.

- **Dow Jones Sustainability Indices**
  The DJSI tracks the financial performance of companies that have committed to long-term sustainability. It is a guide for those who wish to invest in companies that are ethical or that profess a philosophy of sustainability.
- **SERM rating:** This stands for Socio-Ethical Risk Management. It is designed to assess the degree to which companies are actively managing the risk they would be subject to in areas such as abuse of human rights, engagement in bribery and corruption, degradation of the physical environment, negative impacts of new technology, and many other factors.
- **Ethical Investment Research Service (EIRIS)**
  EIRIS carries out research on companies worldwide and provides information to those who wish to invest ethically. It is a charity set up in 1983 by churches and charities who did not wish to invest any of their money in ethically dubious organisations.

The indices are all professionally designed and include checks and tests to ensure that the judgements they contain are valid; this however makes starker the fact that they are judgements rather than measures of social and environmental outcomes.

Webley and More (2003) have sought an empirical answer to the question whether business ethics pays. They faced the technical problem that there is no single and definitive measure of ethical performance. They happily admit that they have had to choose proxy or surrogate measures that are indicative of whether a company is behaving in an ethical and environmentally protective way but not conclusive proof that they are. (Commentators have taken a satirical delight in the fact that Enron was often commended for its ethics policies.) Webley and More chose the following measures:

- Whether a company has a published code of ethics that has been revised within the past five years.

- Companies' SERM rating.

- Companies' ratings on *Management Today*'s 'Britain's Most Admired Companies' survey that is carried out by Michael Brown of Nottingham Business School.

Their analysis showed that companies that had a code of ethics had better ratings on both SERM and the 'Most Admired Company' league tables than those that did not. Therefore, to keep things simple all they needed to check was whether companies with a code performed better financially than those that did not.

It might have been anticipated that when Webley and More (2003) came to consider how to measure the financial performance of companies the task would be easier, but there is a wide range of possible measures. They chose:

- Market value added (MVA) – This is the difference between what investors have put into a company over a number of years and what they would get from it if they sold it at current prices.

- Economic value added (EVA) – This is the amount by which investors' current income from the company is greater or less than the return they would get if they had invested the money in something else of equal risk. In other words it is the opportunity cost of placing money in a particular company.

- Price earnings ratio (P/E ratio) – This is the market value of a share in a company divided by the shareholders' earnings.

- Return on capital employed (ROCE) – This is a measure of the return that the capital invested in a company makes for its owners.

The results of their research into the relationship between a company's ethical standing and its financial performance is shown graphically in Figures 1.1, 1.2, 1.3 and 1.4.

Two cohorts, each a little short of 50, of large companies were chosen from the FTSE 350 for the study. The results indicate, *prima facie*, that companies within the sample that have a code of ethics (and hence score better on the SERM ratings and the 'Most Admired Company' tables than those who do not) also achieved a better MVA and EVA over the four-year period 1997–2000. Between 1997 and 2000 companies without a code had a greater ROCE than those that did, but by 2001 the position had reversed and those with a code performed better. The P/E ratio was more stable over the period of the study for companies with codes than it was for companies without. There is a strong indication that having a code, managing the non-financial risks of a company (as measured by SERM), and being rated by one's peers as a reputable company are associated with higher and more stable financial returns.

1.  **Is having an ethical code consistent with the generation of more added value?**

*Chart 1:    Average Economic Value Added (EVA) by year for major UK quoted companies*

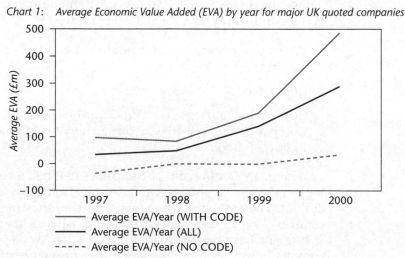

**Figure 1.1** Does business ethics pay: does it add value?

*Source*: Webley and More 2003

**2.  Is having an ethical code consistent with enhanced market value?**

*Chart 2:   Average Market Value Added (MVA) by year for major UK quoted companies*

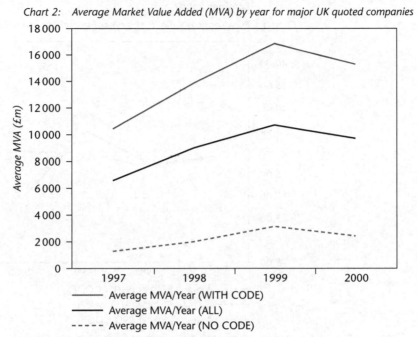

**Figure 1.2** Does business ethics pay: does it enhance market value?

*Source*: Webley and More 2003

**3.  Is having an ethical code consistent with an improved return on capital?**

*Chart 3:   Return on Capital Employed (ROCE) by year for forty-two major UK quoted companies*

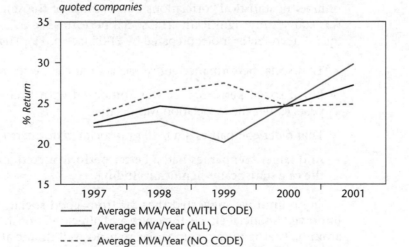

**Figure 1.3** Does business ethics pay? Does It Improve return on capital?

*Source*: Webley and More 2003

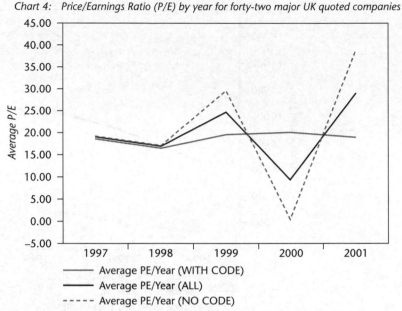

4. **Is having an ethical code consistent with a more stable Price/ Earnings Ratio?**

*Chart 4:   Price/Earnings Ratio (P/E) by year for forty-two major UK quoted companies*

——— Average PE/Year (WITH CODE)
——— Average PE/Year (ALL)
- - - - Average PE/Year (NO CODE)

**Figure 1.4** Does business ethics pay: does it improve the P/E ratio?

*Source*: Webley and More 2003

However, this is not necessarily proof of the business case for business ethics. A statistical association does not mean that the adoption of ethical business practices is the cause of financial improvement. It could be the result of some different, and as yet unconsidered, factor.

Moore (2001) conducted a study of the financial and social performance of eight retail supermarket companies in the UK over a three-year period. He found a number of statistical correlations but, because of the small sample size, only one was statistically significant. The social performance of companies was measured by a sixteen-factor index prepared by EIRIS (see p. 11). The correlations were:

- That social performance got worse as financial performance improved.

- But if social performance was compared with financial performance three years earlier the association was positive.

- That older companies did better on social performance than younger ones.

- And larger companies had a better performance than smaller ones; this was the one statistically significant finding.

These findings suggested that far from good social performance leading to improved financial effects the cause and effect relationship worked the other way around. That is to say, companies that do well financially find themselves with some money that they can spend on good works and improving their social and environmental performance. It takes time to implement these policies, hence the three-year time lag. The Institute of Business Ethics research could not be expected to identify this time lag because their key indicator, the presence or absence of a code of ethics, is not one that would fluctuate year on year, but the index that Moore used would. This direction of causation, from financial to social, is known as the Available Funding Hypothesis (Preston and O'Bannon, 1997). However, giving attention to these new social projects causes companies to take their eye off their main objective, making money. This distraction of attention, plus the fact that these projects can cost a lot of money, causes the financial performance to worsen. In response the companies would return their efforts to financial performance. Commentators within the supermarket industry anticipated that as Sainsbury and Marks and Spencer were performing less well financially their social and environmental efforts would decrease.

These same commentators also speculated whether social and environmental performance might be related to the social class of its customers (Moore and Robson, 2002: 27). Tesco and Morrisons served lower socio-economic groups (on average) who were less likely to be conscious of social and environmental concerns and so there would be no advantage to the company in taking a lead on such matters. The higher status groups who shopped in Sainsbury and Marks and Spencer were more likely to be careful conservers of the natural and social world and might begin to boycott the stores if they were not seen to be sufficiently interested in sustainability.

In a later study (Moore and Robson, 2002: 28–9) a more detailed statistical analysis was carried out between the 16 social performance indicators (instead of the aggregate result as in the first study) and an extended range of financial performance indicators. Negative, and statistically significant, correlations were found between growth in turnover and the league table rank of:

- the mission statements compared with those of others;
- the proportion of women managers compared with other companies;
- the environmental policy;
- the environmental management systems;
- the social performance total.

In summary, this suggests that as companies increase their turnover their social performance worsens, or the obverse, that as their social performance improves their turnover declines. This adds support to the second part of the cycle suggested above, that social performance endangers financial performance, but does not of itself support the first part of the cycle, that companies flush with profits are inclined to spend some of the profits on social performance, even though as we saw above this is precisely what Sir Richard Branson says they should do. These results of course only apply to one industry – retailing and supermarkets.

There is an association between good social performance or ethical business practices and good financial returns. It is not clear, however, that it is the good social performance that increases profits. It may be the other way around. This conclusion is not necessarily dismissive of all concerns with business ethics from an organisational point of view. There may not be a financial case for actively and purposefully seeking to make a better social and environmental world. This does not mean that companies should not seek to minimise the potential costs of being found to have acted unethically or improperly. If a company or government department is sued for damages arising from its negligence or its bad behaviour, the costs of the case and the costs of the award can be very high. It may be wise to seek to avoid those actions and practices that could cost dearly; this management function is known as risk management. If a company can be shown though its risk management procedures to have taken every reasonable precaution to identify a potential malpractice or problem and to do what is reasonable to prevent it, then, even if the problem or malpractice happens and damages others, the company will have a legal defence.

So, unfortunately (fortunately for text book writers for if otherwise we would have to close the book at this point), it is not clear that there is a business case for business ethics, although on the defensive principle there is one for managing the financial risk of unethical or improper organisational behaviour. It is necessary to turn to other ways of deciding whether companies and organisations should act ethically and responsibly. This comes down to the question of whose interests companies and organisations should exist to serve. Should they serve the interests of society generally? Or should they serve the interest of particular groups within society? If so, which groups should they serve? It is the answer to these questions we now turn to.

## Stakeholder theory

### Connexion point

Stakeholder theory is a key and recurring theme in this book because ethics is concerned with the harm or good done to people. As different people may be affected differently by the same action then it is important to take these various impacts, some good and some bad, into account. The simplest way of doing this is to use stakeholder theory. The theory will be used and discussed in Chapters 2, 8 and 12.

If we continue with the storytelling metaphor it is important to know who the characters in the story are. In terms of business ethics stakeholder theory provides an answer. It might be more accurate to say stakeholder theories since there are various interpretations of what the term means. They share one attribute, however, which is that for any organisation there are a number of definable groups who have an interest, or a stake, in the actions of that organisation. There is more disagreement about what constitutes a stake. It is clear that the shareholders, the owners if it has any, have a legitimate stake in an organisation. So do its employees. At the other extreme the 'phishers', who try to gain fraudulently customers' bank account details through fake, spammed emails, obviously have an interest in the banks they attack; but it is hardly a legitimate one. So the issue is three-fold:

- What responsibilities or duties, if any, does an organisation owe to its stakeholders? The fact that a stakeholder group may have a legitimate interest does not, of itself, mean that the organisation owes anything to it. At one extreme of the spectrum of possibilities an organisation may be obliged to do what its stakeholder group requires. If that group is society at large, as it expresses its will through legislation, then the organisation should submit to it. At a level below this stakeholders could have the right to participate in the organisation's decision making. This might be accepted in the case of employees who are expected to commit to the organisation's objectives and decisions. It might not be right in the case of a judicial system's obligations to those being tried in a court. A lesser obligation might be a stakeholder group's right to be consulted before major decisions are taken. If not this, then at least the group might expect the organisation to give them an account of why they did what they did. At the other extreme the organisation might owe the stakeholder group nothing.

- How should an organisation decide between its obligations to two or more stakeholders if they demand incompatible things from an organisation? What criteria should the organisation use when deciding which stakeholder group's wishes it should prioritise? Often in public service organisations the criterion used is a crude one that the group that shouts loudest is the one listened to. There is an interesting issue involved here. What if a constituency is not a person or persons but a thing or collection of things or ideas (these are known in sociological jargon as actants) such as rivers, nature reserves, spirituality? How can these things be given a voice? An easy answer might be that their voices are those of the lobby groups that support each particular cause. There is a problem here though. Some research indicates that, when lobby groups cause too much irritation to the organisation they are trying to influence, their reward is not to be listened to but to be shut out. If the cause of environmentalism is voiced by overaggressive agitation then an organisation might close its ears to the problem when the cause itself is more deserving than its supporters' actions.

- What legitimate interests justify a group of people being regarded as a stakeholder in an organisation? A criterion often proposed is that stakeholders are any group that is affected by an organisation's actions. But this would give a commercial company's competitors a voice in its activities because their performance would be affected by the organisation's performance, which would not seem fair.

The subject matter of business ethics is an attempt to answer these three questions. In the next section we consider four different answers, or perspectives, that are given in modern western, capitalist societies.

## Business and organisational ethics

In this section four broad theories of the firm, and the assumptions and implications of these perspectives for prioritising the various stakeholders' needs and for the exercise of moral agency, are considered.

**DEFINITION**

**Moral agency** within organisations is the ability of individuals to exercise moral judgement *and behaviour* in an autonomous fashion, unfettered by fear for their employment and/or promotional prospects.

Organisation, in the sense we are using the term here, refers to any configuration of people and other resources that has been created to coordinate a series of work activities, with a view to achieving stated outcomes, or objectives. At this stage we make no distinction as to whether an organisation is profit seeking, located within the public sector, or is a charitable/voluntary organisation. The issues we discuss are largely, but not exclusively, sector-blind, although the intensity with which the issues are experienced may vary significantly between organisational types.

As will become evident as we progress through the chapters, the location of an organisation within the public sector does not make it immune from economic constraints, even economic objectives. Likewise, there is a growing body of opinion that argues forcibly that profit seeking organisations should be more accountable to a body of citizens that extends considerably beyond shareholder-defined boundaries. While the distinctions between private sector and public sector, profit seeking and non-profit seeking, have become less clear-cut in recent years, we do not argue that all organisations are equivalent, and that the sector of the economy in which an organisation is located is irrelevant to understanding the ethical, political, economic and social constraints within which it operates. Penalties or sanctions for poor performance are possibly more obvious and severe in the profit seeking sectors, but it can be argued that the multiplicity and complexity of the objectives managers are required to achieve in certain parts of the public sector make managing in such a context a far more demanding and ethically fraught role. Although each perspective assumes that organisational relationships are largely, if not exclusively, mediated by market dynamics, the extent to which 'the market' is relied upon as an exclusive mediating mechanism does vary.

Table 1.1 presents the schema of four perspectives to highlight the point that different imperatives and assumptions may underpin market-based, capitalist economies.

Within the four categories in Table 1.1 different assumptions are made about the relationships between:

- organisations and the state;
- organisations and their employees;
- organisations and their various stakeholder groups (i.e. beyond the employee group).

Table 1.1 Theories of the firm and their ethical implications

| Issue | Classical liberal economic | Pluralist (A and B) | Corporatist | Critical |
|---|---|---|---|---|
| Status of the category | 1. For its advocates it is the only game in town, not merely the most efficient, but the most ethically justifiable. 2. For others the 'pure' model must be tempered by interventions to (a) minimise problems of short-termism, or (b) correct power imbalances. 3. Whilst for others the neo-classical model is a corrupting chimera that acts as a cover to camouflage the interests of the powerful. | 1. Type A. A stakeholder perspective is advocated in corporate decision making, with key interest groups physically represented on decision-making boards. 2. Type B. Individual managers weigh the full ethical and social considerations of their actions and decisions. Stakeholder groups would not necessarily be present at decisions. | Refers to the business relationships in countries such as Germany, Sweden and Japan (although the approaches adopted are not identical). The interests of employee groups, non-equity finance, and sometimes the state, are represented alongside the interests of equity shareholders, on senior decision-making boards. | Ranging from descriptive theories of the firm that portray how organisations appear to be (or are), rather than how they should be, to critical theorists who portray an organisational world beholden to the demands of capitalism or managerialism (these terms are not the same). Both approaches reflect messier and more ethically fraught worlds than tend to be suggested in the other three categories. |
| Number of objectives recognised | One – meeting the demands of equity shareholders. | Multiple, reflecting an array of stakeholder perspectives, although the actual mechanics remain problematic. | A mix of equity shareholder, employee and non-equity finance perspectives, although long-term economic interests of the firm are dominant. | Multiple, reflected by the various coalitions and power groups within an organisation, particularly economic interests. |
| Status of financial targets | Regarded as the organisation's primary or sole objective, because they will reflect the efficiency with which resources are being employed. | Important, but not to the domination of all other considerations. Ethical as well as multiple stakeholder perspectives are weighed in decision making. | Important, but greater attention paid to the medium to longer-term financial implications of decisions than appears to be the general case in Anglo-American corporations. | In highly competitive markets, or during periods of crisis, likely to be the dominant, although not the exclusive, organisational consideration. During periods of relative stability, other considerations will gain in significance and could dominate. |
| Significance of ethical behaviour (both individual and corporate) | Defined by national and international laws, which are seen as both the minimum and maximum of required ethicality. The neo-classical model is argued to be the only approach that allows the primacy of individual interests to be reflected in economic and social coordination. | At the heart of the debate for those who bemoan what is seen as the exclusive, or overly dominant, economic orientation of organisations. | No clear evidence that ethical considerations feature more strongly in corporate decision making, although the lack of an exclusive shareholder perspective might offer greater potential for a broader societal perspective. | An important, but variable, element in defining the reputation of the organisation. Will be shaped by the power of influential individuals and groups within and external to the organisation. |

Table 1.1 Continued

| Issue | Classical liberal economic | Pluralist (A and B) | Corporatist | Critical |
|---|---|---|---|---|
| Role of managers | Portrayed as functionalist, technicist and value neutral. | Type A. Managers come into direct contact with specific sectional interest groups, which should affect decision making. Type B. Individual managers are required to have internalised a societal ethic into their decision making. | The structures of organisations reflect a formal involvement of employee representatives, non-equity financiers, and sometimes state representatives, alongside shareholder interests, on corporate decision-making boards. | Complex, with competing and sometimes/often mutually exclusive interests and demands being required to be satisfied, including the managers' own agendas. |
| Status of employees | Resources to be used by the organisation in its quest to satisfy shareholder interests. | Employees represent an important interest/stakeholder group within the organisation, although economic considerations are not ignored. | Employee representation is guaranteed on some of the organisation's senior decision-making boards, e.g. supervisory boards in Germany. | Operating within a capitalist mode of production, employee interests will vary between organisations, depending upon the power of individuals and groups of individuals. |
| Values | Competition seen as the bulwark against power imbalances. Efficient resource allocation facilitated by profit-maximising behaviour. | Inherently societal in orientation, but the views of those actually making decisions will be important. | Those of the shareholders, employees, non-equity financiers (possibly the state) are likely to dominate. | A complex interaction of multiple individual and corporate values. Critical theorists would single out the values that underpin capitalism. |
| The possibilities for moral agency in organisations | The individual as consumer, as chooser, is the personification of moral agency, but the individual as moral agent when selling his or her labour is troublesome. The atomisation of society, which appears to be an inevitability of this form of individualism, is seen by many as leading to feelings of alienation and anomie. | Type A. Multiple perspectives offer heightened possibilities, but medium to long-term organisational survival will dominate concerns. Type B. Very similar to Type A, but the confidence and integrity of individual managers becomes a critical issue. | With employee representatives on the supervisory boards of organisations (as in Germany), the possibilities again appear stronger than with the liberal-economic perspective. However, economic considerations will remain dominant. | Empirical evidence indicates that the suppression of moral agency might be more than minor and isolated aberrations in an otherwise satisfactory state of organisational affairs. Critical theorists would see these problems as an inevitable consequence of the demands of capitalism. |

We need to understand these perspectives because they are helpful in appreciating the potential for, and the constraints we each face in exercising, moral agency within business contexts.

With the exception of the 'classical-liberal' category, each of the categories is an amalgam of a variety of theories, ideas and practices. The corporatist approach is referred to by Crouch and Marquand (1993) as 'Rhenish'. This latter term refers to a particular (German) approach to a market-based, capitalist-oriented economy, although the writers broaden their consideration beyond Germany to take in a wider group of non-Anglo-American market-based economies. Whilst the German approach displays important differences from the Japanese and the Swedish approaches, they have, for our purposes, been grouped together as representing a more corporatist approach, where the overt involvement of the state and employees in the running of individual organisations is an accepted practice.

This is not to say that the Anglo-American approach to economic development can be simply categorised within the 'classical-liberal-economic' group. Notwithstanding the rhetoric of various UK and US governments, state involvement has been required and forthcoming on many occasions in these two countries, often to overcome what is known as market failure. However, the common belief in the UK and America leans towards the need for less, or minimal, government interference in business, and a drive towards market dynamics to facilitate organisational coordination.

The following is a closer examination of the four theories of the firm and their implications for moral behaviour within, and of, organisations.

## The classical-liberal-economic approach

A classical-liberal theory of the firm places the organisation within an economic system that is made up of a myriad of interconnecting but legally separate parts, and where relationships between these many parts are defined in terms of free exchange. Money acts as the facilitator of exchange, thus performing the role of the oil that greases the economic system's wheels. The 'invisible hand' that Adam Smith spoke of is the force that drives the mass of individual transactions. The argument is that, with no individual person or company able to affect price, the resulting transactions, and the prices that draw both suppliers and customers into the marketplace, reflect people's wishes. This is the strength of the claims for the ethicality of 'free' markets as espoused by writers such as Milton Friedman, Friedrick von Hayek and Ayn Rand. Individual choice, free of government coercion, is seen as the only ethical influence in shaping economic and social development.

Rand is probably the least well known of the three advocates of free markets mentioned above, although her advocacy appears to have been influential. She is reputed to be a favourite writer of Alan Greenspan, the Chairman of the American Federal Reserve at the time of writing. Friedman's arguments in defence of a business world free of government or social obligations beyond those defined in law are considered in more depth in Chapter 8, so a little more time will be given here to consider some of the key thoughts of Rand on the subject of markets as the basis of economic and social coordination.

Ayn Rand was born in Russia in 1905, but she emigrated to America when she was twenty-one, nine years after the 1917 Bolshevik uprising in Russia and four years after the civil war that followed the uprising. On arriving in America, Rand took a variety of low-paid, menial jobs. She is quoted as saying: 'I had a difficult struggle, earning my living at odd jobs, until I could make a financial success of my writing. No one helped me, nor did I think at any time that it was anyone's duty to help me.' Rand depicted man as 'a heroic being, with his own happiness as the moral purpose of his life, with productive achievement as his noblest activity, and reason as his only attribute'.

Such snippets of historical context are helpful in understanding some of the factors that might explain an individual's philosophical position on key issues. Randianism (the term used by followers of Rand) rejects government in anything other than its minimalist form, i.e. that which can be justified to protect individual rights, such as the police, the law courts and national defence forces. All other functions can and should be operated by 'the people', preferably via market mediation, and paid for (or not) by choice.

| Case study 1.2 | **Biography and philosophy** |
|---|---|

Bauman (1994) contrasts two philosophers, Knud Logstrup and Leon Shestov. Logstrup lived a tranquil and civilised life in Copenhagen. He wrote of human nature, 'It is characteristic of human life that we mutually trust each other ... Only because of some special circumstance do we ever distrust a stranger in advance ... initially we believe one another's word; initially we trust one another' (Bauman, 1994: 1). Shestov, on the other hand, experienced great persecution during his life, under both the tsarist and anti-tsarist regimes and as a consequence had a far more pessimistic view of human nature, portraying the individual as one who is vulnerable and must at all times be ready to be betrayed. 'In each of our neighbours we fear a wolf ... we are so poor, so weak, so easily ruined and destroyed! How can we help being afraid?' (Bauman, 1994: 2).

Rand is credited with developing the philosophical position that is known as objectivism. Objectivism has three key elements:

1. '*Reason* is man's [*sic*] only means of knowledge', i.e. the facts of reality are only knowable through a process of objective reason that begins with sensory perception and follows the laws of logic. Objectivism rejects the existence of a God, because it lacks (to date) empirical support. However, in America, some of the most strident advocates of free markets come from politically powerful religious groups.

2. *Rational self-interest* is the objective moral code. Objectivism rejects altruism (i.e. the greatest good is service to others) as an unhelpful and illogical human attribute. Individuals are required to pursue their own happiness, so long as it does not negatively affect anyone else's. This is compatible with negative

freedom, one of Isaiah Berlin's two forms of freedom. It relates to a 'freedom from' approach that grants people a right to be free from interference by others, including, and in particular, government.

3. *Laissez-faire capitalism* is the objective social system. It is important to recognise that laissez-faire capitalism is referred to by its advocates as a social system, and not just an economic system. This is an important issue and one towards which critics of the approach feel unified in their opposition, although such opponents have differing views on how to respond. Some would argue for an overthrow of the capitalist ethic and practice, whilst others would retain a market-based framework, but define boundaries of relevance and ethical justification for markets. The latter is exemplified by writers such as Walzer (1983) and is discussed below.

---

**DEFINITION**

**Laissez-faire** means unrestricted. So laissez-faire capitalism refers to a preparedness to let markets 'sort themselves out', even during periods of disequilibrium and apparent malfunctioning. The belief is that a 'market' will self-correct in time (a natural law, or Darwinist view within economics). Self-correction rather than external intervention is deemed infinitely preferable in the long run for all concerned.

---

The attachment of modern-day libertarian-economists to a myopic focus upon competition can be criticised for ignoring two other significant elements of economic systems, which are:

- *Command* (the extent to which power, coercion and hierarchy affect economic relationships), and

- *Change* (the way that capitalism effects change and is itself affected by change).

These three central elements of capitalism, competition, command and change have ethical and moral implications and it is argued here that they are interconnected, not subject to easy and simplistic separation. However, the classical-liberal perspective eschews these arguments and presents a schema in which the operations of the firm, both those within the firm and how it interacts with its external environment, are treated as if they are value neutral.

Within the simple competitive model of economic behaviour managers are expected to behave in ways that reflect what is known as economic rationality. This normative theory is open to challenge in terms of its descriptive rigour, hence the existence of alternative theories of the firm. Supporters of the neo-classical-economic perspective would accept that actual practice is likely to be variable around the preferred norm, but it is argued that economic rationality is the goal towards which organisations should strive. They argue that those organisations that get closest to the normative position will prosper, with competitors having to respond in a similar fashion, or wither on the economic vine.

## The corporatist approach

The corporatist approach does not deny the primacy of competitive market forces, but an exclusive equity shareholder perspective is eschewed in favour of a broader-based set of perspectives in some of the organisation's decision making. These additional perspectives are those of employee representatives, debt financiers, and in some cases state interests. This broadening of the decision-making base is claimed, and appears to offer, a longer-term view to certain aspects of corporate decision making. For Crouch and Marquand (1993: 3).

> The system as a whole trades-off losses in the short-term efficiency on which the Anglo-American tradition focuses against gains in consensual adaptation and social peace. It owes its extraordinary success to its capacity to make that trade-off ... In a high skilled – or would be high skilled – economy, consensual adaptation and social peace are public goods, for which it is worth paying a price in strict allocative efficiency.

The sphere of inclusion reflected in this approach goes beyond the exclusivity of the shareholder orientation of the classical-liberal perspective espoused by most Anglo-American corporations. Evidence suggests that the corporatist-type approach has avoided, or minimised, many of the worst effects of short-term economic 'adjustments' in world trade that have been experienced since about 1960. This is not to say that countries such as Germany, Sweden and Japan (examples of the corporatist perspective) can be immune from significant movements in world economic activity, but it is argued that significant economic lurches have been avoided in these countries, thus minimising significant rises in unemployment levels, with the attendant impacts upon social cohesion. The significant economic downturns experienced by a number of Asian economies in the late 1990s, including Japan, were associated more with structural factors within these economies than with inherent weaknesses in Japan's more corporatist approach to market coordination.

Whether the corporatist approach is preferred by some because it offers a greater likelihood of economic, and thus political, stability, with the greater apparent value placed upon the interests of individual citizens/employees merely an ancillary benefit, or whether the rationale for employing this approach is reversed (i.e. the ethics of the corporatist approach are argued to be the main reasons for its adoption), is not critical for our discussion. What is relevant is that both the 'classical-liberal-economic' and the 'corporatist' approaches can cite ethical justifications for their superiority as economic and social systems. The former can do so because of the primacy attaching to the notion of individual choice, the latter because of its attachment to social cohesion and the desire to avoid, or minimise, what might be deemed unnecessary social disruption and distress to individual lives during periods of economic correction or recession.

## The pluralist perspectives

There are two main pluralist perspectives. The first (referred to as Type A pluralism) sees broad stakeholder interests being represented (as far as this is possible) by elected or appointed members of corporate boards. This is a development of the corporatist perspective, but with the stakeholder groups being drawn more widely. The corporatist approach is evident in the countries cited above on a reasonable scale, whereas the two pluralist perspectives currently exist as arguments and debates, rather than as practice. Companies such as The Body Shop are very much the exceptions that prove the rule.

In Type A pluralism stakeholder groups are required to do more than argue their particular, vested-interest, case. They are expected to be representative of societal interests. Clearly the extent to which the latter are adequately represented will depend upon the composition of the stakeholder groups. Thus, as compared with the classical-libertarian-economic perspective, where the unconscious forces of individual decisions are deemed to give expression to society's preferences, within Type A pluralism societal preferences are given voice by the presence (or not) of stakeholder groups on company boards or committees.

The second pluralist perspective (referred to as Type B pluralism) does not dispute the possibility of stakeholder groups being physically represented within corporate decision-making processes, but this is neither a prerequisite, nor part of the basic arguments. This second variant of pluralism sees economic rationality being moderated by concerns for, and recognition of, wider social implications of corporate decisions, with these factors being weighed by individual decision makers. Type B perspectives can be presented as a continuum, with writers such as Casson (1991) at one pole, and Maclagan (1998), Maclagan and Snell (1992) and Snell (1993) at the other.

The perspective argued by writers such as Casson is that competition via market-based economies is the preferred economic system, but that reliance upon unadulterated economic rationality as the sole explanation of individual behaviour is both naïve and unhelpful. For the discipline of economics to retain relevance Casson argued that it must recognise behaviours that are explained by drives other than, or in addition to, economic rationality.

> These professional prejudices must be overcome if economics is to handle cultural factors successfully. They are the main reasons why, in spite of its technical advantages ... economics has not contributed more to the analysis of social issues.
>
> (Casson, 1991: 21–2)

Classical-libertarian economics retains a view of human behaviour that sociologists would describe as 'under-socialised' (i.e. unrepresentative of the complexity and variability of actual human behaviour). Type B pluralism argues for a recognition of the realities of everyday market conditions, but also a more socialised set of assumptions of human behaviour. Whilst a market-based economy is seen as the foundation upon which organisational coordination takes place, structural issues and problems within markets are recognised, e.g. power imbalances between competitors; information asymmetry between producers and customers; and the capricious nature of (the owners of) capital. Greater responsibility, ethicality and humanity are required of corporate decision makers.

In a similar vein, but with less of Casson's implicit instrumentalism, Etzioni (1988) employed a moral justification for an overt recognition of broader perspectives beyond short-term profit motives. In the following quotation Etzioni used the term 'deontological'. This is an important word in any consideration of business ethics and it is considered in more depth in Chapter 3. However, we offer a brief definition of the term here to allow you to understand the argument that Etzioni was making.

> **DEFINITION**
>
> A **deontological** approach to moral behaviour is one that believes that moral reasoning and action should be guided by universal principles that hold irrespective of the context in which an ethical dilemma might exist.

Instead of assuming that the economy is basically competitive, and hence that economic actors (mainly firms) are basically subject to 'the market' possessing no power over it (monopolies are regarded as exceptions and aberrations), the deontological 'I & We' paradigm evolved here assumes that power differences among the actors are congenital, are built into the structure, and deeply affect their relationships. We shall see that power differentials are gained both by applying economic power (the power that some actors have over others, directly, within the economy) and by exercising political power (the power that some actors have over others, indirectly, by guiding the government to intervene on their behalf within the economy). These fundamentally different assumptions make up what is referred to here as the I & We paradigm (one of the larger possible set of deontological paradigms). The term [I & We] highlights the assumption that individuals act within a social context, that this context is not reducible to individual acts, and most significantly, that the social context is not necessarily wholly imposed. Instead the social context is, to a significant extent, perceived as a legitimate and integral part of one's existence, a whole of which the individuals are constituent elements ... The deontological paradigm evolved here assumes that people have at least some significant involvement in the community (neo-classicists would say 'surrender of sovereignty'), a sense of shared identity, and commitment to values, a sense that 'We are members of one another'.

(Etzioni, 1988: 5)

Etzioni continued:

The issues explored here range way beyond the technical, conceptual matters of what constitutes a workable theory of decision-making in economic and other matters. At issue is human nature: How wise are we, and what is the role of morality, emotions and social bonds in our personal and collective behaviour.

(Etzioni, 1988: xii)

Progressing along the continuum, past Etzioni's position, one moves towards those who argue for Type B pluralism on the grounds that a broader ethic than that required by classical-liberal economics is desirable, even essential, on the grounds that society as a whole needs organisational decision-makers who understand and can exercise moral judgement in complex situations (Maclagan, 1996,

1998; and Snell, 1993). These writers see management practice as essentially a moral practice, set in a complex and challenging arena (business organisations), for individual moral development.

Thus, our pluralist continuum moves from writers, such as Casson, who argued for theories of decision making to recognise actual human behaviour and instincts in order to make economic theorising more relevant and realistic, to the arguments of writers such Maclagan and Snell, who justify the inclusion of the moral dimensions within business decision making on the grounds of the ethical demands of society as a whole.

## The critical perspective

The critical perspective is composed of many different theories about human and collective behaviour, including the politics of organisations (Simon, 1952, 1953 and 1955); expectation theory (Vroom, 1964); the use of ambiguity and hypocrisy as managerial tools (Brunsson, 1986 and 1989); the theory of coalitions (Cyert and March, 1992); the exploitation of people (Marcuse, 1991); the benefits that people seek at work and the importance of these benefits (Maslow, 1987); power and identity in organisations (Knights and Willmott, 1999); and the range of strategic resources that individual managers draw upon to allow them to cope with managerial life (Watson, 1994). This is far from an exhaustive list, but it gives a flavour of the range of research and theories that have been developed to explain actual behaviour within organisations. What these works share is a picture of organisational life that is far more complex and messy than classical-liberal economics would prefer to work with. The behavioural and critical theories are not normative theories (i.e. theories of how things should be, such as the classical-libertarian-economics perspective), but what are referred to as descriptive theories, i.e. theories of how things actually appear to be. However, behavioural theorists and critical theorists do vary in terms of the intentions of their respective arguments.

Behavioural theories are amoral in their stance in that, unlike the liberal-economic, corporatist and pluralist perspectives, they do not put forward a preferred ethical foundation for their theorising. They might however highlight examples of laudable, contentious or downright immoral behaviour. They do so by acting as organisational windows through which we can observe the ways in which employees at all levels in organisations appear to react, and behave, when faced with ethically complex situations. For example, you become aware that a friend and work colleague, who you know has a very difficult financial situation at home, unlawfully takes a small toy (a company product) home to one of their children. Such situations could involve divided loyalties between either colleagues or concepts, where the ethics of a situation are not clear-cut or neat; or where moral agency is compromised by power imbalances that jeopardise future employment and promotional prospects.

Critical theorists, however, have an avowed commitment to societal change, for the emancipation of employees from the shackles of capitalism. However, critical theorists make different analyses (for example, Foucaudian perspectives, e.g. McKinley and Starkey, 1998, and neo-Marxist perspectives, e.g. Alvesson and

Willmott, 1996) and there is no consensus on the preferred replacement for market-based societies. Habermas (whose ideas are discussed in Chapter 3) does, however, outline the necessary conditions for a societally acceptable economic set of relationships to develop.

## Boundaries of jurisdiction or spheres of justice

The fear of market-based relationships as the bedrock upon which all societal and interpersonal relationships are based is articulated by a number of writers. Walzer (1983), for example, wrote:

> One can conceive of the market as a sphere without boundaries, an unzoned city – for money is insidious, and market relations are expansive. A radically laissez-faire economy would be like a totalitarian state, invading every other sphere, dominating every other distributive process. It would transform every social good into a commodity. This is market imperialism.

> (Walzer, 1983: 119–20)

Taking his cue from Walzer, Keats (1993) argued that:

> It is as if their [liberal economists'] theoretical energy has been so fully utilised in demonstrating the virtues of the market that little has been left to deal with the arguably prior question of what it is that defines the nature – and hence limits – of that 'economic' domain with respect to which market and state are seen as the chief rival contenders.

> (Keats, 1993: 7)

As a way of handling this problem Walzer argued that societal life should be seen as a series of spheres, which contain and constrain differing elements of societal existence. One of these spheres is the economic, in which markets are recognised as the most effective mediating mechanism, and competition the most defensible form of organisational coordination. Whilst markets, contract and competition are seen as appropriate mediating elements, their relevance is largely constrained within this sphere. Within the spheres representing non-economic interpersonal relationships we find notions of trust, care, welfare, sharing, friendship, leisure and possibly even altruism (although this is not highlighted by Walzer). There is some similarity between Walzer and the earlier work of the German philosopher Hegel (1770–1831) who also used the notion of spheres to conceptualise the social world (Singer, 1983). Hegel spoke of the spheres of state, family and civil society, and to these Walzer adds the economic as worthy of consideration.

McMylor comments upon the development of market-based capitalism from feudal societies. He presented the development from non-market societies as a process whereby the economic moved from being enmeshed 'within other domi-nating frameworks' to a situation in market societies when:

the economy, with a capital 'E' is no longer so embedded. The market means that there is in some sense, a differentiation of economic activity into a separate institutional sphere, no longer regulated by norms that have their origin elsewhere. The individual economic agent is free then to pursue economic self-interest, without 'non-economic' hindrance.

(McMylor, 1994: 100)

From a moral perspective one of the problems with dividing the human world into separate spheres is that it might suggest the spheres are independent to the point of allowing differing forms of behaviour to prevail within each. Behaviour might be accepted, or at least tolerated, in one sphere that would not be acceptable in another. It has been argued that this is a recognition that people sometimes act (or feel they need to act), when in 'business mode', in ways that they would not employ within their private, domestic lives. Walzer recognised this and argued that the spheres should not be seen as totally autonomous and independent. Rather, he portrayed a dynamic set of relationships between the spheres in which shifts between spheres of particular facets of societal life do happen, and that a sphere's scope and importance may wax and wane. Boundary conflict thus becomes endemic:

The principles appropriate to the different spheres are not harmonious with one another, nor are the patterns of conduct and feeling they generate. Welfare systems and markets, offices and families, schools and states are run on different principles: so they should be.

(Walzer, 1983: 318)

However, Walzer went on to say that 'the principles must fit within a single culture' (1983: 318). This is highly problematic, unless the single culture is one that recognises difference, a multiplicity of cultures. Within such a complexity of perspectives, the notion of wisdom becomes an important mediating factor, but this has to be an active wisdom, i.e. it is always in a state of emerging through dialogue and debate. Within this perspective the dynamic of change is recognised, is debated and matures through processes that are demanding but which, it must be stressed, are subject to 'social capture' by active groups and voices if participation is shirked by the general polity.

### DEFINITION

**Social capture** is a term used to describe a mechanism, e.g. a committee, a regulatory body or a political process, which is established to oversee a particular facet of social life, but which becomes dominated by, or heavily influenced by, the very sectional interests the mechanism was intended to monitor or control. The original intentions behind the creation of the mechanism thus become at best neutralised, and at worst subverted.

To minimise the risk of social capture and other such distorting influences within political, economic and social systems requires an active citizenry, prepared to be interested in, even involved in, micro- and macro-level debates about equity and justice – the very morality of life's various spheres. Hegel spoke of the dialectic, the processes of debate and argument that are required to surface and (possibly) resolve differences of view and contradictions. The dialectical approach is to be found in the teachings of Socrates, certainly in the way that Plato presents the work of his master. Billig (1996) makes a plea for a resurgence of the practice of rhetoric, not in the pejorative sense in which the term tends to be viewed in contemporary society, but as a return to an engagement in debate and argument, for these are the mechanisms and processes by which civilised societies develop and progress.

## Defining the boundaries of the economic sphere

One of the principal virtues of competitive markets, as the mechanisms by which business and social interaction is mediated, is that the 'invisible hand' of the market is amoral, i.e. value neutral. Although some may suffer as a result of market-based outcomes, through unemployment or loss of capital, the outcomes are not intended from the start. They are simply the unintended consequences of the multitude of transactions that comprise a free market. Sir Keith Joseph, a notable politician of the 1970s and 1980s and an architect of the political period and philosophy referred to as Thatcherism, was a devotee of Hayek and Friedman. As Heelas and Morris (1992: 19) observed:

> Policies designed to effect more equal distribution of resources, Joseph claims, are not only coercive and threaten individual liberty but are counter-productive and give rise to a series of negative consequences (economic, psychological, moral and political) ... Liberty is primarily to be exercised by the self-interested consumer in the market place, including the political, educational and medical 'markets'.

Plant (1992), taking up the theme of markets being the most appropriate mediating mechanism for medical services, explored the possibilities for a free market in body parts (human organs), as well as the justification for a market-based ethos replacing a service ethic in non-voluntary, public service organisations. With regard to a market for human body parts Plant (1992: 91) observed:

> On a strictly capitalist view of market principles, it is very difficult to see why there should not be such a market. The scope for a market is clearly quite wide. There could be a market in blood and blood products; in kidneys; in sperm; in renting out a uterus for surrogate pregnancy; and so forth.

Plant argued that, from a market perspective, at least three principles would favour a market in these areas:

1. There is a clear demand.

2. The current donor system is failing to meet demand.

3. Ownership of the human organs is clear and would not be undertaken by the donor if it were not in their personal interest.

Despite strong advocacy for such markets, broad public support was (and appears to continue to be) lacking. Plant argued that this reluctance reflected a boundary being drawn by society, with human organs currently residing outside the boundary that defines the limits of market application.

Titmuss (1970), in a seminal work on the marketisation/commercialisation of blood donor services, observed, when responding to arguments that blood should be seen as a commodity and thus private blood banks should be introduced to improve the productivity of the blood giving process:

> In essence, these writers,[ ] are making an economic case against a monopoly of altruism in blood and other human tissues. They wish to set people free from the conscience of obligation. Although their arguments are couched in the language of price elasticity and profit maximisation they have far-reaching implications for human values and all 'social service' institutions ... The moral issues that are raised extend beyond theories of pricing and the operations of the marketplace.
>
> (Titmuss, 1970: 159)

Titmuss worried about the wider implications of commercialising the blood donor service in the UK. If the altruism that, it is argued, is reflected in the voluntary and unpaid giving of blood is replaced by a commercial relationship, what, asked Titmuss, fills the space that used to be occupied by the sense of community inherent within the existing system?

> There is nothing permanent about the expression of reciprocity. If the bonds of community giving are broken the result is not a state of value neutralism. The vacuum is likely to be filled by hostility and social conflict, a consequence discussed in another context ... the myth of maximising growth can supplant the growth of social relations.
>
> (Titmuss, 1970: 199)

Titmuss discussed four economic and financial criteria, excluding the much wider and unquantifiable social, ethical and philosophical aspects to concentrate upon those aspects that economists (the focus of his criticism) would recognise. These were:

1. Economic efficiency.

2. Administrative efficiency.

3. Price – the cost per unit to the patient.

4. Purity, potency and safety – or quality per unit.

On all four criteria the commercialised blood market fails. However, paradoxically ... the more commercialised a blood distribution system becomes (and hence more wasteful, inefficient and dangerous) the more will the GNP be inflated. In part, ... this is the consequence of statistically 'transferring' an unpaid service (voluntary blood donors, voluntary workers in the service, unpaid time) with much lower external costs to a monetary and measurable paid activity involving costlier externalities.

(Titmuss, 1970: 205)

The discussion so far in this chapter has laid out the arguments for claiming that the market system is:

- The only defensible economic and social system for protecting the freedom of the individual to exercise personal choice, which allows the development of economic and societal relationships that are free from government coercion and intervention. This is the liberal-economic perspective.

- Something that is preferable to alternative economic systems, but which needs to be carefully watched and, if necessary, modified from time to time to ensure that the economic system is compatible with broader societal aims. This incorporates the corporatist and pluralist perspectives.

- An intrinsically corrupting system that pits human beings against each other, with only an elite few dictating the life chances of the many. This is the critical perspective.

The argument has been about the place of ethics in business life, and the place of business in the ethics of life.

## Descriptive, normative and reflective approaches

Two ways of discussing ethical matters, normatively and descriptively, are often proposed. Normative discussion is concerned with rules and principles that ought to govern our thoughts and actions. Normative arguments are focused in particular on how such prescriptive claims can be shown to be legitimate or valid. Descriptive discussion focuses on how things *are* rather than how they should be. A descriptive approach to ethics would give an account of the values and ethics of particular groups and try to explain how they have emerged. It would analyse value systems to look for norms and the tensions between them. The word normative is troublesome in a subject, such as business ethics, that spans both philosophy and sociology. In sociology, normative refers to that which is the norm within a group or society. The term is both descriptive – the norms are those of a particular group, and also normative – they define right and wrong within that group. In philosophy normative and descriptive are seen as opposing terms. In this book normative will be used in its philosophical sense.

Many business ethics textbooks take a normative approach. They identify ethical difficulties in business, rehearse the arguments about what should be done about them and then present a resolution or a set of principles. Rather than taking a normative and prescriptive approach this textbook takes a descriptive and analytical approach. It attempts to describe how people in organisations interpret and respond to ethical issues at work. It does not propose solutions to the many ethical dilemmas and problems that face managers and organisations. However, by explaining how others think about and respond to ethical matters, and by providing you with the appropriate tools for thinking, we hope the book will enable you to analyse the issues and to come to your own conclusions.

The intention of the book brings us to a third way of talking about business ethics, the reflective and reflexive approach. Reflection implies careful consideration of ethical issues. Reflexive means to turn back on one's own mind and to consider one's own values and personality. This textbook therefore tries to help you examine your own positions and thoughts. This can be done in part by reflecting on the material in this book and other publications. But this is vicarious learning, piggy-backing on the experiences of others. Reflexive learning occurs when you use your values to challenge your actions and your experiences to challenge your values.

## Reflections

One of our concerns in this book is the possibility of the existence of moral agency and ethical practice within organisations. Integrity is one of the concepts that would form part of any definition of business ethics. The importance of integrity within organisational life in general, and executive decision making in particular, is discussed by Srivastva and Cooperrider (1988), although they stress that the way forward is not easily mapped. It can only be navigated and negotiated through dialogue, reflection, learning, tolerance and wisdom.

> Executive integrity is dialogical. Executive integrity is more than the presence of morality or the appropriation of values; integrity involves the process of seeing or creating values. Whereas ethical moralism is blindly obedient, integrity represents the 'insightful assent' to the construction of human values. In this sense, organisation is not viewed as a closed, determined structure but is seen as in a perpetual state of becoming. Dialogue is the transformation of mere interaction into participation, communication, and mutual empathy. Executive integrity is, therefore, a breaking out of a narrow individualism and is based on a fearless trust in what true dialogue and understanding might bring, both new responsibilities and new forms of responsiveness to the other.

> (Srivastva and Cooperrider, 1988: 7)

The big weakness of a heavy reliance upon the notion of a dialectic transformation of society is that the associated processes are subject to the risk of social capture. The best chance of minimising this possibility is for all of us to take ourselves seriously and to believe that our individual voices count in shaping the societies in which we live.

We end this opening chapter on a qualified, optimistic note. Spaemann (1989) refused to accept that conscience is either purely instinct or exclusively a function of upbringing:

In every human being there is the predisposition to develop a conscience, a kind of faculty by means of which good and bad are known.

(Spaemann, 1989: 62–3)

However, Spaemann went on to say that conscience has to be nurtured and supported – shown good practice in order for it to flourish and mature. Fail to do this and the development of a strong conscience becomes 'dwarfed'. The term 'dwarfing' is used by Seedhouse (1988) when discussing the growing attention to a 'business mentality' within UK health care, at the expense of a prioritising of the individual. Both Spaemann and Seedhouse saw the individual as central to any challenge to the primacy of business interests, although, as you will see in Chapter 7, conscience is often the victim of the need to maintain organisational and personal relationships.

Hannah Arendt (cited in Bauman, 1994) also placed the individual at the centre of any developments towards making ethics a live and legitimate subject for debate within organisations. Arendt wrote, 'there are no rules to abide by … as there are no rules for the unprecedented'. Bauman continued

in other words, no one else but the moral person themselves must take responsibility for their own moral responsibility.

(Bauman, 1994: 14)

With this in mind, this book is intended to inform your understanding of some of the key issues that bear upon this critical element of modern society – the possibilities for business ethics.

## Summary

In this chapter the following key points have been made:

- Business ethics issues can be illustrated through stories; sometimes these are expressed as romances, as tragedies, as satire, as comedies and sometimes as farces.

- Many writers, and indeed organisations, argue that there is a business case for companies to behave ethically and responsibly. There is an association between the two, but whether good companies are profitable because they are good, or good because their profitability means they can afford to be, is not easily proven one way or the other.

- Many business ethics issues are best understood by using a stakeholder approach.

- Four different perspectives: the classical-liberal, the corporatist, the pluralist and the critical, on the question of whether organisations, and their role within market systems, are ethically proper.

- The doubts about the classical-liberal model place a premium on the role of the moral agency of individuals within organisations. Moral agency involves reflection on what is right and wrong and working for the good within organisations.

## Quick revision test

1. What is meant by the term 'moral agency'?

2. Ayn Rand is credited with being the founder of the philosophical position known as 'objectivism'. What are objectivism's three core elements?

3. What does the criticism of neo-liberal economics being 'under-socialised' mean?

4. What is the difference between 'normative' theories and 'descriptive' theories of ethical behaviour within organisations?

## Typical assignments and briefs

1. Is there an effective 'business case' for corporations acting in a socially, ethically and environmentally responsible way?

2. Compare and contrast the four approaches to the involvement of stakeholders' business decision making (classical liberal, pluralistic, corporatist and critical) outlined in this chapter.

3. How should a company decide which interest groups should be treated as stakeholders and which should not?

4. What can we learn about business ethics issues at work by studying the stories in which they are reported?

# Sustainability and the responsible corporation

## Learning outcomes

Having read this chapter and completed its associated activities, you should be able to:

- Discuss the importance of sustainability as a concept that applies to social and economic, as well as environmental, aspects of human activity.

- Debate both the principled and consequentialist positions that underpin sustainability arguments.

- Participate in debates concerning various global initiatives on sustainability.

- Evaluate the strength of the ethical egoist arguments for market-based, price-led sustainability solutions.

- Debate the 'enframing of technology' mind-set that represents one of the major obstacles to moving to more sustainable activities, practices and processes.

- Discuss reconceptualising the relationship between shareholder and corporate executives that could allow the stakeholder perspective to become a less problematic issue.

## Introduction

The immediate question we have to address is, 'What do we mean by sustainability?' Sustainability of what, for whom, and over what timescale?

When the term sustainability was first used in the context of social and economic activities it was used exclusively in the context of the use and depletion of environmental resources. There are a number of statements that capture the essence of this notion of sustainability and one of the earliest came from the United Nations Brundtland Commission (1987), which referred to sustainability as

development that meets the needs of the present without compromising the ability of future generations to meet their own needs.

A variation on this theme is to see members of the human race as always in the role of lessees or guardians of the planet. From this perspective, statements such as the following flow, 'We lease nature from our children, and they from their children. We must all act wisely'.

## Significant political initiatives

There have been a number of political initiatives that have attempted to address pressing (environmental) sustainable development issues, culminating in agreements such as the Rio Declaration (1992); the Kyoto Protocol (1997); and the Johannesburg World Summit (2002). Implementation of the Kyoto Protocol was intended to be a major advance in the global approach to climate change issues, with commitments to reduce by 5.2 per cent the 1990 level of global greenhouse gas (GHG) emissions by 2012 and by 50 per cent by 2050.

As indicated above the protocol was drawn up in 1997, but the base line year for calculations was agreed as 1990. However, the subsequent withdrawal of America and Australia from the protocol undermined its status, and the tenth annual UN Conference on Climate Change, held in Buenos Aires in December 2004, witnessed further erosion of its credibility. The purpose of the conference in Buenos Aires was to gain agreement on Kyoto 2, i.e. post-2012. However, the dominant developing economies of India and China joined forces with the USA and Australia to scupper any talks concerning post-2012 GHG emission levels. India and China considered that such levels of GHG emission controls threatened their economic growth and might just be a ploy by the developed economies to slow the economic growth of India and China.

At the present time it is impossible to see the adjustments required to move to a globally sustainable position on natural resource usage without major adjustments being made to people's perceptions of acceptable ways of living. This statement denies neither the claim that present ways of living for many western societies are unsustainable, nor that the adjusted standard of living required is in any way unacceptable to rational human beings. However, it has to be recognised that, at the present time, with ethical egoism such an apparently powerful descriptive theory of human behaviour, for a political leader to claim that their policies will lead to fundamental adjustments and, some might argue, reduced standards of living would be political suicide.

You might ask what types of 'adjustments' are being referred to here. One of the major areas of potential impact would be in terms of modes of transportation. An interesting example is described in Activity 9.1.

### Activity 9.1

For example, an inter-city train can carry many more passengers than a plane on an internal flight, yet, in early 2005, it costs under £27 (including airport taxes) for a scheduled return flight from Nottingham (in England) to Edinburgh (in Scotland), a distance of 260 miles each way. With the round trip amounting

▶

to 520 miles, this works out at 5p per mile! The cheapest return ticket for a train journey from Nottingham to Edinburgh is an Apex ticket that costs £50, but there are always relatively few of these tickets available. The next cheapest ticket costs £85, while the standard return (not first class) is £135. In addition, the train travel time is three hours longer, even allowing for a one-hour early arrival time at the airport. In this context you might like to make enquiries as to the cost of rail travel versus internal air flights in your own part of the UK or your own country.

With the cost of running an average family motor car estimated to be around 30p per mile and rising, and the accepted mileage rate for car travel approved by the Inland Revenue to be 40p per mile, it is puzzling in the extreme to understand how an airline can charge the equivalent of 5p per mile and still find it economically worthwhile. One of the reasons for the difference in price in the UK is that aviation fuel is not taxed. Even though this concession to the airlines is estimated to cost the UK taxpayer £6bn each year (The *Guardian*, 2005), it is not the only concession. In addition, the cost of an airline ticket is 'subsidised' in the sense that no value added tax (VAT) is levied by the government, despite the fact that air travel is the most polluting form of transportation one can choose. Excluding food products, it is difficult to identify any product or service provided by a private sector organisation that is free of VAT. This situation has to say something about the influence the airline industry has in the corridors of power.

While an element of the price differences may have something to do with the respective efficiency levels of the organisations concerned, any government espousing its commitment to a sustainability agenda has to address the cost of air travel. Interestingly, the owners of airports (often local authorities) sometimes offer incentives to airlines to fly to their destination to facilitate local economic development, which once again illustrates the complex intertwining of governments and business and the vulnerability of sustainability issues to economic, social and political interests.

Likewise, the motor car and its place in modern society cannot be exempt from political attention. The taxation of all the different facets of road travel (e.g. fuel costs, road tolls, recycled materials, fuel types, etc.) is a further issue upon which politicians can be said to be dragging their feet. In many societies the motor car has become a fundamental part of modern living, with public transport sometimes barely a viable option. Changing attitudes to reduce dependency upon the motor car is a monumental task and at the present time, potentially, a political suicide note.

## Activity 9.2

Employing the following scale, think about where your position lies on the scale with regard to each of the questions shown below.

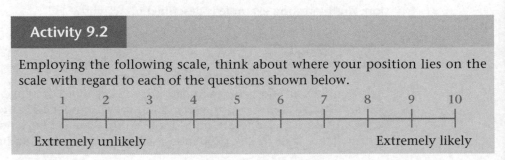

**Questions**

1. Can you envisage *not* owning a car – ever?

2. Would you support an increase in motor fuel tax that would double the price of a litre of fuel?

3. Would you support an increase in motor fuel tax that would quadruple the price of a litre of fuel?

4. Assuming the price adjustment relates to an airline flight that you might take, would you support a levy on aviation fuel that would raise the price of an economy airline ticket from its current price of £300 to £1800?

5. Assuming the price adjustment relates to an airline flight that you might take, would you support a levy on aviation fuel that would raise the price of an internal air flight from, say, £27 to £270?

6. How likely do you think it is that the fuel tax rises suggested in the questions above would address the worldwide issue of GHG emissions?

| Activity 9.3 | A moral choice |
|---|---|

In a radio interview of January 2005, Jonathon Porritt, the UK government's advisor on environmental issues, gave an example of the tension between social ethics and environmental ethics. He argued that, whilst it might be a socially moral act to attend one's sister's wedding in New York, the environmentally moral case is not to attend (but with profuse apologies). What is your reaction to this statement?

The changes required to address the environmental problems facing the world in the early stages of the twenty-first century are not all as startling or lifestyle-changing as these examples and questions imply, but it is probable that many required changes do represent changes of a stepped and profound nature.

Returning to the UN Climate Change Conference in Buenos Aires in December 2004, the problems of achieving an outline agreement on a Kyoto 2 accord were further exacerbated when Italy joined the dissenting countries (Australia, China, India and America) and thereby undermined a previously united EU position. This was clearly a significant setback for the coordinated European position, but the UK's position is itself not wholly consistent. For example, the UK government had previously announced that it had set itself the task of achieving the Kyoto target of GHG emissions by 2010 and by a greater amount than the EU as a whole had agreed. The commitment to achieve higher levels of reduction of carbon dioxide emissions, and two years ahead of the time the EU was requiring its member states to achieve the Kyoto targets, was a demanding commitment by the UK government. However, by doing so the UK government was announcing its commitment to environmental issues.

In April 2004 the UK Secretary of State for the Department of Environment, Food and Rural Affairs (DEFRA) announced that for the period 2004–2007 the UK's reduction in carbon dioxide emissions would be 756m tonnes. However, on 27 October 2004, and after significant lobbying by industry groups, the Secretary of State announced that the UK government had made adjustments to the base line number to allow British industry to remain 'competitive' (i.e. to allow it to spend less on GHG-reducing measures). The reduction in carbon dioxide emissions had been recalculated as 736m tonnes. The overall target reduction for 2010 remained unchanged, which meant that the reductions between 2007 and 2010 would have to be even more significant than before, although maybe that was seen as the next government's problem!

## Emissions Trading Scheme

The commitment to the GHG targets may have been initially well intentioned, but the political will appears to have been found lacking when confronted by powerful industrial pressure groups. However, the story does not end there. The EU Commission refused to accept the UK's revised figures and insisted that the original target be reinstated. After much 'discussion' the UK Government acceded to the EU ruling, but announced that it would challenge the ruling in the courts. This decision allowed the UK to enter the Emissions Trading Scheme (ETS) but left unresolved, for the time being, the reduction in GHG emissions that UK companies would need to achieve. As we write this chapter the situation remains unresolved. The ETS officially began operating on 1 January 2005, although the dispute between the UK government and the EU Commission delayed its start.

The ETS is a market-based response to the need to reduce GHG emissions. As part of the Kyoto Protocol, the EU committed its member states to reduce GHG emissions by 8 per cent by 2012, but as mentioned above the UK government committed itself to achieve a 12 per cent reduction by 2010, so relatively speaking this was a far more ambitious, environmentally sensitive and bold stance than the EU had committed its member states to.

Each EU country has had to develop a National Allocation Plan (NAP). Within the respective NAPs organisations generating more than a certain level of carbon dioxide emissions have to apply for a permit, which may or may not represent the organisation's current carbon dioxide emissions level. If during the year an organisation believes it will exceed its permitted allowance then it will need to enter the ETS and buy additional 'credits'. Alternatively, if an organisation believes that it will not require all its allocated credits (maybe as a result of installing equipment and plant that are very energy efficient) then the organisation can consider selling its surplus 'credits' on the ETS.

Environmental pressure groups and other agencies (including governments) may wish to increase the pressure on companies to replace existing plant with more energy-efficient plant by entering the market and buying credits, thereby reducing the available pool of credits and increasing the price of those credits still available. The intention would be that by driving up the price of credits the cost of purchasing energy-efficient plant and equipment becomes more attractive than buying the GHG credits. In addition, by investing in energy-efficient plant and equipment a company may not need all its credits and thus be able to sell them in, ideally, a rising market for credits. It will be interesting to see the extent to which agencies such as pressure groups and governments act as buyers to push up the price of credits. Without such intervention it is difficult to see how the market will stimulate the desired transfer to energy-efficient plant.

Whether this 'solution' to global warming is the ideal solution, or even a suitable one, is a moot point. It is a business solution to a problem that has profound social, political and, ultimately, survival consequences. As discussed above, unless a market price fully reflects all opportunity and externality costs, including those of future societies, it remains incomplete as an expression of societies' preferences. For example, the approach encourages a highly calculative stance with regard to investment in new energy-efficient plant. As an alternative to possessing sufficient credits that equate with one's GHG emissions, a corporation may simply decide to pay whatever fine is levied upon corporations that fail to comply with the ETS and the Kyoto defined emission levels. Thus, to make engagement with the ETS economically logical, non-compliance fines will need to be high, even punitive. Will governments be strong enough to levy fines of this scale? History does not offer encouragement for this prospect.

Thus, ETS credits could remain only a partial solution to the problem, but be presented as if they were the complete answer. Societies and their governments are likely to have important roles still to play on the issue of global warming.

## When is the environment precious?

The perception that nature is simply a resource at our disposal and that the only factor that will shape our usage of, and attitudes towards, it is the exhaustion of these resources is a very specific view. We will explore a counterview to this stance later in the chapter when we consider the ideas and arguments of Martin Heidegger, but for now it is worth reflecting upon a study by Sterman and Sweeney (2002).

The authors conducted a study of American interviewees' understanding of climate change and global warming issues. Their findings were that, while most who took part in the study accepted that the available facts bear out the claims that climate change and global warming are real phenomena, their understanding of the trajectory of the different issues was usually illogical and/or irrational (the researchers' judgement). Coupled with this was a widespread preference on the part of the study's participants for a wait-and-see policy towards implementing environmental protection policies and practices. The arguments of the researchers were that a 'wait-and-see' approach is inadequate and that merely reducing environmental usage, other than a radical step-change, is unacceptable, but that the interviewees would not consider this as an acceptable position. In terms of the questions posed in Activity 9.2 above, the researchers would argue that, with ozone depletion and global warming occurring at such a pace, nothing short of stopping certain actions and practices is required.

**Connexion point**

The claims of ethical egoism, as discussed in Chapters 3 and 8, are that neo-liberal economics (including free trade, free markets and no government interventions) offers the best prospect for the protection of individual liberties and freedoms and democratic ideals.

Yet, in terms of Activity 9.2, there are, paradoxically, important aspects of a 'business/market-based' solution to GHG emissions and transportation choices that are profoundly undemocratic. Even the intervention of governments by raising fuel taxes by factors of 2, 3, 10, 20, or whatever, but in doing so employing the price mechanism to shape behaviour and achieve a critical environmental policy, suffers the same undemocratic potential.

At one level, by using the price mechanism as a moderator of behaviour, the notion of individual choice is maintained. This, as we have discussed, is the neo-liberal argument regarding the morality of the price mechanism to reflect freedom of choice. However, how democratic is it that only the very wealthy might be able to afford such amenities, and how democratic is it that many, many millions of people may never be able to afford these facilities?

Possibly a more profound question in terms of democratic ideals is, if certain practices and activities are major contributors to ozone depletion and GHG emissions and are thereby harmful to the vast majority of people, possibly even threatening the survival of many species, including *homo sapiens*, why should a few people be allowed to inflict harm upon the vast majority, simply because they are able to use their wealth to exercise their freedom to fly? Is the price mechanism as democratic a tool of resource allocation as it is invariably portrayed?

Redclift (1984, 1987) presented a thoughtful analysis of the tensions and contradictions within the sustainability debates. One of the early statements in his 1987 book asserts, '... the environment, whatever its geographic location, is socially constructed' (1987: 3). What might he have meant by this?

One way to understand this statement is to think of a woodland comprised of ancient trees, glades, brooks, and with special flora and fauna. Today the woodland might be a prized place, maybe designated an SSI (a place of Special Scientific Interest) and consequently protected from exploitation. This is how we see it (socially construct it) today, but that is unlikely to be how it has always been seen by those who have lived by the woodland and in the woodland. At times it might have been seen as a source of social and possibly economic survival. At the social, human existence level, the woodland would have presented wood for building homes and fires, while the animals and bushes would have been the sources of food and sustenance. The notion of a prized place would have been meaningless beyond its relative fruitfulness in terms of hunting, shelter and sustenance. The woodland, and its immediate environs, represented the world as the inhabitants knew it, assuming they had forsaken a nomadic existence. They had neither the time nor the reason to consider the woodland beyond its functionality. If the woodland lacked wildlife it is extremely likely the local people would have held the woodland in low esteem and moved on to more plentiful pastures. A woodland's value would have been determined by its ability to sustain human existence.

At other times the woodland may have been a place of foreboding, a place to be avoided as it could have harboured dangerous and predatory animals and/or people. Highwaymen may have roamed the woodland and trees would have been considered negative elements, providing cover for robbers and brigands. The notion of the woodland as a special place would have been scoffed at and derided. Yet it is the same woodland that we prize today. This is what is meant by the phrase, 'the environment is socially constructed'. In one era the felling of trees (to remove the camouflage that robbers seek) would have been considered desirable and sensible. In another era (today) the felling of many species of trees without special permission is considered a crime and subject to criminal prosecution. With regard to our perceptions of the environment, it is clear that we are once again discussing values, ethics and arguments and not irrefutable and indisputable facts. With regard to issues such as global warming and GHG emissions, while we are discussing (disputed) 'facts', our behaviours and responses to these 'facts' will be reflective of our ethics and our values.

## Broadening the concept of sustainability

For many people the concept of sustainability still refers to the effects of human, particularly corporate, activity on the environment. However, for others the concept needs broadening. With social and political systems so intertwined with economic activity, any hope of addressing the exploitation of people and natural resources has to involve corporate and political forces. In addition, whilst national initiatives on environmental and social issues are important, coordinated international initiatives are equally important, even though the refusal of America and Australia to comply with the Kyoto Protocol (and now India, China and Italy refusing to agree on a Kyoto 2) bears testimony to the problems of achieving meaningful progress on environmental issues. However, the important point is that recognition needs to be given to the engagement of large corporations. It is not enough to highlight that corporate activity (often with governmental support or acquiescence) is the principal cause of many environmental and social problems. The active collaboration of the corporate world has to be an important element in any successful set of initiatives that are implemented to address the world's environmental and social problems.

Part of this argument is that for corporations to remain sustainable (the notion of business sustainability is the interesting twist to current debates) they have to operate within socially acceptable parameters, which include how corporations use and treat the environment and people. This is part of what can be called the 'social contract', as discussed in Chapter 8. The UN Global Compact (1999) and the *Gearing Up* (2004) report are also important documents in attempts to shape thinking, debate and action.

To illustrate some of the tensions that can exist between competitive forces delivering lower prices, but only as the result of what some argue are unsustainable practices, we reflect on the challenges being made against the alleged practices of the supermarkets.

| Case study 9.1 | **Low, low prices – but at whose cost?** |
| --- | --- |

Tesco has risen from the third most significant food retailer in the UK to the UK's largest retailer (not just food) within a 15-year period. In 2005, for every £8 spent in retail outlets in the UK – on all goods – £1 was spent at Tesco. This is a phenomenal growth record and achievement. Tesco has branched out into ▶

clothes and white goods (e.g. fridges and freezers) and other electrical and electronic goods, with good quality goods being sold at prices that customers judge to be excellent value for money. For example, both Tesco and Asda sell good quality jeans for just £3, and a pint of milk cannot be purchased more cheaply than at these stores. However, the low prices of certain goods (not all goods are so 'competitively' priced) come at costs. There are accusations of unethical practices and in some cases illegal practices.

Farmers' unions and allied pressure groups accuse Tesco (and the other large food retailers) of making the farmer carry the burden of the falling price of milk. Tesco is accused of being able to sell milk at the price that it does only because it pressurises the farmer to sell, in some cases, at less than the costs of production.

Tesco has also accepted that quality garden furniture was sold at 'extremely competitive prices', but was made from illegally logged wood from the Indonesian rain forests. In 2003, Friends of the Earth identified that 70 per cent of Tesco's garden furniture was made from illegally logged timber. The Malaysian timber industry has greatly outstripped the supply of suitable Malaysian timber, and highly profitable, but illegal, trafficking in protected Indonesian timber has flourished through Malaysia. However, this was a known phenomenon and having been a signatory to the 95+ Group, which was set up by the World Wildlife Fund (WWF) to protect endangered rain forests, it might have been expected that great care would have been taken by Tesco to ensure that it did not undermine the WWF campaign. A spokesperson for Tesco stated, 'We didn't knowingly buy timber from illegal sources … We haven't done such a good job of checking where the material is coming from, and the ability to track it isn't up to our usual standards' (*Independent on Sunday*, 13 July 2003). Just how rigorous 'usual standards' are was not explained.

The issue is, that while the consumer is able to enjoy low prices, it is the food producer, or the inhabitants of the rain forests, or the garment maker in a sweatshop somewhere, or the assembly worker on an electrical goods production line where health and safety standards bear little resemblance to western conditions, who is shouldering the price cuts, not the superstores. 'Low' and declining prices can rarely be explained exclusively by economies of scales, or the learning curve effect. Someone, somewhere, along the supply chain is being squeezed hard and invariably it will be the least powerful links in the chain.

Tesco, and the other supermarkets, refute these claims and a continuing 'debate' moves back and forth between the companies and their critics.

Interestingly, Bennett (2005) questions why consumers show considerable concern for dolphin-friendly tuna, inappropriately reared prawns or battery-farmed chickens, but express few such qualms regarding jeans that retail at £3 per pair and are sold at the rate of 50,000 pairs per week from Tesco stores alone. National newspapers, so quick to focus upon unsatisfactory farming and harvesting practices when it comes to fish or poultry, laud the cheap, but high-quality garments now on sale, not just at Tesco or Asda, but at designer outlets such as Hennes and Top Shop (Bennett, 2005: 5). The big clothing retailers argue that they meet local employment and payment conditions and often exceed them, but a quick study of local laws and conditions should raise important questions regarding the acceptability of these rules. For example, the internationally agreed Sweatshop Code requires the following conditions in terms of hours of work to be respected if companies are to claim compliance with the Code.

Except in extraordinary business circumstances, employees shall (i) not be required to work more than the lesser of (a) 48 hours per week and 12 hours overtime or (b) the limits on regular and overtime hours allowed by the law of the country of manufacture or, where the laws of such country do not limit the hours of work, the regular work week in such country plus 12 hours overtime and (ii) be entitled to at least one day off in every seven-day period.

Thus, depending upon how vigorously the Code is policed and monitored, company owners can require 60 hours per week as long as they claim that the circumstances are 'extraordinary', or local employment law stipulates a lower ceiling. With regard to the latter, it would be interesting to learn how vigorously the large international corporations lobby for greater employee protection legislation in countries such as Guatemala, Indonesia, China, India, El Salvador and Cambodia, compared with, say, corporate-friendly taxation policies or inward investment incentives.

However, it is not just corporations that should be the focus of attention. As indicated above, while the living conditions of poultry and prawns have grabbed the attention of the media and consumers, the living and working conditions of fellow human beings appear to be less/not important. If we wish markets to reflect different values from those that currently prevail, then it is for individual consumers to exercise their voice. This can be expressed via purchasing decisions or political voting and/or through other media, such as radio and television phone-in programmes etc. These issues are not just issues for businesses to address. Individuals have a part, some would say a responsibility, to express their views. It is too easy to pass all the responsibility for curing the ills of the world on to corporate executives, with consumers accepting no responsibility. If the 'C' in CSR relates only to 'corporate' and not 'consumer' then, should corporations who take their broader social and environmental responsibilities seriously suffer consequential cost increases, but consumers retain price as their primary decision criterion, executives have every right to feel double standards at play in the CSR debate. In such situations the 'market' may need help from governments in the form of differential taxation policies with regard to CSR products or organisations. Contrary to market-fundamentalist belief, maybe this is an example where governments could intervene to reward those companies that operate socially and environmentally sensitive practices and policies, or conversely penalise those organisations that do not. On its own the 'market' cannot equalise the product costs of the different corporate approaches. As the Secretary-General of the United Nations stated at the launch of the UN Global Compact in 1999, 'Markets are not embedded in universal human rights'.

| Activity 9.4 | £3 jeans – a good buy? | | | |
| --- | --- | --- | --- | --- |

|  | | Yes | No | Maybe |
| --- | --- | --- | --- | --- |
| Having read the above discussion, would you: | | | | |
| 1. Now think twice before purchasing jeans at very low prices? | | ☐ | ☐ | ☐ |
| 2. Wait until you are earning a reasonable wage before being able to be a discriminating consumer? or | | ☐ | ☐ | ☐ |
| 3. Not worry about the possible implications of the low prices on the basis that the 'workers' would be worse off without the work? | | ☐ | ☐ | ☐ |

The issue of consumer responsibility, as distinct from corporate responsibility, is an interesting issue to which we will return. However, for the moment, we will concentrate upon environmental sustainability and its various dimensions.

## Environmental sustainability

It might be assumed that concerns at the rate of environmental depletion and contamination are relatively recent, with the levels of social and economic activity of earlier times too limited to have raised concerns over the environmental impacts of human activity. How long ago do you think the following words were written?

> Human beings have been endowed with reason and a creative power so that they can add to what they have been given. But until now they have not been creative, but destructive. Forests are disappearing, rivers are drying up, wildlife is becoming extinct, the climate's being ruined and with every passing day the earth is becoming poorer and uglier.

These are familiar and contemporary concerns, expressed in modern language, but the words were written not five or ten years ago but in 1897 by the Russian dramatist and short-story writer, Anton Chekhov. Does this mean that current concerns over, for example, global warming, deforestation, changes in sea levels and pollution levels are merely a continuation of long-standing worries, and that these concerns underestimate the ability of the environment to absorb and cope with the worst excesses of man?

Even if the answer to the above questions is agreed to be 'No', that is, the depletion of natural resources and evidence of climate change and global warming do pose a threat to political, social and economic structures, the question remains, 'Are these issues really about ethics and morals?' Can we not simply categorise the arguments about pollution levels, climate change and the depletion

of natural resources as commonsense? Will not the logic of adverse developments in any or all of these areas force people to behave sensibly, even if only
out of enlightened self-interest?

We will take these questions separately, with our responses shown in italics,
before returning to the standard font for the general discussion.

**Question 1** – Are we over-reacting and over-estimating the extent of environmental degradation and despoliation and their effects?

*There are a few voices that argue that most, if not all, of the claims over the effects of
environmental degradation and despoliation are misguided and/or exaggerated. An
interesting contribution to the debates has been that of the thriller crime writer Michael
Crichton, whose book 'State of Fear' (2004) tells a fictional but, it is argued, rigorously
researched story of environmental news distortion, exaggeration and manipulation. It
reflects most of the arguments, plus new claims, used by the Kyoto dissenting countries.
However, the counter-view is supported by a considerable weight of evidence. The latter
evidence highlights climate change and global warming and the factors that appear to
be triggering these changes, plus the rate of natural resource depletion. All this evidence
appears to reflect fundamental and potentially destabilising changes. In view of this, the
evidence would argue forcibly for profound changes to our collective and individual
behaviours and practices, particularly on behalf of future generations.*

From an ethical perspective, a response to the above statement can be justified
using both principled (deontological) and consequentialist (utilitarian) arguments.

## The principled argument

Natural justice would be the basis for opposition to what many would argue to
be unsustainable environmental depletion and pollution linked to the double
standards of critical decision-makers. An important factor in this debate is the
issue of property rights. We (societies) have created the construct of property
rights as a way of managing important parts of our lives. This development has
been a significant force in economic development, but it has not been a universal approach. Various groups and societies through time, often but not always
nomadic, have seen man and nature's relationship as far more respectful and
symbiotic than tends to be the case in many contemporary societies. Nature, in
its various forms, has often been represented by gods to be revered and wor-
shipped. Taking from the gods was only possible through compensatory offerings
and devotion to rituals.

Irrespective of contemporary religious (and secular) perspectives on nature, the
social construct of property rights has located control over natural resources (*see*
definition below) in the hands of relatively few people, those with great personal
wealth, or those in critical decision-making roles in business or political organisations. A natural justice argument would see this 'arrangement', at least as it involves
non-politicians, as undemocratic, not just for those members of contemporary societies that are excluded from important decisions by virtue of the existence of
property rights legislation (e.g. because they do not own equity shares in companies), but also members of societies that are denied involvement owing possibly to
their age, gender or ethnicity, or maybe because they have yet to be born.

DEFINITION

The term **resource** is a value-laden concept, carrying with it connotations of something to be used. Even the notion of usage is usually considered in terms of economic usage. This is a particular way of 'seeing' nature – as a resource, as something to be exploited. The notion of nature as a resource will be explored in more depth when we consider the work of Martin Heidegger.

Planning laws have been instituted to address some of these concerns, but the power of 'economic logic' in planning decisions is such that governments, both national and local, are often incapable of resisting proposals to exploit natural resources or to build constructions (including large-scale quarrying) that despoil landscapes or localities. The promise of jobs and the associated economic benefits, or the consequences of losing the proposal to other areas, can be powerful reasons for overriding environmental and other planning considerations. Even Deputy Prime Ministers seem to feel the need to instruct planners to 'take developers' business arguments into account' when considering planning applications (Russell, 2005).

## The double standards argument

This argues that the people who make these decisions rarely live close to, or are affected by, these decisions. Indeed they invariably live in beautiful areas and fight aggressively and generally effectively to defend 'their' environmental habitats. Their access to political networks and their ability to engage influential legal and other resources make their prospects for defending their environments from exploitation by others far greater than is the norm. A defence of this state of affairs might be that it is a system that is open to all, but this would be a very particular form of democratic logic, because many do not possess the networks or financial resources to employ 'the system' so effectively.

The reason that the above is referred to as a principled argument is that it is an argument that is independent of consequentialist issues. No reference has been made to particular decisions being 'wrong' or 'right' because of the specific ramifications of those decisions. To be a principle-based argument, the case has to be that the decisions and/or the processes by which such decisions are made are inadequate and unjust at the general, societal level.

## The consequentialist argument

Opposition to and criticism of current decision-making processes that impact upon sustainability issues that stem from a consequentialist perspective will be as a result of weighing all the ramifications of the decisions in terms of their effects upon various groups. As a result of this calculative approach, the consequentialist perspective is a stance that can be employed to both support and condemn environmental exploitation. Much depends upon how far one draws the boundaries of affected or relevant individuals and groups. Just how far should one allow one's considerations to be stretched before it is agreed that all the relevant parties' interests have been adequately weighed to allow the hypothetical scales of utilitarian justice to show where the balance of the argument lies?

These are often far from easy decisions and decision processes, although utilitarian considerations will often lie at the heart of political and planning decisions. The following case illustrates some of the complexities of such decisions.

---

**Case study 9.2**

## Removing a mountain on the Isle of Harris

The Isle of Harris lies to the north-west of the Scottish mainland and is part of the Outer Hebrides. It is an island, along with the attached Isle of Lewis, of significant natural and archaeological interest and beauty. It is also of considerable geological interest because, unlike the other islands that form the Inner and Outer Hebrides, it was not once part of the Scottish mainland. It 'drifted' to its current position over millennia, as a result of the movement of tectonic plates. The only other areas of the world displaying similar rock formation and composition are to be found in New Zealand and South Africa.

Shortly before this case study was written, the Scottish Parliament announced that it had turned down an application to allow mining of a mountain area on the Isle of Harris. The economic, social and political dimensions to the case were considerable and it is unlikely that the recent decision by the Scottish Parliament is the last act in this unfolding drama.

The mountain in question lies in the south-east corner of the island and is composed of rock that is both extremely hard (wearing) and has luminous qualities, ideal qualities of aggregates to be used in the construction of roads and motorways. With the mining completed the mountain would have effectively been removed, leaving an enormous cavity in the ground. The hole would cover a very wide area and the belief/fear was/is that it would then be a convenient site for the dumping of much of Scotland's 'undesirable' waste, which could include toxic waste.

One of the authors visited the island in 2004 for a holiday and was impressed with the level of opposition to the proposal by islanders in the north of the island, particularly those who were relatively recent inhabitants of the island. Their opposition was based upon environmental and, to a lesser extent, economic considerations. The latter reflected concerns over the impact upon tourism of the massive quarrying and then dumping operations. However, when he visited the south of the island the reaction of the locals was far more mixed, with possibly a majority of those he met (in a very unscientific study!) in favour of the proposal. Their reasoning? It reflected the locals' concern over the significant haemorrhaging of young islanders to the mainland in search of work (although there was a strong argument that the jobs issue could be handled by other approaches). The islands were becoming the repositories of elderly (usually English) people, seeking peaceful retirements and those seeking an alternative lifestyle to the pressures and demands of modern life. In the words of those who supported the proposal, the island was dying as its young people continued to migrate to the mainland.

The following are some of the difficult questions that demand attention if adopting a utilitarian approach to the ethically appropriate decision for the Isle of Harris.

1. Where does the balance of the consequentialist argument lie?

2. Is a simple calculative approach adequate?

3. Is it simply a case of counting the number of people likely to be affected, both negatively and positively, by the decision, and opting for the decision that affects the larger number of people positively?

4. Or should the decision be based upon the option that affects the smaller number of people negatively?

5. If a higher value is placed upon avoiding harm, then avoiding negatively affecting people will carry a higher (political) weighting, which might result in a different decision from that suggested by 3 above.

6. How much attention and weight should be given to the financial implications of the decision?

7. How does one take into account those people who live elsewhere in Scotland or other parts of the UK, who might be affected by a landfill site being located near their homes if the planning application for the Isle of Harris site is refused?

8. Within a utilitarian stance should the views of the indigenous islanders be weighed more significantly than those of the 'newcomers'?

This is a real case with which the Scottish Parliament has had to wrestle and which it might have to revisit, should an appeal be lodged against the planning rejection.

To conclude this section we highlight the murkiness and business–political intrigue at play on the critical subject of environmental sustainability with reference to an article written by Lord May, who in 2005 was President of the Royal Society and between 1995 and 2000 was the UK government's chief scientific advisor. The following case summarises the article.

**Case study 9.3**

## An insider's view

During the 1990s, parts of the US oil industry funded – through the so-called Global Climate Coalition (GCC) – a lobby of professional sceptics who opposed action to tackle climate change by cutting greenhouse gas emissions. The GCC was 'deactivated' in 2001, once President Bush made it clear he intended to reject the Kyoto Protocol. But the denial lobby is still active , and today it arrives in London.

The UK has become a target because the government has made climate change a focus of its G8 presidency this year [2005]. A key player in this decision is chief scientific advisor Sir David King, who became public enemy number one for the denial lobby when he described climate change as a bigger threat than terrorism.

In December [2004], a UK-based group, the Scientific Alliance, teamed up with the George C. Marshall Institute, a body headed by the chairman emeritus of the GCC, William O'Keefe, to publish a document with the innocuous title 'Climate Issues & Questions'. It plays up the uncertainties surrounding climate change science, playing down the likely impact that it will have.

It contrasts starkly with the findings of the Intergovernmental Panel on Climate Change (IPCC) ... the world's most reliable source of information on the effects of greenhouse gas emissions.

(*Source*: Lord May, 2005)

Lord May was pointing out that powerful interest groups in the shape of the major US oil corporations were funding organisations that were seeking to undermine the evidence-based arguments of respected scientific bodies such as the IPCC. You might feel that if the claims being made by organisations such as the George C. Marshall Institute are unfounded and spurious then they will be derided. However, one should not trust reason and logic to prevail when such powerful economic interests are at risk.

Later in his article, Lord May expressed concern that major UK daily newspapers were running articles and leaders in 2005 that undermined the evidence-based arguments of the IPCC. Public opinion becomes influenced by such sources. The American tobacco industry denied for decades the causal link between smoking and different forms of cancer. In the mid-1990s all the CEOs of the seven largest tobacco companies testified before a congressional hearing that in their view there was no causal link, despite the fact the tobacco industries' own (private) research revealed the connections. It was only when one of the tobacco industries' own scientists 'blew the whistle' on the suppressed evidence that the tobacco companies accepted the causal relationship. The oil industry cannot suppress the scientific evidence that is published on climate change, so an alternative strategy is to challenge and undermine the evidence and arguments.

In all discussions on environmental sustainability the American perspective is critical. With America accounting for only 4 per cent of the world's population, but with 22.5 per cent of the world's GHG emissions emanating from the United States, gaining the support of the American political establishment is critical. A different way of looking at this situation is that any American president has an incredibly difficult and high-risk task in making environmental issues a major political issue for the American electorate. Some argue that it would be a political suicide note.

Interestingly, the UK Prime Minister, Tony Blair, when he gave the keynote speech at the opening of the World Economic Forum at Davos, Switzerland, on 26 January 2005, softened his own commitment to making climate change issues his primary challenge, when he asserted that climate change was 'not universally accepted'. Elliot (2005) observed, 'with chief executives of many US firms in the audience, [Blair] said, "the evidence is still disputed"'. Mr Blair went on to state that no significant adjustments to business behaviour towards the environment can be expected if such adjustments threaten economic growth. This may or may not be a realistic assessment of the economic and political power positions (the so-called *realpolitik*), but the assertion is as much puzzling as it is concerning, because it ignores both the morality and the physical consequences of a 'do-nothing' attitude to environmental despoliation and degradation, whether from a principled or consequentialist perspective.

**Question 2** – What are the implications of relying exclusively upon enlightened/rational self-interest to drive sustainable corporate behaviour and practices?

*There has been a variety of evidence available over many years that has highlighted the unsustainability of the rate of environmental depletion and waste across the globe. However, to date, this evidence and official responses have had limited impact upon our practices. For example, in the early 1990s and in response to concerns over carbon dioxide emissions, the Intergovernmental Panel on Climate Change called for carbon dioxide emissions to be 50 per cent lower by 2050 than their 1990 levels. Given the likely increase in global economic activity between 1990 and 2050, such a reduction represents a significant change in consumption and will not be achieved without new technologies and practices, as well as possible revisions to economic growth assumptions. Yet between 1990 and 2004 carbon dioxide emissions actually rose by 8.9 per cent! The implications of these (in)actions and behaviours are likely to affect all members of the human race to some extent, but possibly most significantly, those yet to be born. Thus, a decision based exclusively upon rational self-interest fails to address the wider significance of individual choices and decisions. Whilst our actions and behaviours affect others, they have ethical import.*

The assumptions regarding economic growth rates contained within the calculations regarding carbon dioxide emissions do reflect an economic mind-set that now goes almost unchallenged. Whilst writers such as Dickson (1974), Sawyer (1978) and Schell (1982) presented arguments that challenged the wisdom and sustainability of economic growth assumptions in the 1970s and 1980s, these arguments are far less frequently discussed today, even though the economic growth assumptions have been outstripped – such is the dominance of economic imperatives and their relationships with political objectives. The notion of short-termism in decision making, whether it be related to political or economic decisions (and often they are linked), is a central issue within these debates and can be said to reflect an ethical egoist perspective, as discussed below.

| Activity 9.5 | Putting yourself in the shoes of 'others' |
| --- | --- |

The refusal to recognise the evidence that exists regarding environmental degradation and depletion represents an act with ethical significance. A decision to do nothing is still a decision. What will be the consequences of maintaining existing rates of resource consumption and thus depletion by 2105? If you were to be living in 2105, what do you think would be your attitude towards those living in 2005 who refused/failed to curb their consumption of finite natural resources and/or did little to address global warming and climate change issues?

Ethical egoism (sometimes referred to as possessive egoism), with its reliance upon market signals to reflect social preferences would, at best, appear to require an ambivalent stance towards environmental issues.

## Ethical egoism and sustainability

From an ethical egoist perspective, market-based forms of coordination of economic and social activity are argued to be at the bedrock of basic freedoms. The more all facets of human interaction can be coordinated by market dynamics, the more the resulting outcomes will reflect the independent, 'free' choices of all participants. As we discussed in Chapter 3, this argument has certain strengths, but it also ignores important structural issues which challenge its integrity (principled-based objection) and efficacy (utilitarian-based objection).

Allowing markets to be the dominant forms for allowing societal preferences and choices to become known assumes that prices contain all relevant information and markets are not unduly skewed owing to power imbalances. Yet, as suggested in the Isle of Harris case, there might be certain situations where the opinions and arguments of particular groups might justify higher weightings than other groups in a decision-making process. If it was left to simple market dynamics to reflect these different weightings, then it is likely that the economically powerful would secure the largest weightings, possibly usurping those with higher, principle-based claims to justice, or deservingness.

As mentioned already in this chapter, the voice of the yet to be born is a complex one to include in such debates, but it is almost impossible to envisage how the price mechanism would incorporate the views of future generations, other than perhaps taxes levied by governments on behalf of future generations, to pay for 'clean-ups' or detoxifying processes, reclamation, compensation payments, etc. However, if the voice of future generations was truly able to be heard, it could be that they would be at one in rejecting the decision in its entirety, thus obviating the need for compensation payments or other such contingency plans. Designating areas of special scientific interest is one way of protecting certain parts of the environment for current and future generations, but these designations are vulnerable to powerful interests and can be overridden. One such example is the opening up of a previously protected region of the Arctic Circle in Alaska for oil drilling, as evidenced in Table 8.1 in the previous chapter.

In the context of environmental protection it would seem that market signals have limited application, an example of what can be called 'market failure', making the intervention of governments essential as the representatives of the people and their adjudicators. However, governments' interventions in economic and social affairs are anathema to market fundamentalists, with any exceptions to this principle seen as the start of a very slippery slope. For those with more acceptance of political intervention in such situations, their concerns are with the corruptibility of political processes. The latter are seen as too susceptible to the influence of powerful individuals and corporations.

**Connexion point**

Refer back to Table 8.1 to refresh your memory on the political donations made to the Republican Party during the US Presidential elections of 2000 and the resulting changes to the law that immediately followed President Bush's inauguration.

## A different perspective on environmental issues

If you refer back to Chapter 1, three of the theories of the firm, *Classical liberal economic, Pluralist (A and B)* and *Corporatist*, each locate the business corporation within a capitalist-driven, market-based economy. Each perspective accepts the need for corporations to legitimately seek out new ways to generate profits on behalf of shareholders, but with other interest groups (employees, customers and suppliers) benefiting in differing ways as a result of these corporate activities. Within these perspectives, nature, in all its various forms, is seen as a resource, at the behest of society in general, and corporations in particular, to be employed in whatever ways are deemed socially and legally permissible to facilitate economic activity.

Before these issues are discussed in more detail, we would like you to take a few minutes to undertake the following task.

| Activity 9.6 | Subjects and objects |
| --- | --- |

Try to identify a place or an object that has a special significance for you. The place or object might be very commonplace (e.g. a ring, an ornament, a book, a photograph) or it might be a little unusual, a location for example. Whatever it is, for you it is special. If you cannot identify such a place or object, try to identify a place or object that you know to be special to someone else, your mother or father perhaps, or your brother or sister. If you were then asked to place a value on that place or object, how might you express that value as a number, a monetary value?

Prior to Activity 9.6, the perspective that has so far underpinned our discussions in this chapter has been that of a clear distinction between ourselves (subjects) and the world of objects that surround us. We have assumed that we are separate from nature and nature is separate from us. We possess the technologies to control, manipulate and direct nature, and we possess the capabilities, and some would argue the right, to do with nature as we see fit. The law of property rights underpins this belief. Landowners can prohibit access to their lands because laws have been passed that allow such prohibitions. Countries fight over, or at least contest, ownership of areas of land and sea (the Arctic and Antarctic regions for example) because of their mineral deposits and other valued resources. Even the moon is subject to property rights' claims for its mineral deposits. Currently companies are seeking to decode human DNA so that they can patent and thus 'own' the codes. The ability of humanity to benefit from such 'code-breaking' research will then be subject to commercial exploitation of these medical under-standings. At one level this is no different from the patent rights and copyright constraints existing in many areas of organisational activity, but deeper philo-sophical issues can be argued to be at play when one considers knowledge breakthroughs that can possibly alleviate great human suffering, e.g. in the areas of genetically inherited diseases and disabilities.

Practically everything you see around you, can touch, or what you are wear-ing, represents some form of intervention of human activity on nature. This is not to say that these interventions have been/are bad or wrong. The question is, how do we view nature and, equally importantly, how do we view ourselves with respect to nature?

Martin Heidegger (1959, translation 2000) is the person who is most identified with the perspective we are about to discuss. It is known as Phenomenology.

**DEFINITION**

**Phenomenology** is the belief that the world around us can only be under-stood through our lived experiences. The world does not exist beyond those experiences. We impose understandings and interpretations on that world, or worlds, based upon the values, perspectives and beliefs we hold. The relation-ship between ourselves and nature is a symbiotic one (i.e. mutually dependent) and not one of independence. This perspective has a strong reso-nance with the discussion earlier in the chapter concerning the way a woodland might be perceived through time.

Whilst Heidegger was not the first to challenge the notion that subjects and objects are distinct and separate entities, his analysis was more radical than those who had come before him, for example, Edmund Husserl (1931, 1965), who was Heidegger's teacher. Heidegger died in 1976, so by the standards of notable philosophers his arguments are quite new.

As the definition above indicates, Heidegger's principal argument was that we cannot understand nature other than how we experience it. Nature does not exist beyond our experiences of it. Those experiences might have come to us via first-hand knowledge, or stories, accounts, films, newspapers, books, the Internet, conversations, whatever. When we look at something or hear something, what we see and hear is filtered through our mental faculties, which in turn process information and understanding through many subtle processes including emo-tions, memories, existing values, beliefs and understandings – essentially our experiences. For example, when we look at something, say an NHS hospital, what do we see? Some would simply say that they see a place where those who are unwell or injured are taken in order to receive treatment. Others might see the building as representing a symbol of a civilised society that has created facili-ties to tend to the sick or the injured, irrespective of their ability to pay for their treatment. Others might see the building as representing a bundle of resources, which are outstripped by demand for its services. From the latter perspective, the hospital is a cauldron of ethical dilemmas in terms of the choices over which treatments to prioritise and which to de-prioritise.

The same object can represent different visions to different people. Think back to Acitivity 9.6. Why was the place or object you selected special? The answer will be related to the place or object's history. It is likely to hold memories that are important to you. The place or object keeps you in touch with something or someone you want to hold on to. History and context are central to this debate. Were you able to place a monetary value upon your object or place? For some, the importance of the object or the place will be incalculable because of the memories it reveals, what it represents.

Whilst the argument that different people will have different views about the importance of places and objects is reasonably uncontentious, you might ask, 'Are we moving towards a position that simply admits that all we are likely to agree upon is that we are likely to disagree upon the values we are prepared to place upon various objects?' If so, how is this going to help individuals and corporations make choices over the use of natural resources, whether they be tropical rain forests, a local park, playing field, a set of allotments or the survival of a threatened species of animal? Heidegger does not offer a magic formula, but he does offer a way of thinking, a way of seeing, that could prove helpful.

Heidegger's concern was with what he described as the 'enframing of technology', or what we might call a technology mentality, i.e. the seeing of nature as purely instrumental, as simply a means to an end. If nature represents merely the opportunity to make money, if that is all nature means to us, then, from a Heideggerian perspective, society has become emotionally and spiritually bankrupt.

**DEFINITION**

If an object is viewed in purely **instrumental** terms then it possesses no worth beyond its functional use, that is, what might be obtained for it by either selling it as it is or converting it into another form of tradable object. It is purely a means to an end. The end in this case is to make money, although this is not the only 'end' that can be considered.

Heidegger was not anti-technology. He recognised the contributions that technological advancements had made, and continue to make, to people's lives. Improvements in sanitation, health care, education, etc. can be seen as benefiting either directly or indirectly from technology. In Heidegger's view, we have a symbiotic relationship with nature, i.e. the relationship between humans and nature is one of mutual dependency. As we exploit nature, we cannot avoid, to a greater or lesser extent, having an impact upon ourselves. In this context 'ourselves' is used in a very broad sense, reflecting impacts not necessarily upon our own generation, but those that are yet to come.

The treatment of nature in purely instrumental ways is not limited to profit seeking organisations. Neither is the 'enframing of technology' limited to capitalist systems. Examples of the destruction of the environment in the name of 'progress' can be seen in many different political and economic contexts. However, in an economic system in which:

(a) the *raison d'être* (the reason for being) of business enterprises is to maximise profits on behalf of shareholders, and

(b) the nature of competitive capitalism is that a company incurring additional costs by way of laudable, but not legally required, pollution controls that result in its being put at a cost and price disadvantage to its competitors is likely to fail,

the question has to be asked, 'How is it possible for corporations to view nature in anything other than an instrumental fashion'? In addition, if we cannot expect everyone to value the same objects that we regard as important as highly as ourselves, and vice versa:

- How can a corporation place a value upon any object, other than in terms of its instrumental worth to the corporation?

- How can objects have meaning to a corporation beyond their functional or instrumental worth?

- Where is a corporation's memory that might allow it to attach feelings to objects that transcend their instrumental worth?

- What is the market value of the site of the Parthenon of ancient Greece to a property developer or, for a mining company, a spectacular ravine in a site of special scientific interest that contains valuable mineral deposits?

## A moment of reflection

We are approaching a possibly critical point in our consideration of sustainability, corporate social responsibility and corporate citizenship, certainly in terms of Heidegger's view of a 'technology mentality'. Asking where a corporation's memory might lie, or whether a corporation can possess feelings towards objects, is attributing human characteristics to business enterprises that many would regard as simply unrealistic, as silly. The technical term is reification, that is, giving concrete (human) form to an abstract idea (a corporation). When we use the term 'corporation' in the sense being discussed here, we are referring to the senior decision-makers. A corporation's 'memory' will reside with individuals, or possibly in the form of company stories and myths. The use of 'corporation' is in fact a form of shorthand.

If corporations can only ever view objects in instrumental ways, then society cannot expect corporations to value and to treat nature in ways that it (society) might wish or demand. To repeat, this is not to suggest that all members of society will hold the same views on particular aspects of nature, but at least a debate can ensue between interested parties about the various merits of different choices under debate. And the debate will embrace many value systems that go beyond instrumentality.

Following Heidegger, the fundamental objection is that corporations *cannot* fully act in socially responsible ways because they possess a perspective on nature that is extremely limited. A societal perspective on nature that is compatible with a Heideggerian perspective is denied to a corporation, as long as corporations are constituted in their current form. Corporations cannot be citizens because their value systems are highly constrained and unable to handle concepts of value beyond instrumentality. A corporation's perspective is 'enframed by technology'. However, this does not dismiss corporations as irrelevancies to modern life. Clearly, business, in its many forms, is fundamental to the way we live. In many respects it is the dominant force in modern societies. The central issue concerns the relationship between corporations and society, but is citizenship a realistic or appropriate concept in this debate? Welford (1995), when discussing issues of sustainable development, referred to this issue when, in the six areas that are argued to require shifts of thinking, he stated that a key transformation is the move from 'objects to relationships'.

## Thinking about the Self and Others

Central to any debate concerning objects and subjects is the notion of the Self. We have referred to ethical egoism on a number of occasions in this chapter, with an example of its manifestation reflected in the previous chapter in Table 8.2 on page 303. This table contrasted the remuneration of executive directors of FTSE 100 between January 2000 and December 2002 (up 84 per cent), with the movement in the FTSE 100 index (down 40 per cent). It is intriguing how the behaviour of corporate executives, in relation to their own remuneration, or the ownership of many, many gas-guzzling motor cars by certain wealthy individuals, is sometimes accepted on the basis that, 'Well, I would do the same in their shoes'! Why is there this apparent acceptance of such behaviour and the belittling of one's own ethics? It might have something to do with the promulgation of the Self as a self-serving, myopic, selfish individual as exemplified in agency theory and ethical egoism.

### DEFINITION

**Agency theory**, as used here, refers to the division of ownership and control of corporations, with shareholders the principals and management their agents. With human behaviour assumed to be essentially self-seeking and self-focused and management 'enjoying' a privileged control of information over shareholders, this control is assumed to manifest itself in sub-optimum decision making (from the shareholders' perspective), as reflected in Table 8.2.

This view of human nature was argued for by Thomas Hobbes and David Hume among others. Both were eminent philosophers, but their position on this issue is an argument, not a fact, and it is up to us, individually and collectively, to decide where we stand on this issue. If we are to see as 'natural' a regard for the Self as the primary, maybe sole, driver for determining our collective attitudes towards sustainability, who speaks for those who cannot speak, the dispossessed, the unborn? These tensions are explicitly addressed in the following statement taken from the Sustainability Strategy and Action Plan 2000–2005 of the UK's second largest city, Birmingham. A local authority, like Birmingham City Council, has an immensely difficult task to develop a sustainability strategy or, more accurately, a series of sustainability strategies that cohere and are mutually supportive and sustaining. The statement from which the following extract is taken is headed 'The Challenge'.

A Sustainability Strategy for the City Council could be huge, involving almost every policy and strategy of every department. Clearly this would be undesirably unwieldy. Suffice it to say that Community Safety and Nature Conservation Strategies, policies on Disability, Employment, Equalities and the City's commitment to lifelong learning are a fraction of the existing policies, strategies and actions which are relevant to our drive towards sustainability (p. 3).

Having hinted at the complexity of the task facing the City Council, the 'challenge' is then articulated.

### The Challenge

Delivering sustainability for a large Metropolitan city in the developed world is not an easy or comfortable matter. It is about making choices about the distribution of benefits between generations, and denying people benefits now, for the yet unborn. Such decisions will never be universally popular. There will always be special reasons for not taking the sustainability route. Indeed tensions will sometimes even exist between alternative sustainability options. Facing up to this dilemma is one of the biggest challenges the Council needs to address.

(Sustainability Strategy and Action Plan 2000–2005, Birmingham City Council, p. 4)

Birmingham City Council cite the Brundtland Commission's definition of sustainability (which was shown at the start of this chapter) to define what they mean by sustainability. An interesting definition of sustainable communities and one that offers an insight into the complexity of the notion of sustainable communities is reflected in the UK Government's Sustainable Communities' initiative.

| Sustainable communities | DEFINITION |
|---|---|

Places where people want to live and work, now and in the future. They meet the diverse needs of existing and future residents, are sensitive to their environment, and contribute to a high quality of life. They are safe and inclusive, well planned, built and run, and offer equality of opportunity and good services for all.

The above reflects the challenges that a sustainability commitment involves, but the philosophical position of the ethical egoist position is a powerful one in modern western societies and it is important that we study the issues in more depth. The discussion which follows explores the issues through the lens provided by Adam Smith, who is sometimes referred to as the father of market-based capitalism.

Smith lived during the eighteenth century and was an acquaintance of David Hume. Smith was a prominent Scottish academic who applied his intellect to a number of fields, but he is most notably remembered for his seminal work, the title of which is usually shortened to *The Wealth of Nations*. This treatise argues for the primacy of market-based capitalism to be the basis for social and economic coordination. However, while markets were his principal means of releasing the individual from the demands of kings, governments and religious interference, Smith's advocacy was conditional and dependent on two central elements, that of *competitive* market-based capitalism and *constrained self-love*.

Smith is referred to as a 'classical economist', which means that he considered economic issues from a broader, more socially inclusive perspective than is allowed or recognised in neo-classical economics. In 1751 and at the age of 28, Smith was appointed to the Chair of Logic at Glasgow University. One year later he was appointed to the Chair of Moral Philosophy. It was from the perspective of a Professor of Moral Philosophy that Smith wrote his two seminal treatises. *The Wealth of Nations* has already been referred to, but the second major treatise to flow from Smith's pen was *The Theory of Moral Sentiments*. The importance of this is that, within *The Wealth of Nations*, Smith did not elaborate on his notion of self-love. However, the concept is explored by Smith in *The Theory of Moral Sentiments*, which was first published in 1759, sixteen years before *The Wealth of Nations* was first published, while the final edition of *The Theory of Moral Sentiments* was published in 1790, the year of Smith's death. Thus, it can be seen that the notion of self-love would have developed as a result of Smith's work on his two famous treatises over a period of some forty years. *The Theory of Moral Sentiments* allows us to understand that Smith's conception of self-love was not the distorted version that travels today under the banner of selfishness, nor as it appears to have become corrupted by certain writers, e.g. Levitt (1956), who argued,

> What is important is that the pursuit of Self-interest has become institutionalized ... this is of the greatest importance for the future of capitalism.

> (Levitt, 1956: 109)

As indicated above, although Smith placed competition at the centre of his economic thought, he did not leave his economic ideal to the mercy of rapacious individuals or groups, or imperfections in market conditions. Smith sympathised with Platonic and Aristotelian notions of self-control as a core human virtue in its own right, but his commitment to the importance of self-control within his economic theorising might be argued to be as much prosaic as principled. Self-control was attributed a key position within his economic schema to buttress situations where economic equilibrium would be less than perfect. Self-control was not argued to be regretted, but rather a necessary constraint on human action. Self-control was recognised in respect of freedoms, but not just those of the Self. In sympathy with Aristotelian arguments, the perception of Others was also important.

Smith's recognition of Others was more than a recognition of the plight of others out of a sense of pity. Smith used the term 'sympathy', with this describing a notion of empathy, a 'fellow-feeling'. The opening sentence of *The Theory of Moral Sentiments* reads as follows:

How selfish soever man may be supposed, there are evidently some principles in his nature, which interest him in the fortunes of others, and render their happiness necessary to him, though he derives nothing from it, except the pleasure of seeing it.

(Smith, 2000: I, 3)

The recognition of Others and their interests, whilst not equating to altruism, leads to Smith's important mechanism for operationalising his conception of self-control. The notion of fellow-feeling has been termed 'imaginative sympathy' (Wilson and Skinner, 1976), allowing an understanding to be developed of the position of other people by trying to view our own conduct through their eyes. As Wilson observed,

To use Smith's own imagery, we learn to observe our own behaviour as it might be seen by an imaginary spectator who is at once impartial and well-informed with regard to our motives.

(Wilson, 1976: 74)

Smith used the idea of a 'stranger' or 'spectator' to convey the imagery of an independent arbiter, unfettered by bias and preconceptions.

The constancy or equality of temper which is more valuable for Smith than virtues like humanity, generosity etc., is obtained through a society where everyone has continuously tried to moderate his emotions … everyone is accustomed to think how Others will judge his action and passion and to act accordingly … and … it must be repeated that Self-control in Smith cannot be established without the judgement of strangers.

(Skinner and Wilson, 1975: 122)

In a footnote Skinner and Wilson add,

The stranger is not a friend from whom we can expect any special favour and sympathy. But at the same time he is not an enemy from whom we cannot expect any sympathy at all. Everyone in society is as independent of every other stranger, and is equal with every other as they can exchange the situations. The famous impartial stranger is no one else but the spectator who is indifferent to, and does not take the part of either side.

(Skinner and Wilson, 1975: 122)

Smith argued that man is keen to obtain the respect of Others, but, because this is insufficient to ensure appropriate behaviour, he also argued that man is subject to two forms of jurisdiction, that of conscience (the man within) and that of the 'spectator' (the man without) (Smith, 1776/1982: 20/1).

The above represents a portrayal of Smith's notions of the Self that runs counter to the *a priori* assumptions of man as self-serving, atomised egoist for whom self-love equates with selfishness, traits that are to be found at the root of ethical egoism and agency theory. However, the atomisation of the individual, so dominant in neo-classical economics, is also observable in other disciplines. In political science the elevation of the Self as consumer, but with little other political relevance, was commented upon by Nisbet over fifty years ago.

> The politics of enslavement of man requires the emancipation of man from all the authorities and memberships ... that serve, one degree or another, to insulate the individual from the external political power ... totalitarian domination of the individual will is not a mysterious process, not a form of sorcery based upon some vast and unknowable irrationalism. It arises and proceeds rationally and relentlessly through the creation of new functions, statuses and allegiances which, by conferring community, makes the manipulation of the human will scarcely more than an exercise in scientific, social psychology ... there may be left the appearance of individual freedom, provided it is only individual freedom. All of this is unimportant, always subject to guidance and control, if the primary social contexts of belief and opinion are properly organized and managed. What is central is the creation of a network of functions and loyalties reaching down into the most intimate recesses of human life where ideas and beliefs will germinate and develop.

> (Nisbet, 1953: 202, 208)

Sarason (1986) echoed Nisbet's concerns. The following paraphrases Sarason, setting his argument at the general level of concern about modern conceptions of individualism.

> If *your* ethical dilemma is *your* responsibility according to *my* morality, this is quite consistent with the increasingly dominant ideology of individual rights, responsibility, choice and freedom. If *I* experience the issues as *yours*, it is because there is nothing in my existence to make it *ours*. And by *ours* I mean a social-cultural network and traditions which engender in members an obligation to be part of the problem and possible solution.

One line of thinking has been that the primacy of the Self has been reinforced by the attention given in psychology, and more particularly psychoanalysis, to patients being directed to 'look within' and to see solutions to their personal problems taking the form of much greater attention to the Self – to be far more self-aware and self-actualising. Goodwin (1974: 75), cited in Wallach and Wallach (1983), observed,

> The ideology of individualism is so powerful that we ... look on bonds as restraints; values as opinions and prejudices; customs as impositions.

> (Goodwin, 1974: 75)

Within this conception the Self is seen as a fully autonomous unit that should be responsible to no authority in the forming of its relationships beyond the exercise of its own volition – what it voluntarily wills and wishes to do. The social arrangements remaining that permit a sense of community or shared social purpose 'are assaulted as unjust restraints on liberty, impediments to the free assertion of the self' (Goodwin, 1974: 75). The proper mode of living is to be oneself – to find out who one is and to let no one and nothing interfere with one's self-realisation. This is ethical egoism in its raw form.

Challenging psychoanalysis's focus upon the Self, to the exclusion of broader social relationships and behaviours, Wallach and Wallach (1983) asserted,

> If, ..... human beings can be motivated towards ends quite other than themselves, and it is in fact better for them when this is the case, then perhaps the usual lines of therapeutic advice might well be redirected. The problems and troubles that lead people to seek psychotherapy may derive less than is commonly supposed from not expressing themselves, fulfilling themselves, or satisfying needs directed toward themselves and more from not having a workable way of living in which they participate in and contribute to matters they care about beyond themselves.
>
> (Wallach and Wallach, 1983: 274)

Maybe we need to think more carefully before accepting the arguments of agency theory and ethical egoism that human beings are by nature self-serving, possessively egoistic, with little other consideration than their own well-being. As in psychoanalysis, we need to think afresh about both the empirical and philosophical justification of this position. The assumptions concerning human behaviour explicit within agency theory and ethical egoism to explain the behaviour of senior corporate executives might simply be philosophical camouflage to mask the greed of those in privileged and powerful positions.

Smith was not blind to the risks of competitive capitalism, hence his advocacy of self-control, a virtue that appears to be in very short supply in many corporate board rooms (as evidenced by Table 8.2). What might be the issue is that too many corporate executives lack a fundamental quality of Smith's advocacy of competitive market-based capitalism. Do contemporary corporate executives (as well as politicians) possess the requisite qualities and values that issues, developments and challenges such as the GHG emissions, the power of large corporations, global poverty, and the exploitation of weak and corrupt governments, require?

## Is it all doom and gloom?

There is much within modern experiences to make the heart heavy with concern, but it would clearly be a fundamental mistake to imply that all corporate executives are greedy individuals with no care for the environment, or that corporate activity is exclusively negative, both socially and environmentally. Although one or two examples of impressive individual and/or corporate activity 'do not a summer make', it is important to be aware of the excellent initiatives that are under way at the local and individual (including corporate) level to address sustainability issues, and which in some cases have been established for some time. The following are some examples of organisations that are working with corporations to develop more sustainable processes, practices, attitudes and beliefs. The last two elements are possibly the most important because without them changes to processes and practices are likely to be short-lived and/or poorly implemented and operationalised.

---

**Case study 9.4**

## Capital *One*

In the corporate sector the company Capital *One* is a large credit card organisation. It has a 'corporate responsibility' team of four full-time employees, headed by a 'Corporate Social Responsibility Manager'. The initiative to establish the team came from the main board and replicates its American parent company's belief in corporate responsibility. A 'corporate responsibility' commitment was not the result of the company receiving bad publicity and feeling the need to be 'seen to be doing something'. At one level it might be argued that all the company is displaying is a form of enlightened self-interest, in that by performing good deeds it wishes to attract employment applications from high-quality people who wish to work for such an organisation. The company does not dispute that it hopes to attract 'better' applicants for posts at the company, but the primary stimulus is the belief of the senior management that 'this is the way companies should behave'. The company does not publicise many of the projects in which it becomes involved, the reason being that it does not wish to be accused of merely undertaking the projects to obtain the favourable publicity. It is something of a Catch 22 situation, with the company potentially damned if it does and damned if it doesn't.

An example of one of the projects with which it has been involved relates to the collaboration between the company's programming team and Nottinghamshire Police Force. Following the murder of two young girls in Soham, UK, the Nottinghamshire Police Force wished to create a database of all known paedophiles; however, they lacked the expertise to do this. The programming team of Capital *One*, over a period of some months, developed the database, which has now been adopted by other police forces in the UK. Initially the company kept its involvement in the project low-key. It was only when the system was rolled out to a number of other police forces that it publicly acknowledged its collaboration.

---

**Case study 9.5**

## The Citizen Group

The Citizen Group is an interesting organisation, noted for its watches and other timepieces. The reason for featuring the corporation is not so much for any specific 'good deeds', but rather the company's broader commitment to notions of corporate citizenship. The President of the company heads the 'Citizen CSR Committee', which was instituted in October 2003. The company has developed a 'Citizen Code of Conduct' that speaks to the corporation's values and ethics. The code has eight commitments, with commitments 1–4 concerned with, respectively, products and services; open competition; corporate information; and a respectful environmental policy. These are laudable and hopefully reasonably standard commitments. For our purposes, in terms of corporations that appear to be moving beyond specific but localised CSR initiatives, the Citizen Group displays in commitments 5–8 an articulation of a corporation that does appear to be 'walking the talk' of corporate citizenship (the name of the corporation being highly apposite).

| No. | Commitment |
| --- | --- |
| 5 | Value symbiosis with the regional society as a good corporate citizen, and strive to make a social contribution. |
| 6 | Ensure a safe and good work environment, encourage the development of our employees' abilities and energies while respecting their character and individuality. |
| 7 | Respond to anti-social and corruptive behaviour in a decisive manner. |
| 8 | Value and respect different cultures and customs in foreign countries and contribute to the development of the locale. |

In an extract from the company's 2004 'Environmental and Social Report' (p. 26), the following statements appear.

> In my view [Chair of the CSR Committee] CSR initiatives are an integral part of our business activities. It's not something new that we have to begin. Rather, the way I see it, what we need to do is have a fresh look at our business activities in the context of our relationships with the various stakeholders who support Citizen, and ask anew how we can put this new CSR approach into our business activities ... last year when other companies in Japan suffered from various corporate scandals, I felt that Citizen's culture served us well as a precious asset to help us avoid such problems. Now that Citizen has announced CSR as an important pillar of management, I would like to do my best to help preserve our corporate culture, robustness, honesty and openness.

**Case study 9.6**

## The 'DEEP' fish restaurant chain

A fish restaurant chain was established in 2005, trading under the name 'DEEP'. The menu in the restaurants is limited to only those fish that are *not* 'at risk'. So you will not find Atlantic cod, haddock, blue fin tuna, monkfish or halibut on the menu. Instead there are herring, mackerel and pollack, and others whose stocks are not endangered. The restaurant chain is committed to serving only fish that are taken from the sea within a sustainable fishing policy. Interestingly, fish farms, because of health and safety concerns, as well as the practice of feeding fish sprats to the salmon in the form of food pellets, are not regarded as an appropriate source. In addition, the restaurant chain makes an explicit statement that £1 is added to every bill, which will be used as a donation to a named pressure group that is lobbying for sustainable fishing policies throughout the world.

These are encouraging developments from the corporate world. Moving to the non-profit seeking organisation, a number of interesting developments can be cited, of which the following are but illustrative.

**Case study 9.7**

## The Natural Step Organisation

The Natural Step Organisation was founded in 1989 by Dr Karl-Henrik Robèrt, who at the time was a leading Swedish oncologist (cancer specialist). Dr Robèrt had become concerned about a significant increase in childhood leukaemia cases in particular parts of Sweden, and traced the cause to increasing toxins in the environment. These appeared to have been the result of particular production processes. Dr Robèrt's concern at the production methods used to manufacture so many goods led him to found The Natural Step Organisation to address the systemic causes of environmental problems. Society's apparent preferencing of commercial activity has echoes of Heidegger's 'enframing of technology' or 'technology mindset'.

With the help of fifty Swedish scientists, Dr Robèrt developed a consensus document that described the basic knowledge of the earth's functions and how humans interact with it. The organisation's website tells how the document went through 21 iterations and upon completion was sent to every household and school in Sweden.

In the early 1990s, Dr Robèrt worked with physicist, John Holmberg, to define a set of guiding principles for a sustainable society that are based on the laws of thermodynamics and natural cycles. These principles of sustainability are the foundation of The Natural Step's content and approach. The organisation now has centres in many countries, with its American operations having been established in 1995. The Natural Step Organisation works with corporations and governments in developing sustainable programmes of industrial and commercial activity, but that is not to say that its four guiding principles are easily absorbed within many corporate practices. Changes are required.

**Case study 9.8**

## The Sustainability Institute

The Sustainability Institute was founded in 1996 and possesses an interesting statement of its philosophy.

Unsustainability does not arise out of ignorance, irrationality or greed. It is largely the collective consequence of rational, well-intended decisions made by people caught-up in systems – ranging from families and communities to corporations, governments and economies – that make it difficult or impossible to act in ways that are fully responsible to all those affected in the present and future generations.

(http://www.sustainabilityinstitute.org)

Once again the issue of an 'enframing technology' mind-set underpins the perspective. We are dealing with, in many respects, a need to change people's assumptions about what is possible and acceptable in terms of sustainable systems, communities, economies and societies. However, it must be stressed that what sustainable futures will look like is up to people, individually and collectively, to negotiate, debate and work towards. The mission statement of The Sustainability Institute adopts just this line of reasoning. It possesses three elements, namely:

- to shift mind-sets – values, attitudes and beliefs – when they are out of step with the realities of a finite planet and a globally dominant human race;

- to restructure systems when the rewards and incentives of the system are inconsistent with long-term social, environmental and economic goals; and

- to build the capability to manage and learn in complex, environmental, social and economic systems.

---

**Case study 9.9**

## The Sustainable Business Institute

The Sustainable Business Institute (SBI) is another organisation that seeks to work with corporations to address the challenges of sustainable economic, social and environmental systems.

The SBI was founded in 1994 and aims to educate senior executives about 'what is sustainability' and how sustainable practices are working effectively across industries. In sympathy with the Global Compact's approach of disseminating good practice, the SBI places considerable emphasis upon using workshops, forums and the media, particularly television programmes, to spread its ideas and approaches among senior executives.

---

**Case study 9.10**

## The International Institute for Sustainable Development

The International Institute for Sustainable Development (IISD) was established in 1990 and aims to contribute to sustainable development by advancing policy recommendations in a number of areas, *viz.*

- international trade and investment,

- economic policy,

- climate change,

- measurement and indicators, and

- natural resource management.

By using Internet communications the IISD aims to report on international negotiations and broker knowledge gained through collaborative projects with global partners, resulting in more rigorous research, capacity building in developing countries and better dialogue between North and South.

**Case study 9.11** **The Institute for Market Transformation to Sustainability**

The Institute for Market Transformation to Sustainability (MTS) is another organisation with a commitment to exploring, identifying and supporting sustainable economic activity. However, this organisation is much more upbeat and bullish about the power of markets to be the force in activating change, albeit with an initial helping hand. Its website includes the following statement.

MTS brings together a powerful coalition of sustainable products manufacturers, environmental groups, and key state and local government leaders using market mechanisms [to] increase sales and market share of sustainable products. We have identified consensus protocols for sustainable products such as FSC Certified Wood, Certified Organic Products, and the Clean Car Standard. When such a consensus is reached, the next steps are to increase awareness and sales of these products until profit motives and other marketplace incentives kick in and drive the transformation. Awareness and sales are manageable steps. ... Because the 100 largest companies account for more than 90% of the world's products, our mission is attainable. All companies want to increase their profits while contributing to an unpolluted, safer environment, and improved public welfare. ... Sustainable products increase corporate profits while enhancing society as a whole, because they are cheaper to make, have fewer regulatory constraints, less liability, can be introduced to the market quicker, and are preferred by the public.

(http://mts.sustainableproducts.com)

The commitment to the notion of markets being the primary, if not exclusive, driver of sustainable development is contestable, for such an approach requires that:

(a) all the salient facts can be expressed in numerical form;

(b) all the salient information (including that relating to the preferences of future generations) can be articulated in the final 'market' price; and

(c) all decisions are simply the art, or science, of obtaining the 'right balance' of resource usage and that placing the resource in the hands of those who are able to pay the highest price is the most appropriate 'solution'.

The first two points are concerned with the feasibility of developing inclusive and articulate prices. The third and final point is one that raises profound philosophical issues, both political and ethical.

Moving to the academic community, we find that a number of universities have established sustainability research centres such as:

- the **Sustainable Futures Institute** at Michigan Technological University, USA;

- the **Sustainable Development Research Initiative** at the University of British Columbia, Canada;

- the **World Business Council for Sustainable Development**, which has close links with the Royal Melbourne Institute of Technology, Australia;

- the **Institute of Sustainable Development in Business** at Nottingham Trent University, England; and

- the **Sustainable Development Research Centre**, at Forres, Scotland, which has strong links with St Andrews University, Scotland, and the University of the Highlands and Islands, Scotland.

All of these institutes, and the many more that exist, are important developments. Local, grassroots initiatives are necessary developments for sustainable communities and societies. However, for the national and global sustainability agendas to be adequately addressed, there is an unavoidable need for the active and sincere engagement of large corporations and governments. As the MTS website announces, the largest 100 corporations account for 90 per cent of the world's production output. Without these corporations 'on board' and the active support of governments in encouraging and enforcing sustainable economic, social and environmental policies, all the individual initiatives, as important as they are, will not be anywhere near sufficient to address the pressing sustainability problems.

## The triple bottom line

A phrase that was in vogue in the early 2000s was to talk of organisations having a 'triple bottom line', as distinct from the traditional use of the term 'bottom line' meaning simply profit. The triple bottom line encompasses economic, social and environmental concerns, but its articulation and operationalisation has remained problematic. Explanations of what is meant by 'triple bottom line' do not suggest an equal weighting being given to the three elements. Birch (2001), in reviewing a draft charter of corporate citizenship developed by BP Australia, referred to a statement contained within the draft charter. Under the heading 'sustainable development' the following statement appeared.

> BP is committed to a socially, environmentally and economically responsible business. This means maximising profit in order to create wealth and sustainable jobs, always intending to have a positive social and environmental impact.
>
> (Birch, 2001: 62)

The reference to maximising profit is interesting. Within the draft charter no attempt is made to discuss the tension between this commitment and the commitments made to the social and environmental issues mentioned elsewhere in the draft charter. However, Birch does refer to earlier discussions with BP Australia during which these issues appeared to have been raised.

> The tensions between capitalism and democracy as currently defined are irreconcilable without serious change. We agreed that we could not achieve long-term sustainability without change. Business needs, therefore, significant policy directions to enable this change to occur, not just within business practices but also within society overall.
>
> (Birch, 2001: 59)

The phrase 'business needs … significant policy directions' refers directly to the need for a 'sovereign power', à la Hobbes. There is no suggestion that business can be assumed to resolve these tensions itself. The 'hidden hand' of the market is viewed as too unreliable to be left to its own devices in this context.

The triple bottom line is part of the Global Reporting Initiative (GRI) which in turn is a voluntary initiative that has so far been through two iterations. As we write the second edition of this book, the GRI team is receiving comments and advice from users and preparers as to how the GRI reporting requirements should be developed for the future. The process is open, mirroring the GRI's commitment to a stakeholder approach to corporate reporting. The third version of the GRI is due in 2006.

The current requirements of the GRI require organisations to report on corporate environmental, social and economic performance information, in essence a corporation's sustainability performance. There are five framework documents to the GRI, which are:

- Sustainability reporting guidelines (these are core requirements for all organisations).

- Sector supplements (which indicate additional information for different sectors, if such information is available).

- Technical protocols (these provide details of individual indicators, their definition, formulae and cross-referencing to minimise problems in comparability).

- Issue guidance documents (which are non-sector specific issues affecting a range of organisations, such as 'diversity' and 'productivity'), which all lead to:

- The Sustainability Report.

## A two-way social contract?

What every sustainability and corporate responsibility initiative has to recognise and accept is that with the best will in the world, business corporations, in the form of their chief executives, have to be competitive in their respective marketplaces. Until consumers not only express a wish for corporations to move beyond legal minima, but are prepared, in certain cases, to pay slightly higher prices for products or services produced and delivered in ways that are more socially or environmentally sensitive than rival products, then corporate executives will feel there is too much hypocrisy and double standards in many of the corporate responsibility debates. The social contract, which was discussed in Chapter 8, tends to be presented as a one-way contract, that is, the conditions within the contract are placed exclusively upon corporations for them to maintain their (theoretical) 'licence to operate'. This poses a significant and fundamental question.

---

### A fundamental question

Do the demands of global environmental and social issues, as articulated in the Global Compact, suggest that we must think more carefully about the notion of a two-way social contract?

---

What do we mean by this?

The transfer of production capacity to less-developed economies is not only a reflection of capital seeking out the most profitable investment opportunities, but is also evidence of the perpetual downward pressure on prices. The 'real' (inflation adjusted) cost of many products has been and continues downwards. For most customers, assuming the quality differential is not too marked, then price is a/the critical purchase criterion. Corporate executives need to feel reassured that, assuming any price differential between their own products and those of their competitors can be explained by the more environmentally and/or socially sensitive policies of their organisation, then consumers will respect this and not prejudice the more sustainable policies of the company by switching their purchasing allegiance to companies with lower prices but less sustainable policies. In this respect governments have a potentially important part to play in either rewarding companies that operate with leading-edge environmental and social policies or penalising those that do not. Such interventions could be via grants, tax concessions or tax penalties. Such an approach might be anathema to market fundamentalists, but 'the market' (or more particularly 'the consumer') might be too capricious and fickle a coordinating mechanism in these circumstances to be seen as the principal tool for resource allocation. Is there a need for a term such as 'consumer social responsibility'?

These issues reflect the profoundly important debates that need to be increasingly part of political and social agendas.

## Summary

In this chapter the following key points have been made:

- The notion of sustainability should be seen as the symbiotic relationship between social, economic and environmental issues.

- Different ethical stances can be drawn upon to support particular sustainability positions.

- However, weighting the different claims in a utilitarian analysis can be extremely problematic. Not all those involved in or affected by a decision should necessarily attract the same level of importance.

- The leadership required of all political leaders concerning sustainability issues and the global crises of extreme poverty, child labour, inhuman working conditions, global warming, greenhouse gas emissions and political corruption has been found wanting.

- However, the decision by Global Compact to by-pass the political processes in 1999 and to go directly to the largest corporations to gain their active support in addressing the great global challenges of our time has, with hindsight, been recognised as flawed. Notwithstanding their poor track records, governments have to be a critical part of the strategies to address the many sustainability issues.

- Exclusive reliance upon the price mechanism to adjudicate and reflect societal preferences over sustainability issues has a number of profound weaknesses.

- The 'enframing of technology' mindset has to be successfully challenged.

- Current debates and demands concerning sustainable corporate practices tend to exclude the role consumers and governments can/must play in supporting those corporations employing sustainable and responsible practices and processes.

- The choices before us involve many issues, but above all they are choices that speak to the ethics and morals that we wish to underpin our communities and societies.

## Quick revision test

1. Is the price mechanism without blemish as the key mechanism for resolving societies' preferences for addressing global warming issues?

2. What is meant by the phrase 'the enframing of technology'?

3. What is meant by the environment being socially constructed?

4. Who is the philosopher normally associated with the phrase 'the enframing of technology'?

5. What is the difference between Adam Smith's notion of self-love and selfishness?

6. What might be meant by 'consumer social responsibility'?

7. What is the triple bottom line?

## Typical assignments and briefs

1. In the context of global warming, debate the appropriateness of the price mechanism as the primary democratic tool of resource allocation.

2. Critically evaluate Heidegger's notion of the 'enframing of technology' in terms of its contribution to debates concerning global economic growth rate forecasts.

3. Discuss the notion that 'consumer social responsibility is as important as corporate social responsibility'.

4. Evaluate the usefulness of Adam Smith's 'stranger' to debates concerning corporate executive behaviour and sustainable business practices.

# Topic 2
Information Literacy

# Introduction: Information Literacy

Information literacy is a skill – the ability to find, evaluate and compile information. You may think you are already 'information literate', but are you aware of all the sources of information in your field (and business and management in general)? Can you organise and assimilate information you might find? Can you recognise important bits of information and untrustworthy bits? Can you find the right information quickly? Do your search methods exclude particular types of information?

An information literate person can do more than read textbooks or type words into a search engine or database. The secret to finding good quality and relevant information is to know where to look, which questions to ask and which words to use.

For this particular project you have already been given some sources – but there are many different producers of information, but each will tend to specialise in a particular subject area or type of information and present it according to a specific style. For example, the annual report of a company is as much a marketing tool as an accounting tool, hence the increase in companies producing associated documents such as environmental reports or social responsibility reports. The website of an environmental lobbying group is likely to display a different style when discussing environmental events.

You will need to be realistic about what you can find – not all information is in the public domain, in the format you would like or reported on a regular basis. Much of the most interesting business information will always remain confidential and locked within the internal files of an organisation. Some subjects have not captured the interest of researchers or information providers, and therefore will not have material prepared ready for your enquiry. You may be able to find some of the information, but then need to bring it up to date e.g. check that a piece of legislation has not been amended or repealed by subsequent changes to the law.

Many of the information skills you ultimately develop will be transferable and should help you explore new topics not previously investigated.

In the business environment, information is valued for its role in helping managers to develop or progress commercial endeavour. It enables them to identify new ways of doing things, learn from the lessons of the past and monitor competitor activity. Real commercial benefits can be gained by recognising the importance of finding and utilising relevant information in a timely fashion.

## Categories and Producers of Business Information

The main categories of business information are Company, Market, Financial, Product, Country and Geopolitical. The Producers of the information are the organisations themselves, trade and professional organisations, business publishers , Local and UK government, Multinational organisations and Academic researchers.

The Internet revolution has provided a more readily accessible publishing mechanism for single interest information providers. As a consequence quality vetting of materials has become less consistent, leading to all the inherent dangers of inaccuracy and bias.

## Evaluating material

You should consider all of the following aspects before accepting a piece of information:

1.  AUTHOR: Who is the author? Is there a hidden sponsor with a position on the topic? Don't judge all academics as squeaky clean (they're not all disinterested!) and all web pages as inherently biased (or vice versa).
2.  ACCURACY: You can try to judge this by looking at the coherence of the information; better checks are systems of editorial or peer review control. Further just because there is a clear stream of numbers, you shouldn't assume there isn't inaccuracy or other issues.
3.  OBJECTIVITY: This is the key issue – can you be sure the information hasn't been researched on a biased agenda? A minority of journals, publishers, web pages have a particular agenda. You should also reflect on your own personal assumptions or bias (political, environmental or social) when choosing to use or interpret a particular piece of information.
4.  CURRENCY: Identify the date that the information was created or revised. Is the material of an appropriate age to be useful?
5.  COVERAGE:  A BBC news page will typically have less depth than the original source(s) which the journalist used to write that page
6.  APPROPRIATENESS: Does the information answer / help to answer the question you originally posed, in a format you can make use of? Are you making a commercial business case or testing an academic theory?
7.  MISSING: Identify the strength and weaknesses of the material you've found. What information is still missing, before you can make a balanced judgement? Where might you find such information.

Use these criteria (or Saunders' criteria and any other you can argue to add)  to evaluate all your material in an Information Grid. Critical reflection and judgement is seen as a key attribute of higher-level study. Simply reporting information in itself is limited. It is the evaluation and interpretation of the information and judgement of the validity and credibility of the sources of that information which in part is the value-added thinking you should apply. Be aware of both the power and the limitations of a Google search.

In the Saunders Chapter 3 read up on the purpose of a literature review to develop your information skills by thinking how to refine further questions and objectives and to sample current opinions: the criteria above are reinforced with emphasis on up to date knowledge and clear referencing. Consider the structure of the critical review when evaluating your information resources.  Section 3.3 Literature sources available gives details to add to the producers list above. Section 3.4 Planning your literature search strategy shows how to generate key words for your search can become more focussed.  Because of limited University resources, third year students cannot use Inter-library loan. Saunders appendix 2 shows a good guide to Referencing style. If you would like to refresh your general information skills, try the online training module for Business postgraduates and honours students at : http://gaels.lib.strath.ac.uk/Business/

# Critically reviewing the literature

## LEARNING OUTCOMES

By the end of this chapter you should:

→ understand the importance and purpose of the critical literature review to your research project;

→ know what you need to include when writing your critical review;

→ be aware of the range of primary, secondary and tertiary literature sources available;

→ be able to identify key words and to undertake a literature search using a range of methods including the Internet;

→ be able to evaluate the relevance, value and sufficiency of the literature found;

→ be able to reference the literature found accurately;

→ be able to apply the knowledge, skills and understanding gained to your own research project.

## 3.1 Introduction

As part of your studies, you have almost certainly already been asked by your tutors to 'review the literature', 'write a literature review' or 'critically review the literature' on topics they have specified. Indeed, you may be like many students and have grown to fear the literature review, not because of the associated reading but because of the requirement both to make judgements as to the value of each piece of work and to organise those ideas and findings that are of value into a review. It is these two processes in particular that people find both difficult and time consuming.

Two major reasons exist for reviewing the literature (Sharp *et al.*, 2002). The first, the preliminary search that helps you to generate and refine your research ideas, has already been discussed in Section 2.3. The second, often referred to as the **critical review** or **critical literature review**, is part of your research project proper. Most research textbooks, as well as your project tutor, will argue that this critical review of the literature is necessary. Although you may feel that you already have a good knowledge of your research area, we believe that reviewing the literature is essential. Project assessment criteria usually require you to demonstrate awareness of the current state of knowledge in your subject, its limitations, and how your research fits in this wider context (Gill and Johnson, 2002). In Jankowicz's (2005:161) words:

> There is little point in reinventing the wheel ... the work that you do is not done in a vacuum, but builds on the ideas of other people who have studied the field before you. This requires you describe what has been published, and to marshal the information in a relevant and critical way.

The significance of your research and what you find out will inevitably be judged in relation to other people's research and their findings. You therefore need both to 'map and assess the existing intellectual territory' (Tranfield *et al.*, 2003:208), establishing what research has been published in your chosen area, and, if possible, to try to identify any other research that might currently be in progress. Consequently, the items you read and write about will enhance your subject knowledge and help you to clarify your research question(s) further. This process is called *critically reviewing the literature*.

Recently, we were discussing the difficulties students have when writing their literature reviews for their research projects. Mark summarised what he felt we and fellow project tutors were saying:

'So what happens sometimes is ... a student comes to see her or his project tutor having obviously done a great deal of work. The student presents the tutor with what she or he says is the finished literature review. Yet the purpose of their review is unclear. It is little more than a summary of the articles and books read, each article or book being given one paragraph. Some students have arranged these paragraphs alphabetically in author order, others have arranged them in chronological order. None have linked or juxtaposed the ideas. Their literature reviews look more like adjacent pages from a catalogue rather than a critical review. Just like the items on these pages, each article or book has some similarities in terms of subject matter and so are grouped together. As in the catalogue, the reasons for these groupings are not made explicit. In addition, like the summary descriptions of items on the pages of a home shopping catalogue, each book or article is accorded equal status rather than the amount written reflecting its value to the student's research project.'

*A page from a book catalogue*

He concluded:

'Whilst such an approach obviously makes good sense for a shopping catalogue, it does not work for the critical review of the literature. We obviously need to explain better what we mean by a critical review of the literature to our students.'

For most research projects, your literature search will be an early activity. Despite this early start, it is usually necessary to continue searching throughout your project's life. The process can be likened to an upward spiral, culminating in the final draft of a written critical literature review (Figure 3.1). In the initial stage of your literature review, you will start to define the parameters to your research question(s) and objectives (Section 3.4). After generating key words and conducting your first search (Section 3.5), you will have a list of references to authors who have published on these subjects. Once these have been obtained, you can read and evaluate them (Section 3.6), record the ideas (Section 3.7) and start drafting your review. After the initial search, you will be able to redefine your parameters more precisely and undertake further searches, keeping in mind your research question(s) and objectives. As your thoughts develop, each subsequent search will be focused more precisely on material that is likely to be relevant. At the same time, you will probably be refining your research question(s) and objectives in the light of your reading (Section 2.4).

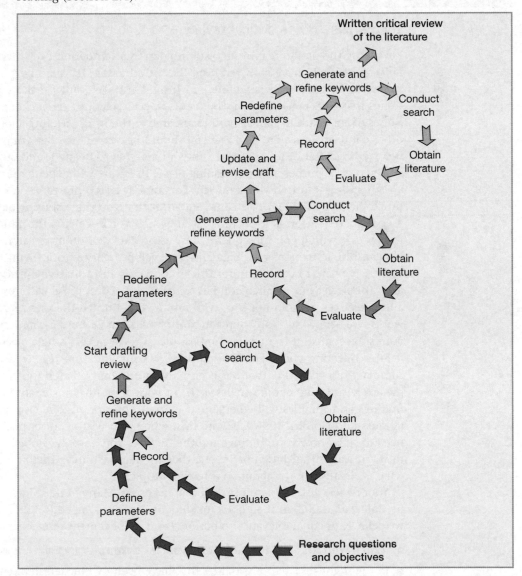

Figure 3.1    The literature review process

*Source*: © Mark Saunders, Philip Lewis, Adrian Thornhill and Martin Jenkins 2003

Unlike some academic disciplines, business and management research makes use of a wide range of literature. While your review is likely to include specific business disciplines such as finance, marketing and human resource management, it is also likely to include other disciplines. Those most frequently consulted by our students include economics, psychology, sociology and geography. Given this, and the importance of the review to your research, it is vital for you to be aware of what a critical literature review is and the range of literature available before you start the reviewing process. For these reasons, we start this chapter by outlining the purpose of your critical review of the literature, its content and what we mean by 'critical' (Section 3.2) and then discussing those literature resources available (Section 3.3).

## 3.2 | The critical review

### The purpose of the critical review

Reviewing the literature critically will provide the foundation on which your research is built. As you will have gathered from the introduction, its main purpose is to help you to develop a good understanding and insight into relevant previous research and the trends that have emerged. You would not expect a scientific researcher inquiring into the causes of cot death to start his or her research without first reading about the findings of other cot death research. Likewise you should not expect to start your research without first reading what other researchers in your area have already found out.

The precise purpose of your reading of the literature will depend on the approach you are intending to use in your research. For some research projects you will use the literature to help you to identify theories and ideas that you will test using data. This is known as a **deductive approach** (Section 4.3) in which you develop a theoretical or conceptual framework, which you subsequently test using data. For other research projects you will be planning to explore your data and to develop theories from them that you will subsequently relate to the literature. This is known as an **inductive approach** (Section 4.3) and, although your research still has a clearly defined purpose with research question(s) and objectives, you do not start with any predetermined theories or conceptual frameworks. We believe such an approach cannot be taken without a competent knowledge of your subject area. It is, however, impossible to review every single piece of the literature before collecting your data. The purpose of your literature review is not to provide a summary of everything that has been written on your research topic, but to review the most relevant and significant research on your topic. If your analysis is effective, new findings and theories will emerge that neither you nor anyone else has thought about (Strauss and Corbin, 1998). Despite this, when you write your critical review, you will need to show how your findings and the theories you have developed or are using relate to the research that has gone before, thereby demonstrating that you are familiar with what is already known about your research topic.

Your review also has a number of other purposes. Many of these have been highlighted by Gall *et al.* (2002) in their book for students undertaking educational research and are, we believe, of equal relevance to business and management researchers:

- to help you to refine further your research question(s) and objectives;
- to highlight research possibilities that have been overlooked implicitly in research to date;

- to discover explicit recommendations for further research. These can provide you with a superb justification for your own research question(s) and objectives;

- to help you to avoid simply repeating work that has been done already;

- to sample current opinions in newspapers, professional and trade journals, thereby gaining insights into the aspects of your research question(s) and objectives that are considered newsworthy;

- to discover and provide an insight into research approaches, strategies (Section 4.3) and techniques that may be appropriate to your own research question(s) and objectives.

## The content of the critical review

As you begin to find, read and evaluate the literature, you will need to think how to combine the academic theories and ideas about which you are reading to form the critical review that will appear in your project report. Your review will need to evaluate the research that has already been undertaken in the area of your research project, show and explain the relationships between published research findings and reference the literature in which they were reported (Appendix 2). It will draw out the key points and trends (recognising any omissions and bias) and present them in a logical way which also shows the relationship to your own research. In doing this you will provide readers of your project report with the necessary background knowledge to your research question(s) and objectives and establish the boundaries of your own research. Your review will also enable the readers to see your ideas against the background of previous published research in the area. This does not necessarily mean that your ideas must extend, follow or approve those set out in the literature. You may be highly critical of the earlier research reported in the literature and seek to discredit it. However, if you wish to do this you must still review this literature, explain clearly why it is problematic, and then justify your own ideas.

In considering the content of your critical review you will therefore need:

- to include the key academic theories within your chosen area of research;

- to demonstrate that your knowledge of your chosen area is up to date;

- through clear referencing, enable those reading your project report to find the original publications you cite.

In addition, by fully acknowledging the research of others you will avoid charges of *plagiarism* and the associated penalties. The content of your critical review can be evaluated using the checklist in Box 3.1.

## What is really meant by being 'critical' about the content

Within the context of your course you have probably already been asked to take a critical approach for previous assignments. However, it is worth considering what we mean by critical within the context of your literature review. Mingers (2000:225–6) argues that there are four aspects of a critical approach that should be fostered by management education:

- critique of rhetoric;
- critique of tradition;

## BOX 3.1 CHECKLIST

### Evaluating the content of your critical literature review

☑ Have you ensured that the literature covered relates clearly to your research question and objectives?

☑ Have you covered the most relevant and significant theories of recognised experts in the area?

☑ Have you covered the most relevant and significant literature or at least a representative sample?

☑ Have you included up-to-date literature?

☑ Have you referenced all the literature used in the format prescribed in the assessment criteria?

- critique of authority;
- critique of objectivity.

The first of these, the 'critique of rhetoric', means appraising or evaluating a problem with effective use of language. In the context of your critical literature review, this emphasises the need for you, as the reviewer, to use your skills both of making reasoned judgements and of arguing effectively in writing. The other three aspects Mingers identifies also have implications for being critical when reading and writing about the work of others. This includes you questioning, where justification exists to do so, the conventional wisdom, the 'critique of tradition' and the dominant view portrayed in the literature you are reading, the 'critique of authority'. Finally, it is likely also to include recognising in your review that the knowledge and information you are discussing are not value free, the 'critique of objectivity'.

Being critical in reviewing the literature is therefore a combination of your skills and the attitude with which you read. In critically reviewing the literature, you need to read the literature about your research topic with some scepticism and be willing to question what you read. This means you need to be constantly considering and justifying with clear arguments your own critical stance. You will therefore have to read widely on your research topic and have a good understanding of the literature. Critically reviewing the literature for your research project therefore requires you to have gained topic-based background knowledge, understanding, the ability to reflect upon and to analyse the literature and, based on this, to make reasoned judgements that are argued effectively. When you use these skills to review the literature, the term 'critical' refers to the judgement you exercise. It therefore describes the process of providing a detailed and justified analysis of, and commentary on, the merits and faults of the key literature within your chosen area. This means that, for your review to be critical, you will need to have shown critical judgement.

Part of this judgement will inevitably mean being able to identify the most relevant and significant theories and recognised experts highlighted in Box 3.1. In addition, Dees (2003) suggests that this means you should:

- refer to and assess research by recognised experts in your chosen area;
- consider and discuss research that supports and research that opposes your ideas;

- make reasoned judgements regarding the value of others' research, showing clearly how it relates to your research;
- justify your arguments with valid evidence in a logical manner;
- distinguish clearly between fact and opinion.

These points are developed in Box 3.2, which contains a checklist to evaluate the extent to which your literature review is critical. The more questions to which you can answer 'yes', the more likely your review will be critical!

---

**BOX 3.2 CHECKLIST**

### Evaluating whether your literature review is critical

☑ Have you shown how your research question relates to previous research reviewed?

☑ Have you assessed the strengths and weaknesses of the previous research reviewed?

☑ Have you been objective in your discussion and assessment of other people's research?

☑ Have you included references to research that is counter to your own opinion?

☑ Have you distinguished clearly between facts and opinions?

☑ Have you made reasoned judgements about the value and relevance of others' research to your own?

☑ Have you justified clearly your own ideas?

☑ Have you highlighted those areas where new research (yours!) is needed to provide fresh insights and taken these into account in your arguments. In particular:

　☑ where there are inconsistencies in current knowledge and understanding?

　☑ where there are omissions or bias in published research?

　☑ where research findings need to be tested further?

　☑ where evidence is lacking, inconclusive, contradictory or limited?

☑ Have you justified your arguments by referencing correctly published research?

---

## The structure of the critical review

The **literature review** that you write for your project report should therefore be a description and critical analysis of what other authors have written (Jankowicz, 2005). When drafting your review you therefore need to focus on your research question(s) and objectives. One way of helping you to focus is to think of your literature review as discussing how far existing published research goes in answering your research question(s). The shortfall in the literature will be addressed, at least partially, in the remainder of your project report. Another way of helping you to focus is to ask yourself how your review relates to your objectives. If it does not, or does only partially, there is a need for a clearer focus on your objectives. The precise structure of the critical review is usually your choice, although you should check, as it may be specified in the assessment criteria. Three common structures are:

- a single chapter;
- a series of chapters;
- throughout the project report as you tackle various issues.

In all project reports, you should return to the key issues from the literature in your discussion and conclusions (Section 14.3).

Within your critical review, you will need to juxtapose different authors' ideas and form your own opinions and conclusions based on these. Although you will not be able to start writing until you have undertaken some reading, we recommend that you start drafting your review early (Figure 3.1). What you write can then be updated and revised as you read more.

A common mistake with critical literature reviews, highlighted at the start of this chapter, is that they become uncritical listings of previous research. Often they are little more than annotated bibliographies (Hart, 1998), individual items being selected because they fit with what the researcher is proposing (Greenhalgh, 1997). Although there is no single structure that your critical review should take, our students have found it useful to think of the review as a funnel in which you:

1 start at a more general level before narrowing down to your specific research question(s) and objectives;

2 provide a brief overview of key ideas and themes;

3 summarise, compare and contrast the research of the key writers;

4 narrow down to highlight previous research work most relevant to your own research;

5 provide a detailed account of the findings of this research and show how they are related;

6 highlight those aspects where your own research will provide fresh insights;

7 lead the reader into subsequent sections of your project report, which explore these issues.

In addition, some writers argue that, in order to improve the transparency of your review process, you should explain precisely how you searched for selected the literature you have included in your review, outlining your choice of key words and of databases used (Tranfield *et al.*, 2003). Within the 'funnel' we have just proposed, this can be thought of as step 0! This is discussed in more detail in sections 3.4 and 3.5.

Whichever way you structure your review you must demonstrate that you have read, understood and evaluated the items you have located. The key to writing a critical literature review is therefore to link the different ideas you find in the literature to form a coherent and cohesive argument, which sets in context and justifies your research. Obviously, it should relate to your research question and objectives. It should show a clear link from these as well as a clear link to the empirical work that will follow. Box 3.3 provides a checklist to help you ensure that the structure of your literature review supports this. Subsequent parts of your project report (Section 14.3) must follow on from this.

## BOX 3.3 CHECKLIST

### Evaluating the structure of your literature review

- ☑ Does your literature review have a clear title which describes the focus of your research rather than just saying 'literature review'?

- ☑ Have you explained precisely how you searched the literature, and the criteria used to select those studies included?

- ☑ Does your review start at a more general level before narrowing down?

- ☑ Is your literature review organised thematically around the ideas contained in the research being reviewed rather than the researchers?

- ☑ Are your arguments coherent and cohesive – do your ideas link in a way that will be logical to your reader?

- ☑ Have you used sub-headings within the literature review to help guide your reader?

- ☑ Does the way you have structured your literature review draw your reader's attention to those issues which are going to be the focus of your research?

- ☑ Does your literature review lead your reader into subsequent sections of your project report?

## BOX 3.4 FOCUS ON MANAGEMENT RESEARCH

### Structure of the literature review

An article published by Mark and Adrian in *Personnel Review* (Saunders and Thornhill, 2003:361–2) includes a review of the literature on organisational justice and trust. The following extract is taken from the introduction of this review and the first subsection. Although your literature review will be longer than this, the extract illustrates:

- the overall structure of starting at a more general level before narrowing down;
- the provision of a brief overview of the key ideas;
- the linking of ideas;
- narrowing down to highlight that work which is most relevant to the research reported.

In their paper, Mark and Adrian subsequently provide more detail about the findings of that research which is most relevant.

**Organisational Justice, Trust and Change: An Overview**
Organisational justice theory (Greenberg, 1987) focuses on perceptions of fairness in organisations, by categorising employees' views and feelings about their treatment and that of others within an organisation. Three types of organisational justice theory have been identified in the literature (Greenberg, 1987; Folger and Cropanzano, 1998). Perceptions about the outcomes of decisions taken form the basis of distributive justice (Homans, 1961; Leventhal, 1976). Perceptions about the processes used to arrive at, and to implement, these decisions form the basis of two further types of justice that are often treated as one in the literature; these are procedural justice and interactional justice (for example Cropanzano and Greenberg, 1997). Procedural justice focuses on employee

perceptions of the fairness of procedures used to make decisions (Thibaut and Walker, 1975). This has been distinguished from interactional justice which focuses on employees' perceptions about the fairness of the interpersonal treatment received during implementation (Bies and Moag, 1986).

Development of trust theory has, to date, been more disparate focusing on a range of levels of analysis from the interpersonal to the inter-organisational (e.g. Rousseau et al., 1998). Although this has resulted in a variety of definitions of trust, these exhibit a number of common elements including notions of 'favourable expectations' and a 'willingness to become vulnerable'. Möllering (2001) has sought to use and develop these elements, arguing that trust develops from favourable expectations that are based upon interpretations of the reality to which trust relates, enabled by a suspension of disbelief and a corresponding leap of faith. This suggests that the process through which trust is developed is informed by socially constructed interpretations of reality that include a willingness to make judgements about as yet unresolved situations and a leap of faith about unknown ones. Trust, according to this approach, is based upon the acceptance of interpretations that includes awareness that information is imperfect. Accordingly, a 'mental leap of trust' is made, or required, from interpretation to expectation for trust to be developed (Möllering 2001: 412).

Herriot et al (1998)'s four manifestations of trust offer a means of relating Möllering's (2001) process based definition to organisational change. Their first manifestation emphasises confidence that expectations of the outcomes of change will be favourable, namely that obligations will be fulfilled. The second relates to a belief about not being deceived. For example, that managers will not be selective with the truth or actively deceive those they manage. In contrast, the third emphasises a willingness to become vulnerable, focusing on the trust placed in the abilities of those managing the change process to undertake this role. Finally, the fourth deals with trust originating from a belief that people are benevolent, will not harm employees (again emphasising vulnerability) and may even care for their welfare during the change process (implying an additional leap of faith). We consider each of the types of organisational justice in turn alongside the likely implications for these manifestations of trust.

*Distributive justice and trust*

Within a change context, distributive justice is concerned with perceptions of fairness arising from organisational allocations and outcomes. Pillai et al (2001) argue that when distributions of organisational outcomes are considered fair, higher levels of trust are likely to ensue. In a similar way, Herriot et al.'s (1998) first manifestation of trust is based on the fulfilment of perceived obligations. According to these formulations the experience of fulfilled obligations is directly related to the generation of trust.

Adams (1965) proposed that feelings of inequity would arise where the ratio of a person's outcomes in relation to their inputs from an exchange were perceived as disproportionate, as the result of a comparison with others. Perceptions of unfairness may lead to positive inequity, where a person perceives that another had a greater claim to a particular allocation leading to a feeling of guilt. In this way an outcome may be favourable but it may not facilitate fairness or trust due to perceptions about lack of integrity in relation to the process (e.g. Bews and Uys, 2002). Alternatively, perceptions of unfairness may lead to negative inequity, where a person feels that they had a greater claim to an outcome compared to the person receiving it, leading to feelings of anger and possibly mistrust.

Perceptions of distributive justice are based largely on comparisons with others (Adams, 1965; Cropanzano and Greenberg, 1997; Greenberg, 1987). Similarly, perceptions about obligations and trust are likely to be related not just to an absolute measure, about whether obligations have been fulfilled, but also to one or more relative, social comparisons. These are termed referent comparisons or standards. Feelings of trust are therefore likely to be affected by the relative treatment of others and by more generalised opportunities available within a person's occupational group, organisation or perhaps even another organisational context.

## 3.3 | Literature sources available

### An overview

The literature sources available to help you to develop a good understanding of, and insight into, previous research can be divided into three categories: primary (published and unpublished), secondary, and tertiary (Figure 3.2). In reality these categories often overlap: for example, primary literature sources, including conference proceedings, can appear in journals, and some books contain indexes to primary and secondary literature.

The different categories of literature resources represent the flow of information from the original source. Often as information flows from primary to secondary to tertiary sources it becomes less detailed and authoritative but more easily accessible. It is because primary literature sources can be difficult to trace that they are sometimes referred to as **grey literature**. Recognising this information flow helps you to identify the most appropriate sources of literature for your needs. Some research projects may access only secondary literature sources whereas others will necessitate the use of primary sources.

The nature of this information flow is typical of traditional printed publications. However, the Internet is changing this situation, providing a more direct means of both publishing and accessing information. Alongside this, moves toward 'freedom of information' mean that what were traditionally 'grey literature', such as some government publications, are increasingly being made available, usually via the Internet. The majority of academic publications still exhibit this information flow, although the final place of publication is increasingly the Internet.

Figure 3.2 also illustrates the reduced currency of secondary literature sources, which are utilising information already published in primary sources. Because of the time taken to publish, the information in these sources can be dated. Your literature review should reflect current thinking as far as possible, so the limitations of such sources must be recognised.

**Primary literature** sources (also known as grey literature) are the first occurrence of a piece of work. They include published sources such as reports and some central and local

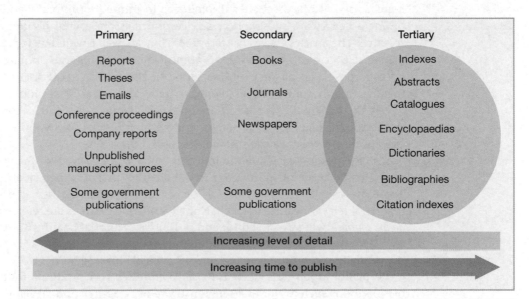

**Figure 3.2** **Literature sources available**

government publications such as White Papers and planning documents. They also include unpublished manuscript sources such as letters, memos and committee minutes that may be analysed as data in their own right (Section 8.2).

**Secondary literature** sources such as books and journals are the subsequent publication of primary literature. These publications are aimed at a wider audience. They are easier to locate than primary literature as they are better covered by the tertiary literature.

**Tertiary literature** sources, also called *search tools*, are designed either to help to locate primary and secondary literature or to introduce a topic. They therefore include indexes and abstracts as well as encyclopaedias and bibliographies.

Your use of these literature sources will depend on your research question(s) and objectives, the need for secondary data to answer them (Section 8.3) and the time available. For some research projects you may use only tertiary and secondary literature; for others you may need to locate primary literature as well. Most research projects will make the greatest use of secondary literature, and so it is this we consider first, followed by the primary literature. Tertiary literature sources are not discussed until Section 3.5, as their major use is in conducting a literature search.

## Secondary literature sources

The number of secondary literature sources available to you is expanding rapidly, especially as new resources are developed or made available via the Internet. Your university's librarians are likely to be aware of a wide range of secondary literature in business and management that can be accessed from your library, and will keep themselves up to date with new resources.

The main secondary literature sources that you are likely to use, along with those primary sources most frequently used for a literature review, are outlined in Table 3.1. The most important when placing your ideas in the context of earlier research are refereed academic journals. Books are, however, likely to be more important than professional and trade journals in this context.

### Journals

**Journals** are also known as *periodicals*, *serials* and *magazines*, and are published on a regular basis. While most are still produced in printed form, many additionally provide online access, via a subscription service. Journals are a vital literature source for any research. The articles are easily accessible. They are well covered by tertiary literature, and a good selection can be accessed from most university libraries either in print, for reference purposes, or via their online services. This online access is usually restricted to members of the university (Table 3.1). Trade and some professional journals may be covered only partially by the tertiary literature (Table 3.2). You therefore need to browse these journals regularly to be sure of finding useful items. Many journals' content pages can also be browsed via the Internet (Section 3.5).

Articles in **refereed academic journals** (such as the *Journal of Management Studies*) are evaluated by academic peers prior to publication, to assess their quality and suitability. These are usually the most useful for research projects as they will contain detailed reports of relevant earlier research. Not all academic journals are refereed. Most *other academic journals* will have an editor and possibly an editorial board with subject knowledge to select articles. The relevance and usefulness of such journals varies considerably, and occasionally you may need to be wary of possible bias (Section 3.6).

**Professional journals** (such as *People Management*) are produced for their members by organisations such as the Chartered Institute of Personnel and Development (CIPD), the

**Table 3.1  Main secondary and primary literature sources**

| Source | Frequency of publication | Format of publication | Coverage by abstracts and indexes (tertiary sources) | Likely availability |
|---|---|---|---|---|
| **Refereed academic journal**<br>**Other academic journal** | Mainly monthly or quarterly |  | Well covered. In addition, content pages often available for searching via publishers' websites | Kept as reference in most university libraries, with many accessible via the Internet through various subscription services. Those not available locally can usually be obtained using inter-library loans. Professional organisations may also provide access to their journals via their own web pages |
| **Professional journal** |  | Mainly printed, but many now available via the Internet. Can be also available on CD-ROM | Increasingly well covered by services such as ABI/Inform and Business Source Premier. In addition, content pages often available for searching via publishers' websites |  |
| **Trade journal** | Mainly weekly or monthly |  |  | Not as widely available in university libraries as academic and refereed journals. Can be obtained using inter-library loans. Most trade associations will have an associated website |
| **Books** | Once; subsequent editions may be published | Mainly printed, occasionally available via the Internet. Can also be available on CD-ROM | Well covered by abstracts and indexes. Searches can be undertaken on remote university OPACs* via the Internet | Widely available. Those not available locally can be obtained using inter-library loans |
| **Newspapers** | Mainly daily or weekly | Most 'quality' newspapers now available on the Internet or through subscription online databases. Also available on CD-ROM and microfilm (for older back-runs) | Specialised indexes available. CD-ROM and Internet format easy to search using key words | Home nation 'quality' newspapers kept as reference in most university libraries. Internet access to stories, often with additional information on the websites, for most national and international 'quality' newspapers |
| **Conference proceedings** | Dependent on the conference, sometimes as part of a journal | As for refereed academic journals. May be published in book form (e.g. Index to Conference Proceedings). Some conference proceedings or abstracts are published on the Internet | Depends on conference, although often limited. Specialist indexes sometimes available |  |
| **Reports** | Once | As for refereed academic journals. Government reports increasingly accessible via the Internet | Poor compared with most secondary sources, although some specialised indexes exist | Not widely held by university libraries. May be possible to obtain using inter-library loans |
| **Theses** | On the awarding of the research degree | Mainly printed | Good for PhD and MPhil research degrees, otherwise poor | Usually obtained using inter-library loans. Often only one copy |

*OPAC, Online Public Access Catalogue

*Source:* © Mark Saunders, Philip Lewis, Adrian Thornhill and Martin Jenkins 2006

**Table 3.2 Tertiary literature sources and their coverage**

| Name | Format | Coverage |
| --- | --- | --- |
| **ABI Inform** | Internet, CD-ROM | Indexes approximately 1000 international business and management journals. Also contains a wide range of trade and professional titles. Covers additional subjects such as engineering, law and medicine. Full text of selected articles from 500 journals may be available depending on subscription (CD-ROM updated monthly) |
| **BIDS** | Internet | Offers access to a wide range of services, including journals' contents pages |
| **British National Bibliography (BNB)** | CD-ROM, print | Bibliographic information for books and serials (journals) deposited at the British Library by UK and Irish publishers since 1950 |
| **British National Bibliography for Report Literature (formerly British Reports, Translations and Theses)** | Microfiche, print | Detailed listings of research and practice reports produced by non-commercial publishers, local and national government, industry, research institutions and charities. Includes UK doctoral theses since 1970 |
| **British Library Public Catalogue** | Internet | Gives access to British Library catalogues including reference collections and document supply collections (books, journals, reports, conferences, theses) |
| **Business Periodicals Index** | Internet, CD-ROM, print | Indexes English language business periodicals (articles and book reviews). North American focus. Selection for indexing is by subscriber preference and has altered over time (since 1959) |
| **EBSCO Business Source Premier** | Internet | Full-text articles from over 2000 management, business, economics and information technology journals, over 600 of which are refereed. Also contains a wide range of trade and professional titles |
| **EMERALD Fulltext** | Internet | 801 full-text journals from MCB University Press |
| **Emerald Management Reviews** | Internet, CD-ROM | Abstracts of articles selected from more than 400 English language publications on the basis of a significant contribution to knowledge |
| **European Business ASAP** | Internet, CD-ROM | 100 journals, mostly full text. Includes a mix of academic journals and business press |
| **Global Books in Print** | Internet | English language bibliographic information for books in print from most of the world |
| **Helecon** | Internet, CD-ROM | Combined indexes from seven European databases on business and management. European focus (updated three times a year) |
| **Index to Conference Proceedings** | CD-ROM, Internet, print | Indexes all conference publications, regardless of subject or language, held by British Library Document Supply Centre (updated monthly – print, quarterly – CD-ROM) |
| **Index to Theses** | Internet, print | Indexes theses accepted for higher degrees by universities in Great Britain and Ireland and by the CNAA (Council for National Academic Awards) |
| **Ingenta** | Internet | Journals contents page service, updated daily |
| **ISI Web of Science** | Internet | Includes access to a wide range of services, including citation indexes |
| **HMSO Monthly Catalogue** | Print | Lists all publications published and distributed through HMSO (includes parliamentary, government department and European) |
| **Key Note Reports** | Internet | Key Note market information reports |
| **Lexis Nexis Executive** | Internet | Worldwide business media database; includes national and regional newspapers, trade journals and company annual reports |
| **MINTEL** | Internet, CD-ROM | Mintel reports plus short business press articles used in the compilation of the reports |
| **Research Index** | Internet, print | Indexes articles and news items of financial interest that appear in the UK national newspapers, professional and trade journals (updated frequently) |
| **Sage Publications/ SRM Database of Social Research Methodology** | CD-ROM | Abstracts of methodological literature published in English, German, French and Dutch since 1970 |
| **Social Science Citation Index** | Internet | Indexes 130 000 articles each year from over 1400 journals in behavioural and social sciences and selected articles from 3100 journals from physical and natural sciences |

Association of Chartered Certified Accountants (ACCA) and the American Marketing Association (AMA). They contain a mix of news-related items and articles that are more detailed. However, you need to exercise caution, as articles can be biased towards their author's or the organisation's views. Articles are often of a more practical nature and more closely related to professional needs than those in academic journals. Some organisations will also produce newsletters or current awareness publications that you may find useful for up-to-date information. Some professional organisations now give access to selected articles in their journals via their web pages, though these may be only accessible to members (see Table 8.2 and Section 3.5). *Trade journals* fulfil a similar function to professional journals. They are published by trade organisations or aimed at particular industries or trades such as catering or mining. Often they focus on new products or services and news items. They rarely contain articles based on empirical research, although some provide summaries of research. You should therefore use these with considerable caution for your research project.

### Books

*Books* and *monographs* are written for specific audiences. Some are aimed at the academic market, with a theoretical slant. Others, aimed at practising professionals, may be more applied in their content. The material in books is usually presented in a more ordered and accessible manner than in journals, pulling together a wider range of topics. They are therefore particularly useful as introductory sources to help clarify your research question(s) and objectives or the research methods you intend to use. Some academic textbooks, such as this one, are now supported by web pages providing additional information. However, books may contain out-of-date material even by the time they are published.

### Newspapers

*Newspapers* are a good source of topical events, developments within business and government, as well as recent statistical information such as share prices. They also sometimes review recent research reports (Box 3.5). The main 'quality' newspapers have websites carrying the main stories and supporting information. Back copies starting in the early 1990s are available on CD-ROM or online via a full-text subscription service, such as *Proquest Newspapers* (Table 3.1). Current editions of newspapers can usually be found via the Internet. Most newspapers have a dedicated website and provide access to a limited full-text service free of charge. Items in earlier issues are more difficult to access, as they are usually stored on microfilm and need to be located using printed indexes. However, you need to be careful, as newspapers may contain bias in their coverage, be it political, geographical or personal. Reporting can also be inaccurate, and you may not pick up any subsequent amendments. In addition, the news presented is filtered depending on events at the time, with priority given to more headline-grabbing stories (Stewart and Kamins, 1993).

## Primary literature sources

Primary literature sources are more difficult to locate, although an increasing number are now being made available via the Internet (Table 3.1). The most accessible, and those most likely to be of use in showing how your research relates to that of other people, are reports, conference proceedings and theses.

## BOX 3.5 RESEARCH IN THE NEWS     FT

### Loan penalties hit 672,000 borrowers

An estimated 672,000 borrowers were hit by penalty fees on personal loans in the past year, according to new research.

The study by Money-Expert.com and Defaqto, financial companies, said people had lost out by having to pay early redemption penalties imposed by banks of up to two months' interest for paying back the money they owed ahead of time. The study also showed 5 per cent of borrowers intended to change their current loan product in 2006 but it believed some people looking to switch loans could pay out again if they did not fully understand how a loan works. The research was carried out by GfK NOP which questioned 957 people.

*Source*: Article by Jane Croft, *Financial Times*, 31 January 2006. Copyright © 2006 The Financial Times Ltd.

### Reports

*Reports* include market research reports such as those produced by Mintel and Keynote, government reports and academic reports. Even if you are able to locate these, you may find it difficult to gain access to them because they are not as widely available as books (Section 8.4). Reports are not well indexed in the tertiary literature, and you will need to rely on specific search tools such as the *British National Bibliography for Report Literature* and the British Library Public Catalogue (see Table 3.2).

The move toward 'freedom for information' by many Western governments has resulted in more information being made available via the web, for example the European Union's (EU) European Commission website and the Commission's Statistics website Eurostat. These and other governmental websites are listed in Table 8.3. European 'grey literature', including reports, conference proceedings, and discussion and policy papers, has been covered since 1980 by SIGLE (System for Information on Grey Literature in Europe) and is available from the publisher OVID.

Individual academics are also increasingly publishing reports and their research on the Internet. These can be a useful source of information. However, they may not have gone through the same review and evaluation process as journal articles and books. It is therefore important to try to assess the authority of the author, and to beware of personal bias.

### Conference proceedings

*Conference proceedings,* sometimes referred to as *symposia*, are often published as unique titles within journals or as books. Most conferences will have a theme that is very specific, but some have a wide-ranging overview. Proceedings are not well indexed by tertiary literature so, as with reports, you may have to rely on specific search tools such as *Index to Conference Proceedings* and the British Library Public Catalogue (Table 3.2) as well as more general search engines such as Google. If you do locate and are able to obtain the proceedings for a conference on the theme of your research, you will have a wealth of relevant information. Many conferences have associated web pages providing abstracts and occasionally the full papers presented at the conference.

### Theses

*Theses* are unique and so for a major research project can be a good source of detailed information; they will also be a good source of further references. Unfortunately, they can be difficult to locate and, when found, difficult to access as there may be only one copy at the awarding institution. Specific search tools are available, such as *Index to Theses* (see Table 3.2). Only research degrees such as PhD and MPhil are covered well by these tertiary resources. Research undertaken as part of a taught masters degree is not covered as systematically.

| 3.4 | Planning your literature search strategy |
|---|---|

It is important that you plan this search carefully to ensure that you locate relevant and up-to-date literature. This will enable you to establish what research has been previously published in your area and to relate your own research to it. All our students have found their literature search a time-consuming process, which takes far longer than expected. Fortunately, time spent planning will be repaid in time saved when searching the literature. As you start to plan your search, you need to beware of information overload! One of the easiest ways to achieve this is to start the main search for your critical review without a clearly defined research question(s), objectives and outline proposal (Sections 2.4 and 2.5). Before commencing your literature search, we suggest that you undertake further planning by writing down your search strategy and, if possible, discussing it with your project tutor. This should include:

- the parameters of your search;
- the key words and search terms you intend to use;
- the databases and search engines you intend to use;
- the criteria you intend to use to select the relevant and useful studies from all the items you find.

Whilst it is inevitable that your search strategy will be refined as your literature search progresses, we believe that such a planned approach is important as it forces you to think carefully about your research strategy and justify, at least to yourself, why you are doing what you are doing.

### Defining the parameters of your search

For most research questions and objectives you will have a good idea of which subject matter is going to be relevant. You will, however, be less clear about the parameters within which you need to search. In particular, you need to be clear about the following (Bell, 2005):

- language of publication (for example, English);
- subject area (for example, accountancy);
- business sector (for example, manufacturing);
- geographical area (for example, Europe);
- publication period (for example, the last 10 years);
- literature type (for example, refereed journals and books).

One way of starting to firm up these parameters is to re-examine your lecture notes and course textbooks in the area of your research question. While re-examining these, we suggest you make a note of subjects that appear most relevant to your research question and the names of relevant authors. These will be helpful when generating possible key words later.

For example, if your research was on the marketing benefits of arts sponsorship to UK banking organisations you might identify the subject area as marketing and sponsorship. Implicit in this is the need to think broadly. A common comment we hear from students who have attempted a literature search is 'there's nothing written on my research topic'. This is usually because they have identified one or more of their parameters too narrowly (or chosen key words that do not match the control language, Section 3.5). We therefore recommend that if you encounter this problem you broaden one or more of your parameters to include material that your narrower search would not have located (Box 3.6).

---

## BOX 3.6 WORKED EXAMPLE

### Defining parameters for a research question

Simon's research question was 'How have green issues influenced the way in which manufacturers advertise cars?' To be certain of finding material he defined each parameter in narrow and, in most instances, broader terms:

| Parameter | Narrow | Broader |
|---|---|---|
| Language | UK (e.g. car) | UK and USA (e.g. car and automobile) |
| Subject area | Green issues | Environmental issues |
| | Motor industry | Manufacturing |
| | Advertising | Marketing |
| Business sector | Motor industry | Manufacturing |
| Geographical area | UK | Europe and North America |
| Publication period | Last 5 years | Last 15 years |
| Literature type | Refereed journals and books | Journals and books |

---

### Generating your key words

It is important at this stage to read both articles by key authors and recent review articles in the area of your research. This will help you to define your subject matter and to suggest appropriate key words. Recent *review articles* in your research area are often helpful here as they discuss the current state of research for a particular topic and can help you to refine your key words. In addition, they will probably contain references to other work that is pertinent to your research question(s) and objectives (Box 3.7). If you are unsure about review articles, your project tutor should be able to point you in the right direction. Another potentially useful source of references is dissertations and theses in your university's library.

After re-reading your lecture notes and textbooks and undertaking this limited reading you will have a list of subjects that appear relevant to your research project. You now need to define precisely what is relevant to your research in terms of key words.

The identification of **key words** or *search terms* is the most important part of planning your search for relevant literature (Bell, 2005). Key words are the basic terms that describe your research question(s) and objectives, and will be used to search the tertiary literature. Key words (which can include authors' surnames identified in the examination of your lecture notes and course textbooks) can be identified using one or a number of different techniques in combination. Those found most useful by our students include:

## BOX 3.7 FOCUS ON MANAGEMENT RESEARCH

### Review articles and systematic review

The *International Journal of Management Reviews* is a major reviews journal in the field of business management and covers all the main management sub-disciplines from accounting and entrepreneurship to strategy and technology management. In 2004 the journal published a special edition containing three reviews relating to innovation and productivity performance with a focus on the United Kingdom (UK):

Edwards, T., Battisti, G. and Neely, A. (2004) 'Value creation and the UK economy: a review of strategic options', *International Journal of Management Reviews* 5: 3&4, 191–213.

Leseure, M.J., Birdi, K., Bauer, J., Neely, A. and Denyer, D. (2004) 'Adoption of promising practices: a systematic review of the evidence', *International Journal of Management Reviews* 5: 3&4, 169–90.

Pittaway, L., Robertson, M., Munir, K., Denyer, D. and Neely, A. (2004) 'Networking and innovation: a systematic review of the evidence', *International Journal of Management Reviews* 5: 3&4, 137–68.

As you can see from the titles, each of these literature reviews adopted a process known as 'systematic review' outlined by Tranfield *et al.* (2003). This process included (Denyer and Neely, 2004):

- the development of clear and precise aims and objectives for the literature review;
- pre-planned search methods;
- a comprehensive search of all potentially relevant articles;
- the use of clear assessment criteria in the selection of articles for review;
- assessment of the quality of the research in each article and of the strength of the findings;
- synthesising the individual studies using a clear framework;
- presenting the results in a balanced, impartial and comprehensive manner.

Each of the three reviews in this special edition contains a section that outlines how the review was undertaken. This includes how the key words used in the search were identified, and what they were; how the key words were combined into search strings using Boolean operators; the databases searched and the total numbers of articles found; and appendices that list the relevance criteria used to exclude and include articles in the review. Denyer and Neely argue that this should enable readers to determine the reasonableness of the decisions taken by the reviewers when writing their reviews as well as the appropriateness of the conclusions in each review.

- discussion with colleagues, your project tutor and librarians;
- initial reading;
- dictionaries, thesauruses, encyclopaedias and handbooks;
- brainstorming;
- relevance trees.

### Discussion

We believe you should be taking every opportunity to discuss your research. In discussing your work with others, whether face to face, by email or by letter, you will be sharing your ideas, getting feedback and obtaining new ideas and approaches. This process will help you to refine and clarify your topic.

### Initial reading, dictionaries, encyclopaedias, handbooks and thesauruses

To produce the most relevant key words you may need to build on your brainstorming session with support materials such as *dictionaries, encyclopaedias, handbooks* and *thesauruses*, both general and subject specific. These are also good starting points for new topics with which you may be unfamiliar and for related subject areas. Initial reading, particularly of recent review articles, may also be of help here. Project tutors, colleagues and librarians can also be useful sources of ideas.

It is also possible to obtain definitions via the Internet. The online search engine Google offers a 'define' search option (by typing 'Define:[enter term]') that provides links to websites providing definitions. Definitions are also offered in free online encyclopaedias such as Wikipedia.[1] These are often available in multiple languages and, although anyone is allowed to edit the entries, inappropriate changes are usually removed quickly (Wikipedia, 2005). However, whilst these websites may be useful for a quick reference or in helping to define keywords, your university will almost certainly expect you to justify the definitions in your research project using refereed journal articles or textbooks.

### Brainstorming

**Brainstorming** has already been outlined as a technique for helping you to develop your research question (Section 2.3). However, it is also helpful for generating key words. Either individually or as part of a group, you write down all the words and short phrases that come to mind on your research topic (Box 3.8). These are then evaluated and key words (and phrases) selected.

---

## BOX 3.8 WORKED EXAMPLE

### Generating key words

Han's research question was 'How do the actual management requirements of a school pupil record administration system differ from those suggested by the literature?' She brainstormed this question with her peer group, all of whom were teachers in Hong Kong. The resulting list included the following key words and phrases:

*schools, pupil records, administration, user requirements, computer, management information system, access, legislation, information, database, security, UK, Hong Kong, theories*

The group evaluated these and others. As a result, the following key words (and phrases) were selected:

*pupil records, management information system, computer, database, user requirement*

Dictionaries and encyclopaedias were used subsequently to add to the choice of key words:

*student record, MIS, security*

Han made a note of these prior to using them in combination to search the tertiary literature sources.

---

[1] The Internet address for Wikipedia is http://www.wikipedia.org/.

### Relevance trees

**Relevance trees** provide a useful method of bringing some form of structure to your literature search and of guiding your search process (Sharp *et al.*, 2002). They look similar to an organisation chart and are a hierarchical 'graph-like' arrangement of headings and subheadings (Box 3.9). These headings and subheadings describe your research question(s) and objectives and may be key words (including authors' names) with which you can search. Relevance trees are often constructed after brainstorming. They enable you to decide either with help or on your own (Jankowicz, 2005):

- which key words are directly relevant to your research question(s) and objectives;
- which areas you will search first and which your search will use later;
- which areas are more important – these tend to have more branches.

To construct a relevance tree:

1 Start with your research question or objective at the top level.

2 Identify two or more subject areas that you think are important.

3 Further subdivide each major subject area into sub-areas that you think are of relevance.

4 Further divide the sub-areas into more precise sub-areas that you think are of relevance.

5 Identify those areas that you need to search immediately and those that you particularly need to focus on. Your project tutor will be of particular help here.

6 As your reading and reviewing progress, add new areas to your relevance tree.

Computer software to help generate relevance trees, such as Inspiration (2005) and MindGenius (2005), is also increasingly available in universities. Using this software also allows you to attach notes to your relevance tree and can help generate an initial structure for your literature review.

## 3.5 | Conducting your literature search

Your literature search will probably be conducted using a variety of approaches:

- searching using tertiary literature sources;
- obtaining relevant literature (Section 3.6) referenced in books and journal articles you have already read;
- scanning and browsing secondary literature in your library;
- searching using the Internet.

Eventually it is likely you will be using a variety of these in combination. However, we suggest that you start your search by obtaining relevant literature that has been referenced in books and articles you have already read. Although books are unlikely to give adequate up-to-date coverage of your research question, they provide a useful starting point and usually contain some references to further reading. Reading these will enable you to refine your research question(s), objectives and the associated key words prior to searching using tertiary literature sources. It will also help you to see more clearly how your research relates to previous research, and will provide fresh insights.

## BOX 3.9 WORKED EXAMPLE

### Using a relevance tree

Sadie's research question asked 'Is there a link between benchmarking and Total Quality Management?' After brainstorming her question, she decided to construct a relevance tree using the key words and phrases that had been generated.

Using her relevance tree Sadie identified those areas that she needed to search immediately (underlined) and those that she particularly needed to focus on (starred*):

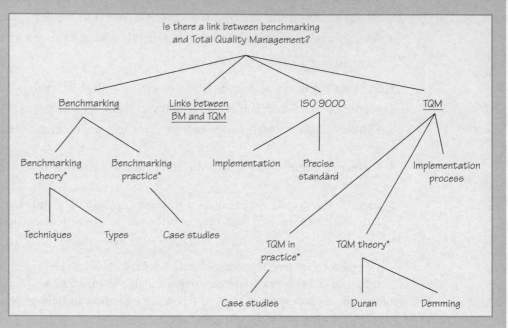

## Tertiary literature sources

A variety of tertiary literature is available to help you in your search. Most of these publications are called indexes and abstracts, and a selection will be accessible via the Internet or held by your university library. It is very tempting with easy access to the Internet to start your literature search with an Internet search engine. Whilst this can retrieve some useful information it must be treated with care. Your project report is expected to be an academic piece of work and hence must use academic sources. Therefore it is essential that you use tertiary sources that provide access to academic literature. Many of these can now be easily accessed via the Internet anyway. An *index* will, as its name suggests, index articles from a range of journals and sometimes books, chapters from books, reports, theses, conferences and research. The information provided will be sufficient to locate the item – for example, for journal articles:

- author or authors of the article;
- date of publication;
- title of the article;
- title of the journal;
- volume and part number of the journal issue;
- page numbers of the article.

Most index searches will be undertaken to find articles using key words, including the author's name. Occasionally you may wish to search by finding those authors who have referenced (cited) a key article after it has been published. A *citation index* enables you to do this as it lists by author the other authors who have cited that author's publications subsequent to their publication.

An **abstract** provides the same information as an index but also includes a summary of the article, hence the term abstract. This abstract can be useful in helping you to assess the content and relevance of an article to your research before obtaining a copy. You should beware of using abstracts, as a substitute for the full article, as a source of information for your research. They contain only a summary of the article and are likely to exclude much of relevance.

Indexes and abstracts are produced in printed and electronic (computerised) formats, the latter often being referred to as *online databases*. This is the term we shall use to refer to all electronic information sources. With the increasing amount of information available electronically, printed indexes and abstracts are often overlooked. Yet they can still provide a valuable resource, providing a varied and sometimes more specific range of information. An increasing number of online databases contain full-text articles. This has helped both to simplify literature searching and to make it a more seamless process, with the searching and retrieval of the full text available from the same source. Most of these online databases will allow you to print, save or email your results. The latter two options will obviously help save you printing costs.

Access to the majority of databases that you will use via the Internet will be paid for by a subscription from your university. There are, however, some pay-as-you-use databases, where the cost of the search is passed on to the user. Online databases provide a wealth of information. Whilst many online databases are intuitive to use, it is still advisable to obtain a librarian's help or to attend a training session prior to your search to find out about the specific features available. It is also vital that you plan and prepare your search in advance so your time is not wasted. For many databases, access is now possible from remote sites such as home or work as well as from your university. Some use a generic username and password specific to your university, although many use the ATHENS service. To gain access via the Internet you will need either your university's specific username and password or to set up an ATHENS account. Your librarian should have more information on this. An additional source of information via the Internet, which our students have found useful, is publishers' web pages. These often include journals' content pages (see Table 3.4 on page 80).

Most university library OPACs (online public access catalogues) are now accessible via the Internet (see Table 3.5 on page 81). These provide a very useful means of locating resources. If you identify useful collections of books and journals, it is possible to make use of other university libraries in the vacations. Within the UK, the SCONUL Vacation Access Scheme gives details of access policies of the libraries in UK higher-education institutions.[2]

To ensure maximum coverage in your search you need to use all appropriate abstracts and indexes. One mistake many people make is to restrict their searches to one or two business and management tertiary sources rather than to use a variety. The coverage of each abstract and index differs in both geographical coverage and type of journal (Section 3.3). In addition, an abstract or index may state that it indexes a particular journal yet may do so only selectively. This emphasises the importance of using a range of databases to ensure a wide coverage of available literature. Some of those more

---

[2] Details of these can be found on the Internet at http://www.sconul.ac.uk/use_lib/vacation.html.

frequently used are outlined in Table 3.2. However, new databases are being developed all the time so it is worth asking a librarian for advice.

## Searching using tertiary literature

Once your key words have been identified, searching using tertiary literature is a relatively straightforward process. You need to:

1 ensure your key words match the controlled index language (unless you can use free text searching);

2 search appropriate printed and database sources;

3 note precise details, including the search strings used, of the actual searches you have undertaken for each database;

4 note the full reference of each item found; this can normally be done by cutting and pasting the references.

Tranfield *et al.* (2003), in their article on **systematic review**, emphasize the importance of reporting your search strategy in sufficient detail to ensure that your search could be replicated (Boxes 3.11, 3.7). Your review will be based on the subset of those items found which you consider are relevant.

### Printed sources

Searching printed indexes and abstracts requires a different technique from electronic databases. The coverage of printed indexes tends to be smaller and possibly more specialised than that of databases. Unlike databases, it is normally only possible to search by author or one broad subject heading, although some cross-references may be included. Because they are paper based, each issue or annual accumulation must be searched individually, which can be time consuming.

### Databases

Most databases, in contrast, allow more precise searches using combinations of search terms. These can include indexed key words, which will need to match the database's **controlled index language** of pre-selected terms and phrases or *descriptors*. These can include specified subject words, author names, and journal titles. If your key words do not match those in the controlled index language, your search will be unsuccessful. You therefore need to check your key words with the *index* or *browse* option prior to searching. This is especially useful to establish how an author is indexed or whether hyphens should be used when entering specific terms. Some databases will also have a *thesaurus* which links words in the controlled index language to other terms. Some thesauruses will provide a definition of the term used as well as indicating other broader subject areas, more specific subject areas or subjects related to the original term. Despite using these tools your searches may still be unsuccessful. The most frequent causes of failure are summarised in Box 3.10 as a checklist.

Once individual key words have been checked, subsequent searches normally use a combination of key words linked using **Boolean logic**. These are known as **search strings** and enable you to combine, limit or widen the variety of items found using *link terms* (Table 3.3). Boolean logic can also be used to construct search strings using dates, journal titles and names of organisations or people. Initially it may be useful to limit your search to journal titles to which your university subscribes. It may also be valuable to narrow your search to specific years, especially if you are finding a wealth of items and

## BOX 3.10 CHECKLIST

### Minimising problems with your key words

✔ Is the spelling incorrect? Behaviour is spelt with a 'u' in the UK but without in the USA.

✔ Is the language incorrect? Chemists in the UK but drug stores in the USA.

✔ Are you using incorrect terminology? In recent years some terms have been replaced by others, such as 'redundancy' being replaced by 'downsizing'.

✔ Are you using recognised acronyms and abbreviations? For example, UK for United Kingdom or ICI instead of Imperial Chemical Industries.

✔ Are you avoiding jargon and using accepted terminology? For example, downsizing rather than redundancy.

✔ Are you avoiding words that are not in the controlled index language?

need to concentrate on the most up to date. By contrast, searching by author allows you to broaden your search to find other work by known researchers in your area.

You can also search just one or more specified fields in the database such as the author, title or abstract. This may be useful if you wish to find articles by a key author in your subject area. Alternatively, many databases allow you to search the entire database rather than just the controlled vocabulary using **free text searching**. Free text searching is

### Table 3.3 Common link terms that use Boolean logic

| Link term | Purpose | Example | Outcome |
|---|---|---|---|
| **AND** | Narrows search | Recruitment AND interviewing AND skills | Only articles containing all three key words selected |
| **OR** | Widens search | Recruitment OR selection | Articles with at least one key word selected |
| **NOT** | Excludes terms from search | Recruitment NOT selection | Selects articles containing the key word 'recruitment' that do not contain the key word 'selection' |
| **\* (truncation)** | Uses word stems to pick up different words | Motivat\* | Selects articles with: Motivate Motivation Motivating |
| **? (wild card)** | Picks up different spellings | behavio?r | Selects articles with: Behavior Behaviour |

increasingly common for electronic publications both on CD-ROM and accessed via the Internet, in particular quality newspapers and journals. These may not have a controlled index language. There are, however, problems with using a free text search. In particular, the context of a key word may be inappropriate, leading to retrieval of numerous irrelevant articles and information overload.

## Scanning and browsing

Any search will find only some of the relevant literature. You will therefore also need to scan and browse the literature. New publications such as journals are unlikely to be indexed immediately in tertiary literature, so you will need to *browse* these publications to gain an idea of their content. In contrast, *scanning* will involve you going through individual items such as a journal article to pick out points that relate to your own research. It is particularly important that you browse and scan trade and professional journals, as these are less likely to be covered by the tertiary literature.

To make browsing and scanning easier you should:

- identify when those journals that are the most relevant are published and regularly browse them;
- browse new book displays in libraries;
- scan new book reviews in journals and newspapers;
- scan publishers' new book catalogues where available;
- discuss your research with your project tutor and librarians, who may be aware of other relevant literature.

Internet access to resources now allows you to browse journals that may not be held in, or accessible from, your university library. Many publishers make the contents pages of their journals available without charge on the web (Table 3.4) and may offer an *article alert* service where they will provide a regular email update of articles in your area of interest. Alternatively, databases such as Ingenta provide access to thousands of journals' contents pages (Table 3.2). Professional journals may also be accessible through the web page of the professional organisation (Table 8.2). Many publishers make their current book catalogues available on the Internet, and these can be accessed either directly (Table 3.4) or through the publishers' catalogues' home page information gateway (see Table 3.5). In addition, websites of bookshops such as Amazon, Blackwell and the Internet Book Shop provide access to catalogues of books in print. These can usually be searched by author, title and subject, and may have reviews attached (Table 3.4). However, as when using electronic indexes and abstracts, it is important that you keep full details of the literature you have scanned and browsed (Box 3.11). As well as enabling you to outline the method you used for your literature review, it will also help prevent you repeating searches you have already undertaken.

## Searching the Internet

The development of the *Internet*, a worldwide network of computers providing access to a vast range of literature and other resources, has revolutionised information gathering, including searching for literature. It will provide you with access to resources that may be of use either for your literature review or as secondary data (Chapter 8). However, you should beware, as these resources may be difficult to locate and the quality of the

**Table 3.4** Selected publishers' and bookshops' Internet addresses

| Name | Internet address | Contents |
|---|---|---|
| **Publishers** | | |
| Blackwell Publishers | http://www.blackwellpublishing.com | Books and journals |
| Cambridge University Press | http://www.cup.cam.ac.uk | Books and journals; links to other university presses and publishing-related services |
| Pearson Education Limited | http://www.pearsoned.co.uk | Business and management books for practitioners and students. Links to book-specific web pages |
| Office of Public Sector Information | http://www.opsi.gov.uk | OPSI publications, including full text of Statutory Instruments and Public Acts |
| MCB University Press | http://www.mcb.co.uk | Over 100 professional and academic management journals |
| Open University Press | http://www.openup.co.uk | Books and journals |
| Oxford University Press | http://www.oup.co.uk | Books and journals, including full-text online journals, a database of abstracts |
| Prentice Hall | http://www.pearsoned.co.uk | Books and other study materials |
| Routledge | http://www.routledge.com | Books |
| Sage | http://www.sagepub.co.uk | Books, journals, software, CD-ROMs |
| Thomson | http://www.thomsonlearning.co.uk | Books, and other study materials |
| **Bookshops** | | |
| Amazon | http://www.amazon.co.uk | Searchable database principally of books (UK site) |
| | http://www.amazon.com | Searchable database principally of books (USA site) |
| Blackwell | http://www.blackwell.co.uk | Searchable database principally of books |
| Internet Book Shop UK | http://www.ibuk.com | Searchable database principally of books |
| The Book Place | http://www.thebookplace.co.uk | Searchable database principally of books |
| TSO (The Stationery Office) | http://www.tsoshop.co.uk | Searchable database of UK books in print. Especially useful for UK government reports |

NB. All services in this table were free at the time of writing.

material is highly variable. This is emphasised by Clausen (1996:4), who likens the Internet to:

> . . . a huge vandalized library where someone has destroyed the catalogue and removed the front matter and indexes from most of the books. In addition thousands of unorganized fragments are added daily by a myriad of cranks, sages and persons with time on their hands who launch their unfiltered messages into cyberspace.

Table 3.5 Selected Internet search tools and their coverage

| Name | Internet address | Comment |
| --- | --- | --- |
| **General search engines** | | |
| Alta Vista Search | http://www.altavista.com<br>http://uk.altavista.com | Searches web and Usenet newsgroups<br>Differentiates between simple and advanced searches and between languages |
| Google | http://www.google.com | Access to over 3 billion documents |
| Google UK | http://www.google.co.uk | |
| Google Scholar | http://scholar.google.com/ | Access to academic journals, theses, books, journals and abstracts from a limited number of academic and professional organisations. Access to the full text is often dependent on an institution's subscription to a journal or service |
| HotBot | http://www.hotbot.co.uk/ | Searches web; useful features include sorting by date and media type |
| Lycos | http://www.lycos.com | Searches web, gopher and ftp sites; offers both key word and subject searching |
| **Meta search engines** | | |
| Dogpile | http://www.dogpile.com | Searches a selection of search engines and subject directories, including Yahoo, Lycos and Yellow Pages |
| **Specialised search engines** | | |
| UK government | http://www.direct.gov.uk | Searches central and local government websites and government agencies |
| **Information gateways** | | |
| Biz/Ed | http://www.bized.ac.uk | Information service, links economics and business students and teachers and information providers |
| BUBL subject tree | http://bubl.ac.uk | Links to a vast range of Internet resources by alphabetical subject list or by class (subject) number order |
| Human Resource Management Resources on the Internet | http://www.nbs.ntu.ac.uk/research/depts/hrm/links.php | Annotated list of links. List split into sub-categories, and provides short description of content |
| HERO (UK Universities and Colleges OPACs) | http://www.hero.ac.uk | Links to UK university and college online public access (library) catalogues (OPACs) |
| Pinakes | http://www.hw.ac.uk/libWWW/irn/pinakes/pinakes.html | Links to major information gateways to Internet resources (especially UK based) |
| Publishers' catalogues homepage | http://www.lights.com/publisher | Links to major publishers' websites, listed alphabetically by country |
| Resource Discovery Network | http://www.rdn.ac.uk/ | Subject-based information and Internet tutorials |
| SOSIG UK Business and Industrial Management Resources | http://www.sosig.ac.uk/roads/subject-listing/World-cat/busgen.html | Detailed descriptions and links to UK business and industrial management sites |
| **Subject directories** | | |
| Yahoo | http://dir.yahoo.com/ | Subject-based directory |
| Yahoo UK | http://uk.yahoo.com | Optionally limits searches to just Great Britain and Ireland |
| | http://uk.dir.yahoo.com/news_and_media/newspapers | Comprehensive listing of newspapers available on the Internet, worldwide |
| Yellow Pages UK | http://www.yell.co.uk | Telephone yellow pages with useful links to UK companies' home pages |

**BOX 3.11 WORKED EXAMPLE**

## Searching electronic indexes and abstracts

Matthew described his research project using the key words 'small business' and 'finance'. Unfortunately, he encountered problems when carrying out his search using one of the online databases of full text and abstracts for business, management and economics journals to which his university subscribed:

■ When he entered the key word 'small business' he retrieved references to over 18,000 items many of which were in trade magazines.

■ He was unsure how to combine his key words into search strings to make his search more specific.

■ Full-text versions were not available for the many of the most recent items retrieved.

After discussing the problem, the librarian showed Matthew how to use the advanced search option of the online database. Using this, Matthew first searched using the terms 'small business' and 'finance' combined as a search string. This resulted in nearly 500 items being highlighted.

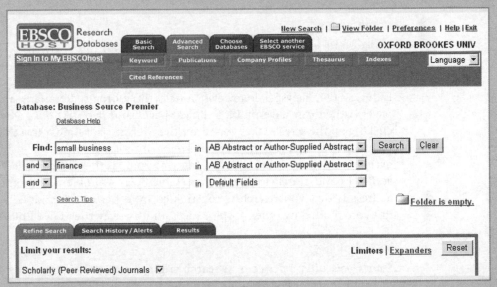

*Source*: EBSCO Information Services, reproduced with permission

He then refined his search further by limiting it to the collection of scholarly (peer reviewed) journals. This resulted in just over 100 items being retrieved. Matthew made a note of the details of his search:

| | |
|---|---|
| Database: | Business Source Premier |
| Collection: | Scholarly (peer reviewed) journals |
| Dates: | 1980 to 2005 |
| Search: | small business AND finance |
| Fields searched: | Abstract |
| Date of search: | 30 November 2005 |
| Total items retrieved: | 103 |

He then copied the references for these items (articles) onto his USB mass storage device. As Matthew scrolled through these he noted that some of them had direct links to copies of the full text stored as a .pdf file. For many of the others, the librarian informed him that he could access the full text using different online databases. However, he still needed to assess each article's relevance to his research.

There are a variety of approaches you can use for searching the Internet. These are summarised in Figure 3.3. Printed guides are available and can be a useful starting point for information. However, because of the rate at which the Internet is growing and the fact that material can literally disappear overnight, these guidebooks are likely to become out of date extremely quickly. Alternatively you can use websites dedicated to providing support information on searching the Internet. One such example that our students have found useful is that provided by Phil Bradley, an information expert.[3] This contains information on different search engines, articles on Internet searching and web page and website design and is regularly updated. Another useful site is hosted by RBA Information Services.[4] This contains an excellent directory of business-related websites as well as a wealth of more generic information on searching the Internet. Once again, we recommend that you keep full details of the Internet searches you have undertaken, making a note of:

- the search engine used;
- the precise search undertaken;
- the date when the search was undertaken;
- the total number of items retrieved.

## Home pages

*Addresses* of Internet sites or *home pages* (such as http://www.brookes.ac.uk) can be the quickest and most direct method of accessing these resources. Addresses can be obtained from many sources, the most frequently used of which are guidebooks (for example, Hahn, 2005), newspaper reviews, articles in journals, librarians and lecturers. Home pages, which can have multiple linked pages and *hypertext links* whereby pointing and clicking on the screen takes you to another website, are similar to a title or contents page. Although home pages often contain publicity for a company or institution, they are an excellent way of navigating around the Internet, as they bring a selection of Internet site addresses and search tools together (Table 3.5). A problem with going directly to one address is that your search is constrained by other people's ideas. Similarly, hypertext links are limited by other people's ideas and the way they have linked pages.

## Search tools

*Search tools*, often referred to as **search engines**, are probably the most important method of Internet searching for your literature review as they will enable you to locate most current and up-to-date items. Although normally accessed through home pages, each search tool will have its own address (Table 3.5).

Most search tools search by key words or subject trees. A *subject tree* is similar to a contents page or index. Some are in the form of alphabetical subject lists, whereas others are in hierarchical groups of subjects that are then further subdivided with links to more narrowly focused subject groups. It is vital that you do not rely on one search tool but use a variety, noting and evaluating each as you use them. Each search tool will have different interfaces, ways of searching and methods of displaying information. They will search different areas of the Internet and are likely to display different results.

Search tools can be divided into four distinct categories (Figure 3.3, Table 3.5):

- general search engines;
- meta search engines;

---

[3] The Internet address of the home page of this site is http://www.philb.com/.
[4] The Internet address of the home page of this site is http://www.rba.co.uk.

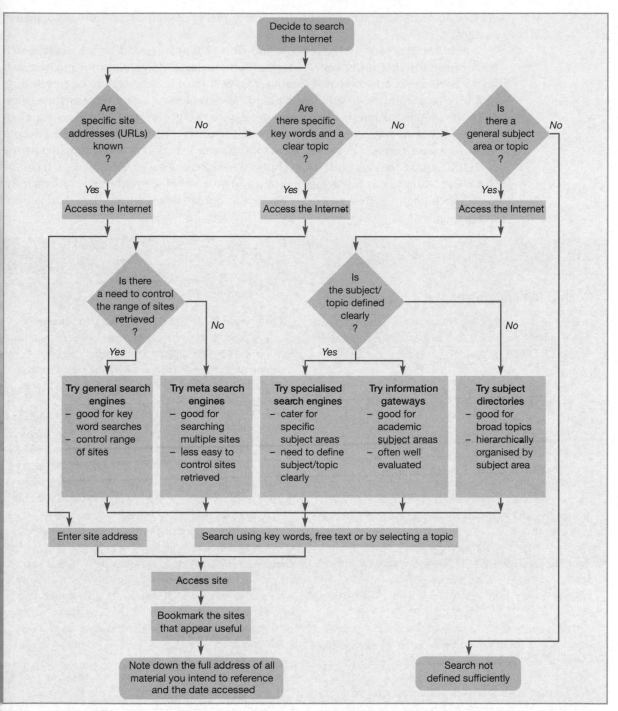

**Figure 3.3    Searching the Internet**

*Source*: © Mark Saunders, Philip Lewis, Adrian Thornhill and Martin Jenkins, 2003

- specialised search engines and information gateways;
- subject directories.

Most search engines index every separate document. In contrast, subject directories index only the 'most important' Internet documents. Therefore, if you are using a clear term to search for an unknown vaguely described document, use a search engine. If you are looking for a document about a particular topic, use a subject directory (Habrakan *et al.*, 2005).

*General search engines* such as Google and Google Scholar (Box 3.12) normally search parts of the Internet using key words and Boolean logic (Table 3.3) or a phrase. Each search engine uses an automated computer process to index and search, often resulting in a very large number of sites being found. As people have not evaluated these sites, many are usually inappropriate or unreliable. As no two general search engines search in precisely the same way it is advisable (and often necessary) to use more than one. In contrast, *meta search engines* allow you to search using a selection of search engines at the same time, using the same interface. This makes searching easier, and the search can be faster. Unfortunately, it is less easy to control the sites that are retrieved. Consequently, meta search engines often generate more inappropriate or unreliable sites than general search engines.

---

## BOX 3.12 RESEARCH IN THE NEWS

### Google to scan universities' library books

Google, the leading service for finding information on the Internet, yesterday set out ambitious plans to become a catalogue and digital library for world literature.

It said it had struck a deal with four leading university libraries and the New York Public Library to scan digitally tens of millions of books from their collections so that users worldwide could search through them using the Google service.

While company officials presented the move as a philanthropic gesture, they also admitted there would be revenue opportunities and that the increased quality of their search results would maintain Google's advantage over its rivals.

In addition to the New York Public Library, books from Harvard, Stanford, Michigan university libraries and Oxford's Bodleian Library will be scanned and indexed as an extension of a project called Google Print.

This year, it launched Google Scholar – a project working with academic publishers to make scientific, technical and medical journals searchable online.

"Even before we started Google, we dreamed of making the incredible breadth of information that librarians so lovingly organise searchable online," said Larry Page, Google co-founder.

Many libraries, including the Library of Congress, have explored digitising part of their collections and have carried out relatively small projects.

But most have been hampered by the cost involved and the slow speed of the scanning technology they have been using.

Google will undertake the scanning for the libraries and significantly increase the amount of searchable material through its engine.

Legally, the task is relatively easy for books published before 1923. Such books are no longer protected by copyright law and are in the public domain. Newer books could be more problematic since Google will have to obtain the permission from the publishers to reproduce the books online.

However, Google hopes to persuade publishers and authors that they will benefit because the scheme will increase the visibility of in and out-of-print books, and generate book sales via "Buy this Book" links, while providing them with a revenue-share of associated advertising.

*Source*: Article by Paul Taylor and Chris Nuttall, *Financial Times*, 15 December 2004. Copyright © 2004 The Financial Times Ltd.

---

*Specialised search engines* cater for specific subject areas. To use these it is necessary to define your general subject area prior to your search. *Information gateways* also require you to define your subject area. Information gateways are often compiled by staff from departments in academic institutions. Although the number of websites obtained is fewer, they can be far more relevant, as each site is evaluated prior to being added to the gateway.

**Subject directories** are hierarchically organised indexes categorised into subject areas, and are useful for searching for broad topics. As people normally compile them, their content has been partly censored and evaluated. Consequently, the number of sites retrieved is fewer but they usually provide material that is more appropriate. Most of the subject directories now offer some form of key word search and links to other search tools.

Search tools are becoming more prolific and sophisticated all the time. Be careful: their use can be extremely time consuming. Your search will probably locate a mass of resources, many of which will be irrelevant to you. It is also easy to become sidetracked to more interesting and glossy websites not relevant to your research needs! There are an increasing number of web-based tutorials to help you learn to search the web. One of these, Marketing Insights' *Smarter Online Searching Guide,* is available via this book's web page. This highlights using search tools, including Advanced search in Google and online e-business resources. Another, which our students have found useful and informative, is hosted by Tilburg University in the Netherlands.[5] This offers interactive tutorials on searching as well as a brief history of the Internet and a glossary of terms.

Companion
Website

### Bookmarking

Once you have found a useful Internet site, you can note its address electronically. This process is termed *bookmarking* or *add to favourites* depending on your Internet software. It uses the software to note the Internet address, and means that you will be able to access it again directly. The vast amount of resources available, and the fact that resources, home pages and sites can be added and deleted by their producers, means it is vital to keep a record of the addresses and a note of the date you accessed it (Section 3.7). These will be needed to reference your sources when you write your critical review (Section 3.2). When sufficient sites have been bookmarked, it is possible to arrange them in whatever hierarchical way you wish.

## 3.6 | Obtaining and evaluating the literature

### Obtaining the literature

After your initial search of books and journal articles, tertiary literature will provide you with details of what literature is available and where to locate it. The next stage (Figure 3.1) is to obtain these items. To do this you need to:

1 check your library catalogue to find out whether your library holds the appropriate publication. Remember many libraries now hold publications such as journals and newspapers in electronic form on CD-ROM or provide access via the Internet;

2 (for those publications that are held by your library or available via the Internet) note their location and:

   a find the publication and scan it to discover whether it is likely to be worth reading thoroughly – for articles it is often possible to make a reasonable assessment of relevance using the abstract; or

---

[5] The Internet address of this site is: http://www.tilburguniversity.nl/services/library/instruction/www/onlinecourse/.

   **b** browse other books and journals with similar class marks to see whether they may also be of use;

**3** (for those items that are not held by your library or available via the Internet) order the item from another library on **inter-library loan**. This is not a free service so make sure you really need it first. Our students have found that, in general, it is only worthwhile to use inter-library loan for articles from refereed journals and books.

## Evaluating the literature

Two questions frequently asked by our students are 'How do I know what I'm reading is relevant?' and 'How do I know when I've read enough?' Both of these are concerned with the process of evaluation. They involve defining the scope of your review and assessing the value of the items that you have obtained in helping you to answer your research question(s). Although there are no set ways of approaching these questions, our students have found the following advice helpful.

You should, of course, read all the literature that is closely related to your research question(s) and objectives. The literature that is most likely to cause problems is that which is less closely related (Gall *et al.*, 2002). For some research questions, particularly for new research areas, there is unlikely to be much closely related literature and so you will have to review more broadly. For research questions where research has been going on for some years you may be able to focus on more closely related literature.

### Assessing relevance and value

Assessing the relevance of the literature you have collected to your research depends on your research question(s) and objectives. Remember that you are looking for relevance, not critically assessing the ideas contained within. When doing this, it helps to have thought about and made a note of the criteria for inclusion and exclusion prior to assessing each item of literature. In contrast, assessing the value of the literature you have collected is concerned with the quality of the research that has been undertaken. As such it is concerned with issues such as methodological rigour and theory robustness as well as the quality of the arguments. For example, you need to beware of managerial autobiographies, where a successful entrepreneur's or managing director's work experiences are presented as the way to achieve business success (Fisher, 2004) and articles in trade magazines. The knowledge presented in such books and articles may well be subjective rather than based upon systematic research.

Box 3.13 provides a checklist to help you in this process.

Remember to make notes about the relevance of each item as you read it and the reasons why you came to your conclusion. You may need to include your evaluation as part of your critical review.

### Assessing sufficiency

Your assessment of whether you have read a sufficient amount is even more complex. It is impossible to read everything, as you would never start to write your critical review, let alone your project report. Yet you need to be sure that your critical review discusses what research has already been undertaken and that you have positioned your research project in the wider context, citing the main writers in the field (Section 3.2). One clue that you have achieved this is when further searches provide mainly references to items you have already read. You also need to check what constitutes an acceptable amount of reading, in terms of both quality and quantity, with your project tutor.

## BOX 3.13 CHECKLIST

### Evaluating the relevance and value of literature to your research

**Relevance**

✔ How recent is the item?

✔ Is the item likely to have been superseded?

✔ Are the research questions or objectives sufficiently close to your own to make it relevant to your own research (in other words, does the item meet your relevance criteria for inclusion)?

✔ Is the context sufficiently different to make it marginal to your research question(s) and objectives (in other words, is the item excluded by your relevance criteria)?

✔ Have you seen references to this item (or its author) in other items that were useful?

✔ Does the item support or contradict your arguments? For either it will probably be worth reading!

**Value**

✔ Does the item appear to be biased? For example, does it use an illogical argument, emotionally toned words or appear to choose only those cases that support the point being made? Even if it is, it may still be relevant to your critical review!

✔ What are the methodological omissions within the work (for example, sample selection, data collection, data analysis)? Even if there are many it still may be of relevance!

✔ Is the precision sufficient? Even if it is imprecise it may be the only item you can find and so still of relevance!

✔ Does the item provide guidance for future research?

*Sources*: Authors' experience; Bell (2005); Fisher (2004); Jankowicz (2005); McNeill (2005)

## 3.7 Recording the literature

The literature search, as you will now be aware, is a vital part of your research project, in which you will invest a great deal of time and effort. As you read each item, you need to ask yourself how it contributes to your research question(s) and objectives and to make *notes* with this focus (Bell, 2005). When doing this, many students download and print copies of articles or photocopy articles and pages from books to ensure that they have all the material. We believe that, even if you print or photocopy, you still need to make notes. The process of note making will help you to think through the ideas in the literature in relation to your research.

In addition to making notes, Sharp *et al.* (2002) identify three sets of information you need to record. These are:

- bibliographic details;
- brief summary of content;
- supplementary information.

Until the advent of inexpensive microcomputers it was usual to write this information on *index cards*. Database software such as Microsoft's Access™ or specialist bibliographic

## BOX 3.14 WORKED EXAMPLE

### Undertaking an Internet search

Elaine's research question was reasonably defined, if somewhat broad. She wanted to assess the impact of European enlargement on small to medium-sized organisations. As part of her search strategy she decided, in addition to the academic databases of business and management journals, also to search the Internet using a general search engine. Her first key word 'European enlargement' revealed that there were nearly 10 million sites and displayed the first 10. Of these, although in the broad topic area, none appeared to be relevant as they were not related specifically to small to medium-sized enterprises (SMEs):

She decided to refine her search using the advanced search feature of the search engine. Although the search engine still found over 200 000 sites, the content of the first 10 appeared more relevant to her research question:

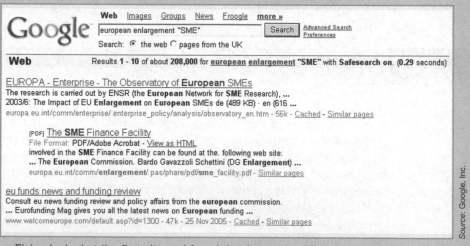

Elaine looked at the first site and found that it contained links to a series of downloadable SME-related reports. These met her relevance criteria. The research for these reports had been carried out by ENSR (the European Network for SME Research) on behalf of the European Union and so were likely to be objective. These reports, coordinated by EIMit, appeared to contain a wealth of information that was useful to her research project. She therefore decided to download and save them as .pdf files prior to assessing their value to her research. She then proceeded to look at the next site in her list.

software such as Reference Manager for Windows™ or EndNote™ provide a powerful and flexible alternative method for recording the literature, although they will probably mean noting it down and transferring it to your database later. Recording can seem very tedious, but it must be done. We have seen many students frantically repeating searches for items that are crucial to their research because they failed to record all the necessary details in their database of references.

## Bibliographic details

For some project reports you will be required to include a **bibliography**. Convention dictates that this should include all the relevant items you consulted for your project, including those not referred to directly in the text. For others, you will be asked to include only a list of **references** for those items referred to directly in the text. The **bibliographic details** contained in both need to be sufficient to enable readers to find the original items. These details are summarised in Table 3.6.

If an item has been taken from an electronic source you need to record as much of the information in Table 3.6 as is available along with details of format (e.g. CD-ROM). If you located the item via the Internet, you need to record the full address of the resource and the date you accessed the information as well (Appendix 2). This address is often referred to as the *URL*, the *unique resource location* or *universal/uniform resource locator*.

Most universities have a preferred *referencing style* that you must use in your project report. This will normally be prescribed in your assessment criteria. Three of the most common styles are the *Harvard system* (a version of which we have used in this book), the *American Psychological Association (APA) System* and the *Vancouver* or *footnotes system*. Guidelines on using each of these are given in Appendix 2.

## Brief summary

A brief summary of the content of each item in your reference database will help you to locate the relevant items and facilitate reference to your notes and photocopies. This can be done by annotating each record with the key words used, to help locate the item and the abstract. It will also help you to maintain consistency in your searches.

**Table 3.6  Bibliographic details required**

| Journal | Book | Chapter in an edited book |
|---|---|---|
| ■ Author(s) – surname, first name initials | ■ Author(s) – surname, first name initials | ■ Author(s) – surname, first name initials |
| ■ Year of publication (in parentheses) | ■ Year of publication (in parentheses) | ■ Year of publication (in parentheses) |
| ■ Title of article | ■ Title and subtitle of book (underlined) | ■ Title of chapter |
| ■ Title of journal (underlined) | ■ Edition | ■ Author(s) of book – surname, first name initials |
| ■ Volume | ■ Place of publication | ■ Title and subtitle of book (underlined) |
| ■ Part/issue | ■ Publisher | ■ Edition |
| ■ Page numbers (preceded by 'p.' for page or 'pp.' for pages) | | ■ Place of publication |
| | | ■ Publisher |
| | | ■ Page numbers of chapter |

## Supplementary information

As well as recording the details discussed earlier, other information may also be worth recording. These items can be anything you feel will be of value. In Table 3.7 we outline those that we have found most useful.

Table 3.7  Supplementary information

| Information | Reason |
| --- | --- |
| **ISBN** | The identifier for any book, and useful if the book has to be requested on inter-library loan |
| **Class number (e.g. Dewey decimal)** | Useful to locate books in your university's library and as a pointer to finding other books on the same subject |
| **Quotations** | Always note useful quotations in full and with the page number of the quote; if possible also take a photocopy |
| **Where it was found** | Noting where you found the item is useful, especially if it is not in your university library and you could only take notes |
| **The tertiary resource used and the key words used to locate it** | Useful to help identify resources for follow-up searches |
| **Evaluative comments** | Your personal notes on the value of the item to your research in relation to your relevance and value criteria |
| **When the item was consulted** | Especially important for items found via the Internet as these may disappear without trace |

## 3.8 │ Summary

■ A critical review of the literature is necessary to help you to develop a thorough understanding of, and insight into, previous research that relates to your research question(s) and objectives. Your review will set your research in context by critically discussing and referencing work that has already been undertaken, drawing out key points and presenting them in a logically argued way, and highlighting those areas where you will provide fresh insights. It will lead the reader into subsequent sections of your project report.

■ There is no one correct structure for a critical review, although it is helpful to think of it as a funnel in which you start at a more general level prior to narrowing down to your specific research question(s) and objectives.

■ Literature sources can be divided into three categories: primary, secondary and tertiary. In reality, these categories often overlap. Your use of these resources will depend on your research question(s) and objectives. Some may use only tertiary and secondary literature. For others, you may need to locate primary literature as well.

■ When planning your literature search you need:
  – to have clearly defined research question(s) and objectives;
  – to define the parameters of your search;

- – to generate key words and search terms;
- – to discuss your ideas as widely as possible.

  Techniques to help you in this include brainstorming and relevance trees.

- ■ Your literature search is likely to be undertaken using a variety of approaches in tandem. These will include:

  - – searching using tertiary sources and the Internet;
  - – following up references in articles you have already read;
  - – scanning and browsing secondary literature in your library.

  Don't forget to make precise notes of the search processes you have used and their results.

- ■ Once obtained, the literature must be evaluated for its relevance to your research question(s) and objectives using clearly defined criteria. This must include a consideration of each item's currency. Each item must be read and noted. Bibliographic details, a brief description of the content and appropriate supplementary information should also be recorded.

## SELF-CHECK QUESTIONS

*Help with these questions is available at the end of the chapter.*

**3.1** The following extract and associated references are taken from the first draft of a critical literature review. The research project was concerned with the impact of direct insurers on the traditional motor insurer.

List the problems with this extract in terms of its:
a content;
b structure.

Jackson (1995) suggests that businesses must be developed from a customer rather than a product perspective. Lindesfarne (1994) demonstrates that direct selling gives the consumer increased control as it is up to them when and if they wish to respond to adverts or direct mail. MacKenzie (1995) comments that free gifts are useful for getting responses to adverts, which is ultimately what all direct insurers need. Bowen (1995) suggests that this type of company can be split into three equally important parts: marketing, insurance and information technology. Motor insurance is particularly price sensitive because of its compulsory nature and its perception by many to have no real 'value' to themselves.

Bowen, I. (1994) 'Short cut to success', *Post Magazine* 2, 26 July.
Jackson, D.R. (1995) 'Prudential's prudent parochialism', *Direct Marketing*, 26–29 April.
Lindisfarne, I. (1995) 'Death of a salesman', *Post Magazine* 15, 30–31 June.
MacKenzie, G. (1995) 'Rise of the freebie', *Post Magazine* 2, 5–6 February.

**3.2** Outline the advice you would give a colleague on:
a how to plan her search;
b which literature to search first.

**3.3** Brainstorm at least one of the following research questions, either on your own or with a colleague, and list the key words that you have generated.
a How effective is profit-related pay as a motivator?
b How do the opportunities available to a first-time house buyer through interpersonal discussion influence the process of selecting a financial institution for the purposes of applying for a house purchase loan?
c To what extent do new methods of direct selling of financial services pose a threat to existing providers?

**3.4**  You are having considerable problems with finding relevant material for your research when searching online databases. Suggest possible reasons why this might be so.

**3.5**  Rewrite the following passage as part of a critical literature review using the Harvard system of referencing:

From what I've read, the English Language Teaching market, which this company serves, remains attractive for publishers despite a decline in growth as this quote shows: 'Overall, the ELT materials market has continued to show growth, because, globally, the demand for English learning persists, albeit on a lower growth track than in the 1980s'.[1] The latest published statistics that I've been able to find (1999) tell us that there are 1,300 million ELT learners worldwide.[2] I therefore think that the need for good ELT authors is growing and, as Francis says: 'the name of the author remains a critical success factor, and an important sub-brand in many cases'.[3]

[1]  R. Francis, 'Youngsters drive ELT growth', *Bookseller*, 23 May 2003, p. 26.
[2]  Gasson, C. (ed.), *Book Publishing in Britain* (London: Bookseller Publications, 1999).
[3]  R. Francis 'ELT Publishing', p. 93 in C. Gasson (ed.), *Book Publishing in Britain* (London: Bookseller Publications, 1999) pp. 86–104.

## REVIEW AND DISCUSSION QUESTIONS

**3.6**  Go to the website of the general search engine Google (http://www.google.com). Use the different Google services such as 'Google Search', 'Google Scholar' and 'University Search' to search for articles on a topic which you are currently studying as part of your course.
 **a**  Make notes regarding the types of items that each of these services finds.
 **b**  How do these services differ?
 **c**  Which service do you think is likely to prove most useful to your research project?

**3.7**  Agree with a friend to each review the same article from a refereed academic journal, which contains a clear literature review section. Evaluate independently the literature review in your chosen article with regard to its content, critical nature and structure using the checklists in Boxes 3.1, 3.2 and 3.3 respectively. Do not forget to make notes regarding your answers to each of the points raised in the checklists. Discuss your answers with your friend.

**3.8**  Visit an online database or your university library and obtain a copy of an article that you think will be of use to an assignment you are both currently working on. Use the checklist in Box 3.13 to assess the relevance and value of the article to your assignment.

## PROGRESSING YOUR RESEARCH PROJECT

### Critically reviewing the literature

☐ Consider your research questions and objectives. Use your lecture notes, course textbooks and relevant review articles to define both narrow and broader parameters of your literature search, considering language, subject area, business sector, geographical area, publication period and literature type.

☐ Generate key words and search terms using one or a variety of techniques such as reading, brainstorming and relevance trees. Discuss your ideas widely, including with your project tutor and colleagues.

☐ Start your search using both database and printed tertiary sources to identify relevant secondary literature. Begin with those tertiary sources that abstract and index academic journal articles and books. At the same time, obtain relevant literature that has been referenced in articles you have already read. Do not forget to record your searches systematically and in detail.

☐ Expand your search via other sources such as the Internet and by browsing and scanning.

☐ Obtain copies of items, evaluate them systematically and make notes. Remember also to record bibliographic details, a brief description of the content and supplementary information on an index card or in your reference database.

☐ Start drafting your critical review as early as possible, keeping in mind its purpose.

☐ Continue to search the literature throughout your research project to ensure that your review remains up to date.

## References

Bell, J. (2005) *Doing Your Research Project* (4th edn), Maidenhead, Open University Press.

Clausen, H. (1996) 'Web information quality as seen from libraries', *New Library World* 97: 1130, 4–8.

Croft, J. (2006) 'Loan penalties hit 672,000 borrowers', *Financial Times,* 31 January.

Dees, R. (2003) *Writing the Modern Research Paper* (4th edn), Boston, MA, Allyn and Bacon.

Denyer, D. and Neely, A. (2004) 'Introduction to special issue: innovation and productivity performance in the UK', *International Journal of Management Reviews* 5/6: 3&4, 131–5.

Fisher, C. (2004) *Researching and Writing a Dissertation for Business Students*, Harlow, Financial Times Prentice Hall.

Gall, M.D., Borg, W.R. and Gall, J.P. (2002) *Educational Research: An Introduction* (7th edn), New York, Longman.

Gill, J. and Johnson, P. (2002) *Research Methods for Managers* (3rd edn), London, Paul Chapman.

Greenhalgh, T. (1997) 'Papers that summarize other papers (systematic reviews and meta-analyses)', *British Medical Journal* 315, 672–5.

Habrakan, A., Schmitz, R. and van Tilberg, P. (2005) 'Searching the World Wide Web: a basic tutorial' [online](cited 27 November 2005). Available from <URL:http://www.tilburguniversity.nl/services/library/instruction/www/onlinecourse/>.

Hahn, H. (2005) *Harley Hahn's Internet Yellow Pages* [online] Accessed 22 November 2005. Available from <URL: http://www.harley.com/yp/home.html>.

Hart, C. (1998) *Doing a Literature Review*, London, Sage.

Inspiration (2005) Inspiration homepage [online] (cited 27 November). Available from <URL:http://www.inspiration.com/>

Jankowicz, A.D. (2005) *Business Research Projects* (4th edn), London, Thomson Learning.

McNeill, P. (2005) *Research Methods* (3rd edn), London, Routledge.

MindGenius (2005) MindGenius homepage [online] (cited 27 November). Available from <URL:http://www.mindgenius.com/>.

Mingers, J. (2000) 'What is it to be critical? Teaching a critical approach to management undergraduates', *Management Learning* 31: 2, 219–37.

Saunders, M.N.K. and Thornhill, A. (2003) 'Organisational justice, trust and the management of change: an exploration', *Personnel Review* 32: 3, 360–74.

Sharp, J.A., Peters, J. and Howard, K. (2002) *The Management of a Student Research Project* (3rd edn), Aldershot, Gower.

Stewart, D.W. and Kamins, M.A. (1993) *Secondary Research: Information Sources and Methods* (2nd edn), Newbury Park, CA, Sage.

Strauss, A. and Corbin, J. (1998) *Basics of Qualitative Research* (2nd edn), Newbury Park, CA, Sage.

Taylor, P. and Nuttall, C. (2004) 'Google to scan universities' library books', *Financial Times*, 15 December.

Tranfield, D., Denyer, D. and Smart, P. (2003) 'Towards a methodology for developing evidence-informed management knowledge by means of systematic review', *British Journal of Management* 14: 3, 207–22.

Wikipedia (2005) Wikipedia home page [online] (cited 27 November). Available from <URL:http://www.wikipedia.org/>.

## Further reading

Bell, J. (2005) *Doing Your Research Project* (4th edn), Maidenhead, Open University Press. Chapter 6 provides a good introduction to the process of reviewing the literature. The section on the critical review of the literature is especially helpful.

Habrakan, A., Schmitz, R. and van Tilberg, P. (2005) 'Searching the World Wide Web: a basic tutorial' [online] (cited 27 November 2005). Available from <URL:http://www.tilburguniversity.nl/services/library/instruction/www/onlinecourse/>. This website provides an introduction to, and history of, the Internet and WWW along with an interactive tutorial. The tutorial offers an explanation of different types of information that you can find on the Internet and how to access them. It also contains a common-sense guide to searching for particular websites.

Sharp, J.A., Peters, J. and Howard, K. (2002) *The Management of a Student Research Project* (3rd edn), Aldershot, Gower. Chapter 4 contains a useful in-depth discussion of the use of relevance trees in your literature search.

Tranfield, D., Denyer, D. and Smart, P. (2003) 'Towards a methodology for developing evidence-informed management knowledge by means of systematic review', *British Journal of Management* 14: 3, 207–22. This paper provides an excellent introduction to the process of systematic review. Although a full systematic review as outlined in this paper may be too time consuming for your research project, there are many useful points made regarding how to plan your search strategy and explain in your project report how your review was undertaken.

For **WEB LINKS** visit
www.pearsoned.co.uk/
saunders

# Topic 3
## Stakeholders

# Introduction: Stakeholders

Use the chapter 'Perspectives on Business Ethics and Values' (Fisher and Lovell) in Topic 1 to give a first introduction to stakeholder analysis, along with chapter 8 that follows the next stage. The following couple of pages gives some pointers for using the concept of Stakeholder in your team project.

Think about the **idea** of **stakeholders** in relation to the team project. As well as the focal organisation or company or industry, what other groups are interested in this issue and might have an effect on how the company or industry deals with the issue? You need to think about the interests and objectives of the business but also about those of selected key stakeholders. Build on previous MDP classes, but make sure the breadth of stakeholders is fully covered.

A stakeholder can very broadly be defined as any group or individual affected by or who can affect the business and the achievement of its objectives. This is a pretty general definition and might extend to a very wide range of groups and individuals. Therefore a major task for managers and those looking to study an issue is to identify the critical stakeholders in relation to the organisation and issue under scrutiny.

In most conventional stakeholder analysis and mapping exercises for business the typical groups of stakeholders broadly identified include:

| | |
|---|---|
| Owners and other investors in the business | Managers and other employees |
| Customers | Suppliers of goods and services to the focal business |
| Competitors | Government and other regulatory agencies |
| Interest and pressure groups (Civil Society) | Local communities where the business is based or does business |

Beyond this is the question of what kinds of stake or interest do these various stakeholder groups have in the organisation and issue?

Sometimes stakeholders are divided into "primary" stakeholders, who have a more direct, immediate and on-going relationship with the organisation and issue under investigation, and "secondary" stakeholders, which in some senses by default are all other groups who you might identify as having a stake but consider on analysis to be less significant.

The company or organisation that each team is looking at in relation to an issue is also a stakeholder although to complicate the matter a bit one might question just who or what is the company? Many large- scale business organisations can be viewed in terms of a number of groups and interests who may share common positions but may have different views about issues or how to deal with these.

Arguably we can think of many groups or individuals who might have an interest and be affected by an issue or what a company does. Sometimes in maps of stakeholder groups, a category such as the local community in which the business is based is identified as a stakeholder. But this term probably obscures the fact that within that local community there are many and varied groups and positions taken on issues, and one needs to look more closely and disaggregate the term. The division between primary and secondary stakeholders may help us identify the groups we think we should focus on, so long as we recognise that this may be a changing picture.

Another example of a stakeholder group, which is sometimes not looked at in enough detail is Government. It often pays to distinguish between different parts since we may find differences of interest and influence.  Local Authorities, the Scottish Executive and Westminster don't always agree!

## Power Interest Matrix

One way of categorising stakeholder groups and seeking to assess their importance on an issue is the Power interest matrix .(Eden and Ackermann, 1998)as previously covered in MDP2 under decision making. This identifies two basic dimensions to look at. One is whether the stakeholder group has a high or low level of interest in the issue. This will have implications for whether a particular group tries to influence outcomes. But having interest in an issue is not enough to influence outcomes unless the group also has some power. This is the second dimension of this analysis. This leads to a fourfold classification:

| Level of INTEREST | High | 'subjects' | 'players' |
|---|---|---|---|
| | Low | 'crowd' | 'leaders' (context setters) |
| | | Low | High |
| | | POWER | |

## Stakeholder Environment

From a business perspective managers need to try to analyse this stakeholder environment. The company itself and its managers will have interests and influence on the situation. Managers may have perspectives as individuals and as members of various groups outside the company as well as acting in the interests of the company. They need to think about what the interests of the company are in relation to an issue both in the short and longer term – and longer term interests sometimes get obscured by immediate pressures and interests – and to read their external environment so that they can analyse, react and maybe anticipate what other groups are wanting and what they might do. Managers are seen as agents of those who own the business and their primary duty and responsibility is to act in the interests of those owners. But how the interests of the owners are defined may be left to the managers, who may be owners or part owners of the company but not necessarily so.

Eden, C. and F. Ackermann (1998). Making Strategy: the journey of strategic management  Sage.

# Topic 4
## Organisation and Management Response

## Introduction: Organisation and Management Response

The following chapter from Fisher and Lovell on Corporate Responsibility, Corporate Governance and corporate citizenship, gives an excellent context for analysing the company aspects of the cases. It introduces Corporate Social Responsibility and counter-arguments to CSR. It also introduces Corporate Manslaughter as an indictable offence and Integrated Social Contract Theory. Typical elements of business ethics management can include:

- Mission or value statements.
- Codes of ethics.
- Reporting or advice channels
- Ethics managers or committees.
- Ethics consultants.
- Ethics education and training.
- Ethics auditing, accounting and reporting.

## Assessing ethical and social performance

We know or think we know how to judge business performance against conventional business criteria such as market share, growth, turnover and profits. But how do we judge social performance? What measure can we use here? We can't depend on the statements of organisations about their ethics and responsibilities.

Ethical or social accounting, auditing and reporting may help here although the issue of who carries this out is important. A critical test is whether companies are prepared to let independent auditors assess and report publicly on ethical and social performance. But other issues include what aspects of social performance do we look at- environmental impacts, employee conditions, health and safety (of employees but also of customers), equal opportunities, human rights, donations to charities and community projects? Do we look at all of these things?

We might look at the actions of a company but we also want to have some idea of the impacts of those actions on affected groups and whether we judge these impacts to be positive or negative. Again involving the key stakeholders in this process of setting appropriate performance targets and measures and evaluating impacts may be a major part in effective social management but may be a difficult process.

Whether companies seriously pursue these is partly a matter of business **leadership** - what do top managers think and what signals do they send down the organisation? And what we might call organisational or company **culture** - the values and beliefs promoted by the organisation. But there can be a credibility gap between formally **espoused** values and what really goes on in organisations either against the wishes of top managers or perhaps even worse with the knowledge and **tacit** approval of top managers. This has been an issue in organisations such as the Greater Manchester Police and other forces where there are strong commitments at the top of the organisation to equal opportunities, valuing diversity and opposing forms of discrimination, but this may not always be apparent in everyday behaviour further down the organisation. Those who have studied the police refer to a "canteen culture" which may be sceptical and even hostile to the formal policies and procedures coming down from the top. Some of you may recall a recent television programme on racist attitudes of some new police recruits (BBC News UK, 2003) at a police training college which covert filming by a reporter posing as a new recruit revealed. The relevant authorities took action but it did raise issues about how such behaviour had been allowed to develop.

To what extent do organisations **anticipate** the critical social and ethical issues facing them and take action at an early stage and to what extent do they **react** to events and external pressures? In responding to such pressures is the approach one of just doing what might be legally required or do organisation seek to take a wider approach to managing social issues and go beyond any basic legal requirements?

To what extent are or should companies be held responsible and accountable for the behaviour of suppliers that they do business with? This kind of issue has been a problem for several companies and the NHS and raises issues of the limits of responsibility and how these can be managed. What kind of monitoring and support would you expect a company to provide to a supplier to ensure that it was meeting certain standards of behaviour? To what extent would demands on companies in this area raise problems in terms of costs, prices and competition?

To what extent are organisations really committed to behaving in socially responsible ways and how much is cosmetic? Be careful of just dismissing such claims from business or going to the other extreme and just accepting them at face value. Like any claim look at it **critically** - what evidence supports it, how has that evidence been produced, can it be independently checked and verified, is it comprehensive in its coverage or does it leave obvious and serious gaps? These kinds of tests should be applied to anything you read and are the kinds of criteria covered in session 2.

BBC News UK (2003) Anger after Police Racism Film http://news.bbc.co.uk/1/uk/3212442.stm accessed 25th June 2007

# Corporate responsibility, corporate governance and corporate citizenship

## Learning outcomes

Having read this chapter and completed its associated activities, you should be able to:

■ Discuss the development of corporate social responsibility (CSR), and the more recent attachment to the notion of corporate responsibility.

■ Critically evaluate the counter-arguments to CSR.

■ Debate the scope and appropriateness of developments in Anglo-American corporate governance since the early 1990s.

■ Discuss the challenges posed to Anglo-American development in corporate governance by the King Report.

■ Review the UN Global Compact and the development in orientation reflected in the 2004 *Gearing Up* report.

■ Understand the notion of the social contract as reflected in *Integrated Social Contract Theory*.

■ Discuss the position of corporate manslaughter as an indictable offence in the UK and America.

## Introduction

Corporate responsibility is a term that is supplanting the term corporate social responsibility. The 'social' is increasingly being omitted in order to emphasise the (claimed) broader responsibilities of business corporations, particularly their responsibilities with regard to the environment, as discussed in the next chapter.

Corporate governance is a phrase with some longevity, but which has gained greater prominence since the early 1990s. The issues of whether corporations can assume the status of citizens and, if so, whether such a development is desirable, will also be discussed. The three terms have been purposely linked in this chapter because, whilst they possess different associations, within corporate governance reforms in the UK and America, there have been strenuous and largely successful attempts to deny their relationship, or at least to contest the notion of corporate responsibility, let alone debate the notion of corporate citizenship.

## The early calls for corporate social responsibility (CSR)

The desire to encourage, nay require, corporations to assume greater responsibility for their actions can be traced back over many decades, and reflects growing concerns regarding the power and influence of corporations over people's lives and even the independence and integrity of governments. For example, Oberman (2000) refers to academic debates over corporate social responsibilities taking place in the 1920s.

As the power and influence of business corporations have assumed ever greater proportions, so too have the calls increased for mechanisms to be put in place that would make corporations more accountable as well as responsible to a wider constituency than merely their shareholders. Within this latter aspect of the debate the use of the term *stakeholder* has gained currency in recent years and is a subject to which we will return later in this chapter.

The development of the argument from one of requiring corporations to act in socially responsible ways, to more recent calls for corporations to be seen as corporate citizens, reflects a desire to lock corporations, both formally and possibly legally, into the responsibilities that this status would confer. As indicated in the definition below, the citizenry is, in theory, sovereign to the state, yet the citizenry has little or no access, and certainly few, if any, rights with respect to corporations. With corporations playing an increasingly influential role over very many aspects of social and political life, the demand for more accountability and responsibility on the part of corporations is unlikely to diminish.

### DEFINITION

The term **citizen** normally relates to the relationship between an individual and the political state in which the individual lives. It carries with it notions of rights and responsibilities on the part of the individual and the state. However, this reciprocity (i.e. two-way relationship) is unlikely to be an equal one. Within democratic theories of the state, citizens have ultimate sovereignty over the state, or at least sovereignty over those who represent the citizenry within government. Practice, however, usually reflects a quite different balance of power.

Being described as a citizen does not of itself imply much about morality. It is a noun in need of an adjective such as 'good' or 'moral' before it can confer a positive societal influence. Wood and Logsdon (2001) referred to this issue when they observed, in the context of the corporate citizen debate,

One important debate distinguishes the concept of citizenship-as-legal-status from the concept of citizen-as-desirable-activity. The minimum requirements to be called a citizen are very different from the requirement to be called a 'good citizen.'

(Wood and Logsdon, 2001: 88)

The role of the citizen can vary from the active notion of citizenship evident in ancient Greece (for those conferred as free men) to a passive acceptance of governance from a sovereign body (à la Hobbes) or from the bureaucratic state (à la Weber). Within the corporate citizen debate, the demands made of corporations vary from a minimalist societally neutral influence, to a proactive role. The societally neutral arguments do not, however, reflect a status-quo situation, or even a single understanding of what might be meant by societally neutral. For example, would being societally neutral mean that:

- Negative and positive effects of corporate activities could be balanced out (possibly involving an international perspective), or would a corporation's impacts need to harm no one or nothing at any time?

- Acting within legal constraints would be acceptable, even if the law was judged by many to be inadequate (as a result of the political lobbying by corporations)?

- There is a general acceptance that corporations do have social responsibilities?

These debates are still developing and represent just some of the issues that make the general area of business and values both dynamic and vital.

Hobbes (*see* Pojman, 1998) held a pessimistic view of human nature, seeing people as essentially selfish and untrustworthy. Thus, Hobbes deemed that a sovereign power was necessary to which the people would owe allegiance. The relationship between the sovereign power and the citizen is, in a Hobbesian world, a subjugated one. In this context, being a citizen within a Hobbesian state is a quite different one from that which would be acceptable in the twenty-first century. However, if the idea of conferring citizenship status upon corporations is one that concerns people, due to their distrust in corporations to act in socially beneficial ways, then a Hobbesian notion of citizenship has some appeal. But much depends upon the constitution and constituent parts of the sovereign power.

As societies have developed and the scope of governments has increased, the lack of possibilities for active participation of citizens has come to be viewed as a weakness of modern conceptions of democratic states. In contemporary societies political citizenship is increasingly limited to periodic elections of political representatives, and even the relevance of these is being questioned. For example, in the 2001 general election in the UK, only 58 per cent of those eligible to vote did so, the lowest turnout for many years. In the UK, local elections and those for the European Union achieve even lower levels of elector participation. In these elections approximately two out of three people do not vote. Thus, when we, or others, use the term citizen, we need to be clear about the form of citizenship we are discussing.

## Activity 8.1

The next time you are in a group – in a seminar room, pub or other social gathering, try to establish how many people voted at the last general election, and if you think the conversation will stand the enquiry, how many people voted at the last local election when it was held independently of a general election. Do you think the percentages you establish sit comfortably in a democratic state?

One of the most widely expressed concerns about modern corporations is that they have relatively unfettered authority, with only limited responsibilities (basically to keep within the laws of the land), but there is a need to be more specific about the form and level of participation in the operations of the state that are being suggested when the phrase corporate citizenship is employed. Given the significance of business organisations within democratic (as well as undemocratic) states, the presumption must be that the notion of corporate citizenship assumed by its advocates would reflect the acceptance of certain societal responsibilities, although whether there is envisaged to be an equal bestowing of citizens' rights on corporations is far from clear.

Before progressing any further, it is worth reflecting upon the observations of Charles Lindblom, a former Professor of Economics and Political Science at Yale University. In his book *Politics and Markets* (1977), Lindblom concluded his analysis of the relationships between large corporations and political systems (and the book itself) with the following paragraph.

It has been a curious feature of democratic thought that it has not faced up to the private corporation in an ostensible democracy. Enormously large, rich in resources ... they can insist that government meet their demands, even if these demands run counter to ... citizens .... Moreover they do not disqualify themselves from playing the role of citizen ..... they exercise unusual veto powers .... The large private corporation fits oddly into democratic theory and vision. Indeed it does not fit.

(Lindblom, 1977: 356)

The final five-word sentence is the last in the book and is particularly piercing. Lindblom was bringing into sharp focus the lack of compatibility between democratic aspirations for political systems and the autocratic, sometimes feudal, systems that operate in many, if not the majority of, corporations, and it is the latter in which most people spend most of their waking lives. Large corporations have influence in and upon even the most significant of political powers. Table 8.1 illustrates the sort of evidence that gives rise to such concerns. The table reflects some of the donations made to the Republican Party during the 2000 American presidential campaign and the actions taken immediately following the inauguration of George W. Bush as President of the United States of America in 2001. All the actions were taken by the President during the first three months of his presidency.

**Table 8.1** Actions taken by President G.W. Bush within three months of his inauguration in 2001

| Industry | $M donated | Actions taken |
|---|---|---|
| Tobacco | 7.0 | Removal of federal lawsuits against cigarette manufacturers |
| Timber | 3.2 | Restrictions on logging roads scrapped |
| Oil and Gas | 25.4 | Restrictions on CO2 emissions abandoned; Kyoto agreement scrapped; moves to open Arctic refuge to drilling |
| Mining | 2.6 | Scrapping of environmental clean-up rules, e.g. arsenic limits in water supply |
| Banks and credit card companies | 25.6 | Bankruptcy bill making it easier for credit card companies to collect debts from bankrupt customers |
| Pharmaceuticals | 17.8 | Medicare (government-supported health insurance) reform removing price controls |
| Airlines | 4.2 | Federal barriers to strikes introduced; back-pedalling on antitrust (mergers and monopolies) legislation |

*Source*: *Guardian* G2, 27 April 2001, p. 2

It would be wrong to imply that concerns are only ever expressed with regard to American corporate–political relationships. The following are just two examples taken from the UK that have raised similar concerns.

1. In 1997, the incoming Labour government had a manifesto commitment to a total ban on tobacco advertising, yet no such proposed legislation was ever formally debated in Parliament during the 1997–2001 administration. By the time the Labour Party's 2001 manifesto was published, the commitment to a complete ban on tobacco advertising was noticeable by its absence, although in March 2002 the Minister for Health announced legislative plans for an almost complete ban on tobacco advertising and sponsorship, the one exception being motor racing sponsorship. It might be just a coincidence that Bernie Ecclestone, who effectively controls world-wide Grand Prix motor racing, donated £1M to the Labour Party, which was subsequently repaid when the donation became public knowledge.

2. The Labour Party's 1997 manifesto also included a commitment to a reform of company law by recognising a stakeholder perspective (as opposed to an exclusively shareholder responsibility). Upon election the Labour government established a committee to consider how the stakeholder commitment could be operationalised. The committee deliberated for nearly two years. An interim report was published after the first year, which retained an attachment to the notion of pluralism in corporate decision making, although the wording can be seen to be becoming a little ambiguous.

The principle arguments are that the present scheme of law fails adequately to recognise that businesses best generate wealth where participants operate harmoniously as teams and that managers should recognise the wider interests of the community.

One year later the committee published its final report, but by now the term pluralism had been lost and in its place appeared the term 'enlightened shareholder value'. The removal of the commitment to pluralism led to the resignation from the committee of the finance director of *The Body Shop*. He described himself as an advocate of social and environmental responsibility and was not prepared to remain a member of the committee once the commitment to enlightened shareholder value had replaced pluralism. Newspaper reports on the outcome of the committee's work talked of frantic lobbying by business interests that ultimately led to not only the retention of the shareholders' interests being the only one formally recognised in UK law, but also the conversion of the committee's proposals for compulsory statements on corporate issues into proposals that would only be voluntary, i.e. at the discretion of directors.

The above examples are not cited to claim that all businesses are corrupt or corrupting. However, just as a few examples of negative or unethical business practices should not tar all businesses with these behaviours, neither should a few examples of positive business behaviour suggest that all is right in the corporate and political worlds. For our purposes the point the cases illustrate is the way the business lobby groups successfully influenced legislative matters. The cases illustrate the significant ramifications for social and democratic processes of the lobbying phenomenon which, by its very nature, is opaque. An image thus emerges of business interests playing an active, although not always transparent, role in political and social, as well as economic, matters.

The question is thus raised, 'To what extent is ethical egoism, with its appeal to emotive and fundamental concepts such as freedom and individuality, merely a convenient façade behind which privileged and powerful self-interests hide?'

### Connexion point

Ethical egoism was discussed in Chapter 3 and relates to the ethical stance that sees the protection of individual freedom as the touchstone of ethics. It draws upon notions of choice, meritocracy and a form of justice, but it can conceal extreme selfishness, protectionism and callousness.

With many large corporations now (and for some time) more powerful than the majority of governments, the feudal nature of corporate realpolitik is masked by the veil of democratic political paraphernalia for the majority of people living on the planet. Thus, if large corporations are to exist within democratic states there have to be certain developments that democratise the corporations and other developments that make them less of a threat to political and social democracy.

When put in this context the subject of corporate governance ceases to be (if it ever was) an arcane and dry technical subject. As we will see, different notions of corporate governance exist in different parts of the world, with some of the most enlightened thinking emanating from South Africa.

## The recurring issue of corporate governance

As with notions of CSR, issues relating to corporate governance have featured regularly through time. For example, the 'Bubble Act' of 1719 came into being as the result of a corporate scandal which, in relative terms, involved sums of money greater than the combined value of Enron and WorldCom.

Lee (1984) and Edey (1984) referred to the manipulation of company accounting information by managers at the expense of the owners' interests during the early nineteenth century, while Carey (1984) referred to the contribution of William Z. Ripley, a Harvard professor, who, in the early 1920s wrote about the 'docility of corporate shareholders permitting themselves to be honeyfuggled'. In relation to the public utilities industries, Ridley referred to 'the hoodwinking of the shareholders', and of accountants Ripley observed, 'accountants are enabled to play ball with figures to an astounding degree' (Carey, 1984: 243).

The concerns over corporate governance continued through the latter part of the nineteenth century and into the early part of the twentieth century, culminating in Berle and Means' seminal publication in 1932. In this publication Berle and Means charted the history and implications of the decoupling of ownership (shareholders) from control (senior management) within the modern corporation. Niebuhr (1932) also wrote powerful critiques of corporate power and the exploitative and alienating tendencies of the capitalist system. Since the early 1990s there has been increasing attention to corporate governance as a result of major corporate scandals such as Maxwell Communications, BCCI and Polly Peck in the late 1980s and in the early 2000s Enron, WorldCom, Global Crossing and Parmalat. We will return to the issues raised by these corporate collapses and scandals shortly, but first we address the issue of whether we should just accept such corporate débacles as a fact of economic life and not be too concerned about them.

## Are not corporate failures just a fact of economic life?

It is clear from the very brief overview above that concerns over corporate governance are not new, but reactions to corporate scandals of the 1990s and early twenty-first century by organisations such as the major stock exchanges, professional accountancy bodies and governments appear to have been more obvious and public than before. Could this reflect a degree of vulnerability and sensitivity that was not felt in the past? It is difficult to say, although débacles such as Enron and WorldCom, Global Crossing and Parmalat pose fundamental problems for securities' markets. Investing in companies is a risky business and any investor must recognise and accept this fact. Thus, it is not the losing of money that is the problem. The problem is the failure of market mechanisms to provide the information and warning signals that the investing public has a right to expect. In all the corporate failures referred to in this chapter the most recent accounts of the corporations concerned gave little if any hint of the financial turmoil the corporations were experiencing.

In the cases of Enron and WorldCom the auditors appear to have been complicit in the deceit, whilst in the cases of Maxwell Communications and BCCI (financial scandals of the late 1980s and early 1990s) the causes of the auditors' performance are more opaque. Whatever the reasons, the important market mechanism that the role of audit is supposed to play (verifying the reliability of the financial information supplied to shareholders) failed. The accounting profession was seen to be, at best, an unreliable scrutineer of financial information. More significantly the independence and integrity of accountants and accounting firms were increasingly being called into question.

In addition to the failings of the audit function, market analysts were still recommending Enron and WorldCom stocks as 'buys' to the investing world until days before the companies crashed, although again the integrity of the market analysts concerned has subsequently been shown to have been heavily compromised. As a result of these failings of the securities' markets, confidence in their fairness, transparency and integrity was undermined, with the risk that investors might turn to other investment options, such as property, currencies, works of art, etc. Thus, while it might only be out of enlightened self-interest, the securities' markets cannot afford to tolerate unethical corporate behaviour. However, at the same time, the intensity of the demands of the securities' markets is unrelenting in terms of the enormous pressures placed upon company executives to deliver improved 'financials' (profits) year upon year, half-year upon half-year, quarter upon quarter.

## Developments in corporate governance

There has been a lot of activity with regard to corporate governance in the UK since the early 1990s and Figure 8.1 presents a schema of the various reports, with the addition of one notable reform in the USA, that of the Sarbanes–Oxley Act in 2002. A brief overview of these reports is provided so that the contestability of corporate responsibility and corporate governance can be discussed.

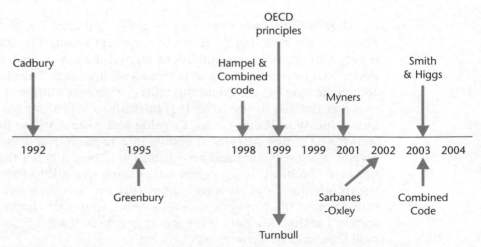

**Figure 8.1** Significant recent reports and developments in corporate governance

The **Cadbury Committee** was established as a response to some significant corporate collapses/scandals in the late 1980s and early 1990s, including BCCI, Polly Peck and Maxwell Communications. Given the comments made above regarding the questioning of the audit function performed by the large accounting firms and the resulting undermining of confidence in the London Stock Exchange, it will come as no surprise to learn that these were the two major sponsoring organisations of the Cadbury Committee. The major recommendations of the committee included the increased use of non-executive directors to counter what is referred to as the agency effect, and the splitting of the roles of chief executive and chairperson.

> **DEFINITION**
>
> The **agency effect** is derived from agency theory, which assumes that people are, at heart, untrustworthy. As a result of the privileged position that executive directors enjoy over shareholders with regard to the control of information, executive directors are deemed likely to exploit this power situation to their own advantage. This might manifest itself in 'managing' information (hence the importance of the audit function) and large remuneration packages.

The **Greenbury Committee** was set up to look into the issue of executive pay (Sir Richard Greenbury was at the time Chief Executive of Marks & Spencer and one of the highest paid directors in the UK). Even at this time the issue of executive pay, sometimes referred to as 'fat-cats pay', was a vexed issue but the work of the Greenbury Committee seems to have had little constraining effect, as indicated by Table 8.2. This table contrasts the movement in the FTSE 100 Index with the average increase in the remuneration of the executive directors of the same top 100 UK corporations. If the movement in a company's market worth is a fair reflection of the performance of the company's senior management, then is it not reasonable to expect that there would be a close correlation between the change in corporate executives' remuneration and the change in market worth of the companies they manage, certainly over a reasonable period of time like three years?

Table 8.2 Average increases in the remuneration of the directors of the FTSE 100 companies for 2000–2002 compared with movements in the FTSE 100 share index over the same period

| Year | Movement in directors' remuneration | Movements in FTSE 100 index |
| --- | --- | --- |
| 2000 | + 28% | – 8% |
| 2001 | + 17% | – 15% |
| 2002 | + 23% | – 23% |
| Overall movements from Jan. 2000 to 31 Dec. 2002 | + 84% | – 40% |

A similar picture is evident in the USA. With the boundaries of self-control removed during the 1990s, but with the retention of the rhetoric of free markets, rapacious has been a frequently used adjective in discussions of corporate and executive behaviour. In both America and the UK stock options became a central part of executive remuneration packages during the 1990s, as attempts were made to tie the pay of senior executives to the performance of their companies, thereby trying to minimise the agency effect. The result was startling, although not necessarily in the way intended. Robert Monks (2003) commented upon the transfer of wealth reflected in the value of stock options held by a very small minority of senior executives in America.

> The most important component of compensation was the grant of options that, according to the accounting rules after 1994, did not have to be accounted for as an expense by the issuing company. Typically, the top five executives in a company held 75% of the total options granted; the ratio of options to the total outstanding rose in the 1990s from 2% to 12%. This must be the greatest 'peaceful' transfer of wealth in recorded history.

(Monks, 2003: 165)

Two per cent or one-fiftieth, of the value of the equity capital of corporate America is a huge figure. Twelve per cent, or nearly one-eighth, is a gargantuan number and this proportion of American equity capital is held by a relatively small number of senior of executives.

Returning to reports on UK corporate governance, the **Hampel Committee** (1998) was formed to take stock of both the Cadbury and Greenbury reports and to suggest how best to implement their recommendations. Interestingly, the Hampel report, while recognising that boards of directors have a responsibility for *relations* with stakeholders, felt the need to emphasise that the *responsibility* of directors is to shareholders. Stakeholders are of concern to directors, but only in as far as they can contribute to the maximisation of shareholder wealth.

The Hampel Report led to the first '**Combined Code**', which was issued by the London Stock Exchange in 1998. The Code specifies the corporate governance practices that quoted companies should follow if they wish to have a listing on the London Stock Exchange. The Code is not backed by law and if a quoted company chooses not to follow the Code the company must explain the rationale for its different practice. For example, the supermarket chain, Morrisons, had, until it bought the Safeway group in 2004, combined the roles of chief executive and chairman, which was contrary to the 1998 Combined Code. Morrisons claimed that combining the two roles made sense for them and this was accepted by the London Stock Exchange.

The 'comply or explain' approach towards corporate governance developments in the UK is different from the approach of the United States, where changes are passed through the legislative processes and are thus legally binding. Such an example is the Sarbanes–Oxley Act of 2002. The latter was the result of two Congressmen formulating their response to a number of financial scandals, notably those of Enron, WorldCom and Global Crossing. The Act places specific responsibilities upon chief executives and the chief financial officers (in UK terms, the finance directors) to personally sign off the accounts. In addition certain accounting services that audit firms might wish to provide to their audit clients have been proscribed by the Act. This reflects the concerns that have been expressed for many years that the level of non-audit fee income earned by accounting firms from their audit clients might compromise their independence and objectivity. The fact that Andersen's (Enron's auditors) generated around $25M of non-audit fee income from Enron, on top of the $25M audit income, was felt by many to have been an unhealthy situation, and it was not unique. Interestingly, Andersen's were also WorldCom's auditors.

The **Turnbull Report** of 1999 concerned itself with internal controls and internal audit, while the **Myners' Committee** was sponsored by the UK Treasury to look into the role of institutional investors in company affairs. With institutional investors (banks, pension funds, unit and investment trusts) such influential players on securities' markets, any hope of improved shareholder activism to challenge the power of directors would need to come from the institutional investors. In a nutshell, Myners recommended that institutional investors *should* be more active, but not a lot more.

The statements of corporate governance principles by the **OECD** (Organisation for Economic Cooperation and Development) in 1999 and 2005 represent a very Anglo-American view of the subject and bear a close resemblance to the 1998 and 2003 UK Combined Codes.

The reports of the **Higgs** and **Smith** Committees were published in 2003, the former being concerned with the roles of non-executive directors (NEDs) and the latter concerned with the work and roles of Audit Committees. Higgs recommended a scaling up of the importance of NEDs, such that the majority of main board directors should be NEDs, presumably to further minimise the agency effect. The Report makes further recommendations with respect to how many NED appointments executive directors can hold etc., but these need not concern us. However, three questions remain unanswered by the Higgs Report and corporate governance developments in general.

1. The majority of directors on Enron's main board were NEDs, but this did not prevent the corruption that appears to have taken place at Enron. So why was the main recommendation of the Higgs Report that the majority of main board directors should be NEDs?

2. NEDs only attend the companies of which they are NEDs on one, possibly two, days each month. Does this not place even more power in the hands of the few remaining executive directors, who agency theory claims should not be trusted?

3. If minimising the agency effect is a key role of NEDs, why is it that the vast majority of NEDs are also executive directors in their primary employment? Why should person 'A', who is an executive director of company 'X' be subject to the agency effect and be untrustworthy in this role, but upon taking on the mantle of NED of company 'B' become a trustworthy individual whose role it is to ensure the integrity of company B's practices? What is the transformation process that turns A from untrustworthy to trustworthy?

As for the Smith Report on Audit Committees, it makes various recommendations, but it stops short of requiring accounting firms to stop providing any of their non-audit services to their audit clients. This is a far less prescriptive or punitive approach than that reflected in the Sarbanes–Oxley Act.

## What have the developments in corporate governance achieved?

What do all these reports and recommendations say about corporate governance and ethics in business? For many they say very little and what they say is inadequate, given the scale of corporate governance issues. A more inclusive view of corporate governance sees the disregard for shareholder interests displayed by executives as but one of the corporate governance issues to be addressed. All the developments in corporate governance since 1992 amount to very little. An increase in NEDs here, some concerns expressed about accounting firms there, but really it is a 'steady-as-she-goes' approach, with only minor adjustments to the tiller.

Frustration with the myopia and impotence displayed by governments to correct what are seen as the inadequate responses to profound corporate governance issues such as child labour, forced labour, inhuman working conditions, despoliation of the environment, and the connivance and corrupt practices of governments (*see* the *Transparency International* website for an examination of the latter) with corporations has led to a series of other initiatives, which are highlighted in Figure 8.2.

## The King Report on corporate governance

Before progressing to the issues reflected in the UN Global Compact, reference will be made to the second King Report, which was published in 2002 (the first having been published in 1994) and which relates to corporate governance in South Africa. The opening of the report is interesting in that it refers to a state-

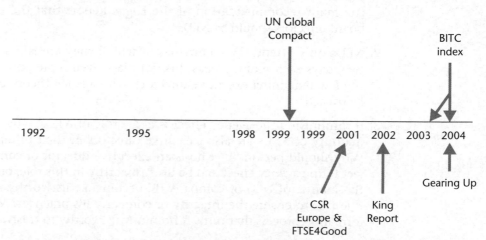

**Figure 8.2** Other interesting developments in corporate governance that have not impacted upon UK and American stock exchange listing requirements

ment made by Sir Adrian Cadbury (the same Cadbury who gave his name to the 1992 UK Cadbury report on corporate governance), but this time the statement was made by Cadbury in the World Bank's 1999 report on corporate governance.

> Corporate governance is concerned with holding the balance between economic and social goals and between individual and community goals. ... The aim is to align as nearly as possible the interests of individuals, corporations and society.
>
> (King, 2002: 6)

This is a much more expansive and inclusive view of corporate governance than that articulated in the 1992 UK Cadbury Report, or in any UK or US financial corporate governance reports since. There are further important features of the King Report that are highly relevant to the considerations of this chapter. The first is the continuation in the second (2002) King Report of the inclusive orientation of the first (1994) King Report. This orientation is reflected in the following extract.

> Unlike its counterparts in other countries at the time, the King Report 1994 went beyond the financial and regulatory aspects of corporate governance in advocating an integrated approach to good governance in the interests of a wide range of stakeholders having regard to the fundamental principles of good financial, social, ethical and environmental practice. In adopting a participative corporate governance system of enterprise with integrity, the King Committee in 1994 successfully formalised the need for companies to recognise that they no longer act independently from the societies and the environment in which they operate.
>
> (King, 2002: 6)

In contrast, Anglo-American reforms to corporate governance have been allowed to concentrate exclusively upon corporations' responsibilities to shareholders. The King Committee took an explicitly inclusive view of a corporation's stakeholders, although it was not a naïve report that ignored or undervalued the economic imperatives faced by companies. It is a thoughtful, scholarly report that distinguishes between accountability and responsibility, which UK reports on corporate governance have failed to articulate. The King Report was not a maverick study located at the margins of South Africa's economic interests. It was a study sponsored by the South Africa Institute of Directors, and whilst operating in the context of a market-based capitalist economy the King Report reflects a very different conception of the business–society debate. This is most intriguingly reflected in paragraph 38 and its subsections where the report focuses upon the values that underpin South African society. This is a dimension to corporate governance that has not only been missed by UK and US corporate governance reports; it would currently not be countenanced as it reflects a profoundly different world view of the business–society relationship.

The very first of the values considered in the King Report is 'spiritual collectiveness'. Paragraph 38.1 reads as follows:

> Spiritual Collectiveness is prized over individualism. This determines the communal nature of life, where households live as an interdependent neighbourhood.

Other values considered include:

Humility and helpfulness to others is more important than criticism of them. (paragraph 38.3)

There is an inherent trust and belief in fairness of all human beings. This manifests itself in the predisposition towards universal brotherhood, even shared by African-Americans. (paragraph 38.6)

High standards of morality are based on historical precedent. These are bolstered by the close kinship observed through totem or clan names and the extended family systems. (paragraph 38.7)

The above claims to community values and beliefs do not deny the historic tribalism that has seen African peoples at war with one another over centuries. However, it draws out the common values that unite rather than separate the tribes (which are effectively mini-nation states in western terms) and seeks to build notions of corporate governance that reflect cultural mores and values, rather than allow more recognisable business values and beliefs to migrate from the economic sphere, driving out the more inclusive, community-oriented values in the process.

Interestingly, paragraph 39 opens with the statement, 'Corporate governance is essentially about leadership', followed by the essential values that a leader should possess and display. The African 'great-soul-man' appears to being alluded to here, who is noticeable by his absence from Anglo-American debates.

The twentieth century was traumatic for South African society. The release of Nelson Mandela in 1990 heralded the ending of the brutal apartheid policies, and the King Report must be seen in this social and cultural context, but it should not be side-stepped or minimised as a result. It is a report that should demand our attention. It offers a very different perspective on corporate governance, arguing that business is a part of society rather than apart from society. This challenge to the assumptions implicit within Anglo-American corporate governance reforms leads us to a consideration of the UN Global Compact.

## The UN Global Compact

In 1999, frustrated by the lack of progress of governments to respond adequately to addressing issues such as child labour and inhuman working conditions in companies located in the developing economies, but which are part of the supply chains of large international organisations, the United Nations set up the UN Global Compact. In the words of Global Compact's Chief Executive, the Global Compact was established to fill a void, to 'respond to demands and needs that governments were either unwilling or unable to meet' (Kell, 2004).

The Compact was, and remains, a voluntary code that is intended to influence corporate practices by:

(i)  gaining the support and membership of leading organisations, and then
(ii) increasing the acceptance and take-up of corporate responsibility by disseminating examples of good practice that hopefully other organisations will adopt.

The Compact focuses upon nine key principles of corporate activity, which are grouped into three categories.

*Human rights*

Principle 1 – Businesses are asked to support the protection of international human rights within their sphere of influence; and

Principle 2 – To ensure their own corporations are not complicit in human rights abuses.

*Labour*

Principle 3 – Businesses are asked to uphold the freedom of association and the effective recognition of the rights to collective bargaining;

Principle 4 – To eliminate all forms of forced and compulsory labour;

Principle 5 – To abolish child labour; and

Principle 6 – To help eliminate discrimination in respect of employment and occupation.

*Environment*

Principle 7 – Businesses are asked to support a precautionary approach to environmental challenges;

Principle 8 – To undertake initiatives to promote greater environmental responsibility;

Principle 9 – To encourage the development and diffusion of environmentally friendly technologies

In 1999 those responsible for the Compact saw the future for social change to be through international corporations, hence the focus on working with significant organisations to both gain their support (patronage) and stimulate corporate responsibility (CR) by highlighting examples of good practice that 'work' and that could be seen to be compatible with being a successful company.

The Foreword to the 2004 report *Gearing Up*, which was commissioned by the executive of Global Compact, reflected a development in this thinking and strategy. There now appears to be a recognition that it was unrealistic to expect corporations to respond to initiatives such as the Global Compact independent of governments. While the original Global Compact may have been a response to political failings, a voluntary initiative that appears to ask businesses to make good the failings of governments, ironically, needs the commitment and positive engagement of governments to help it develop. For this reason *Gearing Up* argues for a greater level of dialogue, collaboration and partnership between businesses and governments for the future development of corporate responsibility.

A more critical voice is that of Christian Aid. In its 2004 report, *Behind the Mask*, Christian Aid dismissed the UN Global Compact as having had 'almost no impact' (p. 16). The lack of transparency associated with the Global Compact and its lack of monitoring and verification are other failings in the initiative's credibility. For Christian Aid it would seem that the Global Compact is an example of the worst sort of CSR initiative, that is one that enjoys a lot of publicity and hype, but is in fact a toothless tiger, with few if any monitoring and/or verification powers or resources. For some it is a sham and governments are complicit, instrumental even, in this charade.

The Global Compact contains the sorts of commitments and aspirations that many supporters and advocates of CSR or CR (corporate responsibility) would welcome, as well as displaying many of the limitations of a number of CR initiatives. Thus, with the important caveat from Christian Aid expressed in the above paragraph, we return to a key aim of the *Gearing Up* report, which is stated as making 'the link between corporate responsibility ... initiatives and wider sustainable development challenges', with the report linked to the Millennium Development Goals (MDGs) (*see* Table 8.3).

The *Gearing Up* report moves on, via a discussion of its findings and case studies, to identify six possible ways (or, probably more accurately, rates of change) that CR could reflect. The six possibilities reflect different levels of engagement by 'business' in economic and non-economic development, including one option (termed 'reverse') which reflects the possibility that businesses might publicly articulate a commitment to being catalysts for change, while, behind the scenes, doing all they can to frustrate and hinder developments.

---

**Table 8.3** The Millennium Development Goals

1  Eradicate extreme poverty and hunger

2  Achieve universal primary education

3  Promote gender equality and empower women

4  Reduce child mortality

5  Improve maternal health

6  Combat HIV/AIDS, malaria and other diseases

7  Ensure environmental sustainability, and

8  Develop a global partnership for development (this relates to trade issues, but also debt relief and access to affordable, essential drugs in developing countries).

---

**Connexion point**

One can construct both consequentialist and deontological arguments to support the development of CSR. Produce two brief justifications for adopting CSR based upon (i) consequentialist arguments, and (ii) deontological arguments. Refer back to Chapter 3 if you need to refresh your memory on these respective ethical stances.

---

**Activity 8.2      An important question**

Notwithstanding the ethical arguments you have raised in response to the above connexion point, is it fair, sensible and/or ethical to ask, let alone expect, business organisations to take on the role of correcting the world's ills? How can organisations, established to fulfil a very specific economic role, take on the responsibility for enacting or at least contributing to roles that might be expected to be the responsibility of governments?

Activity 8.2 raises a fundamental question. To explore both the implications of the question and how one might respond to the question we turn to the arguments of Milton Friedman (1970).

## Milton Friedman's arguments against corporations being charged with social responsibilities

Milton Friedman was a Nobel prize-winning economist, whose ideas were very influential in America and the UK during the 1980s and 1990s. It is worth reading Friedman's oft-cited 1970 article on why the only social responsibility of business is to increase its profits, and not to indulge in social interventions such as sponsorship of community activities, the funding of charities, community activities, or other 'good deeds'.

Friedman's article was a response to what were becoming increasingly frequent calls for corporations to act in socially responsible ways in the late 1960s and early 1970s. Precisely what was meant by 'socially responsible ways' was often left vague and poorly explained, save for concerns being expressed that corporate power was authority without responsibility. Friedman's criticisms were rehearsed by Wolf (2000) thirty years later when the latter accused those (still) calling for greater corporate social responsibility as not only distorting business activity, but confusing and misunderstanding the rationale of business. 'The role of well run companies is to make profits, not save the planet', Wolf argued.

Friedman criticised the arguments for corporate social responsibility on three fronts. The first criticism was an economic one, with ethical undertones. If corporations are required to engage in corporate philanthropy, e.g. making a donation to a charity, school or hospital, these acts will distort allocative efficiency, i.e. the profitability with which capital is employed. Friedman argued that corporations are responsible for using shareholders' funds in profitable ways, in legally acceptable ways – nothing more. Worrying about which charity to support, or which good deed/s to perform, merely 'takes management's eye off the ball', the ball being how to increase profits. Thus, the only form of corporate philanthropy that Friedman's argument would accept is where it could be shown that a donation, or good deed, would improve a company's profitability in ways superior to alternative investment opportunities. We can view this as 'prudential altruism'. In such a case the charitable donation would in fact be described more accurately as a commercial investment. Porter and Kramer (2002) makes a similar point but refers to such acts as 'strategic philanthropy', which, given the points he makes in the article, stretches the notion of philanthropy a little. Windsor (2001) reinforced the philanthropy argument with the demand that all business activities, including 'good deeds', should 'add-value', or more precisely 'add-shareholder-value'. This is most emphatically a Friedmanite position.

The second of Friedman's criticisms draws upon both ethics and political philosophy. It is that it is undemocratic for corporations to use shareholders' funds to support charities or other 'good causes'. Any such donation can only come at the expense of lower dividends, higher prices or lower wages (or a combination of all three). Friedman asked, 'How can it be ethical that a corporation should act first as unpaid tax collector (i.e. levying a tax on the shareholders, customers and/or employees) and then as unaccountable benefactor?' It is either for publicly elected representatives of the people (i.e. national or local politicians) to provide financial support to public services or charities, etc. from public funds, or for individuals to decide to which charities they wish to make private donations.

The third criticism was a philosophical one. It was that corporations cannot possess responsibilities. Corporations are social constructs, i.e. they have been brought into existence by societies passing laws that give legal protection to certain forms of business associations and structures. Without these legal and social devices, corporations could not and would not exist. In Friedman's terms only individuals can have responsibilities, not corporations.

| Activity 8.3 | Challenging Friedman |
|---|---|

Taking the three criticisms that are raised by Friedman, try to develop arguments that challenge Friedman's claims. It is important that you think through the arguments that Friedman is making, so take your time.

## Responding to Friedman's arguments

From the perspective of advocates of unfettered (or as unfettered as possible) market-based economies, which we referred to in Chapter 1 as the *neo-liberal economic position*, or simply neo-liberalism, the best hope for the protection of individual freedoms is the maintenance of open markets (i.e. no barriers to trade) and minimum interference in the workings of business by governments.

**Connexion point**

Adopting the stance that governments should play as small a part as humanly possible in economic and social affairs is the concept known as 'negative freedom', i.e. freedom 'from', as discussed in Chapter 3.

Not only is interference by government seen as economically counter-productive in the medium to long run, but such interventions are themselves argued to be unethical, i.e. they impose a big-brother-knows-best mentality over individual preferences and thus undermine the sovereignty of individual choice. From the perspective of the neo-liberalist position the first and second objections raised by Friedman are both strong objections. Non-accountable tax-raising, whether by government or corporate leaders, is a distortion to allocative efficiency, injurious to the sovereignty of the individual and undemocratic, and thus to be opposed.

Friedman did not argue that corporations should be above the law, but he did argue that corporations should not be expected to exceed what the law defines as minimum levels of behaviour. Laws are assumed to represent what societies deem to be acceptable behaviour (of both individuals and corporations) and only if a society increases the burden upon business in terms of legally defined levels of performance (e.g. increased levels of pollution control) should corporations have to raise their performance. This obviously ignores the pressures for increased performance resulting from normal competitive forces, although such pressures will often present countervailing forces to those emanating from environmental concerns.

Neo-liberal supporters would accept that there are sometimes considerable negative human consequences resulting from economic fluctuations. For example, large-scale redundancies and/or high levels of unemployment can result from significant economic downturns, with resulting impacts upon local infrastructure in the form of, say, lower than desired levels of expenditure on education, health care, transport, etc. The latter would be the economic consequences of lower levels of taxes being collected, coupled with increased social security benefits. These are seen as unfortunate, but unavoidable, consequences that societies must accept in order to protect the overall integrity of the market system. Yet the increasing impact of what is known as globalisation and the powerful moves towards full deregulation of markets across the world by the World Trade Organisation (WTO) have raised the political and social stakes in this debate.

Within the arguments presented by Friedman, either the role and impact of business in general must be benign, or, the more traditional argument, the acknowledged inequities and imperfections in market-based systems are more than counterbalanced by the claimed advancements and advantages that everyone ultimately enjoys, as a result of the market dynamics levering change and economic progress. That everyone does not benefit to the same extent as a result of these claimed economic advances is not disputed, but everyone is argued to be better off, to some extent, in the long run. You may recognise something of the Rawlsian position (which was discussed in Chapter 3) in this argument, that whilst the poorest of society are indeed relatively poor they are better off than they would be, or could be, under any other economic system. This claim can be considered at two levels.

(i) The first is the empirical question. Does the evidence we have of the globalising and deregulating effects on world markets display an overall elevation of people's well-being and is this elevation superior to all other options?

(ii) The second is the ethical question. Does this approach stand up to scrutiny when judged against notions of justice, fairness, wisdom and care?

The evidence that is available with regard to question (i) is incomplete, but at best it is mixed. At worst we are experiencing even greater concentrations of power over resources that lie outside the political arena, with fundamental questions regarding authority, responsibility and accountability remaining unanswered.

**Connexion point**

The observations of Anita Roddick, founder of The Body Shop organisation, are interesting in this context. She was responding to an article by Philippe Legrain that had appeared in the *Guardian* newspaper (on the day before the publication of her letter). Legrain had made the case that the deregulation of world markets, in line with the actions of the WTO, should be welcomed by all, as ultimately all would benefit (the argument outlined above). The words of Ms Roddick are shown on p. 464.

It is always possible to highlight acts by individual people or specific corporations that present a poor image of the groups they are said to represent. Proverbially speaking, bad apples do not necessarily tell us much about the rest of the apples in a barrel. However, if one can point to trends, allegiances, purposeful manipulation of power by large corporations, or groups of corporations, then we might have something more than the odd bad apple. The following are just a selection of possible examples that could be used.

**Case study 8.1**

## The tobacco industry

For many years, medical research had indicated a clear link between the use of tobacco products and various forms of cancer, although these findings had always been contested vigorously by the tobacco industry. Yet, in 2000, the tobacco company Reynolds broke ranks and announced in court that it was accepting liability for certain smokers' ill-health. There is evidence to suggest that the tobacco companies had confirmed the link between their products and cancer-based illnesses many years previously but concealed the evidence. Since sales of tobacco products in most western countries have been either stagnant or in decline since the early 1990s, the tobacco companies had targeted developing countries (and particularly young people) as growth markets for their products.

Notwithstanding the many previous denials of the tobacco companies of the link between cigarettes and cancer, it is now clear that such a link is accepted. This is exemplified by the use made of a study commissioned by the multinational tobacco company, Philip Morris. In 2001 the tobacco firm, one of the world's leading producers of tobacco products, and responsible for 80 per cent of the cigarettes sold in the Czech Republic, felt the need to respond to claims that cigarette smoking was costing the Czech economy significant sums by virtue of high levels of hospitalisation, absenteeism from work and thus lower tax collection levels caused by smoking-related illnesses. The study commissioned by the tobacco company concluded that, rather than impose costs on the Czech economy, cigarettes saved the Czech government over £100M each year. The basis for this assessment was that, because cigarette smokers would be dying earlier than non-smokers, due to smoking-related illnesses, this would save the government hospitalisation costs associated with old age, as well as lower pension costs and lower housing costs.

**Case study 8.2**

## When can genetically modified crops be grown?

In many western countries, including the UK, the planting of genetically modified (GM) crops is limited and tightly controlled by governments. Following a series of trials the UK government announced that only one genetically modified crop had passed its tests. The principal companies concerned had accepted the need to monitor the trials and to develop a thorough body of evidence before large-scale commercial planting could be considered. Yet, at the very time the UK government was proclaiming a moratorium in the UK, in the

Indian state of Andhra Pradesh, a 384 square mile area known as Genome Valley, was being developed for GM crop production, funded by overseas aid from the UK government. In excess of £50M was allocated to this project by the UK government in 2001. Monsanto, the principal company involved in the controlled trials in the UK, was among the companies invited to participate in the development in Andhra Pradesh. Farmers in Andhra Pradesh expressed concerns that development of prairie-style fields would result in the mass migration of millions of small farmers and labourers to the cities in search of work. The Andhra Pradesh project (known as *Vision 2020*) was the result of a study undertaken by a large American consulting firm, which, critics argue, gave little, if any, consideration to alternative forms of raising agricultural efficiency that utilised local resources more effectively and sensitively. Local farmers in Andhra Pradesh wished to control their own destinies, but the fear was that this scheme, with such influential corporate involvement, involvement that will have secured governmental support before it was officially announced, would lead to a social disaster in the region.

The case of the carving up of Indonesia, following the overthrow of President Sukarno in 1966 (reported in Chapter 12), is a further example of what appear to be structural, rather than aberrational, problems in the workings of business-society-political relationships.

| Case study 8.3 | **Markets, prices and need** |
|---|---|

The pharmaceutical industry tends to be the target of a lot of angst when it comes to illustrating the problems/issues raised by global markets and global corporations. Among other things, the pharmaceutical corporations are often criticised for concentrating the overwhelming proportion of their research and development budgets on diseases of the rich. For example, there are new products continually coming to the market which claim to address issues of impotence, hair loss, wrinkles, obesity, etc., whereas diseases such as malaria, Ebola and HIV AIDS either remain under-investigated or the drugs available are too expensive for millions of people experiencing the diseases. However, the drugs companies point out that they are commercial corporations, subject to the disciplines of financial markets. If governments wish them to channel/divert research and development budgets into specific areas of medical treatment, then the pharmaceutical companies need to be compensated for the opportunity cost of this activity. One of the responses to these claims is that generic producers can manufacture HIV-AIDS drugs, for example, for a fraction of the price charged by the global pharmaceutical companies (around one-eighth of the price). The pharmaceutical companies respond by arguing that they need to recover the research and developments costs of those drugs that never reach their intended markets, costs that the generic producers do not incur.

Whilst the ethical weight of the above arguments are not suggested to be equal, we will sidestep offering a view on where the balance lies, but consider one of the ways the pharmaceutical companies (Big Pharma) responded to criticisms of their policies with regard to HIV-AIDS.

In 2001 the South African Government took Big Pharma to court in South Africa over the pricing of retro-viral drugs (the drugs used to treat HIV AIDS). The day before the judicial decision was to be given, the pharmaceutical companies, realising that they were going to 'lose' the decision, effectively began to discuss an 'out-of-court settlement'. This took the form of initially a fifty-word statement, which, after many months of 'debate', became a massive obfuscating document. Many felt the pharmaceutical companies had pulled victory from the jaws of defeat. This feeling was reinforced when in October 2003 the US Senate announced the name of the person who was to head the American AIDS Initiative. It was Randall Tobias, a former head of Eli Lilly, one of the world's big pharmaceutical companies. He was not required to sell his share holding in pharmaceutical companies, meaning that, if Mr Tobias took any decisions that harmed the interests of Big Pharma, he would also be negatively affecting his own wealth position. The question of a conflict of interest was raised by many but never adequately responded to.

The relationship between government and business is complex and in continuous need of scrutiny. It is far more complex than the simplistic call for minimal government that is heard from free-market fundamentalists would suggest. In a market system businesses require the autonomy to respond to market signals and claim the right of freedom from government interference in business decisions. Yet, that claim is disingenuous. It ignores the role of governments in setting fiscal policies; the management of government borrowing and macro-economic affairs; the support given to businesses during times of local or national recessions; the funding provided by governments to support both pure and generic research; and the funding of major projects that might be too large for private capital formation.

In addition, business in general has a vested interest in the maintenance of particular economic and legal conditions. As part of the pluralist political system, business organisations lobby governments and parliaments to achieve the conditions and laws that suit them. In the modern era it is argued that pressure groups, particularly business pressure groups, have a far more significant influence upon the construction of legislation than the polity in general.

The ethical question is immensely complex and not just in terms of disentangling competing notions of justice, fairness and care from one another. However, it is not clear whether this question is being asked at all. The power and influence of large corporations appear to dominate political agendas, stunting debate and maybe thinking.

So, to summarise the argument so far, corporations, via their economic power, have the potential to do significant good and significant harm. The UN Global Compact was initially a reaction to multi-government failure in adequately addressing critical global issues. It was an attempt to by-pass governments and to seek social intervention by large corporations. More recently, in 2004, the *Gearing Up* report has recognised this approach as unrealistic and set itself the task of trying to facilitate greater corporate and government bi-partisanship in tackling the world's great challenges. Are we entering a period when corporate executives become engaged with addressing the world's great social and environmental challenges without jeopardising their economic well-being? It is much too early to say, but what is clear is that the issue of ethics in business has never been more relevant and high profile.

## Profit as the lever and the lure

The types of examples highlighted above regarding globalisation and deregulation issues challenge the claim that the overall effects of liberalism will necessarily be a benefit for all. An application of the Rawlsian original position test might cast doubt upon the efficacy, let alone the ethicality, of the poor being better-off as a result of MNC-influenced globalisation and WTO strictures, rather than the employment of other, more culturally and socially sensitive, approaches to economic development. For example, Chang (2002) makes the case that the principal countries that now fund and direct WTO free-trade policies did not follow WTO-type strictures when they were developing economies. The UK and the USA both employed protectionist policies to allow their economies to grow.

In a similar attack on free-trade ideology, but this time aimed at the IMF and World Bank, Burgo and Stewart (2002) used Malawi as an illustration of enforced privatisation policies that had created a food crisis. The case is explained in more detail in Chapter 13 (*see* Case study 13.3 on p. 513). In summary, in the mid-1990s the IMF insisted on the deregulation of the grain and foodstuffs agency before any further loans and aid finance were to be granted. The result, which Burgo and Stewart attribute principally to the deregulation policy, was a collapse in grain supplies and widespread famine in 2002. Interestingly, the Commerce and Industry Minister of Malawi, Mr Mpasu, was asked by the UK Government to speak to a meeting of G7 ministers in Cancun of the benefits of liberalising the Malawi economy. He stood up and said, 'We have opened our economy. That's why we are flat on our backs' (Elliott, 2003).

An issue emerging from this discussion is the complex question of how can the demands of economic imperatives be tempered within socially acceptable parameters? Nearly 200 years ago, David Ricardo (a significant figure in British economic thinking) described profit as 'the lever and the lure'. The lure because it is the indicator of how successfully capital has been invested, thereby acting as a lure to new capital investment. The notion of the lever, however, speaks to the social, as well as the economic, impact that capital migration can have on whole communities. The migration of capital from one region to another, from one country to another, as it seeks out the most advantageous investment opportunities, can have destabilising impacts upon those areas affected by the capital flows. While Friedman points to the undemocratic nature of corporate social responsibility, the argument to leave business alone ignores the profound influence of corporate decisions and their impact upon, potentially, millions of lives. Corporate decisions are made by unseen and largely unaccountable decision-makers. Critics of Friedman's 'undemocratic' argument see these issues as far more significant and serious threats to democratic processes than those raised by Friedman.

## Friedman's third argument

Moving to the third of Friedman's criticisms, we find that it is open to challenge at the levels of principle, of legal argument and empirical evidence. To remind you, the third of Friedman's arguments was that businesses cannot have responsibilities because they are not real people; they are social constructs, i.e. they are artificial entities. While accepting Friedman's argument that a corporation is a social construct, this does not deny the possibility that the passage of time may confer upon business organisations new constraints, attributes, rights and/or responsibilities. In essence, social constructs can be reconstructed. Therefore, the simple fact that corporations are social constructs does not deny the possibility that the significance of such entities can develop to such an extent that society deems it necessary to place constraints, or responsibilities, upon corporations. There would be nothing philosophically objectionable, or flawed, in such developments. Whether such moves would achieve their desired ends is, however, a quite different question and set of issues.

In addition to challenging the validity of Friedman's third criticism at the level of principle, corporations have themselves undermined the strength of the criticism by their own actions. Corporations in America have claimed the same rights as individuals under the American Constitution. For example, in 1996 the US Supreme Court unanimously overturned a Rhode Island law which had stood for forty years. This law had prohibited businesses advertising the price of beers and spirits. Referring to the First Amendment the Supreme Court ruled that corporations could claim the same rights of protection as individuals. In 1998 in *First National Bank of Boston v. Bellotti* the American Supreme Court ruled again that corporations are protected by the First Amendment in the same way that individuals are in terms of freedom of speech. Thus, notwithstanding that they are social constructs, the corporations involved in these cases were granted the same rights under the American Constitution as those available to individual American citizens.

In the King Report, a further and critical legal point is highlighted. The conventional rhetoric is that corporate executives are required to run corporations in the interests of shareholders. However, the King Report challenges this claim by referring to some jurisdictions in which, upon incorporation,

> the company becomes a separate persona in law and no person whether natural or juristic can be owned. Courts have also held that shareowners have no direct interests in the property, business or assets owned by the company, their only rights being a right to vote and a right to dividends. Shareowners also change from time to time while, as the owner, the company remains constant. Consequently, directors, in exercising their fiduciary duties, must act in the interest of the company as a separate person.
>
> (King Report, 2002: 10)

Following the logic of this separation, the corporate executives are committed to act in the interests of the company, which would suggest that, if they deem it appropriate, this could include acting in ways that could be labelled corporately socially responsible. This approach places the company's long-term economic survival above all others. The interests of shareholders and those of the company would coincide via the process known as 'the correspondence principle', in which investors select companies to invest in on the basis of each company's known objectives and performance. Thus corporate executives do not have to worry about acting in the ways shareholders would prefer. If the actions of corporate executives are consistent with past decisions and rationale, then this will correspond with the interests of the shareowners, because the shareowners would have decided to invest in the company on this very basis.

As a recognisable legal entity, it might also be argued that, if corporations can be assigned the rights of citizenship, why should they not be assigned equivalent levels of responsibilities? If this argument is accepted then it raises questions about how one operationalises a broader view of a corporation's responsibilities and this in turn heralds the notion of stakeholders.

## Stakeholding and stakeholders

The term stakeholding refers to an idea, a principle or argument, whereas the term stakeholder refers to a specifiable person or groups of people (sometimes in an organised form), with clear implications for how the interests of such groups might be incorporated or represented within organisational decisions. This distinction is important because, for some writers who support and argue for the concept of stakeholding, the operationalising of the concept presents enormous problems that possibly cast doubt upon the usefulness of the concept. Writers such as Bucholz (1998) and Rosenthal (1990) are examples of commentators who have expressed support for the stakeholding concept, but also expressed concerns about its real-world potential.

Notwithstanding these concerns, there is growing empirical evidence to suggest that an increasing number of organisations can be said to be adopting more inclusive perspectives into their ways of working that deny an exclusive shareholder focus to their decisions. This does not imply that shareholders are no longer an important consideration of managerial thought and action. Indeed, economic imperatives will often/invariably have to take precedence when stakeholder interests clash, but maybe, just maybe, the interests of shareholders are becoming more of a minimum constraint than a maximising objective.

In many ways a constraint is more demanding than an objective in that a constraint is invariably expressed as a specific number, e.g. the minimum dividend return next year must be 6 per cent, or the minimum earnings yield must be 11 per cent, whereas to state that 'we aim to maximise shareholder wealth' is a very loose statement, with no identifiable performance target. The minimum returns specified in the 'constraints' would need to take account of competing investment opportunities, so what is being suggested here is not 'pie-in-the-sky' wishful thinking, but rather a possible explanation of what might already be happening in some corporate board rooms in an osmotic sort of way. Thus the change process, if it reflects a genuine long-term change rather than something of faddish duration, is not an abrupt sea-change in perspective, which is heralded by a fanfare of trumpets, but rather a more incremental, less obvious change. Clearly more empirical evidence is required to allow more confident statements to be made on this point.

By turning shareholder considerations into a constraint, maybe seeing ordinary shareholders as becoming akin to first-order preference shareholders, managerial attention can then turn to considering how an organisation can become more a part of the societies with which it interacts, rather than apart from them. How might this work in practice?

There are various ways of approaching this issue, but one way that would *not* work is for an organisation to wait until it is confident that it will definitely achieve its shareholder 'constraint' target (i.e. the minimum dividend or earnings return) before debating how it should position itself as a social-economic entity. It might not be until, say, month eleven or later that attainment of the minimum shareholder return can be confirmed, leaving no time to begin thinking about other stakeholder issues.

If stakeholder engagement is to be a realistic and meaningful idea, then a longer-term stakeholder strategy becomes essential, just as a market strategy is essential for product or service development. Organisational development then becomes the sum of the two. To counter the concerns articulated by Friedman (and acolytes such as Elaine Sternberg, 2000), a number of organisations are firmly of the view that employee participation in social projects, which are outside the organisation's normal line of business, has a positive effect upon staff morale and aid organisational performance. The application of staff time in 'social projects' can be shown to be an effective 'value-adding' activity. Case study 8.4 is a specific example.

| Case study 8.4 | **An economically successful corporation with a view of its social position** |
| --- | --- |

Capital *One* is a credit card company that chooses not to publicise its social projects because it is uneasy that it might be accused of only undertaking its social activities in order to gain publicity. Most of its social engagements go unreported and thus unrecognised, but the following example did attract media attention and the company acknowledged its role in the programme.

The projects in question related to the development of sophisticated software to facilitate the interrogation of differing national databases by a local police force in the pursuit of suspected paedophiles. The company supported a number of its programmers in working with the local police force over many months in developing the software, which has subsequently proved to be an important advance in police work and adopted by other police forces. The programmers also committed a lot of their own free time to the project. When talking with people at the company, one of the authors was left in no doubt that everyone was extremely supportive of the project and that its effect upon staff morale had been both positive and significant, manifesting itself in enhanced levels of efficiency and innovation in all areas of the programming division's work.

The Friedmanite response might be that such an example is fine, as long as it is undertaken in the belief that it will positively affect shareholder interests. If this is thought unlikely then such activities should not be undertaken. Interestingly the senior management argued strenuously that the decision to support the project was not taken for Friedmanite reasons. The senior executives argued that decisions relating to their 'social projects' were taken on non-consequentialist grounds. The senior management review projects that have been identified by the 'Social Resonsibility Team' (which comprises four full-time staff). There also appeared to be some consultation with all the employees to help shape the 'social projects' agenda' for the coming year.

The senior management argued that they saw their company as part of the local community and wanted to be regarded as a part of that community. They wanted to be regarded as a good employer, thereby attracting not just 'good' employees, but employees coming with the right approach and commitment. Such a policy did enhance organisational efficiency, but the senior management regarded the policy decision as reflecting more of a principled than an instrumental stance. At its root, the senior management philosophy was an inclusive approach to organisational 'Being'.

The 'everybody wins' feel of the closing sentence of Case study 8.4 does not have to be seen in a cynical light. The basic argument harks back to the original conceptualisation of the word 'company'. The etymology of the word 'company' relates to a community of interest, a mutually beneficial partnership of employers, employees and investors. Such an approach does not deny the significance of competition in an organisation's financial market as well as its product and service markets, but the 'shareholder-as-constraint-perspective' offers a possible way of negotiating the conundrum that the notion of stakeholding appears to present when set in the context of market-based, capitalist systems.

## Corporate governance and trust

We discuss codes of ethics and conduct in Chapter 10, where we make the point that codes of ethics tend to be concerned with values and virtuous qualities. Certainly the most efficient and economic form of corporate governance is a relationship built upon trust, buttressed by the requisite levels of accountability and transparency. As soon as one begins to doubt a person's integrity and trustworthiness then monitoring and control processes come into play, but these are expensive and can themselves exacerbate a situation and breed an air of mistrust.

If an organisation wishes to develop a culture based upon virtues such as integrity, honesty, objectivity, justice and fairness, partly to reduce the costs of monitoring and control processes, then consistency in practices and the avoidance of double standards are essential. Unfortunately this is too often not the case, as indicated by Table 8.4.

**Table 8.4** Organisational principles and human behaviour

| Issue | General employees | Senior executives |
|-------|-------------------|-------------------|
| Working for other organisations | Taking time off to do 'other' work would be described as moonlighting and subject to instant dismissal. Working for other organisations considered to be a vice. | Taking consulting or NED-type role with another organisation invariably seen as broadening for all concerned and a virtue. |
| Pay–motivation relationship | Paying people low wages incentivises employees to work hard. High wages merely breed sloth and inefficiency. | Senior executives need increasing levels of pay to incentivise them. The higher the pay, the higher the motivation. |
| Pensions | It is unreasonable to expect the state or organisations to provide for income after employment. | Generous pension packages are essential to entice the appropriate level of executive talent. |
| Working conditions | General working conditions should reflect basic functional requirements. To do more would reflect an unnecessary diversion of shareholder funds. | Require high-quality accommodation and to provide less will act as a disincentive to prospective appointees. |
| Perks | Very few and where they exist will need to reflect a close relationship between performance and perk. No such thing as a 'free lunch'. | Come in many forms from first-class travel to company cars (when little corporate travel is undertaken by road), to executive boxes at arts or sporting arenas, to company accommodation and company loans. Lunches may still not be free but are paid for by 'others'. |

## Moving the debate forward

So where have we arrived in terms of our consideration of Anglo-American developments in corporate governance and corporate responsibility? It brings us to the point where it is fair to ask, if the Friedmanite position on corporate responsibility can be successfully challenged, how can one operationalise notions of ethics in business which recognise the dynamics of market conditions, but which also recognise the differences in ethical perceptions and stances? Any such framework needs to have at its core some universally held principles relating to human dignity and rights, but also a flexibility to allow certain, 'acceptable' local variations to apply. This might be regarded as the Holy Grail, yet an attempt has been made to develop such a framework. What we are about to discuss is not a prescriptive approach to developing specific ethical principles in complex, multi-cultural contexts, but rather an over-arching framework that at least provides a general structure upon which organisations can begin to shape their respective approaches to managing in ethically complex contexts.

## The social contract and the business case

The social contract is an interesting concept that can be traced back to Plato (Bosanquet, 1906) and Aristotle (Aristotle, 1976), but more recently to Hobbes (1968), Locke (1952) and Rousseau (1913). Lessnoff (1986) provides a good introduction to the history of social contract as an idea and as an argument.

A more recent articulation of the social contract is found in the argument that corporations have to earn and maintain a 'license to operate'. The license to operate reflects a commitment to more than economic imperatives, although the approach does not ignore economic issues. Two interesting writers working in this area are Thomas Donaldson and Thomas Dunfee. They have published in various forms over the past twenty years, for example, Donaldson (1982, 1989, 1990, 1996); Donaldson and Dunfee (1994, 1995 and 1999); Dunfee (1991, 1996); and Dunfee and Donaldson (1995). Donaldson and Dunfee have taken the social contract idea and developed a distinctive approach that they call *Integrative Social Contract Theory* (ISCT). At the core of the theory are four norms, or categories of values. One way to visualise ISCT is in the form of concentric circles, with the core foundational values at the centre (Figure 8.3).

The norms are described as follows.

*Hypernorms*  These are argued to be fundamental human rights or basic prescriptions common to most religions. The values they represent are by definition acceptable to all cultures and all organisations. These have the characteristics of universal norms and in order to be workable will be few in number. What is and what is not a hypernorm would be agreed by rational debate and any contender for 'hypernorm' status would fail if it could be shown not to be universalisable. The issue of universal norms raises all the problems that Kantian ethics encounter, but rather than turning to something akin to Ross's (1930) *prima facie obligations*, Donaldson and Dunfee introduce two 'lower level' norms that allow for 'local' variations to be possible. The first of these is *consistent norms*.

*Consistent norms*  These values are more culturally specific than hypernorms, but they will be consistent with hypernorms and other legitimate norms, the latter being defined as a norm that does not contradict the hypernorm test (Donaldson and Dunfee, 1999: 46). Donaldson and Dunfee cite corporate mission statements as examples of 'consistent norms'.

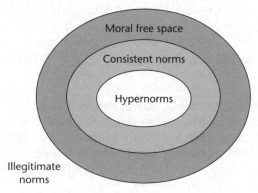

**Figure 8.3** Integrated Social Contract Theory (ISCT)

*Moral free space* This is an interesting concept and allows Donaldson and Dunfee to contain norms that might be in tension (or limited contradiction) with any of the hypernorms within ISCT. An example of such a tension could be the use of child labour. Donaldson and Dunfee cite two examples involving the company Levi-Strauss.

**Case study 8.5**

**Levi-Strauss**

In the first example Levi-Strauss severed its links with the Tan family (and their businesses) because they (the Tan family) reportedly 'held twelve hundred Chinese and Philippine women in guarded compounds working them seventy four hours a week' (*The Clean Clothes Campaign*, 1992). These practices contravened Levi-Strauss's Business Partners Terms of Engagement'. The actions of the Tan family could be said to have contravened the hypernorms of respect for human dignity and justice.

The second example relates to the reaction of Levi-Strauss when it became aware that two of its suppliers in Bangladesh were employing children under the age of fourteen (a generally internationally accepted minimum age of employment). The company did not sever its relationship with the suppliers but chose an alternative course of action. The company required that the children be sent to school, with Levi-Strauss paying the children's tuition and associated fees, but also paying the children's wages to their families, so the latter did not suffer, but only while the children were at school. The company also agreed to re-employ the children when they reached fourteen. Whilst the exploitation of children has to addressed by the hypernorms, ISCT can cope with the actions of Levi-Strauss in this case because, whilst the use of the child labour must have been in contravention of at least one hypernorm, the practice was also recognition of a locally 'accepted' practice, something that might, for the time being, be seen to reside within the 'moral free space'. This is not to say that for all companies the 'right' action would be to react as Levi-Strauss had. For some the use of children under the age of fourteen may have meant a severing of links with the suppliers concerned, irrespective of the ripple effects of this action. In this case the moral free space would not allow the inclusion of the use of children less than fourteen years of age, notwithstanding that it is an 'accepted' local norm. ISCT allows both of these (re)actions because of the relationship of 'moral free space' to 'hypernorms' and 'consistent norms'. The example does illustrate that it is for individual groups and organisations to define what constitutes their 'moral free space'.

*Illegitimate norms* These norms are irreconcilable with *hypernorms*. For some this might be the case with regard to the treatment of women and children in some societies, but for others some of these 'problems' might fit within a 'moral free space' that would allow some development of understanding on all sides to see if a longer-term relationship might be possible with some modification to the 'problems' in question.

**Connexion point**

In this form of application, *moral free space* becomes something of a utilitarian concept (which, you will recall from Chapter 3, weighs ethical decisions in the context of a decision's consequences), but only on the understanding that the intention is to achieve longer-term correction of the offending practice and, to do this most effectively, it is better to work at the offending practice and to achieve change.

It would seem possible for principle-based *hypernorms* to be 'suspended', for some short passage of time, to allow utilitarian considerations to be located within the *moral free space*. This is contentious, and this interpretation might not meet with universal agreement, but it does show the flexibility that would be essential for such a framework to be useful for a multi-national corporation endeavouring to make sense of developing an ethical framework where certain practices, for example nepotism, might be unacceptable in most western cultures, but acceptable and important in others, e.g. Indian society. For an international corporation with operations in many parts of Asia and Europe, how should they handle this tension? They will require a short-term strategy guided by a longer-term principle.

As a result of the above type of example, ISCT has been criticised for being relativist. Donaldson and Dunfee refute this, arguing that ISCT is pluralist, combining the notion of universal norms of behaviour (hypernorms) with the recognition of important cultural differences (consistent norms and moral free space). The authors also recognise that, within the theory, individuals, corporations and communities have to work out for themselves what are their respective 'norms', at all levels.

> Business ethics should be viewed more as a story in the process of being written than as a moral code like the Ten Commandments. It can, and should ... adjust over time – to evolving technology, and to the cultural or religious attitudes of particular economic conditions.
>
> (Donaldson and Dunfee, 1999: viii)

Donaldson and Dunfee go on to say,

> At the heart of social contract effort is a simple assumption, namely that we can understand better the obligations of key social institutions, such as business or government, by attempting to understand what is entailed in a fair agreement or 'contract' between those institutions and society and also in the implicit contracts that exist among the different communities and institutions within society. The normative authority of any social contract derives from the assumption that humans, acting rationally, consent – or at least would consent hypothetically – to the terms of a particular agreement affecting the society or community of which they are a member. In this manner contractarian theories utilise the device of consent, albeit it is often *hypothetical* consent, to justify principles, policies and structures.
>
> (Donaldson and Dunfee, 1999: 16–7)

In order to provide a mechanism that might help operationalise ISCT, Donaldson and Dunfee employ a modified form of Rawls' veil of ignorance. Unlike Rawls' conception of the veil of ignorance, in which those (metaphorically) placed behind the veil have no knowledge of any aspect of their status, ethnic origin, physical abilities, gender, geographic location, political and economic system, etc., in Donaldson and Dunfee's conception only those aspects of a person's identity that are economic in nature, e.g. level of personal skill, nature of economic system, type of employing organisation, employment position held, etc., are concealed. This modified Rawlsian artifice is hoped to facilitate reflection and debate about an 'objective' fairness that should be inherent within an economic system and the ethical and moral base of that system.

ISCT attempts to hold on to both the integrity of universalisable norms (minimum accepted standards of behaviour irrespective of where in the world the norms are being considered), but avoiding the inflexibility of non-consequentialist stances. This is addressed by the introduction of the consistent norms and the moral free space. It is an interesting development, providing as it does a schema or framework that business people can employ to interrogate the ethical and moral issues that might be at stake in a particular situation. Donaldson and Dunfee are emphatic that ISCT is not a framework, let alone an approach, that can be employed unthinkingly. By its very nature it is a framework for facilitating discussion, debate and argument. It is not a decision-making tool, for the type of ethically charged situations that corporations are often faced with are invariably too complex and multi-faceted to lend themselves to easy formulation and calculation. However, the ideas and categories within ISCT do provide a language and a set of concepts that may help parties to a decision think constructively about the different issues and dimensions inherent within a complex business scenario.

## Corporate manslaughter

The concluding major topic in this chapter continues the theme of attempts to hold corporations to account for their roles in, or impacts upon, society. To do this, there is a need to consider both the legal position and the philosophical position of corporations with regard to this issue.

Within the UK the prosecution of corporations, as distinct from individual employees, for claimed acts of wilful neglect of a duty of care has been difficult, at least via criminal law. Actions through the civil courts against corporations have been possible for many years, but the expense and the many years involved in prosecuting such cases make the civil law option one that is rarely taken up by members of the public.

### Recent developments

Recent developments, reflected in proposals to change UK criminal law with respect to corporate manslaughter, by possibly bringing it in line with US criminal law, suggest that corporations might, in future, face the prospect of being held to account for criminal neglect of their duty of care. However, the UK administrations of Prime Minister Tony Blair have been reticent to bring the proposed law to Parliament for debate, despite a manifesto pledge since 1997. The inclusion of a corporate manslaughter bill in the 2004 Queen's Speech (the mechanism that announces the proposed bills to be discussed in the forthcoming parliamentary session) was seen by many as a deceit, because it was generally believed that the Prime Minister would call a general election in May 2005, which proved to be correct, thereby relegating all the proposed bills to the 'bills lost' bin.

Why this reticence to instigate a corporate manslaughter bill? It is difficult to see beyond the power of the corporate lobby persuading government that 'it would not be a good thing'. Yet in the United States it is possible for corporations to be forced to stop trading because of corporate wrongdoings. Such acts, known as charter revocation acts, are very rarely used, but at least they exist. In the UK no such possibilities exist, other than for the Department of Trade and Industry in special situations and for creditors. In America, however, a private citizen can instigate a winding-up procedure as a result of a corporate wrongdoing. There the death penalty exists for corporate acts of murder as it does for individuals. Notwithstanding that the death penalty for citizens has long been abolished in the UK, the possibility of such a punishment in the corporate field raises very different issues and arguments. The possibilities for a charter revocation law in the UK are discussed in a little more detail in Chapter 13 where we introduce our 'modest proposal' for affecting change in the ethics of business.

## The 'identification principle' and the 'guiding mind'

As it currently stands, the first impediment to criminal prosecution for corporate manslaughter in the UK has been the argument, with which you will by now be familiar, that corporations do not commit acts; only individuals do. Thus, individual employees can be charged with manslaughter, e.g. a train driver involved in a rail crash, but charging the relevant rail company is a more difficult task. To do so, one has to be able to prove that an individual, who sits at the nerve centre of corporate decision making, and who should have acted in ways that could have prevented the accident occurring, was negligent in their duties. This is known in law as the *identification doctrine*, i.e. one has to be able to identify the negligent individual who could be said to represent the failure of the corporation as a whole.

In law, as in many other walks of life, one has to be clear about the precise meaning of words. So, when we use the phrase 'who sits at the nerve centre of corporate decision making', what do we mean? For the corporation to be charged, the identified individual has to be shown to be the person with overall responsibility for this particular aspect of corporate activity, for example health and safety matters, or rail track inspection. The need for this requirement is that because the law has, to date, only viewed corporations as being answerable via their employees, the employee concerned must be recognised as the person who was 'guiding' this aspect of corporate activity. This is the second legal principle to recognise, i.e. to be able to prosecute a corporation for corporate manslaughter, the *guiding mind* of the organisation has to be identified, and be shown to be implicated in the negligent act/s. Some real-life examples of this principle will help to illustrate the issues involved.

**Case study 8.6**

## The *Herald of Free Enterprise*

The case has already been mentioned in Chapter 7. It relates to the capsizing of the P&O ferry *Herald of Free Enterprise* outside Zeebrugge harbour in which 192 people lost their lives. It is possible that the captain of the ferry might have been able to be prosecuted for not fully checking that the bow doors were securely closed before the ferry set sail. However, the fact that crew members had, on five previous occasions, expressed concerns to their seniors about the lack of any warning lights on the bridge relating to the position of the bow doors was insufficient to bring a prosecution against the P&O Corporation. It was not possible to prove that these expressions of concern had reached the top echelons of the P&O corporation, the 'guiding mind'. Although comparative evidence was available concerning the (lack of) commitment that P&O was claimed to have towards safety issues, the prosecution lawyers were refused permission by the trial judge to call captains of the Sealink corporation (at the time of the trial Sealink was a rival ferry company), to contrast the safety practices of P&O ferries with those of other ferry operators. Four years after the capsizing of the *Herald of Free Enterprise*, safety issues at P&O were again raised when it was revealed that P&O crew members had to pay for their own basic safety training. One recruit recounted, ' I was sent to a college and given pages of information on things like where lifeboats are kept on a ferry, and how to evacuate in an emergency. But you don't get a chance to practise any of this on a ship. When I worked on a ferry for the first time it was up to me to find out where the evacuation points and passengers' lifejackets were' (Crainer, 1993: 67).

Even actions that might have appeared doubtful did not attract the judge's concerns. For example, while the inquests into the deaths of the 192 passengers and crew were still in progress, the *Herald of Free Enterprise*, which, unaccountably, had been renamed *Flushing Range* and with its bow doors welded together, was being towed to a scrap yard in Taiwan. Members of the Kent police had to fly to South Africa to intercept and inspect the renamed ship. As Crainer (1993) observes, for many concerned in the case, the vessel was 'regarded as an important piece of evidence in a criminal investigation'.

In terms of the 'guiding mind' P&O's marine superintendent admitted that he had misled the original inquiry into the disaster about when he had first heard of a proposal to fit warning lights on ferry bridges. It was also revealed that he discounted warnings from one of the company's senior masters about potential dangers because he thought the captains were exaggerating. Sheen (who chaired the initial enquiry) described Develin's [P&O's marine superintendent] responses to the legitimate concerns of the masters as 'flippant, facetious and fatuous' (Crainer, 1993). Yet Develin was not deemed sufficiently senior to equate with being (or being part of) P&O's 'guiding mind'.

Similar scenarios regarding the chasm that can appear to exist between a corporation's executive and operational management can be seen in other examples. A report in a safety journal during the inquiry into the disaster at *Piper Alpha* oil rig noted,

The whole management evidence from Occidental [the owners of the oil rig] paints a picture of complete ignorance of the problems which existed. The senior management provided no support to the platform staff. They provided no training. They provided no guidance. The laid down no procedures. They did not participate in discussions with the operators. They did not seek the views of their employees.

*(Safety Management*, December, 1989, reported in Crainer, 1993: 116)

Similarly, King (2001) remarked upon the actions of senior management at British Rail following the 1999 Paddington rail crash.

It should come as no surprise that soon after the UK suffered its second worse rail disaster of recent times – the 1999 Paddington crash – it was revealed that the rail companies had resisted calls to introduce a confidential reporting procedure, i.e. 'whistleblowing' procedure through which staff could report safety concerns without fear of recrimination.

(King, 2001: 152)

Of course, if a company has an internal grievance/concerns procedure, and issues are raised by employees within this process, senior management cannot later feign ignorance of any problems that subsequently result in injuries or death to consumers or general members of the public.

A little over 12 months after the Paddington rail crash, in October 2000, another serious incident occurred involving rail transport when a train left the track at Hatfield due to faults in the track. This time four people lost their lives and many more were injured. Again management failures regarding reluctance to heed concerns about the quality of the track and its maintenance were suggested to be a significant feature of the case, but on 23 September 2004 a high court judge announced that no charges would be brought against either the company *Railtrack* (which was later renamed *Network Rail*) and three of its directors, including the former chief executive. The reason – lack of evidence.

## The issue of aggregation

Unlike the situation in the United States, UK courts will not accept the principle of *aggregation*. This relates back to the 'guiding mind' principle. In essence the refusal of UK courts to accept aggregation means that the guiding mind of an organisation needs to be held within a tight area of the corporate structure. However, the US Court of Appeal ruled in 1987 that,

corporations compartmentalise knowledge, subdividing the elements of specific duties and operations into small components. The aggregate of those components constitute the corporation's knowledge of a particular operation.

(Crainer, 1993: 122)

The US Court of Appeal thus recognised the complexity of corporate structures, and allowed that, if responsibility for a particular facet of corporate activity, such as health and safety, was located in many different parts of a corporation, this was not a defence a corporation (as a totality) could employ to deny responsibility for a failure to adhere to acceptable safety practices. As a result of this approach, all the various parts of a corporation that are responsible for safety can be added together (aggregated) to produce the sum of the corporation's health and safety practices (or lack of).

As mentioned above, the past decade has seen calls for a crime of corporate manslaughter grow louder and more frequent in the UK, so much so that in 2000 the UK Government, via the Home Office, published its own proposals, *Reforming the Law on Involuntary Manslaughter*. However, no time in parliamentary sessions could be found. We have already mentioned what happened to the Queen's Speech in the Autumn of 2004. The situation in the UK with regard to corporate manslaughter remains a contentious issue. The influence of industry lobby groups in the stunted progress of a corporate manslaughter bill is a worrying issue for many.

## The UK government's and EU proposals on corporate manslaughter

Notwithstanding the fact that a general election in 2005 frustrated parliamentary time on a bill, the government's proposals do acknowledge the inadequacies of the current law. Four significant disasters were cited in the report *Reforming the Law on Involuntary Manslaughter*. These were: the capsizing of the *Herald of Free Enterprise*; the Kings Cross fire; the Clapham rail crash; and the Southall rail crash, with the implicit view that the law inhibited the successful prosecution of what appeared to be culpability within and of the organisations concerned. The identification doctrine was seen as the principal stumbling block to successful prosecution of companies.

The Government's proposals were based upon the Law Commission Report No. 237, *Legislating the Criminal Code: Involuntary Manslaughters*. The principal proposals were:

- There should be a special offence of corporate killing, broadly corresponding to the proposed offence of killing by gross carelessness.

- The corporate offence should (like the individual offence) be prosecuted only where the corporation's conduct fell far below what could be reasonably expected.

- The corporate offence should not (unlike the individual offence) require that the risk be obvious or that the defendant be capable of appreciating the risk.

- A death should be regarded as having been caused by the conduct of the corporation if it is caused by a 'management failure', so that the way in which its activities are managed or organised fails to ensure the health and safety of persons employed in or affected by its activities.

- Such a failure will be regarded as a cause of a person's death even if the immediate cause is the act or omission of an individual.

- That individuals within a company could still be liable for the offences of reckless killing and killing by gross carelessness, as well as the company being liable for the offence of corporate killing.

## Switching the burden of proof to the corporation

A different approach has been proposed by the Council of Europe (European Union). This proposal would make companies responsible for all offences committed by their employees, but corporations would be allowed a due diligence defence, i.e. corporations would be exempted from liability if they could show that every precaution to avoid or minimise such an act occurring had been implemented. In this proposal the conventional approach to law is turned on its head, i.e. the initial presumption is that of guilt on the part of the accused, and it is then the responsibility of the accused (the corporation) to present evidence of its existing practices that would exempt it from liability. Clarkson (1998) has expressed concern at the implications of this proposal in that (from a legal perspective) it would change the offence committed to one of a lesser order than criminal manslaughter. The new offence would be offset by a possible due diligence defence. The result would be the attribution of lesser sanctions than under a criminal prosecution for manslaughter.

The possibilities for the senior management of corporations to deny personal or corporate responsibility for criminal neglect appear to be entering a new era. In 1993, Crainer observed,

> Sadly the failure of the Zeebrugge corporate manslaughter trial seemed to condone an all-too-prevalent attitude among senior managers: 'Don't tell me what is going on because if I know, I might be held accountable'.

> (Crainer, 1993: 142)

Clarkson made a similar point when he observed,

> If the company's structures are impenetrable or if its policies are so 'sloppy' that no person has been made responsible for the relevant area of activity, a company can still shield itself from corporate criminal liability. In the *P&O* case, where there was no safety manager or director, there would be no person whose acts and knowledge could be attributed to the company.

> (Clarkson, 1998: 6)

Drawing upon the findings of the Sheen Report into the *Herald of Free Enterprise* disaster, in which the corporation was accused by Sheen of 'being infected with the disease of sloppiness' (Department of Transport, 1987), Clarkson observes, 'the worse the disease of sloppiness, the greater is the immunization against criminal liability'. The inference of Clarkson's comments regarding the 'P&O case' (*Herald of Free Enterprise*) is that the interpretation of the identification principle during the trial was too tight. It is not just the weight of the evidence that determines the outcome of legal prosecutions. The interpretations of law and decisions concerning the admissibility of evidence make the judiciary crucial elements within legal processes.

An example of the power of judges to create legal precedent is exemplified in the ruling relating to *Meridian Global Funds Management Asia Ltd v. Securities Commission* (reported in Clarkson, 1998: 3). The presiding judge ruled that the 'directing mind and will' of a company did not have to be a very senior person, if the person committing the act was authorised to undertake the act on the company's behalf. This ruling still leaves identification necessary, at the present time at least, but the clear implication is that the responsible person does not have to be a very senior person in order for a corporation to be held responsible for an act of negligence (Clarkson, 1998: 3).

Twelve years after the *Herald of Free Enterprise* disaster, and following the high-profile rail crashes involving loss of life at Clapham and Southall, two trains collided just outside Paddington Station in 1999, killing 31 people and injuring over 400. In the report published in June 2001 into the causes of the crash, Lord Cullen, the enquiry Chairman, condemned the entire rail industry for 'institutional paralysis'. He described the failure of the track operator, Railtrack, to act on previous reported incidents of train drivers passing through red signals as 'lamentable'. He was extremely critical of one of the train companies involved, Thames Trains (whose driver passed the red signal), and the company's safety culture which he described as 'slack and less than adequate'. Lord Cullen also spoke of the 'significant failures of communication within the organisation'.

The driver of the train operated by Thames Trains was inexperienced and had not been notified by the company of information that was in its possession that the signal just outside Paddington Station had been passed at danger (i.e. on red) eight times before. The problem appears to have been related to the signal being obscured at certain times of day due to the glare of the sun and/or overhanging foliage.

Lord Cullen was also critical of the quality of training given by Railtrack to its signallers, the 'slack and complacent regime at Slough' (the control centre for the signals in question). He was also extremely critical of the Railway Inspectorate which he deemed 'lacked resources, acted without vigour and placed too much faith in Railtrack'. These words carry echoes of those used by Sheen, the chairman of the Department of Trade inquiry into the *Herald of Free Enterprise* disaster. Sheen spread the blame far more widely than those directly involved on the night of the disaster. Guilt lay with 'all concerned in management. From top to bottom, the body corporate was infected with the disease of sloppiness.' No actions were ever brought against the corporations concerned!

The UK Government's earlier proposals allow for criminal prosecutions of corporations, as well as individuals, if practices that a reasonable and careful corporation would employ are absent. The speed with which the Government's proposals move from discussion paper to actual law will be interesting to observe following the 2005 election. American law would be a good precedent to follow in this case.

Clarkson offered a further variation on the quest to hold corporations to account, by the application of what he describes as 'corporate *mens rea*'. Clarkson offers his proposal because he fears that the doctrines of 'identification' and 'guiding mind' remain problematic within the government's proposals.

DEFINITION

*Mens rea* is a legal term that means criminal intention, or knowledge that an act is wrong. Thus, corporate *mens rea* refers to an act or set of practices (or lack of) perpetrated in the name of a corporation that possess the essence of wrongdoing.

Clarkson argued,

> Doctrines – identification, aggregation, etc. – involve fictitious imputations of responsibility. The real question is not whether the question of corporate mens rea involves a fiction, but whether, of all the fictions, it is the one that most closely approximates modern-day corporate reality and perceptions. ... the important point about this approach is that it is not whether any individual within the company would have realised or foreseen the harm occurring but whether in a properly structured and organised, careful company, the risks would have been obvious.
>
> (Clarkson, 1998: 10)

What this argument is saying is, 'Yes, corporate culpability is a fiction, or a problematic concept, but then so are many of the concepts that are involved in this debate'. Clarkson referred to legal concepts such as identification and aggregation as equivalent fictions/problematic concepts, but we could just as easily refer to concepts such as citizenship, democracy, property rights, free trade, a living wage. Property rights are an entirely socially constructed phenomenon, yet this has not prevented millions of lives being lost in its defence over the centuries. It is for societies to decide the laws that are appropriate for their own well-being and development. In many respects the fact that some of the laws relate to human beings, whilst others relate to socially constructed beings, is irrelevant.

**Connexion point**

Earlier in this chapter we discussed one of Milton Friedman's main criticisms of corporations being required to be 'responsible' for their actions beyond economic responsibility. The criticism in question was that as social constructs corporations could not have responsibilities; only people can. The reference, immediately above, to 'It is for societies to decide the laws that are appropriate for their own well-being and development. In many respects the fact that some of the laws relate to human beings, whilst others relate to socially constructed beings, is irrelevant', is extremely apposite in the context of Friedman's objections to calls for CSR.

This still leaves us with the issue of whether corporations can be construed or treated as corporate citizens. From the Heideggerian position (which we discuss in more detail in Chapter 9), corporations cannot be citizens, because the best that can be expected of corporations is that they view nature in exclusively instrumental ways. From a Heideggerian perspective, corporations have to be controlled in ways other than 'wishing' them to act in socially responsible ways. Windsor (2001) supported this view.

> The corporate citizenship notion conflates citizen (which a firm cannot be) and person (which a firm can be, but only as a legal fiction). The portrayal is fictional .... Fictional personhood is not a sound basis for artificial citizenship.
>
> (Windsor, 2001: 41)

The key proposal of the Law Commission report on involuntary manslaughter, which the UK government appears to have accepted, is that management failure to introduce and ensure the application of reasonable safety practices is sufficient to justify the prosecution of corporate manslaughter. This is a fundamental change. Whether it could be cited, retrospectively, against Railtrack and/or Thames Trains is a moot point, but the position of corporations vis à vis the death of their employees and/or members of the public due to actions or inactions of the corporation is undergoing fundamental scrutiny. As mentioned above, whether any alterations to the law will reflect such a fundamental change remains to be seen.

## Summary

In this chapter the following key points have been made:

- The changes in terminology, as reflected in the initial use of corporate social responsibility, which is beginning to mutate into corporate responsibility, while along the way the notion of corporate citizenship has also been employed, reflect an ongoing search for a concept that can encapsulate a business–society set of relationships that satisfies all aspects of the debate, but, particularly, that extends corporate executives' responsibilities beyond those to the providers of equity capital.

- Corporate governance reforms in the UK and America have retained an exclusive focus upon the interests of shareholders, unlike the King Report on corporate governance in South Africa.

- The King Report also raised the issue of values and beliefs as an explicit consideration of corporate governance, which in a South African context emphasised kinship, community and 'an inherent trust and belief in fairness of all human beings'. The issue of values within Anglo-American approaches towards corporate governance is not explicit, but implied. They are underpinned by ethical individualism and (from agency theory) a belief that individuals are self-serving and inherently untrustworthy.

- The 1999 UN Global Compact reflected a frustration with governments to address corporate governance reforms which focused upon basic human rights, such as humane living conditions; freedom of association at work; respectful working conditions, including hours of work; child labour; forced labour; and extreme poverty.

- However, the 2004 *Gearing Up* report reflects a recognition that the initial Global Compact placed too much of the responsibility for making a difference on these issues on to business corporations. The *Gearing Up* report acknowledges that there has to be a genuine bipartisan approach between governments and business if any significant outcome is to be achieved on profound global and national structural problems.

- Integrated Social Contract Theory (ISCT) offers a framework to allow us to begin to identify core organisational values that can stand the test of universalisation, but that retain the flexibility for local variations in customs and values.

- Corporate manslaughter, as a criminal offence, remains profoundly difficult to prosecute under UK law. Proposals to remedy this situation continue to be frustrated and the reasons for this stifling of progress are worrying in terms of democratic principles. The Law Commission and the Council of Europe have both pronounced on the issues and their recommendations await parliamentary time. It is now for government to choose whether or not to act.

- We may be entering, or have already entered, a period when the business–society relationship becomes far more openly debated. As a result we might find that in, say, 10 or 15 years' time the evolution of the limited liability company may have moved on apace from where it was at the turn of the century.

- Within the next 10–15 years, perhaps the notion of shareholder-as-constraint, rather than shareholder-as-maximising-objective, might have become more recognised and part of practice. As a result the notion of stakeholding may have become less of a practical conundrum. Business ethics and values have never been more relevant and centre-stage.

## Quick revision test

1. Have calls for corporations to display greater levels of social responsibility only arisen during the past fifteen years?

2. What was the view of Charles Lindblom regarding the fit of large corporations in democratic states?

3. What is agency theory?

4. What is the paradox concerning non-executive directors that relates to agency theory?

5. What admission was made in the 2004 *Gearing Up* Report concerning the 1999 UN Global Compact?

6. What were Christian Aid's principal criticisms of the UN Global Compact?

# Topic 5
Team Presentations

## Introduction: Team Presentations

Writing and presenting a Team report requires you to build and improve on your previous skills and experience developed in MDP Years one and two as well as in other subjects. The following chapter [Cameron Chapter 11 (Presenting to Others)] is full of lots of useful student-oriented material including the suggestion that the Columbia disaster was due to a PowerPoint slide that led NASA to miss the destructive potential of the crucial loose tile!

- Reflect on your experience so far. Think of how you would make this something that you could include in your CV. What skills and behaviours have you used, and how did you use them to contribute to the achievement of team goals?

- Think how best to co-ordinate writing a team report: it is not a matter of dividing up the tasks among the team, independently writing sections of the report the night before and pasting it together! This will generate an incoherent, inconsistent report, and you will not get the benefits of managing the co-ordination of a final report (perhaps a first draft and revision cycle?)  Note the decisions your team makes and evaluate them after the presentation and submission: did they work? Did everyone follow them? How might they have been improved?

- Planning team report writing: it obviously makes sense to cover all the topics that are going to be assessed, but do research to decide on the report headings – they aren't the same!

Organising your ideas and writing – see CAPLE material at:

http://www.strath.ac.uk/caple/studentdevelopment/

# Presenting to others

Many people are terrified of presenting to a group at first, but with practice come to enjoy it. This chapter looks at the necessary skills, and suggests ways in which you can improve. You may not become a brilliant presenter – such people are rare. But you can become good enough to get good marks and impress employers.

## Learning outcomes

By the end of this chapter you should:

- be alert to the things that can go wrong with presentations
- have assessed your own strengths and weaknesses in this area
- be able to structure a presentation in a way that is appropriate to your audience
- be developing your delivery technique
- be using visual aids to good effect
- be confident in handling questions from your audience
- be able to control nervousness.

The final face-to-face communication skill you need is that of making a presentation to a group of others. Poor presentations can be an ordeal for speaker and audience: good ones can be a delight for both. Furthermore, both good and bad presentations are *remembered*. Whether you are presenting your research results to a group of potential collaborators, talking to a group of senior managers in your own organisation, making a pitch to a potential major client or giving an after-dinner speech for a professional association, it is important to make a good impression. You may pay an invisible price for years to come if you do not. On the other hand, if you do well, unexpected opportunities may come your way far into the future. You will also have an immediate feeling of power and euphoria from having had your audience exactly where you want them.

This chapter addresses the problem of nervousness and the skills that you need. Again, these overlap with skills already covered. Being clear about your objectives, understanding your listeners' (albeit now in the plural) needs, expressing yourself appropriately and clearly and checking understanding will be as important as in one-to-one talking or in making a contribution to a group discussion. But additionally you need to know how to ensure that your audience can see and hear you, to gain and hold their attention and to use visual aids to good effect.

## THE RISKS IN PRESENTATION

Presentations, like written papers or reports, need to be carefully ordered. They need a clear message and should, where possible, use graphs, tables or other illustrations to reinforce the verbal argument. However, the fact that you and your audience are operating in real time makes the risks far greater. If something is difficult to express in writing, you can keep trying until you get it right. If your reader finds that concentration has lapsed, they can go and make a cup of tea, then try reading again from where they 'switched off'. In a live presentation, neither presenter nor audience has a second chance.

There is normally less interchange between speaker and listeners in a formal presentation than in one-to-one or group discussion. Keeping the audience awake, interested and involved is therefore a considerable challenge. You probably know all too well how easy it is to stop concentrating in a lecture and have found sitting still and being 'talked at' a fairly stressful experience. Unfortunately, the older you get, the harder it becomes to be a member of an audience.

As in other areas, the best way to become more aware of what is required is to look at what other people do less than well. You can then look at how those who are more competent do the same thing. Once you are more alert to the different dimensions required, you will be better able to reflect on, and develop, your own skills.

### ACTIVITY 11.1

Think of an unsatisfactory presentation that you have attended recently (lectures are fair game here, as well as presentations by fellow students). List all the factors which contributed to your dissatisfaction. Now think of an experience of a good presentation. List any additional features which distinguished this. (You can go on to do this again at the next presentation you attend.)

**Good features:** _____

_____

**Bad features:** _____

_____

If your experience is anything like mine, your list of bad practice might include the following:

■ The speaker was inaudible, mumbling, whispering or going too fast.

■ Visual aids were illegible, whether overhead transparencies (OHTs) with minute print or computer projection too small and faint to be seen.

■ The speaker faced away from the audience, perhaps while writing on board or flipchart.

- The speech was a hypnotic monotone making sleep irresistible, probably with no visual aids at all.
- Handouts were distributed during the presentation, so that you read these rather than listening.
- The content was jumbled, or incomprehensible, or already familiar to you.
- Questions were barely relevant, but they diverted the speaker from the main point.
- Timekeeping was poor and the speaker went on long beyond the scheduled end.
- Questions deteriorated into argument between the speaker and a single member of the audience.

The remainder of the chapter will address these common faults, as well as covering features which may well have appeared on your list of 'good' points.

---

### ACTIVITY 11.2

Did you mention presentation skills as a strength in your SWOT in Chapter 1? If not, use the following questionnaire to assess your skill level (score 5 if the statement is completely true, 4 if mostly true, 3 if it is neither true nor untrue, 2 if it is not very true, and 1 if it is totally untrue)

I have lots of experience in giving presentations      _____

The presentations I give are usually very well received      _____

I always think carefully about what I need to communicate, and how best to do it to any particular audience      _____

I am good at thinking of how to use visual aids to reinforce my message      _____

I am confident in using PowerPoint to produce effective overheads      _____

I think it is really important to watch the audience, and modify a presentation if it does not seem to be working.      _____

**Total:**      _____

If your score is 25 or above you should not need this chapter – assuming your assessment of your skills is accurate. Below this, you might think about developing an action plan to improve aspects of your skills.

---

## STRUCTURE

The importance of structure was emphasised in the context of written communications, but it is even more important in a presentation. It is very easy for your audience to lose the thread of what you are saying and very hard for them to find it again if they do. They cannot go back and read the difficult bit again. So the classic advice of 'Say what you are going to say, say it, then tell them what you have said' still holds good.

## Introduction

**Good presentations:**
- have a clear structure
- are clearly signposted
- are clearly delivered
- use varied visual aids
- interest the audience
- do not over-run.

You need to settle your audience, so say who you are, what you are aiming to achieve, how long you will be talking and how you plan to operate. Do you want to save all questions except those for clarification to the end, for example, or are you happy to take questions at any point? Will you be handing out copies of your OHTs at the end or do people need to take notes? Once the ground rules have been established, you then need to outline the main points that you will be covering during your presentation. If you can say something that catches your audience's attention at the outset and makes them *want* to hear what follows, then the presentation is likely to go well.

## Main presentation

As with a written report, you need to make clear what situation or topic you are addressing and use evidence to support the arguments you are making. Because of the difficulty of following a spoken argument, you need to make your structure absolutely clear and give your audience as much help as possible on this: 'What I have established thus far is . . . (brief summary). The next point I want to make is . . .'. If you give such pointers at regular intervals, perhaps with OHTs to reinforce them, your audience will find it easier to maintain concentration and to stay with your argument.

## Conclusion

This is the 'tell them what you have said' section. You need to summarise the points you have made, again using visual aids to reinforce them if possible. If you are making a proposal, then it is worth emphasising the main points of this again. It is also good practice to thank the audience for their patience and invite questions or discussion.

# DELIVERY TECHNIQUE

If you do come across good presenters, study them carefully to see if there are ways in which you could improve your own performance. Even if you are not exposed to skilled practitioners, the following guidelines will give you a good foundation.

## Relate to your audience

Talking to a point on the back wall, in an impersonal style, will put an unhelpful distance between you and your audience. Try to sound human in your introduction. Look at people. Say things in the way that they are most likely to understand. Check with them that you are on the right lines: 'Was that point clear?' 'Can you all see this slide?' 'Am I going too fast?'

### Make it easy for people to hear

Speak clearly, without gabbling, and vary your tone. Use short sentences and straightforward language, avoiding unnecessary jargon. Use 'spoken language' not 'written language'. If you have ever heard someone (literally) read a paper they have written, you will probably be all too aware of the difference. If not, try reading part of a journal article out loud, then rephrase it using words you would normally use in talking. Avoid turning your back on your audience (whiteboards are a real hazard here) or being hidden by equipment.

### Try to be interesting

Vary your pace and use a variety of visual aids if there are appropriate ones. Even something as simple as showing a pile of ten books on a subject can reinforce the point that there has been a lot written on it. Occasional humour can be useful, but don't overdo it (unless you are making an after-dinner speech, when a high proportion of jokes seems to be the norm). Above all, make the relevance of what you are saying clear. It may be less obvious to your audience why something is significant than it is to you: you need to *work* at making sure that they see it too.

### Beware of becoming bogged down in detail

It is far harder to absorb detail from a spoken presentation than from a written report. More often, it merely obscures the main point. Try to give only as much detail as you need to make your point. If a fine detail is crucial, it is probably better to give this as a handout for later perusal.

### Avoid giving handouts while you speak

The distribution of handouts distracts people, and you will lose your audience. It doesn't matter how often you say of a handout 'don't read this now' – the temptation to look at it immediately seems universally irresistible. If you distribute handouts before you start, early arrivals will have something to do while they wait. It will also be clear to them how many additional notes (if any) they need to take. Handouts distributed at the end can be a good way of concluding, but you need to tell people at the outset that you are going to do this, otherwise they can feel annoyed if they have taken careful notes which the handout makes superfluous.

### Keep your notes brief

Particularly if you are new to giving presentations, you are likely to be tempted to write out the whole thing. Then you know you can avoid grinding to a stop, because all you have to do is keep reading. Writing it out can be very helpful and the reassurance of knowing you *could* read it if absolutely necessary is very comforting. But try to keep that as an emergency measure. Even if you do write out a 'full text' version, you should also write briefer notes from which, barring the onset of total panic, you will actually speak.

These notes should indicate the key points to be made, in order. Such notes are ideally made on index cards. Number them or join them with a treasury tag just in case you drop them. Trying frantically to reorder a hopeless jumble of cards while facing an audience can be deeply embarrassing! Indicate in your notes each point at which you need to use a visual aid. And cross-refer to your transcript so that you can easily switch to that if necessary. (After a few presentations, when you have never used the full notes, you will probably feel confident enough to dispense with them.)

## Watch your audience

You need feedback on your delivery and people may not tell you in words. But you will be able to see, if you look, whether a glaze of incomprehension is stealing over your audience. If so, you may need to slow down and explain more, or perhaps check understanding by asking a question. If eyelids are drooping, you may be going too slowly already or have under-estimated the prior knowledge of people there. Or you may need to vary your delivery more. If people are tense, tapping feet or fingers with restrained force, you are seriously getting on their nerves and need to find out why. As soon as you pick up signals that all is not well, try to work out why. Unless you are fairly sure what you are doing wrong, *ask* what the problem is. And adapt your presentation in the light of the answers.

## Be honest

Trying to fool people seldom works. If there is a weakness in your case admit it, rather than hoping that no one will notice. If they do notice, they will not think well of you for seemingly failing to spot the weakness yourself. But if you admit to it and have formed a good relationship with your audience, they may help you to strengthen the point. Similarly, pretending to know something when in fact you don't may make you look foolish. But admitting your ignorance may allow someone in the audience who does know to contribute their knowledge – to everyone's advantage.

## Manage your time

Inexperienced presenters are often surprised at how little it is possible to communicate in a specified time. This is because they do not allow for speech being slower than reading, for questions of clarification, for introductions, for interim summaries or for use of visual aids. It is important to judge how long a presentation will take and adjust it if a dry run shows that your guess is wrong. Aim to undershoot slightly. It is generally better to risk allowing slightly too long for questions than to run out of time, and to finish a little early rather than over-running.

# EFFECTIVE VISUAL AIDS

Communication will be far more effective in either writing or speaking if you use images to reinforce your words. Visual aids have already been mentioned several times:

this should have indicated that they are essential in formal presentations of any length or complexity. Such aids have three main functions. They can help the audience *understand* a point, they can help the audience *remember* a point and they can keep your audience *awake*. To make good use of visual aids, you need to think about how each of your points could be reinforced by an actlon, an object or a picture, and then how best to achieve this reinforcement. The best visual aid to use will depend on both the point you are making and the audience to whom you are making it.

**Visual aids can:**
■ reinforce key points
■ clarify meaning
■ aid retention
■ keep audience awake!

Some things can be conveyed far more effectively by means other than words alone. Relationships are more clearly shown in diagrams, while trends are clearly demonstrated in graphs. Other chapters cover representing data visually and diagramming other aspects of a situation, also incorporating the results in written reports. The same principles apply, though within the restrictions of what can be seen from a distance. Revise these principles if you are in doubt. But although you will probably use visual aids similar to those suitable for a report for most of your points, your scope in a spoken presentation is potentially far wider.

Video clips of products, processes, people or places can be hugely effective. Concrete objects can also make a lasting impression. To take an example, when I am running open events to attract potential Open University students, one thing I need to explain is how distance learning works. It is not always obvious that a subject like management can be studied effectively at a distance. So I *show* the audience a course pack, with all the videos, disks, audiotapes and written units. I *show* them course assignments, covered in teaching comments from the tutor. I may *show* them extracts from teaching videos or a video of a tutorial. This allows me to convey far more about the course than would a mere description. If I wanted to make a point about the volume of reading on a conventional course, I might show the audience a pile of the books on the recommended reading list.

I have seen speakers hold up broken items to make a point about quality, or a new product to make a different point. Stephen Pinker held up a comb to make a point about the innate distastefulness of using a comb to stir coffee. Such images make a lasting impression – though the point they demonstrated is not always clearly remembered. If the image is too strong, then it may over-shadow the point (what *was* the significance of this particular distaste?). But this slight caution aside, apart from points which are made better by use of visual aids, people also tend to remember what they see better than what they hear. It is therefore worth using visual aids even to reinforce points which can be made adequately in words in order to aid their retention.

It is also important to incorporate variety to keep people awake and interested. For any presentation longer than, say, half an hour, it is worth using a range of visual aids for this reason alone. You can use some diagrams on prepared OHTs or slides, draw others on a board or flipchart at an appropriate point (do this quickly and avoid talking while drawing) and, if you have the facilities, use video clips and dynamic PC-generated diagrams as well.

If your talk is shorter, you do not need to work so hard at keeping people's attention and too much variety in visual aids can be counterproductive. It is better to reserve them for points that are best made visually, plus those which you really wish to emphasise. More will be a distraction.

## Presentation packages

It is now normal to drive your presentation from your PC. Indeed it would seem unprofessional in many situations to use anything else. PowerPoint is virtually the standard in management presentations, although other packages are available, and some prefer these. The main advantage of a package such as PowerPoint is its flexibility. Suppose you are talking with potential clients prior to a presentation and discover that they have concerns that you had not realised when you prepared your presentation. In a couple of minutes you can add a slide or two to address these. You can easily edit the slides you used on one occasion to provide a slightly modified presentation for another occasion. You can easily incorporate charts and graphs from a report into your presentation, or diagrams from your presentation into a report.

Because you will almost certainly need to give presentations at work using this technology, you should use the opportunities provided by your course to become proficient in using PowerPoint or a similar package. It is remarkably easy to produce basic bullet point slides, and not much harder to animate them, colour them, and add sound effects and clip art. Aim to become proficient at all these as a minimum.

While it is good to explore the possibilities and experiment with what you can do while you have the chance, remember that you should use the facilities advisedly when presenting at work. Your aim is not usually to show how good you are with IT, but to communicate. Over-complexity, too many animations and sound effects and too many slides may actually interfere with communication. Fancy backgrounds distract, and reduce clarity. Animations may look impressive, but are similarly distracting. While it is sometimes extremely useful to build up a picture a bit at a time, you should restrict use of the facility to such times. Words continually flying in from left and right will seldom help your audience to grasp and retain the points you are making. And now that everyone can use PowerPoint, being expert in its use is less impressive than once it might have been. Remember at all times that you are trying to communicate effectively, and use the tools at your disposal to this end alone.

There are less obvious, but perhaps more serious hazards with PowerPoint in terms of the way that it can easily constrain your presentation to an endless series of bullet points. As Naughton (2003) pointed out, it was conceived in a software sales environment. So it tends to turn everything into a sales pitch. There was a version of the Gettysburg address doing the e-mail rounds a while ago that demonstrated this limitation (see **www.norvig.com/Gettysburg**). But Tufte, a Yale professor and expert on visual communication, goes further in his criticism, arguing (in 'The Cognitive Style of PowerPoint', available from **www.edwardtufte.com**) that PowerPoint's ready-made templates tend to weaken verbal and spatial reasoning and corrupt statistical analysis. He attributes the Columbia disaster to a slide that led to Nasa to overlook the destructive potential of the crucial loose tile.

## General requirements for visual aids

Whether or not you are using computer-driven visual aids, there are a number of points to bear in mind.

It may sound blindingly obvious, but many people ignore the requirement for an audience to be able to *see* visual aids if they are to be of use. Even experienced speakers have been known to show OHTs which are photocopies of a full-page table in a book, with perhaps 200 numbers in invisibly small type. The amount of effective information you can convey on a slide is surprisingly small. Experiment with handwriting your drafts of overheads on acetate, then see whether you can read them from the back row. PowerPoint allows you to add points one at a time. If using an OHP you may find it helpful to build up information using a series of OHTs which can be placed one on top of the other. Thus by adding them one at a time you build up the complexity of the picture to a point which would be impossible to grasp if you started with this. Either way it is probably best to aim at no more than four points per slide.

Colour can either enhance or hinder clarity. Think about how you use it. I was once provided with a set of very tasteful, but totally useless, OHTs in shades of blue on blue, the words invisible from more than three paces. PowerPoint slides can be equally illegible if you are not careful. Use both colour and light/dark contrast to enhance legibility and emphasise key points and be careful about fancy backgrounds. They may look good in themselves, but obscure your message.

This is not to argue for refusing to use anything but the hand-scrawled, barely legible exhibits that are still often used. They have their place in 'transient' presentations, for example on group work, where all you are seeking is to convey your thought processes to fellow students. But they would be inappropriate for a formal presentation to a client.

If you are doing an informal presentation to your class, do not have a PowerPoint projector and are discouraged from using the copier, then you can prepare flipchart sheets in the same way as slides and ask a fellow student to be responsible for displaying the right one on cue. (Trying to talk and manage a flipchart is possible, but not easy. It helps considerably to split the responsibility.)

If you are still using OHTs, another obvious point (well, I wish it *were* obvious) is always to use photocopying, not write-on, acetate in a copier. Photocopier acetate is firmer and the box should be clearly labelled as suitable for copying. The write-on sort melts in the machine, making a mess which only the engineer can sort out, and which will make you unpopular all round.

### ACTIVITY 11.3

You can easily assemble an exhibit for your portfolio that addresses both your ability to use images and your ability to read and respond to materials. Take as the basis for this a presentation you make in class, perhaps summarising something you have studied. Your presentation needs to include appropriate visual aids. You also need a way of obtaining feedback from your tutor and/or those present. The exhibit should include the notes for your talk and copies of the images used, together with a description of how you selected both content and images, feedback on their effectiveness and what you would do differently next time in the light of this feedback.

## HANDLING QUESTIONS

Sometimes questions are helpful, but I have seen them wreck a presentation completely. Until you are fairly experienced, and feel confident that you can handle questions during your talk, it is safer to take substantive questions at the end. Make it clear at the outset that during your presentation you will deal only with requests for clarification and that there will be time for questions at the end. Otherwise, you risk being completely side-tracked from your main argument or disconcerted by challenges to what you are saying before you have completed your case. If you want to postpone a question, either take a note of it so that you do not forget or, better still, ask the questioner to ask it again at the end. This means that your brain is not distracted by trying to remember the question while giving the talk.

When you do accept a question, your listening skills will be important. It is hard to listen carefully when you are nervous, particularly if someone is asking a complex multiple question. If this happens, jot down the key parts of the question, otherwise it is easy to answer the first part and forget all the rest. If you are at all uncertain what the question means, clarify this with the questioner. You may feel that it makes you look stupid if you don't understand. But if the questioner is far from clear it is sensible to pick up on this. You may tie yourself in knots if you try to answer a question that you have only partially understood: this does not look all that impressive either.

If a question challenges what you have said, resist the temptation to become either defensive or aggressive. Take the contrasting view seriously, looking for ways to develop your position in the light of it, unless you are convinced that the questioner really has missed the point of what you were saying or is misinformed. If the point has been missed by the questioner, it is possible that others missed it too and finding another way of making it may be helpful. But if you cannot quickly satisfy the questioner, it is usually better to suggest that you discuss it after the presentation is finished, rather than get into an argument that will be of little interest to most of the audience.

People ask questions for many reasons. In work presentations, there will be some who are trying to make an impression on the audience, perhaps with a view to establishing themselves as a rival expert or advertising their own business. Or they may simply like being the centre of attention. Where questions are clearly being asked in the questioner's personal interest, it is simplest to thank them for raising their point, agree with as much of the point as you can, perhaps suggest a discussion outside the meeting and move on to the next question.

If questions reveal a genuine weakness in your presentation, it is usually better to accept this and ask for suggestions from the questioner and the audience for ways around the difficulty. You may find that someone can suggest a way forward. If, however, the difficulty seems to you to be much less significant than the questioner is suggesting, you will need to make sure that the audience does not end up devaluing the bulk of what you have said.

## CONTROLLING YOUR NERVES

It is natural to be nervous when standing up in front of a group of people. The adrenaline it generates can give your performance an excitement that it would otherwise lack, so do not aim to become totally blasé about it. But excess nerves can be a liability, drying your throat and making you physically and verbally clumsy. If you think that you are worrying more than is reasonable, there are several things that can help considerably. Get as much practice as you can. Concentrate on exposing yourself to similar situations, practise deliberate relaxation, and prepare for each specific presentation.

Increase your confidence in presenting by:
- frequent practice
- relaxation techniques
- thorough preparation.

If you *are* over-nervous, you probably avoid all situations where you need to talk in front of people. But the best way to reduce nervousness is to seek out such situations and force yourself to talk. Find the least threatening situations first – talking to a small group of students before addressing the whole class, getting used to the class before giving a paper at a conference . . . . But *do* it. Each time you will feel less nervous.

This is one form of practice which 'desensitises' you to the general trauma of the situation. Another form is to have one or more 'practice runs' of a specific presentation. This will mean that you are confident about the structure of the talk, have practised some of the phrases you will use, know where to use your OHTs or other visual aids and have checked how long it takes, so that you are not worried about having too much or too little material.

Relaxation techniques, discussed as part of stress management in Chapter 2, can help reduce this sort of stress too, though you need to be familiar with the techniques for best effect. If you have not yet practised them, a short period of deep breathing will help. And a *small* alcoholic drink can sometimes be useful.

But your best weapon against nerves is the knowledge that you have done everything possible to prepare for the event, that you have carefully researched your subject and audience, your talk is well structured and your notes are well organised, your visual aids well chosen and you have at your fingertips supporting evidence and examples. Dry runs, described above, can be part of your preparation. Remember, a presentation is a challenge, but it can be exciting and rewarding, and can provoke interesting discussion on a subject dear to your heart. Preparation is so important that more detail is given below.

Even if you have prepared, you may well experience an initial onrush of nerves when you stand up. To get you over this, make sure that you have your introductory remarks written out in full, preferably learned by heart. Take a sip of water and a deep breath, go over your introduction and by then you will have calmed down enough to enjoy yourself.

## PREPARATION

Preparation is the key to successful presentation and you cannot afford to cut corners if you want to do well. You need to have thought carefully about what to include, how to structure it and how to add impact to your arguments by examples and visual aids.

For important presentations, you will want to rehearse your arguments several times. Much of this can be done piecemeal, for example while exercising or in a waiting room, *sotto voce*. But you will need one full-scale, real-time rehearsal to check timing, use of aids and flow of arguments. Ideally, find colleagues or friends to act as an audience for this and ask them to give you feedback afterwards. If this is impossible, then tape yourself and replay the tape after a decent interval, listening critically and noting points where you need to change something.

If you are giving a presentation at work, to clients or potential customers, or a paper at a conference, your preparation needs to extend to ensuring that the location is set up as you want it, temperature is appropriate and equipment working well. You do not want to be hunting for porters or chasing around for a fresh bulb for the projector while half the audience has arrived and is watching your increasing panic. So arrive early and make all the necessary checks.

 Preparation for your *next* presentation should be informed by feedback from the last, so it is important to capture as much feedback as possible. Make a note of your immediate reactions in the light of audience response. Do this as soon as possible after the event, noting points for future action. And if possible, have a friend in the audience charged with giving you their reactions and suggestions. You may even be able to design and distribute a short questionnaire for the audience to complete on leaving. If the presentation is one of a series, this can be extremely useful in helping you to adjust future events to meet audience needs more effectively. If you are preparing an exhibit on your presentation skills, it will be important to include all such feedback.

## SUMMARY

This chapter has argued the following:

- Presentation skills are an important part of communication in the work context and may indeed be tested during selection procedures.

- During your studies you will have many opportunities to develop these skills and they may even influence some of your marks.

- Successful presentation depends on adequate preparation. You need to be clear on your objectives and those of your audience, and structure is even more important than with written communications.

- Good visual aids help audience concentration, comprehension and retention. Using PowerPoint or a similar package to project slides from your PC is flexible and looks professional.

- Audibility, visibility and ability to pace your delivery to suit your audience and your content are essential.

- Questions can be an asset or a disruption. Substantive ones are probably best taken at the end.

- Extreme nervousness can be disabling but lower levels can help. Practice, relaxation and preparation will help you to reduce excessive nerves.

## Further information

- Bradley, A. (2000) *Successful Presentation Skills*, 2nd edn, Kogan Page.
- Collins, J./Video Arts (1998) *Making Effective Presentations*, Kogan Page.
- Conradi, M. and Hall, R. (2001) *That Presentation Sensation*, Financial Times Prentice Hall.
- Leech, T. (2001) *Say it like Shakespeare*, McGraw-Hill – this gives an interestingly different slant on presenting.
- Manchester Open Learning (1993) *Making Effective Presentations*, Kogan Page.
- Williams, J.S. (1995) *The Right Way to Make Effective Presentations*, Eliot Right Way Books.

# Semester 2

## Business Research Proposals and Project Planning

# Introduction: Semester 2
# Business Research Proposals and Project Planning

This semester looks at the business research project process. This aims partly at helping those  students going into honours to prepare for a big element of the honours year, namely the Honours Year Project or Dissertation. The main objective is to bring together those skills which you have been learning in the Management Development Programme to prepare a Business Research Project Proposal: from idea generation through information handling to project planning. Whether  working within a company or for a consultancy the preparation of project plans Is a regular task: research projects are an important type of business project and a proposal has to persuade resource gatekeepers the value of funding your proposal.

For those not considering an honours year, remember that research occurs in many different settings in organisations and many of you will undertake business research projects as part of your employment. Some skills and requirements are similar – the searching for relevant information from existing sources, the need to generate new data and thus think about methods of doing this. The importance of having clearly defined and focussed objectives and questions, the need to critically assess information, data and evidence and arguments, to manage the process and to write effectively. Such Organisation based Business Research is likely to emphasise project planning and detailed objectives whereas Academic Research emphasises creativity of research problem formulation.

| Session | Tasks relating to research project proposal assignment | What you should have written soon after this session |
|---|---|---|
| 1 | Idea generation Generating research objectives | An introduction chapter with context for idea and objectives |
| 2 | Approval of research topic How to use an academic journal article | The review of the literature |
| 3 | Deciding between Qualitative research methods (if any) | Some of the proposed methodology |
| 4 | Deciding between Quantitative approaches (if any) | Complete methodology |
| 5 | Project Planning | Timetable and resources for proposal |

The first stage is to select a research topic. Some brainstorming and creative problem solving skills are designed help at the first session, but it is advisable to come to that session with a few possible ideas, and to leave with an idea you feel confident with which to move forwards. The exercise shows how to generate research objectives from a topic.

The second stage involves critically reviewing literature on your topic. Use systematic methods to check out these sorts of information. Some of the information you will look at for any research project is information, which has been gathered by others and published in some format - a book, journal article, report. This forms what is usually called secondary sources of information. Your project plan should detail plans of what you will do with such Secondary information. The third stage involves collecting your own data and involves two sessions one for qualitative and one quantitative data. The research methodology section of your proposal needs to explain how you have come to your recommendations for the research proposal.

The key learning objectives and outcomes for the second semester are: (1) To develop and enhance your skills in searching for business information and assessing its value: (2) To develop and enhance your skills in planning, conducting and managing business research.

# Topic 1
## Research Topic and Objectives

## Introduction: Research Topic and Objectives – Project Planning

Saunders Chapter 2 addresses how to decide on a research topic. Local factors to be included are resources provided by departments on past topics –  or suggestions of possible topics from supervisors.

It's important to plan the generation of a research proposal – this is a considerable task and needs proper attention over the whole semester. Schedule writing so that  topic, research objectives and research questions are clear after the first session. Do the majority of literature review and evaluation after the second session. In this way staff input can be sought along the way rather than just generating something in the last few days.

A proposal for research should also plan the research project itself. Payne chapter 17 forms a valuable introduction to this: make decisions while developing a research proposal so that there isn't an impossibly long list of activities.

In Saunders Chapter 2 (Formulating and clarifying the research topic), the introduction forms a good context for either business projects or draft honours thesis proposals  The  attributes of a good research topic suggest  good points on outcomes and provide a worked example.

Section 2.3 (Generating and refining research ideas) really will help generate a topic. Section 2.4 (Turning research ideas into research projects) gives valuable details on you to write research questions, and objectives.  The last section describes Writing your research proposal This is also for Session 5, where Cameron Chapter 16 Managing Projects provides good material to help planning.

There are opportunities for creativity and innovation when developing a research project topic. The MDP2 techniques in this area should be valuable. It is also valuable to put your topic in context: in which department are you proposing to do your honours project? Which is the nearest discipline to this business project.

# Writing dissertations or research projects

**Learning outcomes**

After studying this chapter, you should be able to:

- understand the requirements of selecting a research topic
- define a research question
- understand the requirements of a dissertation
- transfer report-writing skills to the presentation of research in a dissertation.

## → Introduction

Many honours degree courses require students to complete a dissertation or research project as part of the final assessment for the degree. A dissertation is a major piece of individual work involving in-depth research about a topic with the end product being a formal report (and in some instances a presentation). Research projects and dissertations often form part of the assessment at later stages in a course, as they require the use of the higher-level cognitive skills of analysis, synthesis and evaluation.

Most of the assessments you will undertake are prescriptive in terms of the topic studied. Dissertations and research projects generally allow greater freedom in what may be done to satisfy the assessment requirements, offering the possibility of choosing an area of particular interest to you within the scope of the course you are studying. Many students feel liberated at the idea of selecting a topic for themselves and relish the opportunity of exploring something of great interest to them. Others will approach the task with trepidation, feeling wary of embarking on a task without the appropriate detail normally provided by tutors. Doing a dissertation means that, instead of knowledge and information being presented and following a prescribed route for answering questions, you are thrust into an active role of managing an investigation into a topic area. This means researching and discovering things for yourself. You will have to set your own targets and parameters, pose your own central research question and decide on the appropriate sources of information to support the research. Dissertations are very time consuming and require a great deal of commitment, but if everything goes to plan they can create a high level of motivation and provide a great sense of achievement on completion of the work.

Many universities or colleges will issue guidelines for the completion of dissertations for the course you are studying. Obtain a copy of these as soon as you can and read them thoroughly so that you are aware from the beginning what is expected of you. It may also be possible to borrow copies of previous dissertations submitted for your course – they are sometimes available for reference in the library. Studying these will help you to get a picture of what you have to produce.

The philosophy underpinning a dissertation is that how you carry out the research (process) is of equal (or possibly greater) importance as the final product. Thus, an understanding of appropriate methodological and analytical techniques is important. There are now many good textbooks available that cover dissertations and the research process in depth. This chapter provides an overview and indicates what may be required of you whilst undertaking such a task.

> **!** **Remember...**
> The research process is as important as the final product.

See
Activity 17.1
**STAGES** OF A
DISSERTATION
in the Online
Study Guide.

### Activity 17.1

## Dissertation requirements for the course

Many courses provide guidelines for completing dissertations. Obtain a copy of dissertation guidelines for your course (if available) and complete the following:

1 What are the limitations, if any, to your choice of topic?

2 Is primary research a requirement?

3 What is the word limit?

4 What is the date of submission?

5 Are there any intermediate submission dates (e.g. research proposal, literature review) and, if so, what and when are they?

6 Are there specific requirements for presentation?

- Font type and size
- Double/single line spacing
- Margins
- Binding
- Number of copies required for submission

7 How are marks allocated for the dissertation (if available)?

8 What support is offered (e.g. individual or group tutorials, etc.)?

## → Selection of a topic

If you are able to choose the topic for your dissertation, you will need to consider this carefully. Start thinking about it as early as possible – keep notes on interesting ideas that you think of during your studies which you can then reflect on as possible research topics. If you are struggling to find a suitable topic, there are a number of possible sources of ideas:

- Visit the library and read the current journals and quality newspapers. These are a good source of topical issues and developments that may provide an idea for your research.

- Look at the end of chapters or articles that you find interesting to see if the author has recommended further research in a particular area.

- Look into an organisation, business or industrial sector in which you have employment experience – perhaps you became aware of a particular problem that the organisation was facing, or recognised that the industry needed to develop in a particular way. Examples such as these can provide a suitable basis for research.

- Consult copies of dissertations completed in previous years – many universities or colleges make these available. The titles or abstracts may suggest something that could be researched further. However, if you do get an idea from a previous dissertation, ensure that your research is sufficiently different from the original and do not be tempted to plagiarise. This is a very serious offence.

- Some universities and colleges may issue a list of staff research interests that may be of interest to you and worth considering for your research. If so, it may be helpful to discuss it with the member of staff concerned.

### Considerations in choosing a topic

See downloadable template 17.1 PLANNING A DISSERTATION for your Personal Development Plan online.

Some students may have difficulty choosing from the wide variety of topics they are interested in, whilst others may struggle to come to terms with the freedom of selecting their own topic. Highlighted below are some of the issues that must be considered when making the final choice for your dissertation.

#### Interest

It is important that you choose something that you are interested in and that will maintain your interest until the work is completed.

#### Philosophy/requirements of the course

The topic you choose should enable you to satisfy the requirements and reflect the philosophy of the course on which you are studying. For example, if you are studying on a business course it may be inappropriate to complete a dissertation about the history of the Roman Empire.

The chosen topic should have sufficient theoretical grounding and secondary sources for a literature review to be carried out. This will form the basis for any primary research you may be required to conduct.

If your course requirements for the dissertation state that your investigation must include primary research, then the topic you choose should allow for this. This is an important consideration – you need to be certain that the collection of the primary data required is possible, given the resource constraints under which you will be working. Gathering primary data can be a very time-consuming and expensive activity.

## Ability/experience

The topic should provide scope for you to demonstrate your abilities to the full but not be so complex that you are unable to complete it successfully. Consider what you know already and avoid any topic or area you find difficult. Try to choose something that will complement your strengths and abilities.

## Resources

Choose a topic that it is possible to research within the limited resources available to you:

- *Time*. Dissertations are very time consuming. It is therefore important that you think carefully about the time required to do the research and the time available. Read Chapter 11 for tips on how to improve time management skills.

- *Information (both primary and secondary)*. Consider the library resources that are readily accessible to you – there is little point attempting a dissertation on the banking system of eastern Malaysia if the library you regularly use has very little or no information about this. To complete such a topic satisfactorily, you will need to be absolutely certain that you have access to information from other sources. Primary data can be very difficult to gather and may require the cooperation of people and organisations external to the university or college. You may need to seek permission to collect the data you need.

- *Money*. Not many student budgets will accommodate a trip to a distant destination to carry out a detailed investigation. Be realistic in your estimation of the costs of travel, postage and telephone calls, etc., needed to collect the information required for the topic you are considering.

- *Support*. What support mechanisms are available to you in completing the research? Some universities and colleges are unable to guarantee that a dissertation tutor will have specific knowledge in the area you are researching. However, tutors will normally have knowledge and experience of the research process. If you are basing your research within an organisation, it is vital that you have its support. Often students have good ideas but they involve the collection of data that are confidential and/or sensitive. It is imperative that permission be obtained from the host organisation for the collection and publication of confidential and sensitive data.

## Moral/ethical considerations

Reflect on any moral or ethical issues surrounding any research that you are proposing to do. Do not attempt to do anything that is likely to bring you or your university or college into disrepute, and ensure that, if you promise confidentiality to any of your sources, you are able to respect that promise. You should also avoid any research that will cause damage to the environment or involves breaking the law. The university or college may have specific guidelines covering this area.

## Activity 17.2

### Ethical considerations

Many universities and colleges now issue guidelines on ethics for dissertations and research projects. Obtain a copy of your institution's guidelines (and those for your course if available). Before finalising your topic area, read the guidelines and assess how they may affect your research.

**Stop and think**
- ○ Does your university or college have an ethical policy relating to research?
- ○ What are the ethical aspects of the research you are proposing to do?
- ○ Do you need to protect confidentiality?

### Life of the topic

It is important that the topic you choose will be 'live' for the duration of the work. Often students choose extremely topical issues that are or have been important in recent times. After six months, the general interest may decline and thus data become inaccessible.

Start thinking about the topic as early as possible. Decide a provisional area of interest, review the relevant literature, and produce a scheme or model of the issues involved (see Chapter 15).

## Activity 17.3

### Identifying suitable topics for research

Identify two topic areas you are interested in investigating for a dissertation. Using the considerations highlighted above and the checklist below, determine the issues surrounding each of the topics you have identified.

### Checklist: determining the suitability of the topic chosen

What is your interest in the topic chosen? ☐

Does the topic provide sufficient scope for you to meet the requirements of your course? ☐

Will the topic allow you to demonstrate your strengths? ☐

Does the university/college library have appropriate information – or can you obtain the information required from other libraries/sources? ☐

Is it possible to collect the appropriate primary data to support the research, if required? ☐

Is it possible to complete the research in the time you have available? ☐

Is it possible to complete the research within your financial budget? ☐

If the research is based on a specific organisation or industry, do you have the support of the appropriate people? Note: organisation/industry personnel change – be sure that you are not reliant on a single individual! ☐

Do you have the support of your tutors to do the research? ☐

Will the topic area remain 'live' until the research has been completed? ☐

## → Defining the research question and objective

Once the topic area has been determined, it will be necessary to refine the research area by defining a research question that will provide a focus and thus avoid the dissertation becoming a mere collection of facts. The research question must be clearly, precisely and unambiguously stated. Students often find that this is the most difficult thing to do, but, once done, everything else can easily fall into place.

It is easy for a project or dissertation to become overly descriptive. In order to avoid this, try to think of a genuine question. You can then analyse the facts and evidence you gather to determine and support the answer to this question.

See
Activity 17.2
DEFINING THE
RESEARCH
QUESTION AND
OBJECTIVE
in the Online
Study Guide.

### Activity 17.4

#### Determining the research question

Identify a suitable topic area for a dissertation and define an appropriate research question and objective for it.

### Feasibility

Once a topic has been identified, some preliminary work needs to be carried out to determine the feasibility of completing the research. This will also help to refine the research area. An initial library search using any key words you have identified for the topic will identify sources and provide an indication of what is readily available that may be of help.

At this stage, the methods to be used to collect the data required need to be identified. Careful consideration needs to be given to the different research methods that may be adopted in order to choose the one that will enable the collection of reliable and valid data in support of the research (see Chapter 9).

---

#### Checklist: the feasibility of a research topic

Is the topic too broad or narrow an area to work with? ☐

Is there a clearly defined research question? ☐

Is there sufficient secondary information easily accessible to you? ☐

Will there be sufficient theoretical content? ☐

Will the collection of primary data be possible (if this is a requirement)? ☐

Are there likely to be problems of confidentiality of data? ☐

Does the topic require the consideration and collation of too much data? ☐

Will it involve statistical analysis work (and problems) which are insurmountable? ☐

Can it be completed in the timescale available? ☐

Has it been done before (some universities and colleges do not allow the same topic to be researched within a certain time frame)? ☐

Do you have the skills necessary to do justice to the work? ☐

Beware of under-focus (ideas not specific enough to form the basis of a good dissertation) at this stage, i.e. you may find that the topic selected is too broad and must therefore be redefined. One of the most common criticisms of initial ideas for student projects and dissertations is that the topic is too broad and lacks sufficient focus. This may result in the final submission providing a descriptive overview rather than an in-depth analysis of the problem or situation.

Beware also of having a single-minded aim of pursuing a particular topic whatever happens. If the feasibility study indicates that there will be problems collecting and analysing the data, or it is not possible to gain permission from the organisation you were hoping to research, do not pursue the idea. Time will be better spent searching for a new topic area.

The initial thinking phase for projects and dissertations is very time consuming. However, it is important to get the research area precisely defined before going too far with the research process.

## → Research proposal

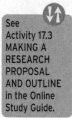

See Activity 17.3 MAKING A RESEARCH PROPOSAL AND OUTLINE in the Online Study Guide.

You may have to submit a proposal or outline for your project or dissertation. A proposal ensures that everyone connected with the research is perfectly clear about and in agreement with the aim of the research, what is going to be done and how it is going to be done. The research proposal or outline should be agreed with your tutor (and employer or sponsor if necessary) before *any* in-depth research is begun. The proposal clearly states the aim of the research, the terms of reference (the steps required to achieve the aim) and the proposed methods of investigation, and gives an indication of an initial bibliography.

Below is a general guide to what to include in a research proposal. Your course may have specific requirements for the research proposal, so check the regulations to see exactly what is required.

### Introduction/background

The introduction should aim to provide a person who has no previous knowledge of the topic with sufficient background information to understand why the research is being undertaken.

### Research aim

The research project or dissertation should have only one aim. This should be stated in a clear, concise and accurate way, indicating the focus of the research and what you hope to achieve. A reader should be left in no doubt as to what you are aiming to do after reading this section of the proposal. Producing such a statement seems to be a very difficult exercise for some students, yet it is crucial to good research that a correctly formulated aim is achieved. Beware of including the word 'and' as this may conceal a multiple aim.

Figure 17.1 **Refinining the research**

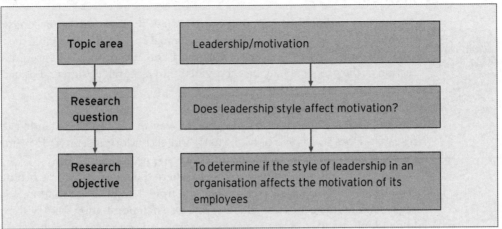

## Terms of reference (objectives)

This is a listing, in logical sequence, of the tasks that will have to be completed in order to achieve the aim. They indicate the data that are required to complete the research. You need to be quite precise in articulating the terms of reference – state exactly what is going to be done in sequence.

Some suggested terms of reference for the research objective identified in Figure 17.1 are:

- to review the different styles of leadership
- to define motivation
- to identify the factors affecting motivation
- to identify the relationship between style of leadership and motivation
- to determine if the style of leadership affects motivation in an organisation.

> **Remember...**
> You may be assessed on how well you have achieved the terms of reference in your dissertation, so ensure that they are achievable.

### Activity 17.5

**Constructing the terms of reference**

For the research objective you defined in the previous activity, determine the terms of reference that would be appropriate in achieving the objective.

## Method

See
Activity 17.4
DECIDING ON
RESEARCH
METHODS
in the Online
Study Guide.

This section outlines how you propose to achieve the aim and the reasons why a particular method was chosen. Sufficient information must be included to enable the reader to determine the validity of the proposed method and the probable degree of accuracy. This section of the proposal may be subdivided into research design and data collection.

### Research design

The research design indicates the general way in which it is intended to carry out the research. Does it involve both primary and secondary research? If primary research is involved, how will this be done – interviews, questionnaires, etc.?

The research design should also state where the research will be conducted and why. For example, is it necessary to gather data from a single organisation, a cross-section of organisations, the general public, etc? The research population from within this also needs to be identified. If you are researching within an organisation, it is necessary to specify which population, from within that organisation, will be used and why. For example, a number of different populations may be identified from within a university – students, academic staff, administrative staff, managers, trade unions, etc. Many of these populations may be subdivided further (e.g. students – full time, part time, etc.). The population you intend to use for your investigation needs to be defined as precisely as possible.

> **Stop and think**
> ○ What is the population for the research topic you are considering?
> ○ How might it be subdivided?

### Data collection

This section should provide a more detailed account of the data required, how they will be collected and any problems anticipated with doing this, such as confidentiality.

- Identify what you intend to achieve from the *secondary* research and highlight the major sources that will be consulted. Indicate which areas the secondary information will support and/or resolve, e.g. theory, background to the organisation or industry, etc.

- Identify the *primary* data that are required and why. Provide more detail about how the data will be collected, including any sampling techniques to be used. For example, if it is intended to interview people, explain how the interviews are to be conducted, what the interviews are intended to achieve, who will be interviewed, how the sample will be constructed, etc. (see Chapter 9).

You should also provide an explanation of how you intend to analyse the data you collect and how this will relate back to the aim of your research.

## Bibliography

At this stage, the bibliography is an indication of the sources you intend to use and the books, journals, etc., already consulted in the selection of the topic and preparation of the proposal (see Chapter 9).

## Planning

Some universities or colleges may also require a section on planning to be included within the proposal. If so, you will need to include details about the timescale involved and the resources required. Be careful not to underestimate the requirements: completing a dissertation takes time and money.

# → Conducting the research

Doing the research for a dissertation is a lengthy process and requires plenty of perseverance, energy and commitment. Do not underestimate the time it will take to gather the data – for example, sending out postal questionnaires and waiting for responses may take several weeks.

Once the topic and aim of the research have been determined, a thorough search and review of the available literature should be conducted. This will help to increase and refine your knowledge of the issues and themes that will inform the primary research. Any research should always start with a review of secondary sources.

See Chapter 9 for more advice on doing the research.

# → Writing up the research

Many students find writing up their research a daunting and difficult task. Writing up the research requires a deep understanding of the topic, which will enable you to explain and present your research in such a way that the reader is able easily to understand and follow the arguments and discussions. The dissertation must incorporate the appropriate elements as set down in the university or college guidelines. Writing up the research will draw on your experience of writing reports, as the final format will reflect many features of a formal report. Refer to Chapter 16 for more detail on report writing.

## Assessment criteria

This section provides an indication of some of the things markers may be looking for when reading a dissertation. However, you should check the course regulations for the specific marking criteria that will be applied to your dissertation.

**Stop and think** ○ What are the marking criteria for your disseration?

### Methodology

This will vary according to the type of dissertation you undertake. The methodology should give details of the method eventually used, a justification for using that particular method, and a discussion of the advantages and limitations of that approach. The final method used may differ from the one outlined in the proposal. If this is the case, you must explain the reasons within the methodology.

The marker may be looking for evidence of the following:

- a thorough discussion and justification of the research method(s) used
- an appropriate research method for the problem being investigated
- a well-defined research population
- a sampling method appropriate for the population
- sufficient information about the population and sampling methods used to determine the validity and reliability of the data collected
- identification and discussion of the limitations (if any) of the method used
- identification of data analysis techniques appropriate for the data.

## Secondary research

The secondary research should indicate that a thorough literature search and/or review of the relevant theory has been undertaken. The marker may be looking for evidence of the following:

- consultation of a range of quality, contemporaneous sources
- no omissions of seminal texts or significant theorists in the area
- collection of information relevant to the terms of reference
- evidence of analysis and critique of the material rather than straightforward acceptance
- where generalisations have been made, are they based on adequate observations?
- are any assumptions explicit?
- correctly referenced sources
- correctly attributed and appropriate quotations where necessary.

## Primary research

If primary research is required, the marker may be looking for evidence of the following:

- collection of data relevant to the terms of reference
- collection of data in an appropriate manner and from an appropriate sample
- recognition of the limitations of the data and that they have been dealt with in an appropriate manner
- the correct application of appropriate data analysis techniques
- an analysis and evaluation of the findings rather than a description
- an explicit relationship between the primary and secondary research.

**Suggestions** for the successful completion of a dissertation or research project

- A sound logical structure should permeate the dissertation.
- Arguments should be lucid and to the point.
- The evidence offered in support of an argument or case should be clearly stated.
- Make clear what use is made of the research undertaken and what it shows.
- Be critically evaluative of the concepts, theories or models considered in light of the data collected.
- Provide continuity by making adequate linkages between the chapters/sections – this may be aided by the use of brief introductions and summaries for each chapter/section.
- Use tables, graphs, charts, etc., where appropriate to enhance presentation of the data.
- Give due recognition to the limitations of the research findings.
- Be rigorous in the development and analysis of the material.
- If the dissertation is based on an organisation, ensure that it meets the academic requirements and do not let the organisation drive the dissertation.

## → Management of the dissertation or research project

The dissertation draws on your abilities to cope as an independent learner. In completing this form of assessment successfully, you will have to decide what you want to know, determine how you are going to find it out, and set your own targets and deadlines. Most universities and colleges will operate some form of supervision, but this will largely be to monitor the process – the management and completion of the final product is up to you.

### Supervision

You may be allocated an academic tutor to supervise your dissertation. This may involve you in a different type of relationship with a tutor than you have experienced before. There may be opportunities to have one-to-one discussions with the tutor/supervisor, whom you have previously encountered only in a classroom situation. It is important to work out a friendly but professional working relationship with your supervisor – find out what they expect from you and work with them to decide what support you may need. Discuss how often you need to meet and if possible work out a schedule with deadlines for particular parts of the work to be completed. Remember that the supervisor is there to guide and advise you, particularly on the process. They are not going to do the research or write the dissertation for you.

Universities or colleges will probably have some guidelines with regard to the supervision of dissertations, but generally supervisors will expect you to:

- work independently – seeking help elsewhere as well as from the supervisor

- attend meetings regularly (and promptly) to keep them informed of your progress
- be prepared for your meetings
- follow their advice
- be committed and enthusiastic.

You may expect your supervisor to:

- be supportive
- be constructively critical
- give you appropriate quality time
- exert influence if necessary on your behalf.

However, remember that it is your dissertation and you are responsible for the final quality of the work you submit, even if it is awarded a poor mark.

→ Summary

This chapter has outlined that:

- the completion of research projects or dissertations is very time consuming and requires planning and dedication
- time spent at the outset to ensure that the research topic meets all the required criteria is time well spent and may save time and effort in later stages
- a course may have specific requirements and it is important to ensure that these are met
- it is essential to understand the criteria by which the dissertation or research project will be assessed.

# Formulating and clarifying the research topic

## LEARNING OUTCOMES

By the end of this chapter you should be able to:

→ generate ideas that will help in the choice of a suitable research topic;

→ identify the attributes of a good research topic;

→ turn research ideas into a research project that has clear research question(s) and objectives;

→ draft a research proposal.

## 2.1　Introduction

Many students think that choosing their research topic is the most exciting part of their course. After all, this is something that they get to decide for themselves rather than having to complete a task decided by their tutors. We will stress in this chapter that it is important to choose something that will sustain your interest throughout the months that you will need to complete it. You may even decide to do some research that is something that forms part of your leisure activities, like playing video games!

Before you start your research you need to have at least some idea of what you want to do. This is probably the most difficult, and yet the most important, part of your research project. Up until now most of your studies have been concerned with answering questions that other people have set. This chapter is concerned with how to formulate and clarify your research topic and your research question. Without being clear about what you are going to research it is difficult to plan how you are going to research it. This reminds us of a favourite quote in *Alice's Adventures in Wonderland*. This is part of Alice's conversation with the Cheshire Cat. In this Alice asks the Cat (Carroll, 1989:63–4):

'Would you tell me, please, which way I ought to walk from here?'

'That depends a good deal on where you want to get to', said the Cat.

'I don't much care where', said Alice.

'Then it doesn't matter which way you walk', said the Cat.

Formulating and clarifying the research topic is the starting point of your research project (Ghauri and Grønhaug, 2005; Smith and Dainty, 1991). Once you are clear about this you will be able to choose the most appropriate research strategy and data collection and analysis techniques. The formulating and clarifying process is time consuming and will probably take you up blind alleys (Saunders and Lewis, 1997). However, without spending time on this stage you are far less likely to achieve a successful project (Raimond, 1993).

In the initial stages of the formulating and clarifying process you will be generating and refining research ideas (Section 2.3). It may be that you have already been given a research idea, perhaps by an organisation or tutor. Even if this has happened you will still need to refine the idea into one that is feasible. Once you have done this you will need to turn the idea into research questions and objectives (Section 2.4) and to write the research proposal for your project (Section 2.5).

However, before you start the formulating and clarifying process we believe that you need to understand what makes a good research topic. For this reason we begin this chapter with a discussion of the attributes required for a good research topic.

## 2.2   Attributes of a good research topic

The attributes of a business and management research topic do not vary a great deal between universities (Raimond, 1993), although there will be differences in the emphasis

The impact of video games on culture and society is a serious research topic, with Copenhagen University's Centre for Computer Games Research at the forefront (Boyd, 2004). This is one of the few places in the world where you can do PhD-level work in video game studies. The centre's purpose is to study how games are both made and played with the aim of using the findings to help design better games in the future. The centre's game room features a giant, flat panel television, complete with surround sound speakers as well as every available console gaming system, whilst shelves are filled with all the latest titles.

*Video games*

Academic interest in computer games has, like the industry, grown rapidly in recent years. Universities have added computer game design and theory courses to their portfolio and academics undertake research. Games similar to that illustrated in the photograph here have been used to explore how players develop hand–eye coordination and in multi-player mode study human rivalries! Researchers have looked at the ethics of games, women and women's issues in gaming and the practice of designing games. The theory that is being developed is influencing and informing game design.

placed on different attributes. If you are undertaking your research project as part of a course of study the most important attribute will be that it meets the examining body's requirements and, in particular, that it is at the correct level. This means that you must choose your topic with care. For example, some universities require students to collect their own data as part of their research project whereas others allow them to base their project on data that have already been collected. You therefore need to check the assessment criteria for your project and ensure that your choice of topic will enable you to meet these criteria. If you are unsure, you should discuss any uncertainties with your project tutor.

In addition, your research topic must be something you are capable of undertaking and one that excites your imagination. Capability can be considered in a variety of ways. At the personal level you need to feel comfortable that you have, or can develop, the skills that will be required to research the topic. We hope that you will develop your research skills as part of undertaking your project. However, some skills, for example foreign languages, may be impossible to acquire in the time you have available. As well as having the necessary skills we believe that you also need to have a genuine interest in the topic. Most research projects are undertaken over at least a six-month period. A topic in which you are only vaguely interested at the start is likely to become a topic in which you have no interest and with which you will fail to produce your best work.

Your ability to find the financial and time resources to undertake research on the topic will also affect your capability. Some topics are unlikely to be possible to complete in the time allowed by your course of study. This may be because they require you to measure the impact of an intervention over a long time period (Box 2.1). Similarly, topics that are likely to require you to travel widely or need expensive equipment should also be disregarded unless financial resources permit.

Capability also means you must be reasonably certain of gaining access to any data you might need to collect. Gill and Johnson (2002) argue that this is usually relatively straightforward to assess. They point out that many people start with ideas where access to data will prove difficult. Certain, more sensitive topics, such as financial performance or decision making by senior managers, are potentially fascinating. However, they may present considerable access problems. You should therefore discuss this with your project tutor after reading Chapter 6.

For most topics it is important that the issues within the research are capable of being linked to theory (Raimond, 1993). Initially, theory may be based just on the reading you have undertaken as part of your study to date. However, as part of your assessment criteria you are almost certain to be asked to set your topic in context (Section 3.2). As a consequence you will need to have a knowledge of the literature and to undertake further reading as part of defining your research questions and objectives (Section 2.4).

Most project tutors will argue that one of the attributes of a good topic is clearly defined research questions and objectives (Section 2.4). These will, along with a good knowledge of the literature, enable you to assess the extent to which your research is likely to provide fresh insights into the topic. Many students believe this is going to be difficult. Fortunately, as pointed out by Phillips and Pugh (2005), there are many ways in which such insight can be defined as 'fresh' (Section 2.5).

If you have already been given a research idea (perhaps by an organisation) you will need to ensure that your questions and objectives relate clearly to the idea (Kervin, 1999). It is also important that your topic will have a **symmetry of potential outcomes**: that is, your results will be of similar value whatever you find out (Gill and Johnson, 2002). Without this symmetry you may spend a considerable amount of time researching your topic only to find an answer of little importance. Whatever the outcome, you need to ensure you have the scope to write an interesting project report.

## BOX 2.1 WORKED EXAMPLE

### The problem of timescale and resources in doing research

Andrew was a part-time student who worked in a large firm of consulting engineers with projects throughout Europe and Asia. The company undertook such major projects as the building of a hospital in Asia and the construction of a major conference centre in a southern European city. Andrew was an operations director and had had particular responsibility for introducing a company intranet three months previous to the time of his research proposal. In part, the intranet was introduced with the idea of forging a sense of shared community between the consultants working on projects, whatever that project may be or wherever it was located. The consultant engineers were from all parts of the world, although English was the language in which the company's business was conducted. English would therefore be the medium for the intranet.

The specific 'shared community' objectives of the intranet were to reduce the feeling of isolation among the engineers, give them an immediate source of important company and technical information, and foster a sense of team spirit at both company and project level.

Andrew knew that the intranet was being used frequently and that informal feedback suggested that people liked it and found it useful. However, he wanted 'harder' evidence that the considerable resources the company had devoted to the introduction and implementation of the intranet were worth while.

He drafted an outline proposal and took it along to the first meeting with Sarah, his project tutor. To Andrew's surprise Sarah was sceptical about his idea. She thought three months was too short a timescale in which to judge the effects of the intranet in relation to the 'softer' anticipated outcomes of lack of isolation and fostering team spirit. She also thought that to meet the objectives Andrew would need to do some qualitative work. That would involve talking to engineers of different nationalities in different locations throughout the world. She felt that the quality of the data from the questionnaire that Andrew had thought about was unlikely to meet his objectives with sufficient authority.

Andrew felt dispirited when he left the meeting with Sarah. He'd agreed to think the matter over and then they would meet again a week later. But Andrew felt that Sarah might be right in her misgivings about the six-month period and he knew that he simply had insufficient time to carry out the primary research in the way Sarah had suggested. Maybe he would have to think of another approach ... or another dissertation topic.

Finally, it is important to consider your career goals (Creswell, 2002). If you wish to become an expert in a particular subject area or industry sector, it is sensible to use the opportunity to develop this expertise.

It is almost inevitable that the extent to which these attributes apply to your research topic will depend on your topic and the reasons for which you are undertaking the research. However, most of these attributes will apply. For this reason it is important that you check and continue to check any potential research topic against the summary checklist contained in Box 2.2.

## 2.3  Generating and refining research ideas

Some business and management students are expected both to generate and to refine their own research ideas. Others, particularly those on professional and post-experience

## Attributes of a good research topic

**Capability: is it feasible?**

☑ Is the topic something with which you are really fascinated?

☑ Do you have, or can you develop within the project time frame, the necessary research skills to undertake the topic?

☑ Is the research topic achievable within the available time?

☑ Will the project still be current when you finish your project?

☑ Is the research topic achievable within the financial resources that are likely to be available?

☑ Are you reasonably certain of being able to gain access to data you are likely to require for this topic?

**Appropriateness: is it worth while?**

☑ Does the topic fit the specifications and meet the standards set by the examining institution?

☑ Does your research topic contain issues that have a clear link to theory?

☑ Are you able to state your research question(s) and objectives clearly?

☑ Will your proposed research be able to provide fresh insights into this topic?

☑ Does your research topic relate clearly to the idea you have been given (perhaps by an organisation)?

☑ Are the findings for this research topic likely to be symmetrical: that is, of similar value whatever the outcome?

☑ Does the research topic match your career goals?

courses, are provided with a research idea by an organisation or their university. In the initial stages of their research they are expected to refine this to a clear and feasible idea that meets the requirements of the examining organisation. If you have already been given a research idea we believe you will still find it useful to read the next subsection, which deals with generating research ideas. Many of the techniques which can be used for generating research ideas can also be used for the refining process.

## Generating research ideas

If you have not been given an initial **research idea** there is a range of techniques that can be used to find and select a topic that you would like to research. They can be thought of as those that are predominantly **rational thinking** and those that involve more **creative thinking** (Table 2.1). The precise techniques that you choose to use and the order in which you use them are entirely up to you. However, like Raimond (1993), we believe you should use both rational and creative techniques, choosing those that you believe are going to be of most use to you and which you will enjoy using. By using one or more creative techniques you are more likely to ensure that your heart as well as your head is in your research project. In our experience, it is usually better to use a variety of techniques. In order to do this you will need to have some understanding of the techniques and the ways in which they work. We therefore outline the techniques in Table 2.1 and suggest possible ways they might be used to generate research ideas. These techniques will generate one of two outcomes:

- one or more possible project ideas that you might undertake;
- absolute panic because nothing in which you are interested or which seems suitable has come to mind (Jankowicz, 2005).

In either instance, but especially the latter, we suggest that you talk to your project tutor. Box 2.3 illustrates how ideas are at the heart of business and management life.

## Examining own strengths and interests

It is important that you choose a topic in which you are likely to do well and, if possible, already have some academic knowledge. Jankowicz (2005) suggests that one way of doing this is to look at those assignments for which you have received good grades. For most of these assignments they are also likely to be the topics in which you were interested (Box 2.1). They will provide you with an area in which to search and find a research idea. In addition you may, as part of your reading, be able to focus more precisely on the sort of ideas about which you wish to conduct your research.

As noted in Section 2.2, there is the need to think about your future. If you plan to work in financial management it would be sensible to choose a research project in the financial management field. One part of your course that will inevitably be discussed at any job interview is your research project. A project in the same field will provide you with the opportunity to display clearly your depth of knowledge and your enthusiasm.

## Looking at past project titles

Many of our students have found looking at *past projects* a useful way of generating research ideas. For undergraduate and taught masters degrees these are often called **dissertations**. For research degrees they are termed **theses**. A common way of doing this is to scan a list of past project titles (such as those in Appendix 1) for anything that captures your imagination. Titles that look interesting or which grab your attention should be noted down, as should any thoughts you have about the title in relation to your own research idea. In this process the fact that the title is poorly worded or the project report received a low mark is immaterial. What matters is the fact that you have found a topic that interests you. Based on this you can think of new ideas in the same general area that will enable you to provide fresh insights.

Scanning actual research projects may also produce research ideas. However, you need to beware. The fact that a project is in your library is no guarantee of the quality of the arguments and observations it contains. In many universities all projects are placed in the library whether they are bare passes or distinctions.

**Table 2.1  More frequently used techniques for generating and refining research ideas**

| Rational thinking | Creative thinking |
|---|---|
| ■ Examining your own strengths and interests<br>■ Looking at past project titles<br>■ Discussion<br>■ Searching the literature | ■ Keeping a notebook of ideas<br>■ Exploring personal preferences using past projects<br>■ Relevance trees<br>■ Brainstorming |

## BOX 2.3 FOCUS ON MANAGEMENT RESEARCH

### The role of ideas in the manager's workplace

The conclusions in a 2004 article in *Management Decision* are not encouraging for part-time students who are practising managers. In this article Rothberg (2004) explores the role of ideas in organisations. He argues that ideas are critical for the ultimate success of organisations. Indeed, they are an essential management resource. He notes that those managers who understand what is happening to ideas in their workplace, and their organisation's environment, will be well placed to benefit from them.

In Rothberg's view ideas may be implicit, taken for granted, encouraged or ignored. He points out that ideas are understood relative to their framework. This includes the interaction of ideas within the framework in use (such as accepted practice), against the framework in use (such as unconventional or hostile activity) and in terms of shifting the framework (such as by changing the rules).

Rothberg's study is an interesting look at how to understand the role of ideas within and upon management and the organisation. It is also a study of the way in which ideas are accommodated in the frameworks used by managers.

Rothberg addresses the topic in four stages: the available frameworks or mindsets within which ideas are approached; the selective framework of mainstream management theory; a survey of what happens to ideas in the workplace; and conclusions from the study.

A pilot survey about what happens to ideas in the workplace was undertaken among 49 managers participating in advanced management programmes at two Australian universities during 2002 and 2003. The exploratory study focused upon the perceived assessment of ideas in the organisations of these managers. The participants had no forewarning of the survey, nor its intent. The managers were from different organisations. They voluntarily and anonymously completed a questionnaire of 23 questions about what was happening to ideas in their organisation. The managers were asked their views about themselves, their workplaces and their managers.

Rothberg's research suggests the following.

1 There is a clear dichotomy of support for ideas in the workplace; in effect, some workplaces are considered friendly and others unfriendly to ideas. Only about half of the respondents thought that it was possible to get ideas considered in their workplace. There was wide reporting of a substantial lack of support, and lack of encouragement for ideas. A significant minority of managers were reported never to offer support for ideas, with a sizable proportion reporting equivocation about the availability of support.

2 The general environment for ideas appears disparate and lax, with managers contributing considerably less than their potential to their enterprises and society. Based on the reported dichotomy among the workplaces, clearly some organisations and their managers are consistently un-engaged in implementing ideas. The findings suggest that the approach managers use in their enterprises shows very wide variation to the point of suppressing, ignoring and being indifferent to ideas.

3 In the functional areas of task and process, there is encouraging evidence that managers know more about improving outcomes than they are sharing. While this may simply be a boast, other evidence suggests that there is sub-optimal encouragement and reward for ideas.

4 Colleagues are not overwhelmingly supportive of each other when it comes to approachability and follow-through with ideas. There is a lack of collegiate confidence, while dependability offers scope for improvement.

## Discussion

Colleagues, friends and university tutors are all good sources of possible project ideas. Often project tutors will have ideas for possible student projects, which they will be pleased to discuss with you. In addition, ideas can be obtained by talking to practitioners and professional groups (Gill and Johnson, 2002). It is important that as well as discussing possible ideas you also make a note of them. What seemed like a good idea in the coffee shop may not be remembered quite so clearly after the following lecture!

## Searching the literature

As part of your discussions, relevant literature may also be suggested. Sharp *et al.* (2002) discuss types of literature that are of particular use for generating research ideas. These include:

- articles in academic and professional journals;
- reports;
- books.

Of particular use are academic **review articles**. These articles contain both a considered review of the state of knowledge in that topic area and pointers towards areas where further research needs to be undertaken. In addition you can browse recent publications, in particular journals, for possible research ideas (Section 3.5). For many subject areas your project tutor will be able to suggest possible recent review articles, or articles that contain recommendations for further work. *Reports* may also be of use. The most recently published are usually up to date and, again, often contain recommendations that may form the basis of your research idea. *Books* by contrast are less up to date than other written sources. They do, however, often contain a good overview of research that has been undertaken, which may suggest ideas to you.

Searching for publications is only possible when you have at least some idea of the area in which you wish to undertake your research. One way of obtaining this is to re-examine your lecture notes and course textbooks and to note those subjects that appear most interesting (discussed earlier in this section) and the names of relevant authors. This will give you a basis on which to undertake a **preliminary search** (using techniques outlined in Sections 3.4 and 3.5). When the articles, reports and other items have been obtained it is often helpful to look for unfounded assertions and statements on the absence of research (Raimond, 1993), as these are likely to contain ideas that will enable you to provide fresh insights.

## Keeping a notebook of ideas

One of the more creative techniques that we all use is to keep a **notebook of ideas**. All this involves is simply noting down any interesting research ideas as you think of them and, of equal importance, what sparked off your thought. You can then pursue the idea using more rational thinking techniques later. Mark keeps a notebook by his bed so he can jot down any flashes of inspiration that occur to him in the middle of the night!

## Exploring personal preferences using past projects

Another way of generating possible project ideas is to explore your *personal preferences* using past project reports from your university. To do this Raimond (1993) suggests that you:

1 Select six projects that you like.
2 For each of these six projects note down your first thoughts in response to three questions (if responses for different projects are the same this does not matter):

   **a**  What appeals to you about the project?

   **b**  What is good about the project?

   **c**  Why is the project good?

**3**  Select three projects that you do not like.

**4**  For each of these three projects note down your first thoughts in response to three questions (if responses for different projects are the same, or cannot be clearly expressed, this does not matter; note them down anyway):

   **a**  What do you dislike about the project?

   **b**  What is bad about the project?

   **c**  Why is the project bad?

You now have a list of what you consider to be excellent and what you consider to be poor in projects. This will not be the same as a list generated by anyone else. It is also very unlikely to match the attributes of a good research project (Box 2.2). However, by examining this list you will begin to understand those project characteristics that are important to you and with which you feel comfortable. Of equal importance is that you will have identified those that you are uncomfortable with and should avoid. These can be used as the parameters against which to evaluate possible research ideas.

## Relevance trees

Relevance trees may also prove useful in generating research topics. In this instance, their use is similar to that of mind mapping (Buzan, 2006), in which you start with a broad concept from which you generate further (usually more specific) topics. Each of these topics forms a separate branch from which you can generate further, more detailed sub-branches. As you proceed down the sub-branches more ideas are generated and recorded. These can then be examined and a number selected and combined to provide a research idea (Sharp *et al.*, 2002). This technique is discussed in more detail in Section 3.4, which also includes a worked example of a relevance tree.

## Brainstorming

The technique of **brainstorming** (Box 2.4), taught as a problem-solving technique on many business and management courses, can also be used to generate and refine research ideas. It is best undertaken with a group of people, although you can brainstorm on your own. To brainstorm, Moody (1988) suggests that you:

**1**  Define your problem – that is, the sorts of ideas you are interested in – as precisely as possible. In the early stages of formulating a topic this may be as vague as 'I am interested in marketing but don't know what to do for my research topic.'

**2**  Ask for suggestions, relating to the problem.

**3**  Record all suggestions, observing the following rules:

   –  No suggestion should be criticised or evaluated in any way before all ideas have been considered.

   –  All suggestions, however wild, should be recorded and considered.

   –  As many suggestions as possible should be recorded.

**4**  Review all the suggestions and explore what is meant by each.

**5**  Analyse the list of suggestions and decide which appeal to you most as research ideas and why.

## BOX 2.4 WORKED EXAMPLE

### Brainstorming

George's main interest was football. When he finished university he wanted to work in marketing, preferably for a sports goods manufacturer. He had examined his own strengths and discovered that his best marks were in marketing. He wanted to do his research project on some aspect of marketing, preferably linked to football, but had no real research idea. He asked three friends, all taking business studies degrees, to help him brainstorm the problem.

George began by explaining the problem in some detail. At first the suggestions emerged slowly. He noted them down on the whiteboard. Soon the board was covered with suggestions. George counted these and discovered there were over 100.

Reviewing individual suggestions produced nothing that any of the group felt to be of sufficient merit for a research project. However, one of George's friends pointed out that combining the suggestions of Premier League football, television rights and sponsorship might provide an idea which satisfied the assessment requirements of the project.

They discussed the suggestion further, and George noted the research idea as 'something about how confining the rights to show live Premiership football to Sky TV would impact upon the sale of Premiership club-specific merchandise'.

George arranged to see his project tutor to discuss how to refine the idea they had just generated.

## Refining research ideas

### The Delphi technique

An additional approach that our students have found particularly useful in refining their research ideas is the **Delphi technique** (Box 2.5). This involves using a group of people who are either involved or interested in the research idea to generate and choose a more specific research idea (Robson, 2002). To use this technique you need:

1  to brief the members of the group about the research idea (they can make notes if they wish);

2  at the end of the briefing to encourage group members to seek clarification and more information as appropriate;

3  to ask each member of the group, including the originator of the research idea, to generate independently up to three specific research ideas based on the idea that has been described (they can also be asked to provide a justification for their specific ideas);

4  to collect the research ideas in an unedited and non-attributable form and to distribute them to all members of the group;

5  a second cycle of the process (steps 2 to 4) in which individuals comment on the research ideas and revise their own contributions in the light of what others have said;

6  subsequent cycles of the process until a consensus is reached. These either follow a similar pattern (steps 2 to 4) or use discussion, voting or some other method.

This process works well, not least because people enjoy trying to help one another. In addition, it is very useful in moulding groups into a cohesive whole.

## BOX 2.5 WORKED EXAMPLE

### Using a Delphi Group

Tim explained to the group that his research idea was concerned with understanding the decision-making processes associated with mortgage applications and loan advances. His briefing to the three other group members, and the questions that they asked him, considered aspects such as:

■ the influences on a potential first-time buyer to approach a specific financial institution;

■ the influence on decision making of face-to-face contact between potential borrowers and potential lenders.

The group then moved on to generate a number of more specific research ideas, among which were the following:

■ the factors that influenced potential first-time house purchasers to deal with particular financial institutions;

■ the effect of interpersonal contact on mortgage decisions;

■ the qualities that potential applicants look for in mortgage advisers.

These were considered and commented on by all the group members. At the end of the second cycle Tim had, with the other students' agreement, refined his research idea to:

■ the way in which a range of factors influenced potential first-time buyers' choice of lending institution.

He now needed to pursue these ideas by undertaking a preliminary search of the literature.

### The preliminary study

Even if you have been given a research idea, it is still necessary to refine it in order to turn it into a research project. Some authors, for example Bennett (1991), refer to this process as a **preliminary study**. For some research ideas this will be no more than a review of some of the literature, including news items (Box 2.6). This can be thought of as the first iteration of your critical literature review (Figure 3.1). For others it may include revisiting the techniques discussed earlier in this section as well as informal discussions with people who have personal experience of and knowledge about your research ideas. In some cases **shadowing** employees who are likely to be important in your research may also provide insights. If you are planning on undertaking your research within an organisation it is important to gain a good understanding of your host organisation (Kervin, 1999). However, whatever techniques you choose, the underlying purpose is to gain a greater understanding so that your research question can be refined.

At this stage you need to be testing your research ideas against the checklist in Box 2.2 and where necessary changing them. It may be that after a preliminary study, or discussing your ideas with colleagues, you decide that the research idea is no longer feasible in the form in which you first envisaged it. If this is the case, do not be too downhearted. It is far better to revise your research ideas at this stage than to have to do it later, when you have undertaken far more work.

## BOX 2.6 RESEARCH IN THE NEWS

### China's increasing influence in IT research and manufacturing

Recent research by economist Jonathan Anderson of UBS suggests that rather than taking over the role in IT supply played by neighbours Japan, South Korea and Taiwan, China has instead become a new link in the supply chain that connects its neighbours to global markets. "Based on broad trade data, China's electronics growth still looks relatively 'friendly' for the rest of the world," Mr Anderson says.

Indeed, much of the shift of production to China has been organised by foreign companies themselves, and they dominate the industry. Overseas-invested companies accounted for more than 87 per cent of China's 2004 exports of "new and high technology" products, a category dominated by IT, according to data from the Ministry of Commerce.

There are plenty of exceptions. Chinese telecoms equipment manufacturers ZTE and Huawei, for example, now compete internationally with global giants such as Nokia and Lucent for contracts to build the newest "third generation" mobile networks.

Both companies are making full use of their ability to hire large corps of engineers for salaries just a fraction of those commanded by counterparts in the US, Europe or Japan.

ZTE and Huawei also spend 10 per cent or more of their revenue on R&D, allowing them to make up ground rapidly on market leaders. Chinese companies can spend less on R&D but get more researchers, says Hou Weigui, chairman of ZTE: "In some ways this is our edge."

The telecom equipment vendors are exceptions however. Few Chinese companies are willing to put as much into R&D. Mr De Luca of Logitech for example, notes that local competitors in the computer peripherals business usually spend less than 1 per cent, while the Swiss-US market leader invests 5.5 per cent. That means it can keep coming up with new features such as laser-equipped mice that command higher prices and fatter margins.

Chinese companies also have no monopoly of access to the 300,000 or so engineers who graduate from the country's universities every year. Clusters of well-funded foreign-owned R&D centres are growing in Beijing, Shanghai and in second-tier cities – and they compete with local ventures for the best talent.

Mr Hou says ZTE's two decades of experience in Chinese R&D is difficult to match, but he acknowledges that this will not be true forever. "It's hard to say for sure, but our advantage will be relatively clear for the next three to five years," he says.

ZTE and its peers have already largely lost any edge gained by using factories in China, as foreign IT manufacturers cut the numbers of their expatriate staff to reduce costs, while often also benefiting from special tax breaks and investment incentives.

*Source*: Article by Mure Dickie, *Financial Times*, 19 October 2005. Copyright © 2005 The Financial Times Ltd.

### Integrating ideas

The integration of ideas from these techniques is essential if your research is to have a clear direction and not contain a mismatch between objectives and your final project report. Jankowicz (2005:34–6) suggests an integrative process that our students have found most useful. This he terms 'working up and narrowing down'. It involves classifying each research idea first into its area, then its field, and finally the precise aspect in which you are interested. These represent an increasingly detailed description of the research idea. Thus your initial area, based on examining your course work, might be accountancy. After browsing some recent journals and discussion with colleagues this becomes more focused on the field of financial accounting methods. With further reading, the use of the Delphi technique and discussion with your project tutor you decide to focus on the aspect of activity-based costing.

You will know when the process of generating and refining ideas is complete as you will be able to say 'I'd like to do some research on . . .'. Obviously there will still be a big gap between this and the point when you are ready to start serious work on your research. Sections 2.4 and 2.5 will ensure that you are ready to bridge that gap.

### Refining topics given by your employing organisation

If, as a part-time student, your manager gives you a topic, this may present particular problems. It may be something in which you are not particularly interested. In this case you will have to weigh the advantage of doing something useful to the organisation against the disadvantage of a potential lack of personal motivation. You therefore need to achieve a balance. Often the project your manager wishes you to undertake is larger than that which is appropriate for your course project. In such cases, it may be possible to complete both by isolating an element of the larger organisational project that you find interesting and treating this as the project for your course.

One of our students was asked to do a preliminary investigation of the strengths and weaknesses of her organisation's pay system and then to recommend consultants to design and implement a new system. She was not particularly interested in this project. However, she was considering becoming a freelance personnel consultant. Therefore, for her course project she decided to study the decision-making process in relation to the appointment of personnel consultants. Her organisation's decision on which consultant to appoint, and why this decision was taken, proved to be a useful case study against which to compare management decision-making theory.

In this event you would write a larger report for your organisation and a part of it for your project report. Section 14.4 offers some guidance on writing two separate reports for different audiences.

## 2.4 | Turning research ideas into research projects

### Writing research questions

Much is made in this book of the importance of defining clear **research questions** at the beginning of the research process. The importance of this cannot be overemphasised. One of the key criteria of your research success will be whether you have a set of clear conclusions drawn from the data you have collected. The extent to which you can do that will be determined largely by the clarity with which you have posed your initial research questions (Box 2.7).

Defining research questions, rather like generating research ideas (Section 2.3), is not a straightforward matter. It is important that the question is sufficiently involved to generate the sort of project that is consistent with the standards expected of you (Box 2.2). A question that prompts a descriptive answer, for example 'What is the proportion of graduates entering the civil service who attended the old-established UK universities?', is far easier to answer than: 'Why are graduates from old-established UK universities more likely to enter the civil service than graduates from other universities?' More will be said about the importance of theory in defining the research question later in this section. However, beware of research questions that are too easy.

It is perhaps more likely that you fall into the trap of asking research questions that are too difficult. The question cited above, 'Why are graduates from old-established UK universities more likely to enter the civil service than graduates from other universities?' is a case in point. It would probably be very difficult to gain sufficient access to the inner portals of the civil service to get a good grasp of the subtle 'unofficial' processes that go

## BOX 2.7 WORKED EXAMPLE

### Defining the research question

Imran was studying for a BA in Business Studies and doing his placement year in an advanced consumer electronics company. When he first joined the company he was surprised to note that the company's business strategy, which was announced in the company newsletter, seemed to be inconsistent with what Imran knew of the product market.

Imran had become particularly interested in corporate strategy in his degree. He was familiar with some of the literature that suggested that corporate strategy should be linked to the general external environment in which the organisation operated. He wanted to do some research on corporate strategy in his organisation for his degree dissertation.

After talking this over with his project tutor Imran decided on the following research question: 'Why does [organisation's name] corporate strategy not seem to reflect the major factors in the external operating environment?'

on at staff selection which may favour one type of candidate over another. Over-reaching yourself in the definition of research questions is a danger.

Clough and Nutbrown (2002) use what they call the '**Goldilocks test**' to decide if research questions are either 'too big', 'too small', 'too hot' or 'just right'. Those that are too big probably need significant research funding because they demand too many resources. Questions that are too small are likely to be of insufficient substance, while those that are too 'hot' may be so because of sensitivities that may be aroused as a result of doing the research. This may be because of the timing of the research or the many other reasons that may upset key people who have a role to play, either directly or indirectly, in the research context. Research questions that are 'just right', note Clough and Nutbrown (2002:34), are those that are 'just right for investigation at *this* time, by *this* researcher in *this* setting'.

The pitfall that you must avoid at all costs is asking research questions that will not generate new insights (Box 2.2). This raises the question of the extent to which you have consulted the relevant literature. It is perfectly legitimate to replicate research because you have a genuine concern about its applicability to your research setting (for example, your organisation). However, it certainly is not legitimate to display your ignorance of the literature.

McNiff and Whitehead (2000) make the point that the research question may not emerge until the research process has started and is therefore part of the process of '*progressive illumination*'. They note that this is particularly likely to be the case in practitioner action research (Section 4.3).

It is often a useful starting point in the writing of research questions to begin with one **general focus research question** that flows from your research idea. This may lead to several more detailed questions or the definition of research objectives. Table 2.2 has some examples of general focus research questions.

In order to clarify the research question Clough and Nutbrown (2002) talk of the Russian doll principle. This means taking the research idea and 'breaking down the research questions from the original statement to something which strips away the complication of layers and obscurities until the very essence – the heart – of the question can be expressed . . . just as the Russian doll is taken apart to reveal a tiny doll at the centre' (Clough and Nutbrown, 2002:34).

Writing your research questions will be, in most cases, your individual concern but it is useful to get other people to help you. An obvious source of guidance is your project

**Table 2.2  Examples of research ideas and their derived focus research questions**

| Research idea | General focus research questions |
| --- | --- |
| Advertising and share prices | How does the running of a TV advertising campaign designed to boost the image of a company affect its share price? |
| Job recruitment via the Internet | How effective is recruiting for new staff via the Internet in comparison with traditional methods? |
| The use of aromas as a marketing device | In what ways does the use of specific aromas in supermarkets affect buyer behaviour? |
| The use of internet banking | What effect has the growth of Internet banking had upon the uses customers make of branch facilities? |

tutor. Consulting your project tutor will avoid the pitfalls of the questions that are too easy or too difficult or have been answered before. Discussing your area of interest with your project tutor will lead to your research questions becoming much clearer.

Prior to discussion with your project tutor you may wish to conduct a brainstorming session with your peers or use the Delphi technique (Section 2.3). Your research questions may flow from your initial examination of the relevant literature. As outlined in Section 2.3, journal articles reporting primary research will often end with a conclusion that includes the consideration by the author of the implications for future research of the work in the article. This may be phrased in the form of research questions. However, even if it is not, it may suggest pertinent research questions to you.

## Writing research objectives

Your research may begin with a general focus research question that then generates more detailed research questions, or you may use your general focus research question as a base from which you write a set of **research objectives**. Objectives are more generally acceptable to the research community as evidence of the researcher's clear sense of purpose and direction. It may be that either is satisfactory. Do check whether your examining body has a preference.

We contend that research objectives are likely to lead to greater specificity than research or investigative questions. Table 2.3 illustrates this point. It summarises the objectives of some research conducted by one of our students. Expression of the first research question as an objective prompted a consideration of the objectives of the organisations. This was useful because it led to the finding that there often were no clear objectives. This in itself was an interesting theoretical discovery.

The second and third objectives **operationalise** the matching research questions by introducing the notion of explicit effectiveness criteria. In a similar way the fourth objective (parts a and b) and the fifth objective are specific about factors that lead to effectiveness in question 4. The biggest difference between the questions and objectives is illustrated by the way in which the fifth question becomes the fifth objective. They are similar but differ in the way that the objective makes clear that a theory will be developed that will make a causal link between two sets of variables: effectiveness factors and team briefing success.

Table 2.3 **Phrasing research questions as research objectives**

| Research question | Research objective |
|---|---|
| 1 Why have organisations introduced team briefing? | 1 To identify organisations' objectives for team briefing schemes. |
| 2 How can the effectiveness of team briefing schemes be measured? | 2 To establish suitable effectiveness criteria for team briefing schemes. |
| 3 Has team briefing been effective? | 3 To describe the extent to which the effectiveness criteria for team briefing have been met. |
| 4 How can the effectiveness of team briefing be explained? | 4a To determine the factors associated with the effectiveness criteria for team briefing being met. |
| | b To estimate whether some of those factors are more influential than other factors. |
| 5 Can the explanation be generalised? | 5 To develop an explanatory theory that associates certain factors with the effectiveness of team briefing schemes. |

This is not to say that the research questions could not have been written with a similar amount of specificity. They could. Indeed, you may find it easier to write specific research questions than objectives. However, we doubt whether the same level of precision could be achieved through the writing of research questions alone. Research objectives require more rigorous thinking, which derives from the use of more formal language.

Maylor and Blackmon (2005) recommend that personal objectives may be added to the list of research objectives. These may be concerned with your specific learning objectives from completion of the research (e.g. to learn how to use a particular statistical software package or improve your word processing ability) or more general personal objectives such as enhancing your career prospects through learning about a new field of your specialism.

Maylor and Blackmon suggest that such personal objectives would be better were they to pass the well-known SMART test. That is that the objectives are:

- *Specific*. What precisely do you hope to achieve from undertaking the research?
- *Measurable*. What measures will you use to determine whether you have achieved your objectives? (e.g. secured a career-level first job in software design).
- *Achievable*. Are the targets you have set for yourself achievable given all the possible constraints?
- *Realistic*. Given all the other demands upon your time, will you have the time and energy to complete the research on time?
- *Timely*. Will you have time to accomplish all your objectives in the time frame you have set?

## The importance of theory in writing research questions and objectives

Section 4.1 outlines the role of theory in helping you to decide your approach to research design. However, your consideration of theory should begin earlier than this. It should inform your definition of research questions and objectives.

**Theory** (Box 2.8) is defined by Gill and Johnson (2002:229) as 'a formulation regarding the cause and effect relationships between two or more variables, which may or may not have been tested'.

## BOX 2.8 FOCUS ON MANAGEMENT RESEARCH

### Clarifying what theory is not

Sutton and Staw (1995) make a useful contribution to the clarification of what theory is by defining what it is not. In their view theory is not:

1 *References.* Listing references to existing theories and mentioning the names of such theories may look impressive. But what is required if a piece of writing is to 'contain theory' is that a logical argument to explain the reasons for the described phenomena must be included. The key word here is 'why': why did the things you describe occur? What is the logical explanation?

2 *Data.* In a similar point to the one above, Sutton and Staw argue that data merely describe which empirical patterns were observed: theory explains why these patterns were observed or are expected to be observed. 'The data do not generate theory – only researchers do that' (Sutton and Staw, 1995:372).

3 *Lists of variables.* Sutton and Staw argue that a list of variables which constitutes a logical attempt to cover the determinants of a given process or outcome do not comprise a theory. Simply listing variables which may predict an outcome is insufficient: what is required for the presence of theory is an explanation of why predictors are likely to be strong predictors.

4 *Diagrams.* Boxes and arrows can add order to a conception by illustrating patterns and causal relationships but they rarely explain why the relationships have occurred. Indeed, Sutton and Staw (1995:374) note that 'a clearly written argument should preclude the inclusion of the most complicated figures – those more closely resembling a complex wiring diagram than a comprehensible theory'.

5 *Hypotheses or predictions.* Hypotheses can be part of a sound conceptual argument. But they do not contain logical arguments about why empirical relationships are expected to occur.

Sutton and Staw (1995:375) sum up by stating that 'theory is about the connections between phenomena, a story about why events, structure and thoughts occur. Theory emphasises the nature of causal relationships, identifying what comes first as well as the timing of events. Strong theory, in our view, delves into underlying processes so as to understand the systematic reasons for a particular occurrence or nonoccurrence'.

In a similar contribution to that of Sutton and Staw (1995), Whetten (1989) contends that if the presence of theory is to be guaranteed, the researcher must ensure that what is passing as good theory includes a plausible, coherent explanation for why certain relationships should be expected in our data.

There is probably no word that is more misused and misunderstood in education than the word 'theory'. It is thought that material included in textbooks is 'theory' whereas what is happening in the 'real world' is practice. Students who saw earlier drafts of this book remarked that they were pleased that the book was not too 'theoretical'. What they meant was that the book concentrated on giving lots of practical advice. Yet the book is full of theory. Advising you to carry out research in a particular way (variable A) is based on the theory that this will yield effective results (variable B). This is the cause and effect relationship referred to in the definition of theory cited above.

The definition demonstrates that 'theory' has a specific meaning. It refers to situations where if A is introduced B will be the consequence. Therefore the marketing manager may theorise that the introduction of loyalty cards by a supermarket will lead to customers being less likely to shop regularly at a competitor supermarket. That is a theory. Yet the marketing manager would probably not recognise it as such. He or she is still less likely to refer to it as a theory, particularly in the company of fellow managers. Many managers are very dismissive of any talk that smacks of 'theory'. It is thought of as something that is all very well to learn about at business school but bears little relation to what goes on in everyday organisational life. Yet the loyalty card example shows that it has everything to do with what goes on in everyday organisational life.

Section 4.1 notes that every purposive decision we take is based on theory: that certain consequences will flow from the decision. It follows from this that every managers' meeting that features a number of decisions will be a meeting that is highly **theory dependent** (Gill and Johnson, 2002). All that will be missing is a realisation of this fact. So, if theory is something that is so rooted in our everyday lives it certainly is something that we need not be apprehensive about. If it is implicit in all our decisions and actions, then recognising its importance means making it explicit. In research the importance of theory must be recognised: therefore it must be made explicit.

Kerlinger and Lee (2000) reinforce Gill and Johnson's definition by noting that the purpose of examining relationships between two or more variables is to explain and predict these relationships. Gill and Johnson (2002:33) neatly tie these purposes of theory to their definition:

> . . . it is also evident that if we have the expectation that by doing A, B will happen, then by manipulating the occurrence of A we can begin to predict and influence the occurrence of B. In other words, theory is clearly enmeshed in practice since explanation enables prediction which in turn enables control.

In our example, the marketing manager theorised that the introduction of loyalty cards by a supermarket would lead to customers being less likely to shop regularly at a competitor supermarket. Following Gill and Johnson's (2002:33) point that 'explanation enables prediction which in turn enables control', the supermarket would be well advised to conduct research that yielded an explanation of why loyalty cards encourage loyalty. Is it a purely economic rationale? Does it foster the 'collector' instinct in all of us? Does it appeal to a sense of thrift in us that helps us cope with an ever more wasteful world? These explanations are probably complex and interrelated. Reaching a better understanding of them would help the marketing manager to predict the outcome of any changes to the scheme. Increasing the amount of points per item would be effective if the economic explanation was valid. Increasing the range of products on which extra points were offered might appeal to the 'collector' instinct. More accurate prediction would offer the marketing manager increased opportunities for control.

The explanations for particular outcomes are a concern for Mackenzie (2000a, 2000b). His argument is that much research (he used the example of employee opinion surveys) yield ambiguous conclusions because they only ask questions which reveal the state of affairs as they exist (in his example, the thinking of employees in regard to, say, their pay). What they do not ask is questions which help those using the research results to draw meaningful conclusions as to why the state of affairs is as it is. If meaningful conclusions cannot be drawn then appropriate actions cannot be taken to remedy such deficiencies (or improve upon the efficiencies) that the research reveals. Usually such additional questions would involve discovering the key implementation processes (in the case of pay these may be the way in which managers make and communicate pay distribution decisions) which may shed light on the reasons why such deficiencies (or efficiencies) exist.

Mackenzie used the metaphor of the knobs on an old-fashioned radio to illustrate his argument. If the radio is playing a station and you are unhappy with what is being received, you will turn the volume knob to alter the volume or the tuning knob to change the station. He argues that the typical questionnaire survey is like the radio without knobs. You cannot make the results more useful, by knowing more about their causes, because you have no means to do so. All you have for your results is a series of what Mackenzie (2000a:136) terms 'knobless items', in which you are asking for respondents' opinions without asking for the reasons why they hold these opinions. What Mackenzie advocates is including **'knobs'** in the data collection process so that the causal relationship between a process and an outcome can be established.

Phillips and Pugh (2005) distinguish between research and what they call **intelligence gathering**, using what Mackenzie (2000a, 2000b) calls 'knobless items'. The latter is the gathering of facts (Box 2.9). For example, what is the relative proportion of undergraduates to postgraduates reading this book? What is the current spend per employee on training in the UK? What provision do small businesses make for bad debts? This is often called descriptive research (Section 4.2) and may form part of your research project. Descriptive research would be the first step in our example of supermarket loyalty card marketing. Establishing that there had been a change in customer behaviour following the introduction of supermarket loyalty cards would be the first step prior to any attempt at explanation.

Phillips and Pugh contrast such 'what' questions with 'why' questions. Examples of these 'why' questions are as follows: Why do British organisations spend less per head on training than German organisations? Why are new car purchasers reluctant to take out extended warranties on their vehicles? Why do some travellers still prefer to use cross-channel ferries as opposed to the Channel Tunnel? Such questions go 'beyond description and require analysis'. They look for 'explanations, relationships, comparisons, predictions, generalisations and theories' (Phillips and Pugh, 2005:48).

It is a short step from the 'why' research question to the testing of an existing theory in a new situation or the development of your own theory. This may be expressed as a hypothesis that is to be tested (Section 4.1), or the eventual answer to your research question may be the development or amendment of a theory (Box 2.10).

Although intelligence gathering will play a part in your research, it is unlikely to be enough. You should be seeking to explain phenomena, to analyse relationships, to compare what is going on in different research settings, to predict outcomes and to gen-

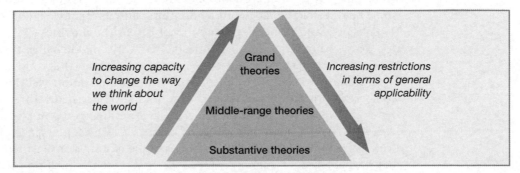

**Figure 2.1    Grand, middle range and substantive theories**

## BOX 2.9 RESEARCH IN THE NEWS

### The increasingly important role of women in Hong Kong business

Although the role and status of women in Hong Kong have come a long way and a growing number of successful businesses are now run by women, some executives say the territory's corporate world is still dominated by men. Women certainly make less money on average.

According to a recent government report, the number of female managers and administrators in Hong Kong rose from 40,300 in 1993 to 73,900 in 2004, while their male counterparts fell from 211,400 in 1993 to 202,000 in 2004.

Meanwhile, the number of male homemakers has risen from 9,100 in 2000 to 11,800 last year, as the number of housewives dropped from 730,000 to 647,500.

Women last year made up 26.8 per cent of all management positions in Hong Kong, compared with 16 per cent in 1993. And although the figure is quite low, it is considered high in Asia.

According to the Switzerland based International Labour Organisation, a quarter of legislators, senior officials and managers in Hong Kong were women in 2003, higher than the 5 per cent in South Korea, 9 per cent in Japan, 20 per cent in Malaysia and 24 per cent in Singapore. The average in Denmark, Finland, Sweden, Canada and the US was 32 per cent.

Executives and human resources professionals say women in Hong Kong enjoy equal opportunities at work. They also say Hong Kong is an easy place for women to work even compared with Europe and the US, thanks to the short distance between homes and offices as well as the availability of domestic helpers and, more importantly, parents. Many people in Hong Kong live close to their parents after they marry, relying on them for everything from meals to childcare.

But in spite of the growing status of women they still earn less than men generally, says the government report. The median monthly incomes for men and women in 2004 were HK$11,000 and HK$8,000 respectively. While a typical female manager earned HK$25,000 per month last year, her male counterpart made HK$30,000. A women professional was paid HK$28,000, but a male one received HK$30,000.

The most senior positions in Hong Kong are still occupied by men. Only 4.5 per cent of board directors in Hong Kong are women, compared with 6 per cent in Singapore and 26.2 per cent in Norway, according to the London-based Ethical Investment Research Service.

A recent survey by the Hong Kong Institute of Certified Public Accountants also shows that although nearly half of the accounting jobs in Hong Kong are held by women, only 22 per cent of the territory's chief financial officials are female.

*Source*: Article by Justine Lau, *Financial Times*, 20 October 2005. Copyright © 2005 The Financial Times Ltd.

eralise; then you will be working at the theoretical level. This is a necessary requirement for most research projects.

You may still be concerned that the necessity to be theory dependent in your research project means that you will have to develop a ground-breaking theory that will lead to a whole new way of thinking about management. If this is the case you should take heart from the threefold typology of theories summarised by Creswell (2002) (see Figure 2.1). He talks of 'grand theories', usually thought to be the province of the natural scientists (e.g. Darwin and Newton). He contrasts these with 'middle-range theories', which lack the capacity to change the way in which we think about the world but are nonetheless of significance. Some of the theories of human motivation well known to managers would be in this category. However, most of us are concerned with 'substantive theories' that are restricted to a particular time, research setting, group or population or problem (Creswell, 2002). For example, studying the reasons why a total quality initiative in a particular organisation failed would be an example of a substantive theory. Restricted they may be, but a host of 'substantive theories' that present similar propositions may lead to 'middle-range theories'. By developing 'substantive theories', however modest, we are

## BOX 2.10 WORKED EXAMPLE

### Writing a research question based on theory

Justine was a final-year marketing undergraduate who was interested in the theory of cognitive dissonance (Festinger, 1957). She wanted to apply this to the consumer purchasing decision in the snack foods industry (for example, potato crisps) in the light of the adverse publicity that the consumption of such foods was having as a result of the 'healthy eating' campaign.

Justine applied Festinger's theory by arguing in her research project proposal that a consumer who learns that snack over-eating is bad for her health will experience dissonance, because the knowledge that snack over-eating is bad for her health is dissonant with the cognition that she continues to over-eat snacks. She can reduce the dissonance by changing her behaviour, i.e., she could stop over-eating. (This would be consonant with the cognition that snack over-eating is bad for her health.) Alternatively, she could reduce dissonance by changing her cognition about the effect of snack over-eating on health and persuade herself that snack over-eating does not have a harmful effect on health. She would look for positive effects of snack over-eating, e.g. by believing that snack over-eating is an important source of enjoyment which outweighs any harmful effects. Alternatively she might persuade herself that the risk to health from snack over-eating is negligible compared with the danger of car accidents (reducing the importance of the dissonant cognition).

Justine's research question was 'How does the adverse "healthy eating" campaign publicity affect the consumer's decision to purchase snack foods?'

doing our bit as researchers to enhance our understanding of the world about us. A grand claim, but a valid one!

This discussion of theory does assume that a clear theoretical position is developed prior to the collection of data (the **deductive approach**). This will not always be the case. It may be that your study is based on the principle of developing theory after the data have been collected (the **inductive approach**). This is a fundamental difference in research approach, and will be discussed in detail in Section 4.3.

## 2.5 Writing your research proposal

At the start of all courses or modules we give our students a plan of the work they will be doing. It includes the learning objectives, the content, the assessment strategy and the recommended reading. This is our statement of our side of the learning contract. Our students have a right to expect this.

However, when we insist on a proposal for a dissertation that is often the equivalent of at least two other modules, there is often a marked reluctance to produce anything other than what is strictly necessary. This is unsatisfactory. It is unfair to your project tutor because you are not making entirely clear what it is you intend to do in your research. You are also being unfair to yourself because you are not giving yourself the maximum opportunity to have your ideas and plans scrutinised and subjected to rigorous questioning.

Writing a research proposal is a crucial part of the research process. If you are applying for research funding, or if your proposal is going before an academic research committee, then you will know that you will need to put a great deal of time into the preparation of your proposal. However, even if the official need for a proposal is not so vital it is still a process that will repay very careful attention.

## The purposes of the research proposal

### Organising your ideas

Section 14.1 notes that writing can be the best way of clarifying our thoughts. This is a valuable purpose of the proposal. Not only will it clarify your thoughts but it will help you to organise your ideas into a coherent statement of your research intent. Your reader will be looking for this.

### Convincing your audience

However coherent your ideas and exciting your research plan, it counts for little if the proposal reveals that what you are planning to do is simply not possible. As part of research methods courses many tutors ask students to draft a research proposal. This is then discussed with a tutor. What usually happens is that this discussion is about how the proposed research can be amended so that something more modest in scope is attempted. Initially work that is not achievable in the given timescale is proposed. The student's task is to amend their initial ideas and convince the module tutor that the proposed research is achievable within the time and other resources available.

### Contracting with your 'client'

If you were asked to carry out a research project for a commercial client or your own organisation it is unthinkable that you would go ahead without a clear proposal that you would submit for approval. Acceptance of your proposal by the client would be part of the contract that existed between you. So it is with your proposal to your project tutor or academic committee. Acceptance implies that your proposal is satisfactory. While this is obviously no guarantee of subsequent success, it is something of comfort to you to know that at least you started your research journey with an appropriate destination and journey plan. It is for you to ensure that you do not get lost!

## The content of the research proposal

### Title

This may be your first attempt at the title. It may change as your work progresses. At this stage it should closely mirror the content of your proposal.

### Background

This is an important part of the proposal. It should tell the reader why you feel the research that you are planning is worth the effort. This may be expressed in the form of a problem that needs solving or something that you find exciting and has aroused your curiosity. The reader will be looking for evidence here that there is sufficient interest from you to sustain you over the long months (or years) ahead.

This is also the section where you will demonstrate your knowledge of the relevant literature. Moreover, it will clarify where your proposal fits into the debate in the literature. You will be expected to show a clear link between the previous work that has been done in your field of research interest and the content of your proposal. In short, the literature should be your point of departure. This is not the same as the critical literature review (Section 3.2) you will present in your final project report. It will just provide an overview of the key literature sources from which you intend to draw.

### Research questions and objectives

The background section should lead smoothly into a statement of your research question(s) and objectives. These should leave the reader in no doubt as to precisely what it is that your research seeks to achieve. Be careful here to ensure that your objectives are precisely written and will lead to observable outcomes (look again at Table 2.3, e.g., 'to describe the extent to which the effectiveness criteria specified for the team briefing scheme have been met'). Do not fall into the trap of stating general research aims that are little more than statements of intent (e.g. 'to discover the level of effectiveness of the team briefing scheme').

### Method

This and the background sections will be the longest sections of the proposal. It will detail precisely how you intend to go about achieving your research objectives. It will also justify your choice of method in the light of those objectives. These two aims may be met by dividing your method section into two parts: research design and data collection.

In the part on research design you will explain where you intend to carry out the research. If your earlier coverage has pointed out that your research is a single-organisation issue, then this will be self-evident. However, if your research topic is more generic you will wish to explain, for example, which sector(s) of the economy you have chosen to research and why you chose these sectors. You will also need to explain the identity of your research population (for example, managers or trade union officials) and why you chose this population.

This section should also include an explanation of the general way in which you intend to carry out the research. Will it be based, for example, on a questionnaire, interviews, examination of secondary data or use a combination of data collection techniques? Here again it is essential to explain why you have chosen your approach. Your explanation should be based on the most effective way of meeting your research objectives.

The research design section gives an overall view of the method chosen and the reason for that choice. The data collection section goes into much more detail about how specifically the data are to be collected. For example, if you are using a survey strategy you should specify your population and sample size. You should also clarify how the survey instrument such as a questionnaire will be distributed and how the data will be analysed. If you are using interviews you should explain how many interviews will be conducted, their intended duration, whether they will be audio-recorded, and how they will be analysed. In short, you should demonstrate to your reader that you have thought carefully about all the issues regarding your method and their relationship to your research objectives. However, it is normally not necessary in the proposal to include precise detail of the method you will employ, for example the content of an observation schedule or questionnaire questions.

You will also need to include a statement about how you are going to adhere to any ethical guidelines. This is particularly important in some research settings, such as those involving medical patients or children.

## Timescale

This will help you and your reader to decide on the viability of your research proposal. It will be helpful if you divide your research plan into stages. This will give you a clear idea as to what is possible in the given timescale. Experience has shown that however well the researcher's time is organised the whole process seems to take longer than anticipated (Box 2.11).

## BOX 2.11 WORKED EXAMPLE

### Louisa's research timescale

As part of the final year of her undergraduate business studies degree Louisa had to undertake an 8000–10 000-word research project. In order to assist her with her time management she discussed the following outline timescale with her tutor.

| Target date | Month number | Task to be achieved |
|---|---|---|
| Start October | 1 | Start thinking about research ideas (latest start date) |
| End November | 2 | Literature read |
| | | Objectives clearly defined with reference to literature |
| End December | 3 | Literature review written |
| | | Methodology literature read for dissertations involving secondary/primary data |
| End January | 4 | Secondary/primary data collected and analysed (analysis techniques linked to methodology/research literature) |
| | | Literature review extended further |
| Mid-February | 5 | Further writing up and analysis |
| End March | 6 | Draft completed including formatting bibliography etc. |
| Mid-May | 8 | Draft revised as necessary |
| End May | 8 | Submission |

As part of this section of their proposal, many researchers find it useful to produce a schedule for their research using a **Gantt chart**. Developed by Henry Gantt in 1917, this provides a simple visual representation of the tasks or activities that make up your research project, each being plotted against a time line. The time we estimate each task will take is represented by the length of an associated horizontal bar, whilst the task's start and finish times are represented by its position on the time line. Figure 2.2 shows a Gantt chart for a student's research project. As we can see from the first bar on this chart, the student has decided to schedule in two weeks of holiday. The first of these occurs over the Christmas and New Year period, and the second occurs while her tutor is reading a draft copy of the completed project in April. We can also see from the second and fourth bar that, like many of our students, she intends to begin to draft her literature review while she is still reading new articles and books. However, she has also recognised that some activities must be undertaken sequentially. For example, bars 9 and 10 highlight that before she can administer her questionnaire (bar 10) she must complete all the revisions highlighted as necessary by the pilot testing (bar 9).

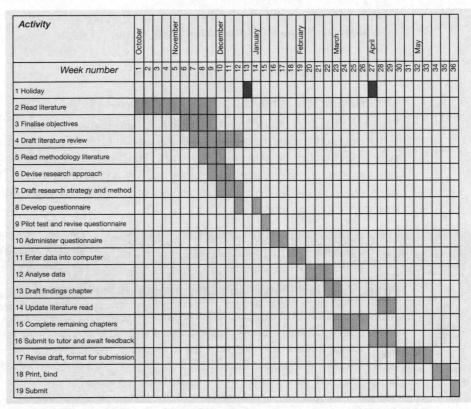

**Figure 2.2  Gantt chart for a research project**

## Resources

This is another facet of viability (Box 2.2). It will allow you and the reader to assess whether what you are proposing can be resourced. Resource considerations may be categorised as finance, data access and equipment.

Conducting research costs money. This may be for travel, subsistence, help with data analysis, or postage for questionnaires. Think through the expenses involved and ensure that you can meet these expenses.

Assessors of your proposal will need to be convinced that you have access to the data you need to conduct your research. This may be unproblematic if you are carrying out research in your own organisation. Many academic committees wish to see written approval from host organisations in which researchers are planning to conduct research. You will also need to convince your reader of the likely response rate to any questionnaire that you send.

It is surprising how many research proposals have ambitious plans for large-scale data collection with no thought given to how the data will be analysed. It is important that you convince the reader of your proposal that you have access to the necessary computer hardware and software to analyse your data. Moreover, it is necessary for you to demonstrate that you have either the necessary skills to perform the analysis or can learn the skills in an appropriate time, or you have access to help.

## References

It is not necessary to try to impress your proposal reader with an enormous list of references (Robson, 2002). A few key literature sources to which you have referred in the background section and which relate to the previous work that is directly informing your own proposal should be all that is necessary.

## Criteria for evaluating research proposals

### The extent to which the components of the proposal fit together

Your rationale for conducting the research should include a study of the previous published research, including relevant theories in the topic area. This study should inform your research question(s) and objectives. Your proposed methodology should flow directly from these research question(s) and objectives (Box 2.12). The time that you have allocated should be a direct reflection of the methods you employ, as should the resources that you need.

---

**BOX 2.12  WORKED EXAMPLE**

### Fitting together the various components of the research proposal

Jenny was a middle manager in a large insurance company. She was very interested in the fact that electronic forms of communication meant that organisations could move information-based administrative work round different locations. Her company was scanning paper applications for insurance policies onto their computer system and delivering these into a central electronic bank of work. The company had employees in three different locations in the UK, and work was drawn from the bank on the basis of workload existing in each particular location. Recently senior management had been considering developing work locations in South Asian cities, where it felt the standard of English meant that such functions could be fulfilled effectively. Jenny anticipated that this would pose certain logistical problems, for example staff training and communications. Knowledge of these problems would give her a clear picture of the limit of complexity of the work that could be done. This was particularly important since the complexity range went from the simple to the technically complex. Research into the literature on cross-cultural training justified Jenny's concern. As a consequence of her thought and reading she developed her research question as: 'What cross-cultural problems may be posed by international electronic work transfer in the insurance industry, and how may these problems limit the complexity of the work that may be transferred?'

Through her reading of the practitioner journals Jenny was aware that some other financial services organisations had been sending their work to Asia for some time. She decided that approaching these companies and interviewing their key personnel would be a fruitful approach. The main problem that Jenny would have with this research would be the time that the interview work would take, given that such companies were located all over the UK and North America. She was unsure how many interviews would be necessary. This would become clearer as she progressed in the research. However, it was unlikely that fewer than 10 companies would yield sufficient valuable data. She thought that she could collect the necessary data in a four-month period, which fitted in with her university deadline. There were no specific resources that Jenny needed other than finance and time. Since her research would be of immediate benefit to her employer she thought that neither would pose a problem.

---

### The viability of the proposal

This is the answer to the question: 'Can this research be carried out satisfactorily within the timescale and with available resources?'

## The absence of preconceived ideas

Your research should be an exciting journey into the unknown. Do not be like the student who came to Phil to talk over a research proposal and said 'Of course, I know what the answer will be'. When asked to explain the purpose of doing the research if he already knew the answer he became rather defensive and eventually looked for another supervisor and, probably, another topic.

## BOX 2.13 WORKED EXAMPLE

### A written research proposal

Puvadol was a student from Thailand who returned home from the UK to complete his MA dissertation. His proposed dissertation concerned the applicability of Western methods of involving employees in decision-making in Thai organisations.

An abbreviated version of Puvadol's proposal follows:

#### Title
The influences of Thai culture on employee involvement.

#### Background
Involving employees in the decision making of their employing organisations has been increasingly popular in Europe and North America in recent years. The influx of American organisations into Thailand has meant that similar approaches are being adopted. However, this assumes that Thai employees will respond to these techniques as readily as their European and American counterparts.

Doubts about the validity of these assumptions derive from studies of Thai national culture (Komin, 1990). Using Rokeach's (1979) conceptual framework, Komin characterised Thai culture in a number of ways. I have isolated those that relate to employee involvement. These are that Thais wish to:

a save face, avoid criticism and show consideration to others;

b exhibit gratitude to those who have shown kindness and consideration;

c promote smooth, conflict-free interpersonal relations;

d interpret 'rules' in a flexible way with little concern for principles;

e promote interdependent social relations;

f be seen to be achieving success through good social relations rather than individual success.

I intend to demonstrate in this section that these six cultural values contradict the values of employee involvement (e.g. employee involvement may involve employees in openly criticising managers, which directly contradicts **a** above).

#### Research objectives
1 To examine the assumptions behind the management technique of employee involvement.

2 To establish the characteristics of the Thai national culture.

3 To identify the opinions of Thai employees and their managers, working in American-owned organisations in Thailand, towards values underpinning employee involvement.

4 To draw conclusions about the applicability of employee involvement to Thai employees.

### Method

1 Conduct a review of the literatures on employee involvement and Thai national culture in order to develop research hypotheses.

2 Carry out primary research in three American-owned petrochemical and manufacturing organisations in Thailand to assess the opinions of Thai employees and their managers towards values underpinning employee involvement. Informal approval has been gained from three organisations. American-owned organisations are relevant because it is in these that employee involvement is most likely to be found and values underpinning employee involvement exhibited. Petrochemical and manufacturing organisations are chosen because the occupations carried out in these organisations are likely to be similar, thus ensuring that any differences are a function of Thai national culture rather than of occupational culture.

A questionnaire will be developed with questions based on the Thai values a–f in the Background section above. Each value will lead to a hypothesis (e.g. employee involvement may not be appropriate to Thai culture because it may mean that employees openly criticise their managers). The questions in the questionnaire will seek to test these hypotheses. The questionnaire will be distributed to a sample (size to be agreed) of employees and of managers across all three organisations.

Data analysis will use the SPSS software. Statistical tests will be run to ensure that results are a function of Thai cultural values rather than of values that relate to the individual organisations.

### Timescale

January–March 2006: review of literature
April 2006: draft literature review
May 2006: review research methods literature and agree research strategy
June 2006: agree formal access to three organisations for collection of primary data
July–August 2006: compile, pilot and revise questionnaire
September 2006: administer questionnaire
October–November 2006: final collection of questionnaires and analysis of data
November 2002–February 2007: completion of first draft of project report
March–May 2007: final writing of project report

### Resources

I have access to computer hardware and software. Access to three organisations has been negotiated, subject to confirmation. My employer has agreed to pay all incidental costs as part of my course expenses.

### References

Komin, S. (1990) *Psychology of the Thai People: Values and Behavioral Patterns*, Thailand, National Institute of Development Administration (in Thai).

Rokeach, M. (1979) *Understanding Human Values: Individual and Society*, New York, The Free Press.

If it is absolutely crucial that your proposal is of the highest quality then you may wish to use an **expert system** such as Peer Review Emulator™. This software is available either on its own or as part of the Methodologist's Toolchest™ suite of programs. It asks you a series of questions about your proposed research. The program then critiques these answers to ensure that common research standards are achieved (idea Works, 2005).

## 2.6  Summary

- The process of formulating and clarifying your research topic is the most important part of your research topic.
- Attributes of a research topic do not vary a great deal between universities. The most important of these is that your research topic will meet the requirements of the examining body.
- Generating and refining research ideas makes use of a variety of techniques. It is important that you use a variety of techniques, including those that involve rational thinking and those that involve creative thinking.
- The ideas generated can be integrated subsequently using a technique such as working up and narrowing down.
- Clear research questions, based on the relevant literature, will act as a focus for the research that follows.
- Research can be distinguished from intelligence gathering. Research is theory dependent.
- Writing a research proposal helps you to organise your ideas, and can be thought of as a contract between you and the reader.
- The content of the research proposal should tell the reader what you want to do, why you want to do it, what you are trying to achieve, and how you to plan to achieve it.

## SELF-CHECK QUESTIONS

*Help with these questions is available at the end of the chapter.*

**2.1**  For the workplace project for her professional course, Karen had decided to undertake a study of the effectiveness of the joint consultative committee in her NHS Trust. Her title was 'An evaluation of the effectiveness of the Joint Consultative Committee in Anyshire's Hospitals NHS Foundation Trust'. Draft some objectives which Karen may adopt to complement her title.

**2.2**  You have decided to search the literature to 'try to come up with some research ideas in the area of Operations Management'. How will you go about this?

**2.3**  A colleague of yours wishes to generate a research idea in the area of accounting. He has examined his own strengths and interests on the basis of his assignments and has read some review articles, but has failed to find an idea about which he is excited. He comes and asks you for advice. Suggest two techniques that your colleague could use, and justify your choice.

**2.4**  You are interested in doing some research on the interface between business organisations and schools. Write three research questions that may be appropriate.

**2.5**  How may the formulation of an initial substantive theory help in the development of a research proposal?

**2.6**  How would you demonstrate the influence of relevant theory in your research proposal?

## REVIEW AND DISCUSSION QUESTIONS

**2.7**  Together with your colleagues, decide on the extent to which a set of research topics constitute a 'good research topic' according to the checklist in Box 2.2. The set of topics you choose may be past topics obtained from your tutor which relate to your course. Alternatively they may be those which have been written by you and your colleagues as preparation for your project(s).

**2.8**  Look through several of the academic journals which relate to your subject area. Choose an article which is based upon primary research. Assuming that the research question and objectives are not made explicit, infer from the content of the article what the research question and objectives may have been.

**2.9**  Watch the news on television. Most bulletins will contain stories on research which has been carried out to report the current state of affairs in a particular field. Spend some time investigating news sites on the Internet (for example http://www.news.google.com) in order to learn more about the research which relates to the news story. Study the story carefully and decide what further questions the report raises. Use this as the basis to draft an outline proposal to seek answers to one (or more) of these questions.

## PROGRESSING YOUR RESEARCH PROJECT

### From research ideas to a research proposal

☐ If you have not been given a research idea, consider the techniques available for generating and refining research ideas. Choose a selection of those with which you feel most comfortable, making sure to include both rational and creative thinking techniques. Use these to try to generate a research idea or ideas. Once you have got some research ideas, or if you have been unable to find an idea, talk to your project tutor.

☐ Evaluate your research ideas against the checklist of attributes of a good research project (Box 2.2).

☐ Refine your research ideas using a selection of the techniques available for generating and refining research ideas. Re-evaluate your research ideas against the checklist of attributes of a good research project (Box 2.2). Remember that it is better to revise (and in some situations to discard) ideas that do not appear to be feasible at this stage. Integrate your ideas using the process of working up and narrowing down to form one research idea.

☐ Use your research idea to write a general focus research question. Where possible this should be a 'why?' or a 'how?' rather than a 'what?' question.

☐ Use the general focus research question to write more detailed research questions and your research objectives.

☐ Write your research proposal making sure it includes a clear title and sections on:

  ☐ the background to your research;

  ☐ your research questions and objectives;

  ☐ the method you intend to use;

  ☐ the timescale for your research;

  ☐ the resources you require;

  ☐ references to any literature to which you have referred.

## References

Bennett, R. (1991) 'What is management research?', in Smith, N.C. and Dainty, P. (eds) *The Management Research Handbook*, London, Routledge, pp. 67–77.

Boyd, C. (2004) 'Academics take on video games', 21 October [online] (cited 11 February 2006). Available from <URL:http://news.bbc.co.uk/1/hi/technology/3727932.stm>.

Buzan, T. (2006) *The Ultimate Book of Mind Maps*, London, Harper Thorsons.

Carroll, L. (1989) *Alice's Adventures in Wonderland*, London, Hutchinson.

Clough, P. and Nutbrown, C. (2002) *A Student's Guide to Methodology*, London, Sage.

Creswell, J. (2002) *Qualitative, Quantitative, and Mixed Methods Approaches* (2nd edn), Thousand Oaks, CA, Sage.

Dickie, M. (2005) China's challenge changes the rules of the game, *Financial Times*, 18 October.

Festinger, L (1957) *A Theory of Cognitive Dissonance*, Stanford, CA, Stanford University Press.

Ghauri, P. and Grønhaug, K. (2005) *Research Methods in Business Studies: A Practical Guide* (3rd edn), Harlow, Financial Times Prentice Hall.

Gill, J. and Johnson, P. (2002) *Research Methods for Managers* (3rd edn), London, Sage Publications.

idea Works (2005) 'Methodologist's Toolchest features' [online] (cited 11 February 2006). Available from <URL:http://www.ideaworks.com/MToolchestFeatures.shtml>.

Jankowicz, A.D. (2005) *Business Research Projects* (4th edn), London, Thomson Learning.

Kerlinger, F. and Lee, H. (2000) *Foundations of Behavioral Research* (4th edn), Fort Worth, TX, Harcourt College Publishers.

Kervin, J.B. (1999) *Methods for Business Research* (2nd edn), New York, HarperCollins.

Lau, J. (2005) 'In Hong Kong, women "just have to work harder"', *Financial Times*, 20 October.

Mackenzie, K.D. (2000a) 'Knobby analyses of knobless survey items, part I: The approach', *International Journal of Organizational Analysis* 8: 2, 131–54.

Mackenzie, K.D. (2000b) 'Knobby analyses of knobless survey items, part II: An application', *International Journal of Organizational Analysis* 8: 3, 238–61.

Maylor, H. and Blackmon, K. (2005) *Researching Business and Management*, Basingstoke, Palgrave Macmillan.

McNiff, J. with Whitehead, J. (2000) *Action Research in Organizations*, London, Routledge.

Moody, P.E. (1988) *Decision Making: Proven Methods for Better Decisions* (2nd edn), Maidenhead, McGraw-Hill.

Phillips, E.M. and Pugh, D.S. (2005) *How to get a PhD* (4th edn), Maidenhead, Open University Press.

Raimond, P. (1993) *Management Projects*, London, Chapman & Hall.

Robson, C. (2002) *Real World Research* (2nd edn), Oxford, Blackwell.

Rothberg, G. (2004) 'The role of ideas in the manager's workplace: theory and practice', *Management Decision* 42: 9, 1060–81.

Saunders, M.N.K. and Lewis, P. (1997) 'Great ideas and blind alleys? A review of the literature on starting research', *Management Learning* 28: 3, 283–99.

Sharp, J., Peters, J. and Howard, K. (2002) *The Management of a Student Research Project* (3rd edn), Aldershot, Gower.

Smith, N.C. and Dainty, P. (1991) *The Management Research Handbook*, London, Routledge.

Sutton, R. and Staw, B. (1995) 'What theory is not', *Administrative Science Quarterly* 40: 3, 371–84.

Whetten, D. (1989) 'What constitutes a theoretical contribution?', *Academy of Management Review* 14: 4, 490–5.

## Further reading

Fisher, C. (2004) *Researching and Writing a Dissertation for Business Students*, Harlow, Financial Times Prentice Hall. Chapter 1 has some very practical tips on choosing your research topic.

Maylor, H. and Blackmon, K. (2005) *Researching Business and Management*, Basingstoke, Palgrave Macmillan. Chapter 3 covers similar ground to this chapter and has some useful ideas on generating research topics and some very interesting examples of student topics.

Sutton, R. and Staw, B. (1995) 'What theory is not', *Administrative Science Quarterly* 40: 3, 371–84. This is an excellent article which makes very clear what theory is by explaining what theory is not. The authors draw on their experience as journal editors who constantly have to examine articles submitted for publication. They report that the reason for refusals is usually that there is no theory in the article. This leads to some very clear and practical advice for us all to follow.

**For WEB LINKS visit www.pearsoned.co.uk/ saunders**

Whetten, D. (1989) 'What constitutes a theoretical contribution?', *Academy of Management Review* 14: 4, 490–5. Whetten also comments as a journal editor and covers similar ground to Sutton and Staw. Again, this is clear and straightforward advice and, read together with Sutton and Staw, gives a pretty clear idea of how to avoid criticisms of a lack of theory in research writing.

# Topic 2
# Information Sources

For Saunders Chapter 3, please refer to Semester 1 Topic 2

## Introduction: Information Sources

A key area of developing a research proposal (whether academic or business) is to write the literature review. The literature review needs to be organised in a way which carries an argument forward. Avoid merely reporting what you have read; review the material with explicit criteria; sequence the review to tell a story of how each source addresses the research objectives: assess the strengths and weakness in the literature.

Section **3.1 Introduction** of Saunders Chapter 3 suggests information searches should start early, involve a wide range of literature, and should be iteratively refined.

The iterative process of literature review involves generating **information criteria** to plan your search and then to accommodate what has been found and what are the remaining gaps.

The literature review should serve several purposes:
1    it locates the research topic in the context of what has been written; and should develop understanding of key issues, ideas and evidence in the field
2    it should focus the research topic and objectives
3    it should identify appropriate ways of gathering evidence and generating data by looking at what others have done and replicating or adapting.
4    For a replication study it identifies the method and/or analysis to apply to different data.

The proposal should describe and critique those information sources. In addition it can identify some sources that you have been unable to find, review and use due to time limitations. To show that you have thought about other information use the Information Grid to set out a plan to identify and review other information, citing the further sources you plan to use.

Generate **information criteria** that will help identify and organise all the information included in the literature review. You can obtain criteria from the department subject references in the Library system (http://www.lib.strath.ac.uk/busweb.htm ). Information can be categorised into four types

| | | |
|---|---|---|
| 1) | Theoretical | – How should we do Y? |
| 2) | Practical | – How to do Y? |
| 3) | Anecdotal | – How does X do Y? |
| 4) | Statistical | – How many do Y? |

Each type of information is likely to come from different sources. For example, the majority of **theoretical** writing will be found in good quality academic journals. **Practical** or **anecdotal** information can be found in trade journals, interviews, programme transcripts, newspapers, websites and internal documents from companies. **Statistical** information is produced by official bodies, government departments, multinational organisations, such as the EU, or professional and trade associations.

The **information grid** is a tool to manage information. Use it to:
•    Identify the main concepts / search topics
•    Identify the keywords relevant to the main concepts – useful when using databases and indexes in textbooks
•    Identify the information types providing information on the main concepts
•    Suggest the timescale required to access the main sources of information

It is advisable to include an Information Grid in your report to allow you to proceed to the critical review of all your information sources (minimum six!). Blank and example grids will be provided on the VLE.

Steps to **select a journal article:** (use the issued lists of department approved journals)

1    Does the title sound relevant or interesting? Does it contain keywords from your research problem and objectives?
2    Does the abstract sound useful? Does it involve data or is it theoretical only
3    From a quick look online ask whether the article looks worth reading and evaluating

**Use Abstracts** to evaluate possible journal articles. – Do not select until you check the following:

- Aims & Objectives of the study
- Methodology / techniques used in the study
- Conclusions of the study

The research proposal  literature reviews should not only describe your information sources but also critically evaluate them. The information grid will help you do the following:

1.  Identify types of information required for the research
2.  Identify areas of information which may take longer to find
3.  Identify main subjects / concepts within the research proposal
4.  Identify keywords to use in databases / indexes
5.  Identify preliminary reading material
6.  Identify if research is possible in timescale
7.  A planning tool to record what needs to be done and the order.

In section 3.2 of Saunders the **critical review** tells you explicitly what is meant by being 'critical' about the content. The example literature review in Box 3.4 shows a good example for how to pitch it. Section 3.3 surveys the range of information sources available; section 3.4 shows how to plan your literature search, 3.5 how to conduct your literature search, 3.6 and 3.7 show how to record and register the process.

Many departments provide guidelines on their preferred style of referencing material. Strathclyde Library give some help at: http://www.lib.strath.ac.uk/bibref.htm pointing to the American Psychological Association guidelines. For Harvard referencing you could use the online learning exercise at http://www.lmu.ac.uk/skills/open/sfl/content/harvard/  Saunders Appendix 2  gives further helpful examples. Make sure you know how to cite the range of information sources: Books, Academic journal articles and web pages.

# Systems of referencing

Four points are important when referencing:

- Credit must be given when quoting or citing other work.
- Adequate information must be provided to enable a reader to locate each reference.
- References must be consistent and complete.
- References must be recorded in the precise format required by your university.

## The Harvard system

### Referencing in the text

The *Harvard system* is an *author–date system*, a variation of which we use in this book. It was developed at Harvard University in the 1930s (Anderson and Poole, 2001) and usually uses the author's name and year of publication to identify cited documents within the text. The system for referencing work in the text is outlined in Table A2.1.

### Referencing in the references or bibliography

In the references or bibliography the publications are listed alphabetically by author's name, and all authors' surnames and initials are listed in full. If there is more than one work by the same author, these are listed chronologically. The system for referencing work in the references or bibliography is outlined in Table A2.2. While it would be impossible for us to include an example of every type of reference you might need to include, the information contained in this table should enable you to work out the required format for all your references.

For copies of journal articles from printed journals that you have obtained electronically via the Internet it is usually acceptable to reference these using exactly the same format as printed journal articles (Table A2.2), provided you have obtained and read a facsimile (exact) copy of the article. Exact copies of journal articles have precisely the same format as the printed version, including page numbering, tables and diagrams. They are usually obtained by downloading the article via the Internet as a .pdf file that can be read on the screen and printed using Adobe Acrobat Reader.

Finally, remember to include a, b, c etc. immediately after the date when you are referencing different publications by the same author from the same year. Do not forget to ensure that these are consistent with the letters used for the references in the main text.

**Table A2.1 Using the Harvard system to reference in the text**

| To refer to | Use the general format | For example |
| --- | --- | --- |
| A single author | (Surname date) | (Saunders, 1993) |
| Dual authors | (Surname and Surname, date) | (Saunders and Thornhill, 2006) |
| More than two authors | (Surname *et al.*, date) | (Lewis *et al.*, 2004) |
| Work by different authors generally | (Surname, date; Surname, date) in alphabetical order | (Cassell, 2004; Dillman, 2000; Robson, 2002) |
| Different authors with the same surname | (Surname, Initial., date) | (Smith, J., 2006) |
| Different publications by the same author | (Surname, date; date) in ascending date order | (Saunders, 2004; 2005) |
| Different publications by the same author from the same year | (Surname, date letter), make sure the letter is consistent throughout | (de Vita, 2005a) |
| An author referred to by another author where the original has not been read (*secondary reference*) | (Surname, date; cited by Surname, date) | (Granovetter, 1974; cited by Saunders, 1993) |
| A corporate author | (Corporate name, date) | (Harley-Davidson Inc., 2003) |
| A newspaper article with no obvious author | (Newspaper name, date) | (The Guardian, 2006) |
| Another type of publication with no obvious author | (Publication title, date) | (Labour Market Trends, 2005) |
| An Internet site | (Site title, date) | (Financial Times, 2006) |
| A television or radio programme | (Television or radio programme series title, date) | (Little Britain, 2005) |
| A commercial DVD or video that is part of a series | (DVD or video series title, date) | (The Office, Series 1 and 2, 2005) |
| A commercial DVD or video that is not part of a series | (DVD or video title, date) | (One Flew Over the Cuckoo's Nest, 2002) |
| A publication for which the year of publication cannot be identified | (Surname or Corporate name, nd), where 'nd' means no date (Surname or Corporate name, c. date) where 'c.' means circa | (Woollons, nd) (Hattersley, c. 2004) |
| A direct quotation | (Surname or Corporate name, date, p. number) where 'p.' means 'page' and number is the page in the original publication on which the quotation appears | 'Whenever an employee's job ceases to exist it is potentially fair to dismiss that person.' (Lewis *et al.*, 2003, p. 350) |

Table A2.2  **Using the Harvard system to reference in the references or bibliography**

| To reference | | Use the general format | For example |
|---|---|---|---|
| **Books and chapters in books** | Book (first edition) | Surname, Initials and Surname, Initials (date) *Title*, Publisher, Place of publication | Saunders, MNK and Cooper, SA (1993) *Understanding Business Statistics*, DP Publications Ltd, London |
| | Book (other than first edition) | Surname, Initials and Surname, Initials (date) *Title* (? edn), Publisher, Place of publication | Morris, C (2003) *Quantitative Approaches to Business Studies* (6th edn), Financial Times Pitman Publishing, London |
| | Book (no obvious author) | Corporate name or Publication name (date) *Title*, Publisher, Place of publication | Mintel Marketing Intelligence (1998) *Designerwear: Mintel Marketing Intelligence Report*, Mintel International Group Ltd, London |
| | Chapter in a book | Surname, Initials and Surname, Initials (date) *Title*, Publisher, Place of publication, Chapter ? | Robson, C (2002) *Real World Research* (2nd edn), Blackwell, Oxford, Chapter 3 |
| | Chapter in an edited book | Surname, Initials (date) 'Chapter title', *in* Surname, Initials and Surname, Initials (eds), *Title*, Publisher, Place of publication, page numbers | King, N (2004) 'Using templates in the thematic analysis of text' *in* Cassell, C. and Symon, J. (eds), *Essential Guide to Qualitative Methods in Organizational Research*, Sage, London, pp. 256–270 |
| **Journal articles** | Journal article | Surname, Initials and Surname, Initials (date) 'Title of article', *Journal name*, volume number: part number, pages | Storey, J, Cressey, P, Morris, T and Wilkinson, A (1997) 'Changing employment practices in UK banking: case studies', *Personnel Review*, 26:1, 24–42 |
| | Journal article (no obvious author) | Corporate name or Publication name (date) 'Title of article', *Journal name*, volume number: part number, pages | Local Government Chronicle (1993) 'Westminster poised for return to AMA fold', *Local Government Chronicle*, 5 November, p. 5 |
| **Government publications** | Parliamentary papers including acts and bills | Country of origin (date) *Title*, Publisher, Place of publication | Great Britain (2005) *The Prevention of Terrorism Act*, The Stationery Office, London |
| | Others (with authors) | As for books | As for books |
| | Others (no obvious authors) | Department name or Committee name (date) *Title*, Publisher, Place of publication | Department of Trade and Industry (1992) *The Single Market: Europe Open for Professions, UK Implementation*, HMSO, London |
| **Newspapers, including CD-ROM databases** | Newspaper article | Surname, Initials and Surname, Initials (date) 'Title of article', *Newspaper name*, place of printing, day, month, pages (where known) | Roberts, D (1998) 'BAe sells property wing for £301m', *The Daily Telegraph*, London, 10 October, p. 31 |

Table A2.2 (continued)

| To reference | | Use the general format | For example |
|---|---|---|---|
| **Newspapers including CD-Rom databases continued** | Newspaper article (no obvious author) | Newspaper name (date) 'Title of article', *Newspaper name*, place of printing, day, month, pages (where known) | Guardian (1992) 'Fraud trial at Britannia Theme Park', *The Guardian*, Manchester, 5 February, p. 4 |
| | Newspaper article (from CD-ROM database) | Newspaper name or Surname, Initials (date) 'Title of article', *Newspaper name* (CD-ROM), day, month, pages (where known) | Financial Times (1998) 'Recruitment: lessons in leadership: moral issues are increasingly pertinent to the military and top corporate ranks', *Financial Times* (CD-ROM), London, 11 March, p. 32 |
| **Other CD-ROM publications** | | Title of CD-ROM or Surname, Initials (date) (CD-ROM), Publisher, Place of publication | Encarta 2006 Encyclopaedia (2005) (CD-ROM), Microsoft, Redmond, WA |
| **Unpublished conference papers** | | Surname, Initials and Surname, Initials (date) 'Title of paper', *paper presented at the Conference name*, days, month, location of conference | Saunders, MNK, Thornhill, A and Lewis, P (2001) 'Employees' reactions to the management of change: an exploration from an organisational justice framework', *paper presented at the Eighth Annual International Conference on Advances in Management*, 11–14 July, Athens |
| **Letters, personal emails and electronic conferences/ bulletin boards** | Letter | Surname, Initials and Surname, Initials (date) 'Unpublished letter: Subject matter' | McPartlin, A (2005) 'Unpublished letter: Reviewer's feedback' |
| | Personal email | Sender's surname, Sender's initials (sender's email address) (date) 'Subject of message' (email to recipient's initials and surname) (recipient's email address) | McPartlin, A (amcpartlin@abcdef.com) (2005) 'Reviewer's feedback' (email to MNK Saunders) (mnksaunders@abcdef.com) |
| | Electronic conference/Bulletin Boards | Site host, (date) 'subject matter', *name of electronic conference/bulletin board* [online] (cited day month year) Available from <URL:http://www. remainder of full Internet address> | GPO Access (2005), *Federal Bulletin Board* [online] (cited 6 April 2005) Available from <URL:http://fedbbs.access.gpo.gov/> |
| **Internet items excluding emails** | Journal published on the Internet | <URL:http://www. remainder of full Internet electronic conference/bulletin board> | <URL:http://www.stingray.ivision.co.uk/groups/emu/frindex.htm> |
| | Journal article published on the Internet | Surname, Initials and Surname, Initials (date) 'Title of article', *journal name*, volume number, part number [online] (cited day month year) Available from <URL:http://www. remainder of full Internet address> | Illingworth, N (2001) 'The Internet matters: exploring the use of the Internet as a research tool', *Sociological Research Online* 6: 2 [online] (cited 20 March 2002) Available from <URL:http://www.socresonline.org.uk/6/2/illingworth.html> |

**Table A2.2 (continued)**

| To reference | | Use the general format | For example |
|---|---|---|---|
| **Internet items excluding emails** *continued* | Internet site/specific site pages | Site title (date) 'Title of page within site where applicable' [online] (cited day month year) Available from <URL:http://www. remainder of full Internet address> | Chartered Institute of Personnel and Development [online] (cited 7 January 2002) Available from <URL:http://www.cipd.co.uk> |
| | Internet article | Surname, Initials and Surname, Initials (date) 'Title of article' [online] (cited day month year) Available from <URL:http://www.remainder of full Internet address> | Jones, A and Smith, A (eds) (2001) 'What exactly is the Labour Force Survey? [online] (cited 20 December 2001) Available from <URL:http//www.statistics.gov.uk/ nsbase/downloads.theme_labour/ what_exactly_is_LFS1.pdf> |
| **Audio-visual material** | Television or radio programme | Series title. Series number (Year of production) *Programme title*, Place of publication, transmitting organisation, date of transmission | Little Britain. Series 3 (2005) *Little Britain*, London, British Broadcasting Corporation, 1 December 2005 |
| | Commercial DVDs and videos that are part of a series | DVD or video series title Series number (Year of production) *Episode title*, Place of publication, Publisher [medium: format] | The Office Complete Series 1 and 2 and the Christmas Specials (2005) *Series 1 Christmas Special*, London, British Broadcasting Corporation [video: DVD] |
| | Commercial DVDs and videos that are part of a series | DVD or video title (Year of production) *DVD or video title*, Place of publication, Publisher [medium: format] | Bruce Springsteen Live in New York City (2003) *Bruce Springsteen Live in New York City*, New York, Sony [video: DVD] |

# The American Psychological Association (APA) system

The *American Psychological Association system* or *APA system* is a variation on the author–date system. Like the Harvard system it dates from the 1930s and 1940s, and has been updated subsequently. The latest updates are outlined in the latest edition of the American Psychological Association's (2001) *Publication Manual of the American Psychological Association*, which is likely to be available for reference in your university's library.

Relatively small but significant differences exist between the Harvard and APA systems, and many authors adopt a combination of the two systems. The key differences are outlined in Table A2.3.

**Table A2.3 Key differences between Harvard and APA systems of referencing**

| Harvard system | APA system | Comment |
|---|---|---|
| **Referencing in the text** | | |
| (Lewis 2001) | (Lewis, 2001) | Note punctuation |
| (Saunders and Williams 2001) | (Saunders & Williams, 2001) | '&' not 'and' |
| (Williams *et al*. 1999) | (Williams, Saunders & Staughton, 1999) | For first occurrence |
| (Williams *et al*. 1999) | (Williams *et al*., 1999) | For subsequent occurrences; note punctuation |
| **Referencing in the references or bibliography** | | |
| Thornhill A, Lewis P, Millmore M and Saunders MNK (2000) *Managing Change: A Human Resource Strategy Approach*, FT Prentice Hall, Harlow | Thornhill, A., Lewis, P., Millmore, M. & Saunders, M.N.K. (2000) *Managing change: A human resource strategy approach*. Harlow: FT Prentice Hall. | Note full stops and commas Note use of 'and', '&' Note use of capitals in title Note order, use of colon, comma and full stop |

# Footnotes

## Referencing in the text

When using *footnotes*, sometimes referred to as the *Vancouver system*, references within the research report are shown by a number. This number refers directly to the references, and it means it is not necessary for you to include the authors' names or date of publication:

'Recent research[1] indicates that . . .'

## Referencing in the references

These list sequentially the referenced works in the order they are referred to in your research report. This can be useful as it enables you to include comments and footnotes as well as the references (Jankowicz, 2005). It does, however, mean that the references are unlikely to be in alphabetical order. When using the footnotes system you need to ensure that:

- the layout of individual references is the same as that for the Harvard system (Table A2.2), other than that they are preceded by a number, for example:

    [1] Ritzer, G (1996) *The McDonaldization of Society* (revised edn), Thousand Oaks, CA, Pine Forge Press

- the publications referred to include only those you have cited in your report. They should therefore be headed 'References' rather than 'Bibliography';
- you refer to the same item more than once using standard bibliographic abbreviations to save repeating the reference in full (Table A2.4).

**Table A2.4  Bibliographic abbreviations**

| Abbreviation | Explanation | For example |
|---|---|---|
| *op. cit.* *(opere citato)* | Meaning 'in the work cited'. This refers to a work previously referenced, and so you must give the author and date and, if necessary, the page number. | Robson (2002) *op. cit.* pp. 23–4 |
| *loc. cit.* *(loco citato)* | Meaning 'in the place cited'. This refers to the same page of a work previously referenced, and so you must give the author and date. | Robson (2002) *loc. cit.* |
| *ibid.* *(ibidem)* | Meaning 'the same work given immediately before'. This refers to the work referenced immediately before, and replaces all details of the previous reference other than a page number if necessary. | *ibid.* |

## References

American Psychological Association (2001) *Publication Manual of the American Psychological Association* (5th edn), Washington, American Psychological Association.

Anderson, J. and Poole, M. (2001) *Assignment and Thesis Writing* (4th edn), Brisbane, John Wiley and Sons.

## Further reading

American Psychological Association (2001) *Publication Manual of the American Psychological Association* (5th edn), Washington, American Psychological Association. The most recent version of this manual contains full details of how to use this form of the author–date system of referencing as well as how to lay out tables, figures, equations and other statistical data. It also provides guidance on grammar and writing.

Anderson, J. and Poole, M. (2001) *Assignment and Thesis Writing* (4th edn), Brisbane, John Wiley and Sons. Chapter 13 provides a thorough, up-to-date discussion of the layout required for a wide range of information sources using the Harvard, American Psychological Association and footnotes referencing systems.

Branscomb, H.E. (2001) *Casting Your Net: A Student's Guide to Research on the Internet* (2nd edn), Boston, MA, Allyn and Bacon. Appendix 2 provides a detailed discussion of documenting a wide range of sources from the Internet.

# Topic 3
## Qualitative Research Methods

# Introduction: Qualitative Research Methods

Although reviewing the literature is an important part of Research, the majority of proposals have an element of new data (primary research) which needs to be collected to address the research problem and objectives. An important part of planning research is to estimate the resources required. This session and the next cover Primary Research, giving you an introduction to skills and required resources so that you can describe the value and cost of the techniques you select for your Research Proposal. This session looks at qualitative approach to research. Qualitative research stresses richness and depth of data over concepts like reliability and representativeness which are addressed more directly in quantitative analysis.

| Qualitative Research | |
|---|---|
| Collects data which is not easy to measure in a numerical fashion | Involved where research objectives are to gain a greater understanding of an issue, or to map out the range of behaviours or influences |
| If questions like Why, What If, & What influenced your decision are key to your research objectives, you are more likely to need Qualitative Research | Use Qualitative Research to get behind results. The company share price increased 50% in Jan 2007, but why? Could asking an informed respondent help tell you? |

The most frequently used qualitative methods used in student projects are in-depth interviews and focus groups: other techniques are the Delphi Technique, Cognitive Mapping & Repertory Grids. Chapter 10 Saunders (Collecting primary data using semi-structured, in-depth and group interviews) provides good background reading – all focussed around interviews, and includes lots of useful checklists.

Other qualitative research techniques include Observation and Case Study Research

| Observation | |
|---|---|
| Observation of relevant people, actions and situations | A technique that is 'non-reactive' - doesn't involve interacting with respondents. |
| Observing visitors to shops by following them with CCTV | Informed Consent issues. |

One form of observation is **participant observation** where you are actually part of the group you are observing. Some students say that part of their research approach is to use participant observation, based on their workplace. But this only counts as systematic research if you **plan** it as part of your approach to collecting data.

The **case study** is often seen as part of the qualitative approach because it involves going into one or a few organisations over a period of time to collect data from various sources within that setting. But it is more an approach or context rather than a single method and typically case study based research will use a range of techniques to collect data - interviews, observation, documentary analysis and sometimes surveys.

## Stages and Planning

| Stages of Qualitative research | Resources |
|---|---|
| **Prepare** topic guide and prompts, arrange taping/ recording, recruit respondents (and incentives), arrange time and place. Address Ethical and Consent issues. | Researcher time and costs. Travel costs, Incentives, Equipment. Hiring discussion space. |
| **Collect** information, recordings, tapes, notes, data sheets. Get to the interview as well as time, arrange for clients to observe discussions. | Researcher time and travel |
| **Analyse** first transcribe information, Interpretation, Coding – themes, time lines | Transcription time, coding effort, researcher time |
| **Report** Generate printed report, present results to client | Researcher time, travel to client organisation, presentation equipment |

The kind of data you will generate using qualitative methods is text rather than numbers. The text is detailed, verbatim interview transcripts or notes of your observations.

**Project Planning** is how to put together a research plan: timing, resources, contingencies, phases, transcription, prompting structures, interview/ topic guides. By now you should start to have a primary & secondary research plan (where appropriate) to be like a consultant pitching for a project. Issues include:

- Prioritising objectives: Are they some objectives already answered and others that need specific primary research?
- Identify the best method of research and the key gaps in secondary data and the literature
- Identify additional objectives where necessary - e.g. if the literature has exposed to opposing approaches to the problem
- An honours student doesn't typically have sufficient resources (mainly of time) to fully use more than one method, and needs to make a reasoned choice between alternatives (both between qualitative and quantitative and within each). Hybrid proposals using multiple methods are sometimes valuable, but need justification – using concepts like triangulation.

# Collecting primary data using semi-structured, in-depth and group interviews

## LEARNING OUTCOMES

By the end of this chapter you should be:

→ able to classify research interviews in order to help you to understand the purpose of each type;

→ aware of research situations favouring the use of semi-structured and in-depth interviews, and their limitations;

→ able to analyse potential data quality issues and evaluate how to overcome these;

→ able to consider the development of your competence to undertake semi-structured and in-depth interviews, and the logistical and resource issues that affect their use;

→ aware of the relative advantages of using one-to-one and group interviews, including focus groups, in particular contexts;

→ aware of the issues and advantages of conducting interviews by telephone and via the Internet or intranet.

## 10.1　Introduction

An interview is a purposeful discussion between two or more people (Kahn and Cannell, 1957). The use of interviews can help you to gather valid and reliable data that are relevant to your research question(s) and objectives. Where you have not yet formulated such a research question and objectives, an interview or interviews may help you to achieve this. In reality, the research interview is a general term for several types of interview. This fact is significant since the nature of any interview should be consistent with your research question(s) and objectives, the purpose of your research and the research strategy that you have adopted. We provide an overview of types of interview in the next section of this chapter (Section 10.2) and show how these are related to particular research purposes. However, as indicated by this chapter's title, our main focus is semi-structured, in-depth and group interviews, structured interviews (interviewer administered questionnaires) being discussed in Chapter 11.

Section 10.3 considers situations favouring the use of semi-structured and in-depth interviews. The following three sections examine issues associated with the use of these types of interview. Section 10.4 identifies data quality issues associated with their use and discusses how to overcome them. Section 10.5 considers the areas of competence that you will need to develop. Section 10.6 discusses logistical and resource issues and how to manage these. Throughout the discussion of issues related to the use of semi-structured and in-depth interviews our focus is on what you will need to think about in order to be able to conduct these interviews. Section 10.7 considers the particular advantages and issues associated with the use of group interviews and focus groups. Finally, Section 10.8 explores the advantages and issues associated with telephone, Internet and intranet-mediated (electronic) interviews.

## 10.2  Types of interview and their link to the purposes of research and research strategy

### Types of interview

Interviews may be highly formalised and structured, using standardised questions for each **respondent** (Section 11.2), or they may be informal and unstructured conversations. In between there are intermediate positions. One typology that is commonly used is thus related to the level of formality and structure, whereby interviews may be categorised as one of:

There is probably not a day that goes by without you reading about, listening to and watching interviews. We read interviews such as those given by business leaders in quality newspapers, listen to interviews such as those with celebrities on radio programmes and watch interviews such as those with politicians on television programmes. However, despite the seeming ease with which they are conducted, using the interview to collect research data requires considerable skills.

Interviewer skills are regularly demonstrated by presenters such as the BBC's Jeremy Paxman. His interview with the UK government's Home Secretary, Michael Howard, on 13 May 1997 is still remembered as one of the toughest political interviews ever conducted (BBC, 2005) and resulted subsequently in Paxman winning the 1998 Interviewer of the Year award. During the interview, Paxman was questioning Howard about the management of the UK Prison Service and, in particular, his account of the recent dismissal of the Head of the Prison Service at that time, Derek Lewis. During the interview Paxman asked the former Home Secretary the question 'Did you threaten to overrule him [i.e. Lewis]?'

*Jeremy Paxman on* Newsnight

twelve times, the question relating to a decision about a particular prison. Before moving on to the next part of the interview Paxman commented: 'With respect, you have not answered the question of whether you threatened to overrule him.' At the time, this interview and, in particular, Howard's responses to this question were thought likely to have contributed to the stalling of Howard's political career.

- structured interviews;
- semi-structured interviews;
- unstructured or in-depth interviews.

Another typology (Healey, 1991; Healey and Rawlinson, 1993, 1994) differentiates between:

- standardised interviews;
- non-standardised interviews.

Robson (2002), based on the work of Powney and Watts (1987), refers to a different typology:

- respondent interviews;
- informant interviews.

There is overlap between these different typologies, although consideration of each typology adds to our overall understanding of the nature of research interviews.

**Structured interviews** use questionnaires based on a predetermined and *standardised* or identical set of questions and we refer to them as interviewer-administered questionnaires (Section 11.2). You read out each question and then record the response on a standardised schedule, usually with pre-coded answers (Sections 11.4 and 12.2). While there is social interaction between you and the respondent, such as the preliminary explanations that you will need to provide, you should read out the questions exactly as written and in the same tone of voice so that you do not indicate any bias. As structured interviews are used to collect quantifiable data they are also referred to as *quantitative research interviews*.

By comparison, semi-structured and in-depth (unstructured) interviews are *non-standardised*. These are often referred to as *qualitative research interviews* (King, 2004). In **semi-structured interviews** the researcher will have a list of themes and questions to be covered, although these may vary from interview to interview. This means that you may omit some questions in particular interviews, given a specific organisational context that is encountered in relation to the research topic. The order of questions may also be varied depending on the flow of the conversation. On the other hand, additional questions may be required to explore your research question and objectives given the nature of events within particular organisations. The nature of the questions and the ensuing discussion mean that data will be recorded by audio-recording the conversation or perhaps note taking (Section 10.5).

**Unstructured interviews** are informal. You would use these to explore in depth a general area in which you are interested. We therefore refer to these as *in-depth interviews* in this chapter and elsewhere in this book. There is no predetermined list of questions to work through in this situation, although you need to have a clear idea about the aspect or aspects that you want to explore. The interviewee is given the opportunity to talk freely about events, behaviour and beliefs in relation to the topic area, so that this type of interaction is sometimes called *non-directive*. It has been labelled as an **informant interview** since it is the interviewee's perceptions that guide the conduct of the interview. In comparison, a **respondent interview** is one where the interviewer directs the interview and the interviewee responds to the questions of the researcher (Easterby-Smith *et al.*, 2002; Ghauri and Grønhaug, 2005; Healey and Rawlinson, 1994; Robson, 2002).

We can also differentiate between types of interview related to the nature of interaction between the researcher and those who participate in this process. Interviews may be conducted on a one-to-one basis, between you and a single participant. Such interviews are most commonly conducted by meeting your participant 'face to face', but there may be some situations where you conduct an interview by telephone or electronically via the Internet or an organisation's intranet. There may be other situations where you conduct a semi-structured or in-depth interview on a group basis, where you meet with a small number of participants to explore an aspect of your research through a group discussion that you facilitate. These forms of interview are summarised in Figure 10.1. The discussion throughout most of this chapter applies to each of these forms. However, the final two sections (10.7 and 10.8) include specific consideration of the issues and advantages related to the use of group interviews and focus groups and to the use of a telephone and Internet-mediated interviews as an alternative to a 'face-to-face' meeting, respectively.

## Links to the purpose of research and research strategy

Each form of interview outlined above has a distinct purpose. Standardised interviews are normally used to gather data, which will then be the subject of quantitative analysis (Sections 12.3–12.5), for example as part of a survey strategy. Non-standardised (semi-structured and in-depth) interviews are used to gather data, which are normally analysed qualitatively (Sections 13.2–13.6), for example as part of a case study strategy. These data are likely to be used not only to reveal and understand the 'what' and the 'how' but also to place more emphasis on exploring the 'why'.

In Chapter 5 we outlined how the purpose of your research could be classified as exploratory, descriptive and explanatory studies (Section 5.2). By examining these categories we can see how the various types of interview may be used to gather information for, and assist the progress of, each kind of study:

- In an exploratory study, in-depth interviews can be very helpful to 'find out what is happening [and] to seek new insights' (Robson, 2002:59) (Box 10.1). Semi-structured interviews may also be used in relation to an exploratory study.

- In descriptive studies, structured interviews (Section 11.2) can be used as a means to identify general patterns.

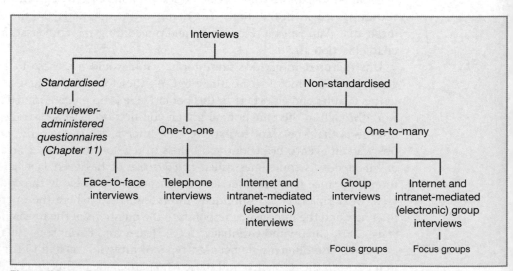

Figure 10.1    Forms of interview

- In an explanatory study, semi-structured interviews may be used in order to understand the relationships between variables, such as those revealed from a descriptive study (Section 5.2). Structured interviews may also be used in relation to an explanatory study, in a statistical sense (Section 12.5).

This is summarised in Table 10.1.

Your research may incorporate more than one type of interview. As part of a survey strategy, for example, you may decide to use in-depth or semi-structured interviews initially to help identify the questions that should be asked in your questionnaire. The data that you gather from such exploratory interviews will be used in the design of your questionnaire or structured interview. Semi-structured interviews may be used to explore and explain themes that have emerged from the use of your questionnaire (Wass and Wells, 1994). In addition to this staged approach, Healey and Rawlinson (1994:130) state that a combination of styles may be used within one interview: 'one section of an interview may ask a common set of factual questions . . . while in another section a semi-structured qualitative approach may be used to explore [responses]'. Wass and Wells (1994) make the point that interviews, presumably semi-structured or in-depth ones, may also be used as a means to validate findings from the use of questionnaires. We can therefore see that the various types of interview have a number of potentially valuable uses in terms of undertaking your research project. The key point for you to consider is the consistency between your research question and objectives, the strategy you will employ and the methods of data collection you will use – their fitness for purpose.

## 10.3 Situations favouring non-standardised (qualitative) interviews

There are many situations in which the use of non-standardised (qualitative) research interviews as a method of data collection may be advantageous. These can be grouped into four aspects related to interview:

- the purpose of the research;
- the significance of establishing personal contact;
- the nature of the data collection questions;
- length of time required and completeness of the process.

We examine each of these in turn.

**Table 10.1  Uses of different types of interview in each of the main research categories**

|  | Exploratory | Descriptive | Explanatory |
|---|---|---|---|
| Structured |  | ✓✓ | ✓ |
| Semi-structured | ✓ |  | ✓✓ |
| Unstructured | ✓✓ |  |  |

✓✓ = more frequent, ✓ = less frequent

## BOX 10.1 FOCUS ON MANAGEMENT RESEARCH

### Continuity and change in mergers and acquisitions

A recent paper by Johannes Ulrich, Jan Wieseke and Rolf Van Dick in the *Journal of Management Studies* (2005) examines the role of a sense of continuity for employees' organisational indentification after an organisational merger in a Germany-based global organisation. Prior to this, the two merged companies had been operating as competitors in the same market. In-depth interviews were conducted with a probability sample of 16 top managers, 12 months after the merger. This sample was drawn from a population of 50 managers identified as having high potential by the company's internal leadership development system. Nine of the sample came from one of the merger partners and seven from the other.

The interview guide used in the research consisted of open-ended questions and brainstorming cues. These were divided into four sections (2005:1556–7):

- 'feelings towards and acceptance of the new company structure' – where participants were encouraged to say what came into their mind but with a focus on emotional reactions, acceptance of the new structure and issues associated with its implementation;

- 'hot spots' – where respondents were asked to identify places on the new organisation chart where things did not run smoothly;

- 'organisational identification' – where participants were asked to describe how much they and their subordinates identified with different foci before and after the merger;

- 'outlook' – where participants were asked to project the future situation of the company in 12 months' time and what they would have done differently if they had been in charge of creating the new company structure.

Interviews were conducted at five different company locations in Western Germany. Each interview lasted between one and two hours, all but one being audio-recorded. All interviews were voluntary, with assurances of confidentiality being given. Subsequently the interview findings were discussed and validated by in-depth interviews with the company's change agent and triangulated using 40 company newspapers published both before, during and after the merger.

## The purpose of the research

Where you are undertaking an exploratory study, or a study that includes an exploratory element, it is likely that you will include non-standardised (qualitative) research interviews in your design (Blumberg *et al.*, 2005). Similarly, an explanatory study is also likely to include interviews in order for the researcher to be able to infer causal relationships between variables (Sections 5.2 and 11.4). Essentially, where it is necessary for you to understand the reasons for the decisions that your research participants have taken, or to understand the reasons for their attitudes and opinions, it will be necessary for you to conduct a **qualitative interview**.

Semi-structured and in-depth interviews provide you with the opportunity to 'probe' answers, where you want your interviewees to explain, or build on, their responses. This is important if you are adopting an interpretivist epistemology, where you will be concerned to understand the meanings that respondents ascribe to various phenomena (Section 4.2). Interviewees may use words or ideas in a particular way, and the opportunity to probe these meanings will add significance and depth to the data you obtain. It may also lead the discussion into areas that you had not previously considered but which are significant for your understanding, and which help you to address your research question and objectives, or indeed help you formulate such a question. They also afford each interviewee an opportunity to hear herself or himself 'thinking aloud' about things she or he may not have previously thought about. The result should be that you are able to collect a rich and detailed set of data.

## The significance of establishing personal contact

We have found that managers are more likely to agree to be interviewed, rather than complete a questionnaire, especially where the interview topic is seen to be interesting and relevant to their current work. An interview provides them with an opportunity to reflect on events without needing to write anything down. Other researchers report similar conclusions, where participants prefer to be interviewed rather than fill in a questionnaire (North *et al.*, 1983, cited in Healey, 1991). This situation also provides the opportunity for interviewees to receive feedback and personal assurance about the way in which information will be used (Sections 6.2 and 6.4, Box 6.1).

Potential research participants who receive a questionnaire through the post may be reluctant to complete it for a number of reasons. They may feel that it is not appropriate to provide sensitive and confidential information to someone they have never met. They may also not completely trust the way in which the information they provide is used. They may be reluctant to spend time providing written explanatory answers, where these are requested, especially if the meaning of any question is not entirely clear. The use of personal interviews, where appropriate, may therefore achieve a higher response rate than using questionnaires. Healey (1991:206) also makes the point that 'the interviewer . . . has more control over who answers the questions' in comparison with a questionnaire, which may be passed from one person to another.

## The nature of the questions

An interview will undoubtedly be the most advantageous approach to attempt to obtain data in the following circumstances (Easterby-Smith *et al.*, 2002; Healey, 1991; Jankowicz, 2005):

- where there are a large number of questions to be answered;
- where the questions are either complex or open-ended;
- where the order and logic of questioning may need to be varied (Box 10.2).

A semi-structured or in-depth interview will be most appropriate for the latter two types of situation.

## Length of time required and completeness of the process

Apart from the difficulty of trying to design a viable questionnaire schedule to cope with issues that are complex, unclear, or large in number, the time needed for the respondent to complete the questionnaire may mean that an interview is in any case the best or only alternative. In our experience, where expectations have been clearly established about the length of time required and participants understand and agree with the objectives of the research interview, they have generally been willing to agree to be interviewed. Some negotiation is, in any case, possible and the interview can be arranged at a time when the interviewee will be under least pressure. We have found that our respondents tend to be

**BOX 10.2 WORKED EXAMPLE**

### The need to vary the order and logic of questioning

Val undertook a series of semi-structured interviews into the approach used to manage public relations (PR) activities in 30 organisations. It soon became evident that it would not be meaningful to ask exactly the same questions in each organisation. For example, some organisations had centralised PR as part of the marketing function, whereas in other organisations it was devolved to individual business units. Another significant variable was associated with the public relations styles adopted. Some organisations adopted a 'press agency' approach where the main focus was to get the organisation or product mentioned in the media as often as possible, the nature of the mention being of secondary importance. Others adopted a 'public information' approach where the main aim was to get media exposure for the organisation or product.

The impact of these and other variables meant that it was not sensible to ask exactly the same questions at each interview, even though many questions remained applicable in all cases and the underlying intention was to ensure consistency between interviews. It was not until each interview had started that Val was able to learn which of these different variables operated within the particular organisation. Fortunately, the flexibility offered by semi-structured interviews enabled her to do this.

generous with their time, and sometimes when interviews have been arranged to start at mid-morning they often arrange for lunch, which can allow the discussion and exploration of issues to continue. However, for those of you who fancy a free lunch, we do not want to raise your expectations falsely, and the start time for an interview should not be set with this in mind!

Your aim will be to obtain data to enable you to answer all your research questions, allowing for the right of participants to decline to respond to any question you ask. Where you conduct the event skilfully an interview is more likely to achieve this than the use of a self-administered or interviewer-administered questionnaire. Where your respondent does not provide an answer to a particular question or questions in a non-standardised interview, you should be able to form some indication of why a response could not be provided. This may even lead you to modify the question or to compose another where this would be appropriate. Section 6.4 provides a consideration of the ethical issues associated with seeking to obtain answers.

While there are a number of situations favouring the use of non-standardised (qualitative research) interviews, you still need to decide whether or not to use these types of interview and to justify your choice. Box 10.3 provides a checklist to help you in your deliberations.

## 10.4 Data quality issues and preparing for the interview

### Data quality issues

A number of data quality issues can be identified in relation to the use of semi-structured and in-depth interviews, related to:

- reliability;

**BOX 10.3** CHECKLIST

## To help you decide whether to use semi-structured or in-depth interviews

☑ Does the purpose of your research suggest using semi-structured and/or in-depth interviews?

☑ Will it help to seek personal contact in terms of gaining access to participants and their data?

☑ Are your data collection questions large in number, complex or open-ended?

☑ Will there be a need to vary the order and logic of questioning?

☑ Will it help to be able to probe interviewees' responses to build on or seek explanation of their answers?

☑ Will the data collection process with each individual involve a relatively lengthy period?

- forms of bias;
- validity and generalisability.

These are discussed in turn.

The lack of standardisation in such interviews may lead to concerns about *reliability*. In relation to qualitative research, reliability is concerned with whether alternative researchers would reveal similar information (Easterby-Smith *et al.*, 2002; Healey and Rawlinson, 1994). The concern about reliability in these types of interview is also related to issues of bias. There are various types of bias to consider. The first of these is related to **interviewer bias**. This is where the comments, tone or non-verbal behaviour of the interviewer creates bias in the way that interviewees respond to the questions being asked. This may be where you attempt to impose your own beliefs and frame of reference through the questions that you ask. It is also possible that you will demonstrate bias in the way you interpret responses (Easterby-Smith *et al.*, 2002). Where you are unable to develop the trust of the interviewee, or perhaps where your credibility is seen to be lacking, the value of the information given may also be limited, raising doubts about its validity and reliability.

Related to this is **interviewee** or **response bias**. This type of bias may be caused by perceptions about the interviewer, as referred to above, or in relation to perceived interviewer bias. However, the cause of this type of bias is not necessarily linked to any perception related to the interviewer. Taking part in an interview is an intrusive process. This is especially true in the case of in-depth or semi-structured interviews, where your aim will be to explore events or to seek explanations. The interviewee may, in principle, be willing to participate but may nevertheless be sensitive to the unstructured exploration of certain themes. Interviewees may therefore choose not to reveal and discuss an aspect of the topic that you wish to explore, because this would lead to probing questions that would intrude on sensitive information that they do not wish, or are not empowered, to discuss with you. The outcome of this may be that the interviewee provides a partial 'picture' of the situation that casts himself or herself in a 'socially desirable' role, or the organisation for which they work in a positive or even negative fashion.

Bias may also result from the nature of the individuals or organisational participants who agree to be interviewed (Box 10.4). The time-consuming requirements of the interview process may result in a reduction in willingness to take part on behalf of some of those to whom you would like to talk. This may bias your sample from whom data are collected (Robson, 2002). This is an issue that you will need to consider carefully and attempt to overcome through the approach taken to sampling (Sections 7.2 and 7.3).

## BOX 10.4 WORKED EXAMPLE

### Willingness (or otherwise) to be interviewed

Saffron's research project involved her interviewing people about their perceptions of the real benefits of different hair products. She decided that the best way to conduct these interviews was, with the permission of the owner, to interview customers at her local hairdresser. Saffron discovered that although some of the customers were willing to be interviewed, others were not. A minority of customers, often smartly dressed in business suits, refused outright, saying that they had insufficient time. In contrast, others, particularly pensioners, were happy to answer her questions in considerable detail and appeared to wish to prolong the interview.

There is also likely to be an issue about the generalisability of the findings from qualitatively based interview studies, although the validity of such studies is not raised as an issue. If we consider *validity* first, this refers to the extent to which the researcher gains access to their participants' knowledge and experience, and is able to infer a meaning that the participant intended from the language that was used by this person. The high level of validity that is possible in relation to non-standardised (qualitative) interviews that are conducted carefully is made clear by the following quotation:

> The main reason for the potential superiority of qualitative approaches for obtaining information is that the flexible and responsive interaction which is possible between interviewer and respondent(s) allows meanings to be probed, topics to be covered from a variety of angles and questions made clear to respondents.
>
> (Sykes, 1991:8, cited in Healey and Rawlinson, 1994:132)

However, qualitative research using semi-structured or in-depth interviews will not be able to be used to make *generalisations* about the entire population (whatever this may be in the context of the research topic) where this is based on a small and unrepresentative number of cases. This is often the situation when adopting a case study strategy (Yin, 2003).

## Overcoming data quality issues

### Reliability

One response to the issue of reliability is that the findings derived from using non-standardised research methods are not necessarily intended to be repeatable since they reflect reality at the time they were collected, in a situation which may be subject to change (Marshall and Rossman, 1999). The assumption behind this type of research is that the circumstances to be explored are complex and dynamic. The value of using non-standardised interviews is derived from the flexibility that you may use to explore the complexity of the topic. Therefore an attempt to ensure that qualitative, non-standardised research could be replicated by other researchers would not be realistic or feasible without undermining the strength of this type of research. Marshall and Rossman (1999) suggest that researchers using a qualitative, non-standardised approach need to make this clear – perhaps to transform an aspect perceived to be a weakness by some into a strength based on realistic assumptions about the ability to replicate research findings.

However, they suggest that where you use this approach you should make and retain notes relating to your research design, the reasons underpinning the choice of strategy and methods, and the data obtained. This will be referred to by other researchers in order to understand the processes that you used and your findings and, where appropriate, to enable them to reanalyse the data you collected. The use of non-standardised interviews should not lead to a lack of rigour in relation to the research process – if anything, greater rigour is required to overcome the views of those who may be wedded to the value of quantitative research to the exclusion of any other approach.

## Preparation

Like all research methods, the key to a successful interview is careful preparation. When using non-structured interviews the five Ps are a useful mantra: prior planning prevents poor performance. In particular, we believe it is critical that you plan precisely how you are going to demonstrate your credibility and obtain the confidence of the interviewees. Issues associated with this are discussed in the following subsections and summarised in Box 10.12 on page 328 as a checklist.

**Level of knowledge**   You need to be knowledgeable about the organisational or situational context in which the interview is to take place. A prior search in your university library (Sections 3.4 and 3.5) may reveal journal articles written by senior employees of the organisation that is participating in your research. There may also be other material about the organisation, and this is particularly likely to be found on the Internet, in the 'trade' press and the quality newspapers. It may also be appropriate to look at company reports and other publications, or financial data relating to the organisation. The ability to draw on this type of information in the interview should help to demonstrate your credibility and thereby encourage the interviewee to offer a more detailed account of the topic under discussion. A further benefit of this is made clear by Healey and Rawlinson (1994:136): 'A well informed interviewer has a basis for assessing the accuracy of some of the information offered.'

Your level of knowledge about your research topic should also help to establish your credibility in the view of your research participant. This knowledge may be gleaned through the review of the literature that you undertake. As you undertake a number of interviews, you will also be able to draw on the initial analysis that you make of data previously collected.

**Level of information supplied to the interviewee**   Credibility may also be promoted through the supply of relevant information to participants before the interview. Providing participants with a list of the interview themes before the event, where this is appropriate, should help this. The list of themes (Boxes 10.1 and 10.5) should also promote validity and reliability by enabling the interviewee to consider the information being requested and allowing them the opportunity to assemble supporting organisational documentation from their files. We can testify to this approach and the value of allowing participants to prepare themselves for the discussion in which they are to engage. Access to organisational documentation also allows for triangulation of the data provided (Sections 8.2 and 8.3). Our experience is that participants are generally willing to supply a photocopy of such material, although of course it will be necessary to conceal any confidential or personal details that this contains.

## BOX 10.5 WORKED EXAMPLE

### Developing interview themes

Karl was interested in understanding why some employees in his organisation used the IT Help Desk whilst others did not. This subject was felt to be significant in relation to the perceptions of service level agreements, service relationships and service quality. He decided to provide his interviewees with a list of themes that he wished to explore during the interviews. After some deliberation and reading of the academic literature he came up with the following list (extract):

- what employees understand by the term 'IT Help Desk';
- the extent to which the IT Help Desk is meeting employees' needs;
- the nature of support employees feel they are receiving;
- the extent to which employees feel they know how to use the IT Help Desk;
- the services employees feel the IT Help Desk should be providing;
- knowledge of service level agreements.

He subsequently used these to develop his interview guide (Box 10.6).

Interview themes may be derived from the literature that you read, the theories that you consider, your experience of a particular topic, common sense, discussions with co-workers, fellow students, tutors and research participants, or some combination of these approaches. You will need to have some notion of the theme or themes that you wish to discuss with your participants even if you intend to commence with exploratory, in-depth interviews and adopt a grounded theory approach to your research project (Section 13.6). Without at least some focus, your work will clearly lack a sense of direction and purpose. It will be necessary for you to formulate a focus if your work is to make progress. You should therefore start with a set of themes that reflect the variables being studied, or at least one or more general questions related to your research topic that you could use to start your interview. These can be incorporated into your *interview guide* (Box 10.6). This lists topics that you intend to cover in the interview along with initial question and probes that may be used to follow up initial responses and obtain greater detail from the participants (King, 2004). When creating your guide, you need to try to ensure that the order of questions is likely to be logical to your participants and that the language you use will be comprehensible. Using your guide, you will be able to develop and/or explore research themes through the non-standardised interviews that you conduct to see whether you can identify and test relationships between them (Chapter 13).

**Appropriateness of location**    It is possible that the place you conduct your interviews may influence the data you collect. As we discussed in Section 6.4, you should choose the location for your interviews with regard to your own personal safety. However, it is also important that you think about the impact that the location will have upon your participants and the responses they are likely to give. In particular, you should choose a location which is convenient for your participants, where they will feel comfortable and where the interview is unlikely to be disturbed (Box 10.7). Finally, you need to choose a place that is quiet so that outside noise will not reduce the quality of your audio-recording of the interview. Mark recalls an interview in a room outside which building work was taking place. Although he was able to hear the participant's responses clearly whilst the interview was taking place, for much of the audio-recording these responses were unintelligible due to the sound of a very loud pneumatic drill!

**BOX 10.6 WORKED EXAMPLE**

### Extract from an interview guide

Karl was interested in understanding why some employees in his organisation used the IT Help Desk whilst others did not. Using his interview themes (Box 10.5) he began to develop his guide:

**Help Desk Support**

1 To what extent does the IT Help Desk meet your needs?

*Probe: In what ways? [ask for real-life examples]*

*Probe: Can you give me an example (if possible) of when you received good support from the IT Help Desk?*

*Probe: Can you give me an example (if possible) of when you received insufficient support from the IT Help Desk?*

2 Do you consider you have enough support from the IT Help Desk?

*Probe: How is this support provided (e.g. telephone, face to face)?*

*Probe: What else (if anything) could usefully be done?*

**BOX 10.7 WORKED EXAMPLE**

### Choosing an appropriate location

Anne was pleased that the manufacturing company in which she was undertaking her research had arranged for her to use a room in the Human Resources Department. The room contained a low table and chairs, had an electric plug socket for her audio-recorder and she had been provided with bottled water and glasses as well. However, after her third interview she was beginning to doubt her own interviewing skills. Her participants, the company's production line workers, seemed unwilling to be open in their responses. She began to wonder if something was wrong with the interview location and decided to ask the next participant about this. At the end of that interview she had her answer. Her participants were unhappy with the interview location. Prior to being interviewed by Anne, the only time they or their colleagues had visited the Human Resources Department was to receive a reprimand. The location was therefore inappropriate!

**Appropriateness of the researcher's appearance at the interview**  Your appearance may affect the perception of the interviewee. Where this has an adverse affect on your credibility in the view of interviewees, or results in a failure to gain their confidence, the resulting bias may affect the reliability of the information provided. Robson (2002) advises researchers to adopt a similar style of dress to those to be interviewed. Essentially, you will need to wear clothing that will be generally acceptable for the setting within which the interview is to occur (Box 10.8).

**Nature of the opening comments to be made when the interview commences**  Where the interviewee has not met you before, the first few minutes of conversation will have a significant impact on the outcome of the interview – again related to the issue of your credibility and the level of the interviewee's confidence. Often such interviews occur in

## BOX 10.8 WORKED EXAMPLE

### Checking out the dress code

Mel arranged to visit the administration centre of a large insurance comapny on a Friday to conduct a group interview with staff drawn from one of its telephone sales divisions and two one-to-one interviews with senior managers. He felt that it was appropriate to wear fairly 'formal' clothes to match what he thought would be the dress code of the organisation. Indeed, for four days of the working week this assumption would have been appropriate. However, the organisation had recently introduced the practice of not wearing such formal work clothes on Fridays. Thus he found himself the only one dressed formally in the organisation on the day of his visit. Taking lunch proved to be a memorable experience, as he intermingled with everyone else dressed in jeans and tee shirts, etc. His 'mistake' proved to be an amusing opening at the start of each interview rather than a barrier to gaining access to participants' data. Indeed, it might not have been appropriate for him to match too closely the 'dress-down' style of participants. Nevertheless, it does provide a useful example of the way in which expectations about appearance are likely to be noticed.

a setting that is unfamiliar to you. Despite this, it is your responsibility to shape the start of the discussion. You will need to explain your research to the participant and, hopefully, gain their consent (Section 6.4, Box 6.12). As part of this you will need to establish your credibility and gain the interviewee's confidence. During these initial discussions we have found that the interviewee often has some uncertainties about sharing information, and about the manner in which these data may be used. Alternatively, she or he may still need clarification about the exact nature of the data that you wish to obtain. We have found that a pre-prepared participant information sheet (Section 6.4, Box 6.12) and consent form (Box 6.13) are both extremely helpful in reducing anxieties. There may also be a degree of curiosity on the part of the interviewee and probably a genuine level of interest in the research, related to the reason why the request to participate was accepted. This curiosity and interest will offer an opening for both parties to start a conversation, probably before the 'intended discussion' commences. You may find it appropriate to follow the initial discussion by demonstrating interest in the interviewee by asking about their role within the host organisation (Ghauri and Grønhaug, 2005). However, you need to make sure that these opening moves to demonstrate credibility and friendliness, and to relax and develop a positive relationship, are not overstated, so that too much time is used and the interviewee starts to become bored or restive.

The start of the intended discussion therefore needs to be shaped by you. It is your opportunity to allay, wherever possible, the interviewee's uncertainties about providing information, establish the participant's rights and, based upon this, hopefully, obtain informed consent. Box 10.9 provides a structure that you can adapt for starting your interviews.

Healey and Rawlinson (1994) say that an assurance from you that confidential information is not being sought should make interviewees more relaxed and open about the information that they are willing to discuss. Combined with assurances about anonymity, this should increase the level of confidence in your trustworthiness and reduce the possibility of interviewee or response bias. You can also demonstrate your commitment to confidentiality by not naming other organisations that have participated in your research, or by talking about the data you obtained from them.

## BOX 10.9 WORKED EXAMPLE

### Opening a semi-structured interview

As part of her research project Bethan undertook a series of semi-structured interviews with freelance IT consultants working for a range of organisations. She covered the following points at the start of each interview:

■ The participant was thanked for considering the request for access and for agreeing to the meeting.

■ The purpose of the research and its progress to date were outlined briefly. As part of this, the participant was given an information sheet to keep.

■ The previously agreed right to confidentiality and anonymity was reiterated by stating that nothing said by the participant would be attributed to her or him without first seeking and obtaining permission.

■ The participant's right not to answer any question was emphasised and that the interview would be stopped if they wished.

■ The participant was told about the nature of the outputs to which the research was intended to lead and what would happen to the data collected during and after the project.

■ The offer to provide a summary of the research findings to the interviewee was also restated, as was when this would happen.

■ The request to record the interview electronically was restated and, where agreed, this was used subsequently.

■ Before the substantive discussion started, Bethan again requested permission to undertake the interview, summarised the themes to be covered, confirmed the amount of time available and requested that the participant read and signed the informed consent form.

All of these points were dealt with within five minutes.

**Approach to questioning**   When conducted appropriately, your approach to questioning should reduce the scope for bias during the interview and increase the reliability of the information obtained. Your questions need to be phrased clearly, so that the interviewee can understand them, and you should ask them in a neutral tone of voice. Easterby-Smith *et al.* (2002) point out that the use of open questions (Section 10.5) should help to avoid bias. These can then be followed up by the use of appropriately worded probing questions (Section 10.5). The use of these types of question will help you to explore the topic and to produce a fuller account. Conversely, questions that seek to lead the interviewee or which indicate bias on your part should be avoided. Perceived interviewer bias may well lead to interviewee or response bias. Long questions or those that are really made up of two or more questions should also be avoided if you are to obtain a response to each aspect that you are interested to explore (Robson, 2002).

Questions should also avoid too many theoretical concepts or jargon since your understanding of such terms may vary from that of your interviewees. Where theoretical concepts or specific terminology need to be used, you will have to ensure that both you and the interviewee have the same understanding (Box 10.10; Easterby-Smith *et al.*, 2002; Ghauri and Grønhaug, 2005).

When asking questions it is important that wherever possible these are grounded in the real-life experiences of your participants rather than being on an abstract concept. One approach to questioning which makes use of key participant experiences is the

**critical incident technique**, in which respondents are asked to describe in detail a critical incident or number of incidents that are key to the research question. A **critical incident** is defined as an activity or event where the consequences were so clear that the respondent has a definite idea regarding the effects (Keaveney, 1995).

---

### BOX 10.10 WORKED EXAMPLE

#### (Mis)understanding terminology

Sven was conducting an interview with the European sales manager of a large multinational corporation. Throughout the interview the sales manager referred to the European Division. Sven assumed that the sales manager meant continental Europe. However, by chance, later questions revealed that, for this organisation, Europe extended into parts of Asia, including Turkey, the United Arab Emirates, Saudi Arabia, Kuwait and Israel. Until this point in the interview, Sven had assumed that these countries were the responsibility of another sales manager!

---

Healey and Rawlinson (1994:138) suggest that 'it is usually best to leave sensitive questions until near the end of an interview because this allows a greater time for the respondent to build up trust and confidence in the researchers'. They report cases where the first part of an interview is used by participants to assess the level of trust that can be placed in the researcher. Others have witnessed this experience, as Box 10.11 illustrates, affecting the nature of the questions that may be asked during the early part of an interview.

---

### BOX 10.11 WORKED EXAMPLE

#### Establishing trust and asking sensitive questions

Sam recalls an occasion when her treatment by her participants altered as her group interview progressed. For the first hour of a two-hour interview it appeared to her that the participants were convinced that she was really there to sell them a consultancy service. When they accepted that she was not going to try to sell them something, the mood of the interview changed and they became much more relaxed and responsive to the questions that Sam wished to ask. It was at this point that she was able to ask and pursue more sensitive questions that could have led to the interview being terminated during the period when the participants mistrusted her motives.

---

Once this position of trust has been reached and you wish to seek responses to potentially sensitive questions, Ghauri and Grønhaug (2005) point out that the wording of these deserve very particular attention in order to avoid any negative inferences related to, for example, responsibility for failure or error. Care taken over the exploration of sensitive questions should help towards the compilation of a fuller and more reliable account.

*Nature and impact of the interviewer's behaviour during the course of the interview*
Appropriate behaviour by the researcher should also reduce the scope for bias during the interview. Comments or non-verbal behaviour, such as gestures, which indicate any bias in your thinking should be avoided. A neutral (but not an uninterested) response should be projected in relation to the interviewee's answers in order not to provide any lead that

may result in bias. Robson (2002) says that you should enjoy the interview opportunity, or at least appear to do so. An appearance of boredom on your part is hardly likely to encourage your interviewee!

Your posture and tone of voice may also encourage or inhibit the flow of the discussion. You should sit slightly inclined towards the interviewee and adopt an open posture, avoiding folded arms. This should provide a signal of attentiveness to your interviewee (Torrington, 1991). Tone of voice can also provide a signal to the interviewee. You need to project interest and enthusiasm through your voice, avoiding any impression of anxiety, disbelief, astonishment or any other negative signal.

**Demonstration of attentive listening skills**    The purpose of a semi-structured or in-depth interview will be to understand the participant's explanations and meanings. This type of interaction will not be typical of many of the conversations that you normally engage in, where those involved often compete to speak rather than concentrate on listening. You therefore need to recognise that different skills will be emphasised in this kind of interaction. Torrington (1991:43) says that listening involves people being 'on the look-out for signals and willing to spend the time needed to listen and build understanding, deliberately holding back our own thoughts, which would divert or compete with the other's'.

It will be necessary for you to explore and probe explanations and meanings, but you must also provide the interviewee with reasonable time to develop their responses, and you must avoid projecting your own views (Easterby-Smith *et al.*, 2002; Ghauri and Grønhaug, 2005; Robson, 2002). Careful listening should allow you to identify comments that are significant to the research topic and to explore these with the interviewee (Torrington, 1991).

**Scope to test understanding**    You may test your understanding by summarising an explanation provided by the interviewee. This will allow the interviewee to 'evaluate the adequacy of the interpretation and correct where necessary' (Healey and Rawlinson, 1994:138). This can be a powerful tool for avoiding a biased or incomplete interpretation. It may also act as a means to explore and probe the interviewee's responses further.

In addition to this opportunity to test understanding at the interview, you may also ask the interviewee to read through the factual account that you produce of the interview. Where the interviewee is prepared to undertake this, it will provide a further opportunity for you to test your understanding and for the interviewee to add any further points of relevance that may occur to them.

**Approach to recording data**    As well as audio-recording your interview (discussed in Section 10.5), we believe it is important to also make notes as the interview progresses. In addition to providing a back-up if your audio-recording does not work, this provides another way for you to show that your participant's responses are important to you. If possible, immediately after the interview has taken place you should compile a full record of the interview (Healey, 1991; Healey and Rawlinson, 1994; Robson, 2002). Where you do not do this, the exact nature of explanations provided may be lost as well as general points of value. There is also the possibility that you may mix up data from different interviews, where you carry out several of these within a short period of time and you do not complete a record of each one at the time it takes place (Ghauri and Grønhaug, 2005). Either situation will clearly lead to an issue about the trustworthiness of any data. You therefore need to allocate time to write up a full set of notes soon after the event. In addition to your notes from the actual interview, you should also record the following **contextual data**:

- the location of the interview (e.g. the organisation, the place);
- the date and time;
- the setting of the interview (e.g. was the room quiet or noisy, could you be overheard, were you interrupted?);
- background information about the respondent (e.g. their role, post title, gender);
- your immediate impression of how well (or badly) the interview went (e.g. was the participant reticent, were there aspects about which you felt you did not obtain answers in sufficient depth?).

You are probably wondering how, if you are also recording these data, you can still help ensure confidentiality and anonymity of your participants where this has been promised. As we outlined in Section 6.4, the best course of action is likely to be ensuring that your data are completely and genuinely anonymised. This means that you should store the contextual data separately from your interview transcripts. We suggest that you should be able to link these two sets of data only by using a 'key' such as a code number. We also suggest that if a key to identify participants by name which can link them to these data is absolutely necessary, this should not be retained by those who control these data and should, again, be kept separately. In addition, as pointed out in Section 6.4, you will need to take great care in the way you report your findings to help preserve anonymity and confidentiality.

Cultural differences and bias   As a final note to this particular discussion, we need to recognise that it is often difficult to attempt to control bias in all cases. Other factors may become significant. For example, there may be misinterpretation of responses because of cultural differences between the interviewee and the interviewer (Marshall and Rossman, 1999). This issue is not exclusively related to interviews and can be associated with a number of data collection methods. For example, we encountered it in relation to the interpretation of the data produced from a cross-national survey. An in-depth interview at least offers the opportunity to explore meanings, including those that may be culturally specific, but you will need to be aware of cultural differences and their implications (see, for example, Hofstede, 2001).

## Generalisability

In the first part of this section, which described data quality issues relating to semi-structured and in-depth interviews, we stated that there is likely to be a concern surrounding the generalisability of findings from qualitative research, based on the use of a small and unrepresentative number of cases. However, two arguments have been advanced that seek to clarify and modify the approach often adopted to the generalisability or transferability of qualitative research. The first of these relates to the situation where a single case study is used because of the unstructured nature of the research. Bryman (1988:90) states that 'within a case study a wide range of different people and activities are invariably examined so that the contrast with survey samples is not as acute as it appears at first glance'. The single case may in fact encompass a number of settings, where for example it involves a study in a large organisation with sites across the country, or even around the world. By contrast, Bryman (1988) points out that many research projects adopting a survey strategy use samples restricted to one particular locality. A well-completed and rigorous case study is thus more likely to be useful in other contexts than one that lacks such rigour.

The second argument with the approach that questions the generalisability of qualitative research or a case study is related to the significance of this type of research to

## BOX 10.12 CHECKLIST

### To help you prepare for your semi-structured or in-depth interview

☑ How might your level of preparation and knowledge (in relation to the research context and your research question) affect the willingness of the interviewee to share data?

☑ What will be the broad focus of your in-depth interview, or what are the themes that you wish to explore or seek explanations for during a semi-structured interview?

☑ What type of information, if any, will it be useful to send to your interviewee prior to the interview?

☑ What did you agree to supply to your interviewee when you arranged the interview? Has this been supplied?

☑ How will your appearance during the interview affect the willingness of the interviewee to share data?

☑ Have you considered the impact that your interview location may have on participants' responses and on your own personal safety?

☑ How will you prepare yourself to be able to commence the interview with confidence and purpose?

☑ What will you tell your interviewee about yourself, the purpose of your research, its funding and your progress?

☑ What concerns, or need for clarification, may your interviewee have?

☑ How will you seek to overcome these concerns or provide this clarification?

☑ In particular, how do you intend to use the data to which you are given access, ensuring, where appropriate, its confidentiality and your interviewee's anonymity?

☑ What will you tell your interviewee about their right not to answer particular questions and to end the interview should they wish?

☑ How would you like to record the data that are revealed to you during the interview? Where this involves using a tape recorder, have you raised this as a request and provided a reason why it would help you to use this technique?

☑ How will you seek to overcome potential issues related to the reliability of the data you collect, including forms of interviewer bias (related to your role and conduct), interviewee bias (the level of access that you gain to the data of those whom you interview) and sampling bias?

theoretical propositions (Bryman, 1988; Yin, 2003). Where you are able to relate your research project to existing theory you will be in a position to demonstrate that your findings will have a broader theoretical significance than the case or cases that form the basis of your work (Marshall and Rossman, 1999). It will clearly be up to you to establish this relationship to existing theory in order to be able to demonstrate the broader significance of your particular case study findings.

This relationship will allow your study to test the applicability of existing theory to the setting(s) that you are examining and where this is found wanting to suggest why. It will also allow theoretical propositions to be advanced that can then be tested in another context. However, as Bryman (1988) points out, this also has implications for the relationship between theory and research, since the identification of existing theory and its application will be necessary before the researcher embarks on the collection of data.

## 10.5 | Interviewing competence

There are several areas where you need to develop and demonstrate competence in relation to the conduct of semi-structured and in-depth research interviews. These areas are:

- opening the interview;
- using appropriate language;
- questioning;
- listening;
- testing and summarising understanding;
- recognising and dealing with difficult participants;
- recording data.

Most of these competence areas have already been discussed in relation to over-coming interviewer and interviewee bias in Section 10.4. However, there is scope to discuss further approaches to questioning, recognising and dealing with difficult participants and recording information in order to be able to develop your competence. These are summarised as a checklist in Box 10.14 at the end of this sub-section.

### Questioning

Even in an in-depth interview, as well as in a semi-structured one, you will need to consider your approach to questioning. Allowing the interviewee to talk freely throughout an in-depth interview is unlikely to lead to a clearly focused discussion on issues relevant to the research topic (Easterby-Smith *et al.*, 2002; Robson, 2002) unless the purpose is simply to discover important concerns relating to the topic at a given time. It will therefore be necessary to devise relevant interview themes (Section 10.4), even though you can adopt a flexible approach about the way these are dealt with during the interview. The use of this approach demands a significant level of competence on your part. Formulating appropriate questions to explore areas in which you are interested will be critical to achieving success in this type of interviewing. We shall now discuss the types of question that you will use during semi-structured and in-depth interviews.

### Open questions

The use of **open questions** will allow participants to define and describe a situation or event. An open question is designed to encourage the interviewee to provide an extensive and developmental answer, and may be used to reveal attitudes or obtain facts (Grummitt, 1980). It encourages the interviewee to reply as they wish. An open question is likely to start with, or include, one of the following words: 'what', 'how' or 'why'. Examples of open questions include:

'Why did the organisation introduce its marketing strategy?'

'What methods have been used to make employees redundant?'

'How has corporate strategy changed over the past five years?'

### Probing questions

**Probing questions** can be used to explore responses that are of significance to the research topic. They may be worded like open questions but request a particular *focus* or direction. Examples of this type of question include:

'How would you evaluate the success of this new marketing strategy?'

'Why did you choose a compulsory method to make redundancies?'

'What external factors caused the corporate strategy to change?'

and, from Box 10.13:

'How would you describe David Brent?'

These questions may be prefaced with, for example, 'That's interesting . . .' or 'Tell me more about . . .'.

Probing questions may also be used to seek an *explanation* where you do not understand the interviewee's meaning or where the response does not reveal the reasoning involved. Examples of this type of question include:

'What do you mean by "bumping" as a means to help to secure volunteers for redundancy?'

'What is the relationship between the new statutory requirements that you referred to and the organisation's decision to set up its corporate affairs department?'

The use of *reflection* may also help you to probe a theme. This is where you will 'reflect' a statement made by the interviewee by paraphrasing their words. An example of this might be:

'Why don't you think that the employees understand the need for advertising?'

The intention will be to encourage exploration of the point made without offering a view or judgement on your part.

Where an open question does not reveal a relevant response, you may also probe the area of interest by using a *supplementary* question that finds a way of rephrasing the original question (Torrington, 1991).

### Specific and closed questions

These types of question are similar to those used in structured interviews. They can be used to obtain specific information or to confirm a fact or opinion (Section 10.4). Examples of these types of question include:

'How many people responded to the customer survey?'

This question is designed to obtain a specific piece of data.

'Did I hear you say that the new warehouse opened on 25 March?'

This, like the following question from Box 10.13, is a closed question seeking a yes or no answer.

'You're talking about [collaborator] Stephen Merchant?"'

In phrasing questions, remember that you should avoid using leading or proposing types of question in order to control any bias that may result from their use (Section 10.4).

## BOX 10.13 RESEARCH IN THE NEWS

### Office outing

Outside Coda, a swank little Manhattan bar at 34th and Madison, New Yorkers had started lining up more than an hour before show time to get good seats to see Ricky Gervais.

Gervais hasn't come to do stand-up comedy, which he certainly wouldn't mind doing in the US at some point, but rather to be interviewed on stage by *The New Yorker*'s television critic, Nancy Franklin, as part of the magazine's annual festival of arts talks. The audience (young/youngish, hip, pretty good-looking and over-whelmingly white) has paid $35 each to see Gervais, a creator of the BBC/HBO sitcom *Extras* and of the BBC sitcom *The Office*, the cult series that has made Gervais a transatlantic star. The 170 tickets to his Coda appearance sold out in four minutes.

He has won the crowd over before he walks into the room. They cheer not in prim welcome but warmly, familiarly. His hilariously tragic *Office* character David Brent – and Gervais's brilliantly subtle portrayal of him – will be studied, parodied and ripped off, probably, for generations to come. "David Brent is a name that's become part of the popular culture as a type," Franklin says as she and Gervais settle into the spotlight. "How would you describe David Brent?"

Gervais gazes into the middle distance and says, "He's a good-looking guy," scoring the first of countless big laughs.

He continues: Brent is a bad boss but not a bad man; he tries too hard; he's a bit wounded because his life hasn't turned out as he thought it should. "He wants you to think he's clever, thoughtful, sensitive, a philosopher." The answer goes on and on, suggesting not just Gervais's intimate understanding of the character but also his fascination and even regard for him. "He's one of those people that just really wants to be accepted," Gervais says. "I'd have a drink with him. I quite like David Brent. There's a bit of Brent in all of us."

It is 10pm on a Saturday night and Coda's drink special is an orangeish "orchard martini", featuring maple syrup. Gervais drinks a bottled beer. He wears a black knit shirt, black trousers, black shoes, and is clean shaven with slicked-back hair.

What everyone wants to know, among other things, is how much of David Brent exists in Ricky Gervais, whether Gervais will exhibit any of the embarrassingly insecure, self-aggrandising, interpersonal tics that made Brent so excruciatingly enjoyable and addictive to watch. But no.

For all Brent's self-consciousness, Gervais is smooth and collected and naturally complements Franklin's droll interviewing style with sardonic, exquisitely timed come-backs. When Franklin asks about casting and writing, Gervais says, "We like doing everything ourselves."

"You're talking about [collaborator] Stephen Merchant?" Franklin asks.

"No, I talk about myself like the Queen," Gervais replies.

"Where is Stephen Merchant now?"

"Exactly," Gervais responds, and swigs his beer.

On screen, Gervais's comedic style centres on what he calls "body-language acting". He demonstrates a look of surprise – a subtle flick of the eyes and silent twitch of the lips, signature David Brent. "We were a slave to realism," he says.

Americans tend to obsess over origins so Franklin asks about Gervais's background. He gives the basics – son of a bricklayer and housewife, raised in the industrial city of Reading, went to university followed by knockabout jobs. "In America they tell you, 'You can be president!' In England we're told, 'Your dad's got a perfectly good lumberyard.' The English – we're scared of failing. It would be embarrassing," he says. "Americans aren't embarrassed."

If the inherent Englishness is a large part of what makes Gervais so funny, his facile wit and unpretentiousness are what makes him so winning before a live audience.

Someone asks if *Office* cast members ever cracked themselves up on camera. Gervais recalls that one scene – in which Brent tells Tim, "Who knows, in a few years' time you could be in the hot seat" – required no fewer than 25 takes. Gervais cracks himself and the entire room up just remembering the crack-up. Watching him tell it is like watching the actual blooper.

By the end of the evening I sense that Gervais is enjoying not just his popularity but rather the revelation of having found his way to work that fascinates and energises him – or as Faulkner puts it, having created "out of the materials of the human spirit something which did not exist before".

Judging by the New York reception, Gervais is the admired, beloved funnyman David Brent always wanted to be.

*Source*: Article by Paige Williams, *Financial Times*, 5 November 2005. Copyright © 2005 The Financial Times Ltd.

**BOX 10.14 CHECKLIST**

## To help you think about the questions you are going to ask in your semi-structured or in-depth interview

✔ How long will you have to conduct the interview?

✔ How do you wish to conduct (or structure) the interview?

✔ How will you use appropriate language and tone of voice, and avoid jargon when asking questions or discussing themes?

✔ How will you word open questions appropriately to obtain relevant data?

✔ How will you ask appropriately worded probing questions to build on, clarify or explain your interviewee's responses?

✔ How will you avoid asking leading questions that may introduce forms of bias?

✔ Have you devised an appropriate order for your questions, where the early introduction of sensitive issues may introduce interviewee bias?

✔ How will you avoid over-zealously asking questions and pressing your interviewee for a response where it should be clear that they do not wish to provide one?

✔ How will you listen attentively and demonstrate this to your interviewee?

✔ How will you summarise and test your understanding of the data that are shared with you in order to ensure accuracy in your interpretation?

✔ How will you allow your interviewee to maintain control over the use of a tape recorder, where used, where they may wish to exercise this?

✔ Have you practised to ensure you can carry out a number of tasks at the same time, including listening, note taking and the identifying where you need to probe further?

✔ How might you identify actions and comments made by your interviewee that indicate an aspect of the discussion that should be explored in order to reveal the reason for the response?

✔ How will you avoid projecting your own views or feelings through your actions or comments?

✔ How will you maintain a check on the Interview that you intend to cover and to steer the discussion where appropriate to raise and explore these aspects?

✔ How do you plan to draw the interview to a close within the agreed time limit and to thank the interviewee for their time and the data they have shared with you?

## Recognising and dealing with difficult participants

Inevitably, during the course of your interviews you will meet some participants who are more difficult to interview. Although it is impossible for us to highlight all the possible variations, the most prevalent difficulties are summarised in Table 10.2, along with suggestions regarding how to address them. However, whilst reading Table 10.2 will give you some ideas of what to do, the best advice we can give is to undertake practice interviews in which a colleague introduces one or more of these 'difficulties' and you have to deal with it!

**Table 10.2 Difficult interview participants and suggestions on how to address them**

| Recognised difficulty | Suggestion |
|---|---|
| Participant appears willing only to give monosyllabic answers, these being little more than 'yes' or 'no' | Reasons for this are varied.<br><br>If it is due to limited time, or worries about anonymity, then this can be minimised by careful opening of the interview (Box 10.9).<br><br>If the participant gives these answers despite such precautions, try phrasing your questions in as open a way as possible; also use long pauses to signify that you want to hear more |
| Participant repeatedly provides long answers which digress from the focus of your interview | Although some digression should be tolerated, as it can lead to aspects about which you are interested, you will need to impose more direction.<br><br>This must be done subtly so as not to cause offence such as by referring back to an earlier relevant point and asking them to tell you more, or requesting that they pause so you can note down what they have just said |
| Participant starts interviewing you | This can suggest that you have created rapport. However, you need to stress that you are interested in their opinions and that, if they wish, they can ask you questions at the end |
| Participant is proud of their status relative to you and wants to show off their knowledge, criticising what you do | This is extremely difficult and at times like this you will have to listen attentively and be respectful.<br><br>Remember that you are also likely to be knowledgeable about the research topic so be confident and prepared to justify your research and the research design you have chosen |
| Participant becomes noticeably upset during the interview and, perhaps, starts to cry | Another difficult one for you.<br><br>You need to give your respondent time to answer your question and, in particular, do not do anything to suggest that you are feeling impatient.<br><br>If your respondent starts crying or is obviously very distressed it is probably a good idea to explain that the question does not have to be answered.<br><br>Do not end the interview straight away as this is likely to make them even more upset |

*Sources*: King (2004), authors' experiences

## Recording information

The need to create a full record of the interview soon after its occurrence was identified in Section 10.4 as one of the means to control bias and to produce reliable data for analysis. This particular discussion and the accompanying checklist (Box 10.15) look briefly at the use of audio-recorders and the need to develop the skill of making notes during the interview. Most interviewers audio-record their interviews, where permission is given, although, as summarised in Table 10.3, this has both advantages and disadvantages. As an interviewer, you will be interested in both what your participants say and the way in which they say it. By audio-recording your interview, you will be able to concentrate more fully and listen attentively to what is being said and the expressions and other non-verbal cues your interviewee is giving when they are responding. However, as we pointed out earlier, we believe it is also helpful to make brief notes as well in order to

**Table 10.3** Advantages and disadvantages of audio-recording the interview

| Advantages | Disadvantages |
|---|---|
| ■ Allows interviewer to concentrate on questioning and listening | ■ May adversely affect the relationship between interviewee and interviewer (possibility of 'focusing' on the audio-recorder) |
| ■ Allows questions formulated at an interview to be accurately recorded for use in later interviews where appropriate | |
| ■ Can re-listen to the interview | ■ May inhibit some interviewee responses and reduce reliability |
| ■ Accurate and unbiased record provided | ■ Possibility of a technical problem |
| ■ Allows direct quotes to be used | ■ Time required to transcribe the audio-recording (Section 13.3) |
| ■ Permanent record for others to use | |

*Sources*: Authors' experience; Easterby-Smith *et al.* (2002); Ghauri and Grønhaug (2005); Healey and Rawlinson (1994)

maintain your concentration and focus (Ghauri and Grønhaug, 2005). This is important because, although audio-recordings can capture the tone of voice and hesitation, they do not record facial expressions and other non-verbal cues. Most people have their own means of making notes, which may range from an attempt to create a verbatim account to a diagrammatic style that records key words and phrases, perhaps using mind mapping (Section 2.3). The task of note making in this situation will be a demanding one. As you seek to test your understanding of what your interviewee has told you, this will allow some time to complete your notes concurrently in relation to the particular aspect being discussed. Most interviewees recognise the demands of the task and act accordingly. However, the interview will not be the occasion to perfect your style, and you may be advised to practise in a simulated situation: for example, by watching an interview on television and attempting to produce a set of notes.

Permission should always be sought to audio-record an interview. Healey and Rawlinson (1994) report an earlier study that advises that you should explain why you

## BOX 10.15 CHECKLIST

### Issues to consider regarding your recording of interview data

☑ How do you intend to record the data that are shared with you? What rights will your interviewee have in relation to the use of an audio-recorder where they have agreed in principle to let you use one?

☑ What reference do you need to make about sending your interviewee an output from your data analysis and when this is due to occur?

☑ How will you prepare your approach to note making so that you may recall the interviewee's responses for long enough to make an accurate and more permanent record?

☑ Has your schedule of work been formulated to permit you to find sufficient time in order to write up your notes/transcribe your interview recordings and to analyse them before undertaking further data collection?

☑ How will you organise your material so that you retain a copy of your original notes and interview recordings, an extended version of your notes after writing them up or a transcript of relevant material, and a set of additional notes or memos relating to the interview and your learning from that particular experience? (Section 13.3) would prefer to use a recorder rather than simply requesting permission. Where it is likely to have a detrimental effect, it is better not to use a recorder. However, most interviewees adapt quickly to the use of the recorder. It is more ethical to allow your interviewee to maintain control over the recorder so that if you ask a question that they are prepared to respond to, but only if their words are not audio-recorded, they have the option to switch it off (Section 6.4). It will inevitably be necessary to make notes in this situation.

## 10.6 | Managing logistical and resource issues

### Logistical and resource issues

Interviewing is a time-consuming process. Where the purpose of the interview is to explore themes or to explain findings, the process may call for a fairly lengthy discussion. In such cases the time required to obtain data is unlikely to be less than one hour and could easily exceed this, perhaps taking two hours or longer. This may have an adverse impact on the number and representativeness of those who are willing to be interview participants, as we discussed earlier. Where managers or other potential participants receive frequent requests to participate in research projects, they will clearly need to consider how much of their time they may be willing to devote to such activities. This issue may arise in relation to either the completion of a questionnaire or participation in an interview. However, there will be more flexibility about when and where to fill in a questionnaire. It is therefore incumbent on you to establish credibility with, and to engender the interest of, potential interviewees.

Your choice of an approach that involves data collection through interviewing will have particular resource issues. Conducting interviews may become a costly process where it is necessary to travel to the location of participants, although this can be kept to a minimum by cluster sampling (Section 7.2) or using the Internet (Section 10.8). Interviews are almost certainly likely to be more expensive than using self-administered or telephone questionnaires to collect data. Choice of method should be determined primarily by the nature of the research question and objectives rather than by cost considerations. This highlights the need to examine the feasibility of the proposed question and research strategy in relation to resource constraints, including time available and expense, before proceeding to the collection of data. Where your research question and objectives require you to undertake semi-structured or in-depth interviews, you need to consider the logistics of scheduling interviews. Thought needs to be given to the number of interviews to be arranged within a given period, and to the time required to compose notes and/or transcribe audio-recordings of each one, and undertake an initial analysis of the data collected (Section 13.3).

### Managing logistical and resource issues

In the preceding subsection, the issue of time required to collect data through interviewing was raised. You need to consider very carefully the amount of time that will be required to conduct an interview. In our experience, the time required to undertake qualitative research interviews is usually underestimated. The likely time required should be clearly referred to in any initial contact, and it may be better to suggest that interviews are envisaged to last up to, say, one, one and a half, or two hours, so that a willing participant sets aside sufficient time. They may then be in a position to recoup time not required from a shorter interview should this be the case. Some negotiation is in any case possible with an interested participant who feels unable to agree to a request for, say, two hours but who is prepared to agree to a briefer meeting. The interview can also be arranged at a time when the interviewee will be under least pressure.

Another possible strategy is to arrange two or more shorter interviews in order to explore a topic thoroughly. This might have the added advantage of allowing participants to reflect on the themes raised and questions being asked, and therefore to provide a fuller account and more accurate set of data. In order to establish this option it may be beneficial to arrange an initial meeting with a potential participant to discuss this request, where you will be able to establish your credibility. A series of exploratory interviews may then be agreed. Consideration also needs to be given to the number of interviews that may be undertaken in a given period. It is easy to overestimate what is practically possible, as Box 10.16 highlights.

These are all factors that need to be considered in the scheduling of semi-structured and in-depth interviews. Where you are involved in a study at one establishment, it may be more practical to undertake a number of interviews in one day, although there is still a need to maintain concentration, to make notes and write up information and to conduct your initial analysis. Phil found that undertaking three interviews per day in this type of study was enough.

## BOX 10.16  WORKED EXAMPLE

### Calculating the number of non-standardised (qualitative) interviews to be undertaken in one day

Feroz arranged two interviews in a capital city during the course of a day, which involved travelling some miles across the city during the lunch hour. Two interviews appeared to be a reasonable target. However, a number of logistical issues were experienced even in relation to the plan to undertake two such interviews in one day. These issues included the following: the total travelling time to and from the city; the time to find the appropriate buildings; the transfer time during a busy period; the time to conduct the interviews; the need to maintain concentration, to probe responses, to make initial notes and then to write these up without too much time elapsing. Because of his experience, Feroz took a decision not to conduct more than one interview per day where significant travel was involved, even though this necessitated more journeys and greater expense.

The nature of semi-structured or in-depth interviews also has implications for the management of the time available during the meeting. The use of open-ended questions and reliance on informant responses means that, while you must remain responsive to the objectives of the interview and the time constraint, interviewees need the opportunity to provide developmental answers. You should avoid making frequent interruptions but will need to cover the themes and questions indicated and probe responses in the time available (Ghauri and Grønhaug, 2005). The intensive nature of the discussion and the need to optimise one's understanding of what has been revealed means that time must be found to write up notes as soon as possible after an interview. Where an audio-recorder has been used, time will be required to produce a transcription, and Robson (2002) states that a one-hour recording may take up to ten hours to transcribe.

## 10.7 Group interviews and focus groups

Non-standardised interviews may also be conducted on a group basis, where the interviewer asks questions to a group of participants. Figure 10.1 summarised these variations earlier in this chapter. Currently there are a variety of terms that are used interchangeably to describe group interviews and which are often assumed to have equivalent meanings (Boddy, 2005). These include focus group, group interview, group discussion and various combinations of these words! In this section we use *group interview* as a general term to describe all non-standardised interviews conducted with two or more people. In contrast, and as suggested by Figure 10.1, the term *focus group* is used to refer to those group interviews where the topic is defined clearly and precisely and there is a focus on enabling and recording interactive discussion between participants (Carson *et al.*, 2001).

Typically group interviews (and focus groups) involve between four and eight participants, or perhaps even 12, the precise number depending upon the nature of the participants, the topic matter and the skill of the interviewer. Inevitably, the more complex the subject matter the smaller the number of interviewees. Participants are normally chosen using non-probability sampling, often with a specific purpose in mind (Section 7.3). For many group interviews this purpose is because you feel that you can learn a great deal from these individuals. Krueger and Casey (2000:25) refer to such participants as being 'information rich'.

If you are thinking about using group interviews, or specifically focus groups, consideration of the following issues may help.

- Where your research project (or part of it) occurs within an organisation the request to participate in a group interview may be received by individuals as an instruction rather than allowing them a choice about whether to take part. This may be the case where an organisation is acting as a host for your research and the request is sent out on official notepaper or in the name of a manager, or because of your own position in the organisation. Where this is the case it is likely to lead to some level of non-attendance, or to unreliable data. In our experience, participants often welcome the chance to 'have their say'. However, where any request may be perceived as indicating lack of choice, to gain their confidence and participation you will need to exercise care over the wording to be used in the request that is sent to them to take part. You will also need to exercise similar care in your introduction to the group when the interview occurs in order to provide a clear assurance about confidentiality.

- Once your sample have been selected, respondents should be grouped so as not to inhibit individuals' possible contributions. Inhibitions may be related to lack of trust, to perceptions about status differences, or because of the dominance of certain individuals. The nature and selection of each group will affect the first two elements. We would advise using a series of *horizontal slices* through an organisation so that, within each group, participants have a similar status and similar work experiences. (Using a *vertical slice* would introduce perceptions about status differences and variations in work experience.) In this way, group interviews can be conducted at a number of levels within an organisation. A reference may be made about the nature of the group to provide reassurance, and you may consider asking people to introduce themselves by their first name only without referring to their exact job.

- Where one or two people dominate the discussion, you should seek to reduce their contributions carefully and to bring others in. Torrington (1991) suggests that this may be attempted in a general way:

'What do you think, Barry?'

'What do other people think about this?'

Alternatively, more specifically:

'How does Sally's point relate to the one that you raised, Sheila?'

A question posed to other group members should also have the effect of inhibiting the contribution of a dominant member:

'What do you think about Johan's suggestion?'

- You will need to ensure that participants understand each other's contributions and that you develop an accurate understanding of the points being made. Asking a participant to clarify the meaning of a particular contribution, where it has not been understood, and testing understanding through summarising should help to ensure this.

- You will need to consider the location and setting for a group interview. It is advisable to conduct the interview in a neutral setting rather than, say, in a manager's office, where participants may not feel relaxed. There should be no likelihood of interruption or being overheard. You should consider the layout of the seating in the room where the interview is to be held. Where possible, arrange the seating in a circular fashion so that everyone will be facing inward and so that they will be an equal distance from the central point of this circle.

- Finally, students often ask, 'When will I know that I have undertaken sufficient group interviews or focus groups?' Writing about focus groups, Krueger and Casey (2000) suggest that you should plan to undertake three or four group interviews with any one type of participant. If after the third or fourth group interview you are no longer receiving new information, this means that you have heard the full range of ideas and reached *saturation*.

The demands of conducting all types of group interview, including focus groups, and the potential wealth of ideas that may flow from them mean that it is likely to be difficult to manage the process and note key points at the same time. We have managed to overcome this in two ways: by audio-recording the group interviews or using two interviewers. Where two interviewers are used, one person facilitates the discussion and the other person makes notes. We would recommend that you use two interviewers even if you are audio-recording the group interview as it will allow one interviewer to concentrate fully on managing the process whilst the other ensures the data are recorded. Where you cannot audio-record the group interview, you will need to write up any notes immediately afterwards so as not to lose data. As with one-to-one interviews, your research will benefit from the making of notes about the nature of the interactions that occur in the group interviews that you conduct. We would not advise you to undertake more than one group interview in a day on your own because of the danger of losing or confusing data.

## Group interviews

In a **group interview** your role will be to ensure that all participants have the opportunity to state their points of view and answer your question and that these data are captured. This type of interview can range from being highly structured to unstructured, although it tends to be relatively unstructured and fairly free-flowing (Zikmund, 2000) in terms of both breadth and depth of topics. The onus will be placed firmly on you to explain its purpose, to encourage participants to relax, and to initiate their comments and, with focus groups, detailed discussion. The use of this method is likely to necessitate a balance between encouraging participants to provide answers to a particular question or questions that you introduce and allowing them to range more freely in discussion where this may reveal data that provide you with important insights. Thus once you have opened the interview (Box 10.9) and the discussion is established, it will need to be managed carefully. Group interactions may lead to a highly productive discussion as interviewees respond to your questions and evaluate points made by the group. However, as your opportunity to develop an individual level of rapport with each participant will not be present (compared with a one-to-one interview), there may also emerge a group effect where certain participants effectively try to dominate the interview. This situation will leave you with the task of trying to encourage involvement by all group members and of maintaining the interview's exploratory purpose. A high level of skill will therefore be required in order for you to be able to conduct this type of discussion successfully, as well as to try to record its outcomes.

Despite this reference to the potential difficulties of using group interviews, there are distinct advantages arising from their use. Because of the presence of several participants, this type of situation allows a variety of points of view to emerge and for the group to respond to these views. A dynamic group can generate or respond to a number of ideas and evaluate them, thus helping you to explain or explore concepts. You are also likely to benefit from the opportunity that this method provides in terms of allowing your participants to consider points raised by other group members and to challenge one another's views. In one-to-one interviews, discussion is of course limited to the interviewer and interviewee. The use of group interviews may also provide an efficient way for you to interview a larger number of individuals than would be possible through the use of one-to-one interviews (Box 10.17). Linked to this point, their use may allow you to adopt an interview-based strategy that can more easily be related to a representative sample, particularly where the research project is being conducted within a specific organisation or in relation to a clearly defined population. This may help to establish the credibility of this research where an attempt is made to overcome issues of bias associated with interviews in general and this type in particular.

Group interviews can also be used to identify key themes that will be used to develop items that are included in a survey questionnaire. This particular use of group interviews may inform subsequent parts of your data collection, providing a clearer focus. For example, in an attitude survey the initial use of group interviews can lead to a 'bottom-up' generation of concerns and issues, which helps to establish the survey.

## Focus groups

Focus groups are well known because of the way they have been used by political parties to test voter reactions to particular policies and election strategies, and through their use in market research to test reactions to products. A **focus group**, sometimes called a *focus group interview*, is a group interview that focuses clearly upon a particular issue, product, service or topic and encompasses the need for interactive discussion amongst participants (Carson *et al.*, 2001). This means that, in comparison with other forms of group interview, individual group members' interactions and responses are both encouraged and more closely controlled to maintain the focus. Participants are selected because they have certain characteristics in common that relate to the topic being discussed and they are encouraged to discuss and share their points of view without any pressure to reach a

## BOX 10.17 FOCUS ON MANAGEMENT RESEARCH

### Using group interviews in exploratory research

Resarch by Gary Packham, David Brooksbank, Christopher Miller and Brychan Thomas (2005) examined how growth-oriented firms in Wales had adopted management practices to build the entrepreneurial capacity necessary to sustain growth. Because of the exploratory nature of their research, they decided to use group interviews to collect data from owner-managers of small to medium-sized enterprises whose firms had achieved consistent growth for the previous five years. These were divided into three broad industrial classifications:

- manufacturing;
- construction;
- services.

In total, 18 firms divided equally between the three industrial classifications participated in the research. Two group interviews were held for each of the three industrial sectors, in which a moderator chaired the meetings. Group interviews were principally unstructured and participants were asked to consider how and why management practices had contributed to their firms' successes. These included:

- management development;
- planning and control;
- financial management;
- marketing.

Group interviews were scheduled to last no more than one hour owing to the participants' time constraints. Each firm was given a pseudonym to preserve confidentiality. Each meeting was video-recorded and transcribed later, participants being sent the transcription of their group interview to confirm validity.

consensus (Krueger and Casey, 2000). These discussions are conducted several times, with similar participants, to enable trends and patterns to be identified when the data collected are analysed.

If you are running a focus group, you will probably be referred to as the **moderator** or *facilitator*. These labels emphasise the dual role of the person running the focus group, namely to:

- keep the group within the boundaries of the topic being discussed;
- generate interest in the topic and encourage discussion, whilst at the same time not leading the group towards certain opinions.

Where focus groups are being used this is likely to be associated with a higher level of interviewer-led structure and intervention to facilitate discussion than where group interviews are being used. The size of groups may also be related to topic. Thus a focus group designed to obtain views about a product range (Box 10.18) is likely to be larger than a group interview that explores a topic related to a more emotionally involved construct, such as attitudes to performance-related pay or the way in which employees rate their treatment by management. You may also choose to design smaller groups as you seek to develop your competence in relation to the use of this interviewing technique to collect qualitative data.

## BOX 10.18 RESEARCH IN THE NEWS     FT

### McDonald's finds ready appetite for fruit and veg

Images of fruit and vegetables will be featured in McDonald's advertisements in a marketing revamp that seeks to position the fast food company as an authority on nutrition.

Peter Beresford, chairman and chief executive of McDonald's in the UK, said yesterday the company would spend £7.4m on moves to promote healthier eating.

The announcement follows the publication of a white paper calling on food marketers to do more to help prevent obesity in children.

Mr Beresford said McDonald's was acting in response to calls from parents who felt overwhelmed "by the barrage of information that is coming at them about nutrition".

He said: "They asked us to use our marketing expertise to make things simpler for them . . . I think we can show leadership and make fruit and veg a fun part of any diet."

He said McDonald's would be adding five healthier options to its Happy Meals, which are aimed at children. However, the company would continue to give out toys with Happy Meals.

The changes mean children will be able to eat carrot sticks instead of french fries with their burgers and chicken McNuggets.

Other new items include Chicken Grills, Wobble-icious Fruit Jelly made with 99 per cent fruit juice, Robinson's Apple Fruit Shoot and no-added-sugar Sprite Z.

All Happy Meal television advertisements will feature a fruit or a vegetable, Mr Beresford said, promising to spend £3.65m on commercials promoting fruit and vegetables.

McDonald's also has created a Happy Meals Choice Chart that lists the calories, fat, saturated fat, salt and added sugar in 108 potential Happy Meal combinations.

The options range from a 100-calorie meal consisting of Chicken Grills, carrot sticks and Evian water to a 717-calorie offering featuring a cheeseburger, fries and a milk shake.

Mr Beresford said the initiatives would help parents to craft healthy diets for their children. "All our food is healthy and all the information is in this brochure," he said.

He said McDonald's has had great success with new offerings such as fruit and salads, and there would be more new salads in the UK.

Mr Beresford added that McDonald's had been late in responding to the change in consumer tastes; something that became clear to him after he took part in focus group discussions with consumers.

"In the last two to three years we have lagged behind others in terms of innovation," he said. "We could have responded more quickly."

McDonald's has sold about 10m bags of fruit since introducing it in the UK about 18 months ago. Salads account for 10 per cent of the product mix.

"The mums love the salad choices," Mr Beresford said.

*Source*: Article by Gary Silverman, *Financial Times*, 9 March 2005. Copyright © 2005 The Financial Times Ltd.

## 10.8   Telephone, Internet- and intranet-mediated interviews

Most non-standardised interviews occur on a face-to-face basis. However, such qualitative interviews may also be conducted by telephone or electronically via the Internet or intranet. These pose particular problems as well as providing advantages in certain circumstances that we discuss in this section.

### Telephone interviews

Attempting to conduct non-standardised interviews by telephone may offer potential advantages associated with access, speed and lower cost. This method may allow you to make contact with participants with whom it would be impractical to conduct an interview on a face-to-face basis because of the distance and prohibitive costs involved and time required. Even where 'long-distance' access is not an issue, conducting interviews by telephone may still offer advantages associated with speed of data collection and lower cost. In other words, this approach may be seen as more convenient.

However, there are a number of significant issues that militate against attempting to collect qualitative data by telephone contact. We have already discussed the importance of establishing personal contact in this type of interviewing. The intention of non-standardised interviewing is to be able to explore the participant's responses. This is likely to become more feasible once a position of trust has been established, as discussed earlier. This situation, of establishing trust, will become particularly important where you wish to ask sensitive questions. For these reasons, seeking to conduct qualitative interviews by telephone may lead to issues of (reduced) reliability, where your participants are less willing to engage in an exploratory discussion, or even a refusal to take part.

There are also some other practical issues that would need to be managed. These relate to your ability to control the pace of a telephone interview and to record any data that were forthcoming. Conducting an interview by telephone and taking notes is an extremely difficult process and so we would recommend using audio-recording. In addition, the normal visual cues that allow your participant to control the flow of the data that they share with you would be absent. With telephone interviews you lose the opportunity to witness the non-verbal behaviour of your participant, which may adversely affect your interpretation of how far to pursue a particular line of questioning. Your participant may be less willing to provide you with as much time to talk to them in comparison with a face-to-face interview. You may also encounter difficulties in developing more complex questions in comparison with a face-to-face interview situation. Finally, attempting to gain access through a telephone call may lead to ethical issues, as we discussed in Section 6.4.

For these reasons, we believe that non-standardised interviewing by telephone is likely to be appropriate only in particular circumstances. It may be appropriate to conduct a short, follow-up telephone interview to clarify the meaning of some data, where you have already undertaken a face-to-face interview with a participant with whom you have been able to establish your integrity and to demonstrate your competence. It may also be appropriate where access would otherwise be prohibited because of long distance, where you have already been able to establish your credibility through prior contact, perhaps through correspondence, and have made clear that your requirements are reasonable and guided by ethical principles. Where this situation involves a request to undertake a telephone interview with a participant from another country, you will need to be aware of any cultural norms related to the conduct and duration of telephone conversations.

## Internet- and intranet-mediated interviewing

Morgan and Symon (2004) use the term **electronic interviews** to refer to interviews held both in real time using the Internet and organisations' intranets as well as those that are, in effect, undertaken off-line. This subdivision into asynchronous and synchronous (Figure 10.2) offers a useful way of categorising electronic interviews as there are significant differences in electronic interviews dependent upon whether the interview is undertaken in real time (**synchronous**) or offline (**asynchronous**).

Using the Internet or an organisation's intranet has significant advantages where the population you wish to interview are geographically dispersed. In addition, with all forms of electronic interview the software automatically records as they are typed in,

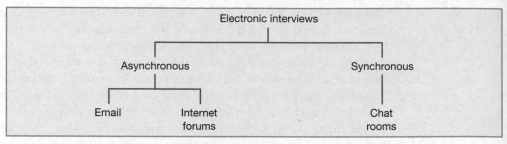

Figure 10.2     **Forms of electronic interview**

thereby removing problems associated with audio-recording and transcription such as cost, accuracy and participants' apprehension.

Web conferencing software can be used for both synchronous (real time) and asynchronous one-to-one and group interviews. Where this requires participants to have the software loaded onto their computers this can cause problems, especially where they are unfamiliar with the software or there is incompatibility with hardware or operating systems. Internet forums and emails can be used for asynchronous interviews. In contrast, a **chat room** is an online forum operating in synchronous mode.

By far the most common form of chat room is instant messaging such as MSN Messenger™. Although some would argue that this is not a true chat room as conversations are restricted to those named in a user's list, such instant messaging can be used to undertake real-time one-to-one and group interviews, providing netiquette is observed. The considerable debate regarding the suitability of Internet- and intranet-mediated communication for synchronous interviewing has been reviewed by Mann and Stewart (2000). Some researchers argue that interviewing participants online such as through web conferencing or chat rooms is unlikely to achieve the same high levels of interactivity and rich and spontaneous communication that can be obtained with face-to-face interviewing. This is often explained by the relatively narrow *bandwidth* of these electronic media when compared with face-to-face communication, it being argued that electronic media transmit fewer social cues. Others argue that this is not the case and that, after the initial invitation to participate, it is possible to build up considerable rapport between the interviewer and the interviewee during an online interview. It has also been suggested that the relative anonymity of online interviews facilitates more open and honest responses, in particular with regard to sensitive issues where participants have adopted pseudonyms (Sweet, 2001). Where group interviews or focus groups are being conducted, participants are less likely to be influenced by characteristics such as age, ethnicity or appearance. Overbearing participants are less likely to predominate, although variations in keyboard skills are likely to impact on participation levels.

For asynchronous interviewing, email and **Internet forums** or discussion groups mean that interviews are normally conducted over an extended time period of weeks. A **forum** usually deals only with one topic and personal exchanges are discouraged. Forums are commonly referred to as web forums, message boards, discussion boards, discussion forums, discussion groups and bulletin boards. Although forums do not allow people to edit each other's messages, there is usually a moderator or forum administrator who typically is responsible for netiquette being observed (Section 6.4 and 11.5) and has the ability to edit, delete or modify any content.

An **email interview** consist of a series of emails each containing a small number of questions rather than one email containing a series of questions (Morgan and Symon, 2004). Although you can send one email containing a series of questions, this is really an Internet- or intranet-mediated questionnaire (Sections 11.2 and 11.5). After making contact and obtaining agreement to participate, you initially email a small number of questions or introduce a topic to which the participant will (hopefully) reply. You then need to respond to these ideas, specifically asking further questions, raising points of clarification and pursuing ideas that are of further interest. Morgan and Symon (2004) emphasise that, because of the nature of email communications, such interviews may last for some weeks, there being a time delay between a question being asked and its being answered. This, they argue, can be advantageous as it allows both the interviewer and the interviewee to reflect on the questions and responses prior to providing a considered response.

## 10.9 | Summary

- The use of non-standardised (qualitative) research interviews should allow you to collect a rich and detailed set of data, although you will need to develop a sufficient level of competence to conduct these and to be able to gain access to the type of data associated with their use.

- Interviews can be differentiated according to the level of structure and standardisation adopted. Different types of interviews are useful for different research purposes.

- Non-standardised (qualitative) research interviews include two broad types that are generally referred to as in-depth or unstructured interviews and semi-structured interviews. You can use non-standardised interviews to explore topics and explain other findings.

- Your research design may incorporate more than one type of interview.

- In-depth and semi-structured interviews can be used in quantitative as well as qualitative research.

- There are situations favouring non-standardised (qualitative) interviews that will lead you to use this method to collect data. Apart from the nature of your research strategy, these are related to the significance of establishing personal contact, the nature of your data collection questions, and the length of time required from those who provide data.

- Data quality issues, your level of competence and logistical and resource matters will all need to be considered when you use in-depth and semi-structured interviews.

- Apart from one-to-one interviews conducted on a face-to-face basis, you may consider conducting such an interview by telephone or electronically in particular circumstances. In addition, you may consider using group interviews such as focus groups. There may be particular advantages associated with group interviews, but these are considerably more difficult to manage than one-to-one interviews.

## SELF-CHECK QUESTIONS

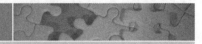

*Help with these questions is available at the end of the chapter.*

**10.1** What type of interview would you use in each of the following situations:
- **a** a market research project?
- **b** a research project seeking to understand whether trade union attitudes have changed?
- **c** following the analysis of a questionnaire?

**10.2** What are the advantages of using semi-structured and in-depth interviews?

**10.3** During a presentation of your proposal to undertake a research project, which will be based on semi-structured or in-depth interviews, you feel that you have dealt well with the relationship between the purpose of the research and the proposed methodology when one of the panel leans forward and asks you to discuss the trustworthiness and usefulness of your work for other researchers. This is clearly a challenge to see whether you can defend such an approach. How do you respond?

**10.4** Having quizzed you about the trustworthiness and usefulness of your work for other researchers, the panel member decides that one more testing question is in order. He explains that qualitatively based work isn't an easy option. 'It is not an easier alternative for those who want to avoid statistics', he says. 'How can we be sure that you're competent to get involved in interview work, especially where the external credibility of this organisation may be affected by the impression that you create in the field?' How will you respond to this concern?

**10.5** What are the key issues to consider when planning to use semi-structured or in-depth interviews?

**10.6** What are the key areas of competence that you need to develop in order to conduct an interview successfully?

# REVIEW AND DISCUSSION QUESTIONS

**10.7** Watch and, if possible, video-record a television interview such as one that is part of a chat show or a documentary. It does not matter if you only record an interview of 10 to 15 minutes' duration.
   **a** As you watch the interview, make notes about what the participant is telling the interviewer. After the interview review your notes. How much of what was being said did you manage to record?
   **b** If you were able to video-record the television interview, watch the interview again and compare your notes with what was actually said. What other information would you like to add to your notes?
   **c** Either watch the interview again or another television interview that is part of a chat show or a documentary. This time pay careful attention to the questioning techniques used by the interviewer. How many of the different types of question discussed in Section 10.5 can you identify?
   **d** How important do you think the non-verbal cues given by the interviewer and the interviewee are in understanding the meaning of what is being said?

**10.8** With a friend, each decide on a topic about which you think it would be interesting to interview the other person. Separately develop your interview themes and prepare an interview guide for a semi-structured interview. At the same time, decide which one of the 'difficult' participants in Table 10.2 you would like to role play when being interviewed.
   **a** Conduct both interviews and, if possible, make an audio-recording. If this is not possible the interviewer should take notes.
   **b** Listen to each of the audio-recordings – what aspects of your interviewing technique do you each need to improve?
   **c** If you were not able to audio-record the interview, how good a record of each interview do you consider the notes to be? How could you improve your interviewing technique further?

**10.9** Obtain a transcript of an interview that has already been undertaken. If your university subscribes to online newspapers such as ft.com, these are a good source of business-related transcripts. Alternatively, typing 'interview transcript' into a search engine such as Google will generate numerous possibilities on a vast range of topics!

a Examine the transcript, paying careful attention to the questioning techniques used by the interviewer. To what extent do you think that certain questions have led the interviewee to certain answers?

b Now look at the responses given by the interviewer. To what extent do you think these are the actual verbatim responses given by the interviewee? Why do you think this?

## PROGRESSING YOUR RESEARCH PROJECT

### Using semi-structured or in-depth interviews in your research

☐ Review your research question(s) and objectives. How appropriate would it be to use non-standardised (qualitative) interviews to collect data? Where it is appropriate, explain the relationship between your research question(s) and objectives, and the use of such interviews. Where this type of interviewing is not appropriate, justify your decision.

☐ If you decide that semi-structured or in-depth interviews are appropriate, what practical problems do you foresee? How might you attempt to overcome these practical problems?

☐ What threats to the trustworthiness of the data collected are you likely to encounter? How might you overcome these?

☐ Draft a list of interview themes to be explored and compare these thoroughly with your research question(s) and objectives.

☐ Ask your project tutor to comment on your judgement about the use of non-standardised (qualitative) interviews, the issues and threats that you have identified, your suggestions to overcome these, and the fit between your interview themes and your research question(s) and objectives.

## References

BBC News (2005) 'Paxman versus Howard' [online] (accessed 24 January 2006). Available from <URL:http://news.bbc.co.uk/1/hi/programmes/newsnight/newsnight25/4182569.stm#>.

Blumberg, B., Cooper, D.R. and Schindler, P.S. (2005) *Business Research Methods*, London, McGraw-Hill.

Boddy, C. (2005) 'A rose by any other name may smell as sweet but "group discussion" is not another name for "focus group" nor should it be', *Qualitative Market Research* 8: 3, 248–55.

Bryman, A. (1988) *Quantity and Quality in Social Research*, London, Unwin Hyman.

Carson, D., Gilmore, A., Perry, C. and Grønhaug, K. (2001) *Qualitative Marketing Research*, London, Sage.

Easterby-Smith, M., Thorpe, R. and Lowe, A. (2002) *Management Research: An Introduction* (2nd edn), London, Sage.

Ghauri, P. and Grønhaug, K. (2005) *Research Methods in Business Studies: A Practical Guide* (3rd edn), Harlow, Financial Times Prentice Hall.

Healey, M.J. (1991) 'Obtaining information from businesses', *in* Healey, M.J. (ed.), *Economic Activity and Land Use*, Harlow, Longman, pp. 193–251.

Healey, M.J. and Rawlinson, M.B. (1993) 'Interviewing business owners and managers: a review of methods and techniques', *Geoforum* 24: 3, 339–55.

Healey, M.J. and Rawlinson, M.B. (1994) 'Interviewing techniques in business and management research', *in* Wass, V.J. and Wells, P.E. (eds), *Principles and Practice in Business and Management Research,* Aldershot, Dartmouth, pp. 123–46.

Hofstede, G. (2001) *Culture's Consequences: Comparing Values, Behaviours, Institutions and Organisations Across Nations,* London, Sage.

Jankowicz, A.D. (2005) *Business Research Projects* (4th edn), London, Business Press Thomson Learning.

Kahn, R. and Cannell, C. (1957) *The Dynamics of Interviewing,* New York and Chichester, Wiley.

Keaveney, S.M. (1995) 'Customer switching behaviour in service industries: an exploratory study', *Journal of Marketing* 59: 2, 71–82.

King, N. (2004) 'Using interviews in qualitative research', *in* Cassell, C. and Symon, G. (eds), *Essential Guide to Qualitative Methods in Organizational Research,* London, Sage, pp. 11–22.

Krueger, R.A. and Casey, M.A. (2000) *Focus Groups: A Practical Guide for Applied Research* (3rd edn), Thousand Oaks, CA, Sage.

Mann, C. and Stewart, F. (2000) *Internet Communication and Qualitative Research: A Handbook for Researching Online,* London, Sage.

Marshall, C. and Rossman, G.B. (1999) *Designing Qualitative Research* (3rd edn), Thousand Oaks, CA, Sage.

Morgan, S.J. and Symon, G. (2004) 'Electronic interviews in organizational research', *in* Cassell, C. and Symon, G. (eds), *Essential Guide to Qualitative Methods in Organizational Research,* London, Sage, pp. 23–33.

North, D.J., Leigh, R. and Gough, J. (1983) 'Monitoring industrial change at the local level: some comments on methods and data sources', *in* Healey, M.J. (ed.), *Urban and Regional Industrial Research: The Changing UK Data Base,* Norwich, Geo Books, pp. 111–29.

Packham, G., Brooksbank, D., Miller, C. and Thomas, B. (2005) 'Climbing the mountain: management practice adoption in growth oriented firms in Wales', *Journal of Small Business and Enterprise Development* 12: 4, 482–97.

Powney, J. and Watts, M. (1987) *Interviewing in Educational Research,* London, Routledge and Kegan Paul.

Robson, C. (2002) *Real World Research* (2nd edn), Oxford, Blackwell.

Silverman, G. (2005) 'McDonald's finds ready appetite for fruit and veg', *Financial Times,* 9 March.

Sweet, C. (2001) 'Designing and conducting virtual focus groups', *Qualitative Market Research* 4: 3, 130–35.

Sykes, W. (1991) 'Taking stock: issues from the literature in validity and reliability in qualitative research', *Journal of Market Research Society* 33: 1, 3–12.

Torrington, D. (1991) *Management Face to Face,* London, Prentice Hall.

Ulrich, J., Wieseke, J. and Van Dick, R. (2005) 'Continuity and change in mergers and acquisitions: a social identity case study of a German industrial merger', *Journal of Management Studies* 42: 8, 1549–69.

Wass, V. and Wells, P. (1994) 'Research methods in action: an introduction', *in* Wass, V.J. and Wells, P.E. (eds), *Principles and Practice in Business and Management Research,* Aldershot, Dartmouth, pp. 1–34.

Williams, P. (2005) 'The performance: office outing', *Financial Times,* 5 November.

Yin, R.K. (2003) *Case Study Research: Design and Methods* (3rd edn), Beverly Hills, CA, Sage.

Zikmund, W.G. (2000) *Business Research Methods* (6th edn), Fort Worth, TX, Dryden Press.

## Further reading

Cassell, C. and Symon, G. (2004) (eds) *Essential Guide to Qualitative Methods in Organizational Research*, London, Sage. Chapter 2 by Nigel King and Chapter 3 by Stephanie Morgan and Gillian Symon are readable accounts of interviews and electronic interviews, respectively, both with extremely useful detailed case studies.

Healey, M.J. and Rawlinson, M.B. (1994) 'Interviewing techniques in business and management research', *in* Wass, V.J. and Wells, P.E. (eds), *Principles and Practice in Business and Management Research*, Aldershot, Dartmouth, pp. 123–46. This is an excellent contribution and a 'must' for those of you intending to use qualitative research and interviews.

Krueger, R.A. and Casey, M.A. (2000) *Focus Groups: A Practical Guide for Applied Research* (3rd edn), Thousand Oaks, CA, Sage. A very useful work for those considering the use of this method of group interviewing.

Mann, C. and Stewart, F. (2000) *Internet Communication and Qualitative Research: A Handbook for Researching Online*, London, Sage. Chapter 6 provides a useful guide to using online interviews and Chapter 5 to online focus groups.

For WEB LINKS visit
www.pearsoned.co.uk/
saunders

# Topic 4
## Quantitative Research Methods

# Introduction: Quantitative Research Methods

Chapter 11 Saunders (Collecting primary data using questionnaires) provides lots of detailed examples ,boxes and question design material. Important issues to cover in your proposal if you decide on a quantitative primary research are sampling, and questionnaires.

You may be planning econometric or financial analysis of numerical data – whatever you need to know how to analyse and write up your results. A few rules of thumb to help you interpret tables are included here.

## Sampling

Sampling addresses the point 'Who to ask?' 'Random Sampling' describes probability sampling and should only be used to describe methods where a population (to which you want to generalise the results) is defined and listed: a sample is then taken using random numbers.

## Questionnaires

Questionnaires are the main tool in quantitative research. The Workplace Employment Relations Survey(WERS)questionnaire for an example (http://www.dti.gov.uk/employment/research-evaluation/grants/wers/ ). A major advantage in using questionnaires is that they provide a highly structured and standardised tool, which can be used on large-scale samples of a population.

Questionnaires can be self- administered (on paper or on the web), that is, completed by the respondents themselves but can also be administered face to face. With questionnaires you need to bear in mind the costs of production, distribution and data analysis.

Look at other questionnaires that have been carried out in your area. Adopt and adapt from these where appropriate. This replication of previous studies allows you to compare findings. Of course any use of questions from past research must be clearly cited and referenced to avoid the charge of plagiarism.

**Remember to always have in mind the purpose of your research and your overall research questions and aims when designing questionnaires. Your methodology section should show how your research objectives will be met.**

## Rules of thumb for interpreting tables.

An important part of quantitative research is interpretation: telling a story based on the numbers in tables. The following rules of thumb suggest ways to make sense of tables, giving you an idea of what resources are required to interpret the tens or hundreds of tables your research could involve.

- Is the question analysed nominal, ordinal or interval. Nominal means that there is no order to the answers. Ordinal that there is an order to the answers. Interval it makes sense to calculate averages of the question.
- Is the question multiple response – Can one respondent validly give more than one answer to a question.

- Be careful of missing values – percentages either do, or do not include them in the total!
- Is the table just concerning one question (univariate), or more than one question (multivariate)?
- For an ordinal, univariate table: look for largest categories (The Mode). This works for Nominal and Ordinal. You can then write sentences such as 'Most respondents (xx%) fell in the YY category.
- Look for the category which contains 50% in the Cumulative Percent column. You can then say 'at least half the sample answered at least YY to the question'
- When quoting percentages use just two significant numbers – don't quote 37.7%, say 38%. (i.e. use rounding).
- If the question is multiple response note that the sum of all the percents doesn't necessarily come to 100% - it depends on the average number of responses given by each respondent. You can't add two percentages as there is unknown overlap.
- If a table has means make sure you know what a high and low value indicate. You could try looking to see where the largest mean is for each column, and see if for each row the means are in the same order. Highlight when they are not with a sentence. For example say "In all rows except X Column Y had the highest mean, showing that in almost all cases Y is associated with a high mean." This describes the result – then interpret (with a degree of speculation) what does this mean
- For Cross-tabulations compare the percentage for each cell with the total sample percent at the foot of the column. For each column indicate the highest and lowest rows with percentages. Similarly for Each row highlight which column has high and low values. Make statements up to describe all the interesting effects. Are they rows with similar patterns across columns? Or Columns with similar patterns across rows? What do the results and patterns suggest? Don't just describe the numbers – you should also write a story to make it make sense – preferably in the context of the research objectives.

## Quantitative Primary research proposals – finance and economics Departments

Clearly indicate and justify your chosen source of data (e.g. Data Stream) and inform the process which selects the variables and ratios you propose to use. Then indicate and justify the modelling or statistical procedures that you plan and the suggest the value of the outputs that you expect to produce. Describe the Research Design, and describe how it's proposed to select measures and develop models.

## Ethical issues in Research Proposals

Other honours students will find they need to follow departmental ethics procedures. This ensures compliance with University regulations when they are doing research with human subjects. The issues to be considered are how to obtain access and age restrictions, but the primary criteria is informed consent. Respondents should be clearly informed of what will be done with the information they provide: problems such as deception and threats to privacy must clearly be avoided. Most organisations have ethical research policies.

# Collecting primary data using questionnaires

## LEARNING OUTCOMES

By the end of this chapter you should:

→ understand the advantages and disadvantages of questionnaires as a data collection method;

→ be aware of a range of self-administered and interviewer-administered questionnaires;

→ be aware of the possible need to combine techniques within a research project;

→ be able to select and justify the use of appropriate questionnaire techniques for a variety of research scenarios;

→ be able to design, pilot and administer a questionnaire to answer research questions and to meet objectives;

→ be able to take appropriate action to enhance response rates and to ensure the validity and reliability of the data collected;

→ be able to apply the knowledge, skills and understanding gained to your own research project.

## 11.1  Introduction

Within business and management research, the greatest use of questionnaires is made within the survey strategy (Section 5.3). However, both experiment and case study research strategies can make use of these techniques. Although you probably have your own understanding of the term 'questionnaire', it is worth noting that there are a variety of definitions in common usage (Oppenheim, 2000). Some authors (for example, Kervin, 1999) reserve it exclusively for questionnaires where the person answering the question actually records their own answers. Others (for example, Bell, 2005) use it as a more general term to include interviews that are administered either face to face or by telephone.

In this book we use **questionnaire** as a general term to include all techniques of data collection in which each person is asked to respond to the same set of questions in a predetermined order (deVaus, 2002). It therefore includes both structured interviews and telephone questionnaires as well as those in which the questions are answered without an interviewer being present, such as TGI Friday's online questionnaire. The range of techniques that fall under this broad heading are outlined in the next section (11.2), along with their relative advantages and disadvantages.

The use of questionnaires is discussed in many research methods texts. These range from those that devote a few pages to it to those that specify precisely how you should construct and use them, such as Dillman's (2000) **tailored design method**. Perhaps not surprisingly, the questionnaire is one of the most widely used data collection techniques within the survey strategy. Because each person (*respondent*) is asked to respond to the same set of questions, it provides an efficient way of collecting responses from a large sample prior to quantitative analysis (Chapter 12). However, before you decide to use a questionnaire we should like to include a note of caution. Many authors (for example, Bell, 2005; Oppenheim, 2000) argue that it is far harder to produce a good questionnaire than you might think. You need to ensure that it will collect the precise data that you require to answer your research question(s) and achieve your objectives. This is of paramount importance because, like TGI Friday's, you are unlikely to have more than one opportunity to collect the data. In particular, you will be unable to go back to those individuals who choose to remain anonymous and collect additional data using another questionnaire. These issues are discussed in Section 11.3.

Questionnaires are a part of our everyday lives. For modules in your course, your lecturers have probably asked you and your fellow students to complete module evaluation questionnaires, thereby collecting data on students' views. Similarly, when we visit a tourist attraction or have a meal in a restaurant there is often the opportunity to complete a comment card. Some restaurants, such as TGI Friday's, also use online questionnaires administered via their website as a way of collecting data from, and keeping in contact with, customers. As can be seen from the illustration, TGI Friday's online questionnaire collects details about the restaurant and time of visit, as well as opinions regarding the quality of the food received and perceptions

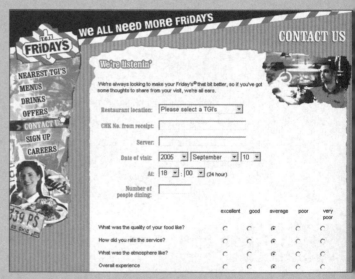

*Extract from TGI Friday's online questionnaire*

of service quality, atmosphere and the overall experience. In addition to asking for these data, the TGI Friday's questionnaire provides space for general comments/feedback as well as for customers to ask questions. Andy Rodgers, from TGI Friday's Consumer Insight Team, says that such questionnaires provide TGI Friday's with valuable information about customers' views and help to reinforce the company's customer service ethos. All people completing the questionnaire are asked to tick a box and provide contact details if they would like the company to respond to their comments. Responding promptly to these, Andy Rodgers argues, helps TGI Friday's to maintain high levels of customer satisfaction.

The design of your questionnaire will affect the response rate and the reliability and validity of the data you collect. Response rates, validity and reliability can be maximised by:

- careful design of individual questions;
- clear layout of the questionnaire form;
- lucid explanation of the purpose of the questionnaire;
- pilot testing;
- carefully planned and executed administration.

Together these form Sections 11.4 and 11.5. In Section 11.4 we discuss designing your questionnaire. Administering the actual questionnaire is considered in Section 11.5 along with actions to help ensure high response rates.

## 11.2 | An overview of questionnaire techniques

### When to use questionnaires

We have found that many people use a questionnaire to collect data without considering other methods such as examination of secondary sources (Chapter 8), observation (Chapter 9), and semi-structured or unstructured interviews (Chapter 10). Our advice is to evaluate all possible data collection methods and to choose those most appropriate to your research question(s) and objectives. Questionnaires are usually not particularly good for exploratory or other research that requires large numbers of open-ended questions (Sections 10.2 and 10.3). They work best with standardised questions that you can be confident will be interpreted the same way by all respondents (Robson, 2002).

Questionnaires can therefore be used for descriptive or explanatory research. *Descriptive research*, such as that undertaken using attitude and opinion questionnaires and questionnaires of organisational practices, will enable you to identify and describe the variability in different phenomena. In contrast, *explanatory* or *analytical research* will enable you to examine and explain relationships between variables, in particular cause-and-effect relationships. These two purposes have different research design requirements (Gill and Johnson, 2002), which we shall discuss later (Section 11.3).

Although questionnaires may be used as the only data collection method, it is usually better to link them with other methods in a multiple-methods research design (Section 5.4). For example, a questionnaire to discover customers' attitudes can be complemented by in-depth interviews to explore and understand these attitudes (Section 10.3). In addition, questionnaires, if worded correctly, normally require less skill and sensitivity to administer than semi-structured or in-depth interviews (Jankowicz, 2005).

### Types of questionnaire

The design of a questionnaire differs according to how it is administered and, in particular, the amount of contact you have with the respondents (Figure 11.1). **Self-administered questionnaires** are usually completed by the respondents. Such questionnaires are administered electronically using the Internet (**Internet-mediated questionnaires**) or intranet (**intranet-mediated questionnaires**), posted to respondents who return them by post after completion (**postal** or *mail* **questionnaires**), or delivered

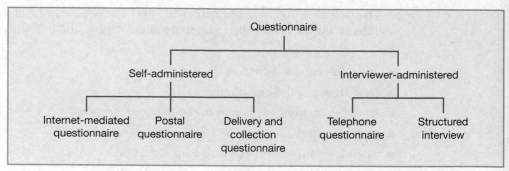

**Figure 11.1  Types of questionnaire**

by hand to each respondent and collected later (**delivery and collection question-naires**). Responses to **interviewer-administered questionnaires** are recorded by the interviewer on the basis of each respondent's answers. A growing number of surveys, particularly in the area of market research, contact respondents and administer questionnaires using the telephone. These are known as **telephone questionnaires**. The final category, *structured interviews* (sometimes known as *interview schedules*), refers to those questionnaires where interviewers physically meet respondents and ask the questions face to face. These differ from semi-structured and unstructured (in-depth) interviews (Section 10.2), as there is a defined schedule of questions, from which interviewers should not deviate.

## The choice of questionnaire

Your choice of questionnaire will be influenced by a variety of factors related to your research question(s) and objectives (Table 11.1), and in particular the:

- characteristics of the respondents from whom you wish to collect data;
- importance of reaching a particular person as respondent;
- importance of respondents' answers not being contaminated or distorted;
- size of sample you require for your analysis, taking into account the likely response rate;
- types of question you need to ask to collect your data;
- number of questions you need to ask to collect your data.

These factors will not apply equally to your choice of questionnaire, and for some research questions or objectives may not apply at all. The type of questionnaire you choose will dictate how sure you can be that the respondent is the person whom you wish to answer the questions and thus the reliability of responses (Table 11.1). Even if you address a postal questionnaire to a company manager by name, you have no way of ensuring that the manager will be the respondent. The manager's assistant or someone else could complete it! Internet- and intranet-mediated questionnaires, and in particular those administered in conjunction with email, offer greater control because most users read and respond to their own mail at their personal computer (Witmer *et al.*, 1999). With delivery and collection questionnaires, you can sometimes check who has answered the questions at collection. By contrast, interviewer-administered question-naires enable you to ensure that the respondent is whom you want. This improves the reliability of your data. In addition, you can record who were non-respondents, thereby avoiding unknown bias caused by refusals.

| Attribute | Internet and intranet mediated | Postal | Delivery and collection | Telephone | Structured interview |
|---|---|---|---|---|---|
| Population's characteristics for which suitable | Computer-literate individuals who can be contacted by email, Internet or intranet | Literate individuals who can be contacted by post; selected by name, household, organisation etc. | | Individuals who can be telephoned; selected by name, household, organisation etc. | Any; selected by name, household, organisation, in the street etc. |
| Confidence that right person has responded | High if using email | Low | Low but can be checked at collection | High | High |
| Likelihood of contamination or distortion of respondent's answer | Low | May be contaminated by consultation with others | | Occasionally distorted or invented by interviewer | Occasionally contaminated by consultation or distorted/invented by interviewer |
| Size of sample | Large, can be geographically dispersed | Large, can be geographically dispersed | Dependent on number of field workers | Dependent on number of interviewers | Dependent on number of interviewers |
| Likely response rate[a] | Variable, 30% reasonable within organisations/via intranet, 11% or lower using Internet | Variable, 30% reasonable | Moderately high, 30–50% reasonable | High, 50–70% reasonable | High, 50–70% reasonable |
| Feasible length of questionnaire | Conflicting advice; however, fewer 'screens' probably better | 6–8 A4 pages | 6–8 A4 pages | Up to half an hour | Variable depending on location |
| Suitable types of question | Closed questions but not too complex, complicated sequencing fine if uses IT, must be of interest to respondent | Closed questions but not too complex, simple sequencing only, must be of interest to respondent | | Open and closed questions, but only simple questions, complicated sequencing fine | Open and closed questions, including complicated questions, complicated sequencing fine |
| Time taken to complete collection | 2–6 weeks from distribution (dependent on number of follow-ups) | 4–8 weeks from posting (dependent on number of follow-ups) | Dependent on sample size, number of field workers, etc. | Dependent on sample size, number of interviewers, etc., but slower than self-administered for same sample size | |
| Main financial resource implications | Web page design, although automated expert systems offered online and by software providers are reducing this dramatically | Outward and return postage, photocopying, clerical support, data entry | Field workers, travel, photocopying, clerical support, data entry | Interviewers, telephone calls, clerical support. Photocopying and data entry if not using CATI[c]. Programming, software and computers if using CATI | Interviewers, travel, clerical support. Photocopying and data entry if not using CAPI[c]. Programming, software and computers if using CAPI |
| Role of the interviewer/field worker | None | None | Delivery and collection of questionnaires, enhancing respondent participation | Enhancing respondent participation, guiding the respondent through the questionnaire, answering respondents' questions | |
| Data input[b] | Usually automated | Closed questions can be designed so that responses may be entered using optical mark readers after questionnaire has been returned | | Response to all questions entered at time of collection using CATI[c] | Response to all questions can be entered at time of collection using CAPI[d] |

[a]Discussed in Chapter 7  [b]Discussed in Section 12.2  [c]Computer-aided telephone interviewing  [d]Computer-aided personal interviewing

Sources: Authors' experience; Dillman (2000); Hewson et al. (2003); Oppenheim (2000); deVaus (2002); Witmer et al. (1999)

Any *contamination* of respondents' answers will reduce your data's reliability (Table 11.1). Sometimes, if they have insufficient knowledge or experience they may deliberately guess at the answer, a tendency known as *uninformed response*. This is particularly likely when the questionnaire has been incentivised (Section 11.5). Respondents to self-administered questionnaires are relatively unlikely to answer to please you or because they believe certain responses are more **socially desirable** (Dillman, 2000). They may, however, discuss their answers with others, thereby contaminating their response. Respondents to telephone questionnaires and structured interviews are more likely to answer to please owing to contact with you, although the impact of this can be minimised by good interviewing technique (Section 10.5). Responses can also be contaminated or distorted when recorded. In extreme instances, interviewers may invent responses. For this reason, random checks of interviewers are often made by survey organisations.

The type of questionnaire you choose will affect the number of people who respond (Section 7.2). Interviewer-administered questionnaires will usually have a higher response rate than self-administered questionnaires (Table 11.1). The size of your sample and the way in which it is selected will have implications for the confidence you can have in your data and the extent to which you can generalise (Section 7.2).

Longer questionnaires are best presented as a structured interview. In addition, they can include more complicated questions than telephone questionnaires or self-administered questionnaires (Oppenheim, 2000). The presence of an interviewer means that it is also easier to route different subgroups of respondents to answer different questions using a filter question (Section 11.4). The suitability of different types of question also differs between techniques.

Your choice of questionnaire will also be affected by the resources you have available (Table 11.1), and in particular the:

■ time available to complete the data collection;

■ financial implications of data collection and entry;

■ availability of interviewers and field workers to assist;

■ ease of automating data entry.

The time needed for data collection increases markedly for delivery and collection questionnaires and structured interviews where the samples are geographically dispersed (Table 11.1). One way you can overcome this constraint is to select your sample using cluster sampling (Section 7.2). Unless your questionnaire is administered online, or **computer-aided personal interviewing (CAPI)** or **computer-aided telephone interviewing (CATI)** is used, you will need to consider the costs of reproducing the questionnaire, clerical support and entering the data for computer analysis. For postal and telephone questionnaires, cost estimates for postage and telephone calls will need to be included. If you are working for an organisation, postage costs may be reduced by using *Freepost* for questionnaire return. This means that you pay only postage and a small handling charge for those questionnaires that are returned by post. However, the use of Freepost rather than a stamp may adversely affect your response rates (see Table 11.4).

Virtually all data collected by questionnaires will be analysed by computer. Some packages (for example, SNAP™ and SphinxSurvey™) allow you both to design your questionnaire and to enter and analyse the data within the same software. Once your data have been coded and entered into the computer you will be able to explore and analyse them far more quickly and thoroughly than by hand (Section 12.2). As a rough rule, you should analyse questionnaire data by computer if they have been collected from 30 or more respondents. For larger surveys, you may wish to automate the capture and input of data. For Internet- and intranet-mediated questionnaires (**electronic questionnaires**), this is normally undertaken at the questionnaire design stage and, where the software is automated, costs are minimal. For example, SurveyMonkey™, an online software tool for creating and administering web-based questionnaires, at the time of writing charged $19.99 for up to 1000 responses a month, whilst a survey of 10 or fewer questionnaires and with 100 or fewer responses is free (SurveyMonkey, 2005). For self-administered questionnaires, data capture and input is most straightforward for closed questions where respondents select and mark their answer from a prescribed list (Box 11.1).

---

## BOX 11.1  WORKED EXAMPLE

### Closed question designed for an optical mark reader

Ben's research project involved sending out a questionnaire to a large number of people. Because of this he obtained permission to use his university's optical mark reader to input the data from his questionnaire. In his questionnaire, respondents are given clear instructions on how to mark their responses:

Please use a pencil to mark your answer as a solid box like this: [—]

If you make a mistake use an eraser to rub out your answer.

1  Please mark **all** the types of       Rock and Pop        [  ]
   music that you regularly              Dance and Urban     [  ]
   listen to:                            Soundtracks         [  ]
                                         Jazz and Blues      [  ]
                                         Country             [  ]
                                         Easy listening      [  ]
                                         Folk                [  ]
                                         World               [  ]
                                         Classical           [  ]
                                         Other               [  ]
                                         (please describe):
                                         ........................................

---

The mark is read using an **optical mark reader**, which recognises and converts marks into data at rates often exceeding 200 pages a minute. Data for interviewer-administered questionnaires can be entered directly into the computer at the time of interview using CATI or CAPI software. With both types of software you read the questions to the respondent from the screen and enter their answers directly into the computer. Because of the costs of high-speed and high-capacity scanning equipment, software and pre-survey programming, CATI and CAPI are financially viable only for very large surveys or where repeated use of the hardware and software will be made.

In reality, you are almost certain to have to make compromises in your choice of questionnaire. These will be unique to your research as the decision about which questionnaire is most suitable cannot be answered in isolation from your research question(s) and objectives and the population that you are surveying.

## 11.3 | Deciding what data need to be collected

### Research design requirements

Unlike in-depth and semi-structured interviews (Chapter 10), the questions you ask in questionnaires need to be defined precisely prior to data collection. Whereas you can prompt and explore issues further with in-depth and semi-structured interviews, this will not be possible for questionnaires. In addition, the questionnaire offers only one chance to collect the data, as it is often difficult to identify respondents or to return to collect additional information. This means that the time you spend planning precisely what data you need to collect, how you intend to analyse them (Chapter 12) and designing your questionnaire to meet these requirements is crucial if you are to answer your research question(s) and meet your objectives.

For most management and business research the data you collect using questionnaires will be used for either descriptive or explanatory purposes. For questions where the main purpose is to describe the population's characteristics either at a fixed time or at a series of points over time to enable comparisons, you will normally need to administer your questionnaire to a sample. The sample needs to be as representative and accurate as possible where it will be used to generalise about the total population (Sections 7.1–7.3). You will also probably need to relate your findings to earlier research. It is therefore important that you select the appropriate characteristics to answer your research question(s) and to address your objectives. You therefore need to have:

- reviewed the literature carefully;

- discussed your ideas with colleagues, your project tutor and other interested parties.

For research involving organisations, we have found it essential to understand the organisations in which we are undertaking the research. Similarly, for international or cross-cultural research it is important to have an understanding of the countries or cultures in which you are undertaking the research. Without this it is easy to make mistakes, such as using the wrong terminology or language, and to collect useless data. For many research projects an understanding of relevant organisations can be achieved through browsing company publications or their Internet sites (Section 8.3), observation (Chapter 9) and in-depth and semi-structured interviews (Chapter 10).

Explanatory research requires data to test a theory or theories. This means that, in addition to those issues raised for descriptive research, you need to define the theories you wish to test as relationships between variables prior to designing your questionnaire. You therefore need to have reviewed the literature carefully, discussed your ideas widely, and conceptualised your own research clearly prior to designing your questionnaire (Ghauri and Grønhaug, 2005). In particular, you need to be clear about which relationships you think are likely to exist between variables:

- a variable is *dependent* – that is, it changes in response to changes in other variables;

- a variable is *independent* – that is, it causes changes in dependent variables;

- a variable is *extraneous* – that is, it might also cause changes in dependent variables, thereby providing an alternative explanation to your independent variable or variables (Box 11.2).

As these relationships are likely to be tested through statistical analysis (Section 12.5) of the data collected by your questionnaire, you need to be clear about the detail in

**BOX 11.2 WORKED EXAMPLE**

### Defining theories in terms of relationships between variables

As part of her research Marie-Claude wished to test the theory that the incidence of repetitive strain injury (RSI) was linked to the number of rest periods that keyboard operators took each working day.

The relationship that was thought to exist between the variables was that the incidence of RSI was higher when fewer or no rest periods were taken each day. The dependent variable was the incidence of RSI and the independent variable was the number of rest periods taken each day. Marie-Claude thought that extraneous variables such as the use of proper seating and wrist rests might also influence the incidence of RSI. Data were therefore collected on these variables as well.

which they will be measured at the design stage. Where possible, you should ensure that measures are compatible with those used in other relevant research so that comparisons can be made (Section 12.2).

## Types of variable

Dillman (2000) distinguishes between three types of data variable that can be collected through questionnaires:

- opinion;
- behaviour;
- attribute.

These distinctions are important, as they will influence the way your questions are worded (Box 11.3). **Opinion** variables record how respondents feel about something or what they think or believe is true or false. In contrast, data on behaviours and attributes record what respondents do and are. When recording what respondents do, you are recording their **behaviour**. This differs from respondents' opinions because you are recording a concrete experience. Behavioural variables contain data on what people (or their organisations) did in the past, do now or will do in the future. By contrast, **attribute** variables contain data about the respondents' characteristics. Attributes are best thought of as things a respondent possesses, rather than things a respondent does (Dillman, 2000). They are used to explore how opinions and behaviour differ between respondents as well as to check that the data collected are representative of the total population (Section 7.2). Attributes include characteristics such as age, gender, marital status, education, occupation and income.

## Ensuring that essential data are collected

A problem experienced by many students and organisations we work with is how to ensure that the data collected will enable the research question(s) to be answered and the objectives achieved. Although no method is infallible, one way is to create a **data requirements table** (Table 11.2). This summarises the outcome of a process:

1  Decide whether the main outcome of your research is descriptive or explanatory.

2  Subdivide each research question or objective into more specific investigative questions about which you need to gather data.

**BOX 11.3** WORKED EXAMPLE

### Opinion, behaviour and attribute questions

Sally was asked by her employer to undertake an anonymous survey of financial advisors' ethical values. In particular, her employer was interested in the advice given to clients. After some deliberation she came up with three questions that address the issue of putting clients' interests before their own:

**2** How do you feel about the following statement? 'Financial advisors should place their clients' interest before their own.'

| | | |
|---|---|---|
| | strongly agree | ☐ |
| | mildly agree | ☐ |
| (please tick the appropriate box) | neither agree or disagree | ☐ |
| | mildly disagree | ☐ |
| | strongly disagree | ☐ |

**3** In general, do financial advisors place their clients' interests before their own?

| | | |
|---|---|---|
| | always yes | ☐ |
| | usually yes | ☐ |
| (please tick the appropriate box) | sometimes yes | ☐ |
| | seldom yes | ☐ |
| | never yes | ☐ |

**4** How often do you place your clients' interests before your own?

| | | |
|---|---|---|
| | 80–100% of my time | ☐ |
| | 60–79% of my time | ☐ |
| (please tick the appropriate box) | 40–59% of my time | ☐ |
| | 20–39% of my time | ☐ |
| | 0–19% of my time | ☐ |

Sally's choice of question or questions to include in her questionnaire were dependent on whether she needed to collect data on financial advisors' opinions or behaviours. She designed question 2 to collect data on respondents' opinions about financial advisors placing their clients' interest before their own. This question asks respondents how they feel. In contrast, question 3 asks respondents whether financial advisors in general place their clients' interests before their own. It is therefore concerned with their opinions in terms of their individual beliefs. Question 4 focuses on how often the respondents actually place their clients' interests before their own. Unlike the previous questions, it is concerned with their actual behaviour rather than their opinion.

To answer her research questions and to meet her objectives Sally also needed to collect data to explore how ethical values differed between subgroupings of financial advisors. One theory she had was that ethical values were related to age. To test this she needed to collect data on the attribute age. After some deliberation she come up with question 5:

**5** How old are you?

| | | |
|---|---|---|
| | Less than 30 years | ☐ |
| | 30 to less than 40 years | ☐ |
| (please tick the appropriate box) | 40 to less than 50 years | ☐ |
| | 50 to less than 60 years | ☐ |
| | 60 years or over | ☐ |

Table 11.2  **Data requirements table**

| Research question/objective: | | | |
|---|---|---|---|
| Type of research: | | | |
| Investigative questions | Variable(s) required | Detail in which data measured | Check measurement question included in questionnaire ✓ |
| | | | |

3  Repeat the second stage if you feel that the investigative questions are not sufficiently precise.

4  Identify the variables about which you will need to collect data to answer each investigative question.

5  Establish the level of detail required from the data for each variable.

6  Develop measurement questions to capture the data at the level of data required for each variable.

**Investigative questions** are the questions that you need to answer in order to address satisfactorily each research question and to meet each objective (Blumberg *et al.*, 2005). They need to be generated with regard to your research question(s) and objectives. For some investigative questions you will need to subdivide your first attempt into more detailed investigative questions. For each you need to be clear whether you are interested in respondents' opinions, behaviours or attributes (discussed earlier), as what appears to be a need to collect one sort of variable frequently turns out to be a need for another. We have found the literature review, discussions with interested parties and pilot studies to be of help here.

You then need to identify the variables about which you need to collect data to answer each investigative question and to decide the level of detail at which these are measured. Again, the review of the literature and associated research can suggest possibilities. However, if you are unsure about the detail needed you should measure at the more precise level. Although this is more time consuming, it will give you flexibility in your analyses. In these you will be able to use computer software to group or combine data (Section 12.2).

Once your table is complete (Box 11.4), it must be checked to make sure that all data necessary to answer your investigative questions are included. When checking, you need to be disciplined and to ensure that only data that are essential to answering your research question(s) and meeting your objectives are included. We added the final column to remind us to check that our questionnaire actually includes a measurement question that collects the precise data required!

## 11.4 | Designing the questionnaire

The internal validity and reliability of the data you collect and the response rate you achieve depend, to a large extent, on the design of your questions, the structure of your questionnaire, and the rigour of your pilot testing (all discussed in this section). A valid questionnaire will enable accurate data to be collected, and one that is reliable will mean that these data are collected consistently. Foddy (1994:17) discusses validity and reliability in terms of the questions and answers making sense. In particular, he emphasises

## BOX 11.4 WORKED EXAMPLE

### Data requirements table

As part of his work placement Greg was asked to discover customer attitudes to the introduction of a smoking ban in restaurants and bars. Discussion with senior management and colleagues and reading relevant literature helped him to firm up his objective and investigative questions. A selection of these is included in the extract from his table of data requirements:

**Research question/objective**: To establish customers' attitudes to the introduction of a smoking ban in restaurants and bars

**Type of research**: Predominantly descriptive, although wish to examine differences between restaurants and bars, and between different groups of customers

| Investigative questions | Variable(s) required | Detail in which data measured | Check included in questionnaire ✓ |
|---|---|---|---|
| Do customers feel that they should be able to smoke in restaurants and bars as a right? (opinion) | Opinion of customer to smoking in restaurants and bars as a right | Feel. . . should be allowed, should not be allowed, no strong feelings [N.B. will need separate questions for restaurants and for bars] | |
| Do customers feel that restaurants and bars should provide a smoking room for smokers? (opinion) | Opinion of customer to the provision of a smoking room for smokers | Feel. . . very strongly that it should, quite strongly that it should, no strong opinions, quite strongly that it should not, very strongly that it should not [N.B. will need separate questions for restaurants and for bars] | |
| Do customers' opinions differ depending on | (Opinion of employee – outlined above) | (Included above) | |
| • age? (attribute) | • Age of employee | • To nearest 5-year band (youngest 16, oldest 65) | |
| • whether or not a smoker? (behaviour) | • Smoker | • Non-smoker, smokes but not in own home, smokes in own home | |
| How representative are the responses of customers? (attributes) | Age of customer Gender of customer Job [Note: must be able to compare with National Statistics Socio-Economic Classification (Rose and Pevalin, 2003)] | (Included above) Male, female Higher managerial and professional occupations, Lower managerial and professional occupations, Intermediate occupations, Small employers and own account workers, Lower supervisory and technical occupations, Semi-routine occupations, Routine occupations, Never worked and long-term unemployed | |

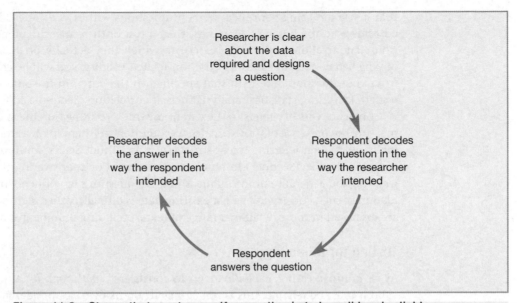

**Figure 11.2    Stages that must occur if a question is to be valid and reliable**

*Source*: Developed from Foddy (1994) *Constructing Questions for Interviews and Questions*. Reproduced with permission of Cambridge University Press.

that 'the question must be understood by the respondent in the way intended by the researcher and the answer given by the respondent must be understood by the researcher in the way intended by the respondent'. This means that there are at least four stages that must occur if the question is to be valid and reliable (Figure 11.2). It also means that the design stage is likely to involve you in substantial rewriting in order to ensure that the respondent decodes the question in the way you intended. We therefore recommend that you use a word processor or survey design software such as SNAP or SphinxSurvey.

## Assessing validity

*Internal validity* in relation to questionnaires therefore refers to the ability of your questionnaire to measure what you intend it to measure. This means you are concerned that what you find with your questionnaire actually represents the reality of what you are measuring. This presents you with a problem, as if you actually knew the reality of what you were measuring there would be no point in designing your questionnaire! Researchers get round this problem by looking for other relevant evidence that supports the answers found using the questionnaire, relevance being determined by the nature of their research question and their own judgement.

Often, when discussing the validity of a questionnaire, researchers refer to content validity, criterion-related validity and construct validity (Blumberg *et al.*, 2005). **Content validity** refers to the extent to which the measurement device, in our case the measurement questions in the questionnaire, provides adequate coverage of the investigative questions. Judgement of what is 'adequate coverage' can be made in a number of ways. One is through careful definition of the research through the literature reviewed and, where appropriate, prior discussion with others. Another is to use a panel of individuals to assess whether each measurement question in the questionnaire is 'essential', 'useful but not essential', or 'not necessary'.

**Criterion-related validity**, sometimes known as **predictive validity**, is concerned with the ability of the measures (questions) to make accurate predictions. This means that if you are using your measurement questions within your questionnaire to predict customers' future buying behaviours, then a test of these measurement questions' criterion-related validity will be the extent to which they actually predict these customers buying behaviours. In assessing criterion-related validity, you will be comparing the data from your questionnaire with that specified in the criterion in some way. Often this is undertaken using statistical analysis such as correlation (Section 12.5).

**Construct validity** refers to the extent to which your measurement questions actually measure the presence of those constructs you intended them to measure. This term is normally used when referring to constructs such as attitude scales, aptitude and personality tests and the like (Section 11.4) and can be thought of as answering the question: 'How well can you generalise from you measurement questions to your construct?' Because validation of such constructs against existing data is difficult, other methods are used. These are discussed in more detail in a range of texts, including Blumberg *et al.* (2005).

## Testing for reliability

As we outlined earlier, *reliability* refers to consistency. Although for a questionnaire to be valid it must be reliable, this is not sufficient on its own. Respondents may consistently interpret a question in your questionnaire in one way, when you mean something else. As a consequence, although the question is reliable, it does not really matter as it has no internal validity and so will not enable your research question to be answered. Reliability is therefore concerned with the robustness of your questionnaire and, in particular whether or not it will produce consistent findings at different times and under different conditions, such as with different samples or, in the case of an interviewer-administered questionnaire, with different interviewers.

Mitchell (1996) outlines three common approaches to assessing reliability, in addition to comparing the data collected with other data from a variety of sources. Although the analysis for each of these is undertaken after data collection, they need to be considered at the questionnaire design stage. They are:

- test re-test;
- internal consistency;
- alternative form.

*Test re-test* estimates of reliability are obtained by correlating data collected with those from the same questionnaire collected under as near equivalent conditions as possible. The questionnaire therefore needs to be administered twice to respondents. This may result in difficulties, as it is often difficult to persuade respondents to answer the same questionnaire twice. In addition, the longer the time interval between the two questionnaires, the lower the likelihood that respondents will answer the same way. We therefore recommend that you use this method only as a supplement to other methods.

*Internal consistency* involves correlating the responses to each question in the questionnaire with those to other questions in the questionnaire. It therefore measures the consistency of responses across either all the questions or a subgroup of the questions from your questionnaire. There are a variety of methods for calculating internal consistency, of which one of the most frequently used is Cronbach's alpha. Further details of this and other approaches can be found in Mitchell (1996) and in books about more advanced statistical analysis software such as Field (2005).

The final approach to testing for reliability outlined by Mitchell (1996) is *alternative form*. This offers some sense of the reliability within your questionnaire through comparing responses to alternative forms of the same question or groups of questions. Where questions are included for this purpose, usually in longer questionnaires, they are often called *check questions*. However, it is often difficult to ensure that these questions are substantially equivalent. Respondents may suffer from fatigue owing to the need to increase the length of the questionnaire, and they may spot the similar question and just refer back to their previous answer! It is therefore advisable to use check questions sparingly.

## Designing individual questions

The design of each question should be determined by the data you need to collect (Section 11.3). When designing individual questions researchers do one of three things (Bourque and Clark, 1994):

- adopt questions used in other questionnaires;
- adapt questions used in other questionnaires;
- develop their own questions.

Adopting or adapting questions may be necessary if you wish to replicate, or to compare your findings with, another study. This can allow reliability to be assessed. It is also more efficient than developing your own questions, provided that you can still collect the data you need to answer your research question(s) and to meet your objectives. Some survey design software includes questions that you may use. Alternatively, you may find questions and coding schemes that you feel will meet your needs in existing questionnaires or in *question banks* such as the ESRC Question Bank. This consists of a database of questions and question methodology of UK social surveys going back to 1991 and is available from <URL http://qb.soc.surrey.ac.uk>.

However, before you adopt questions, beware! There are a vast number of poor questions in circulation, so always assess each question carefully. In addition, you need to check whether they are under copyright. If they are, you need to obtain the author's permission to use them. Even where there is no formal copyright you should note where you obtained the questions and give credit to their author.

Initially, you need only consider the type and wording of individual questions rather than the order in which they will appear on the form. Clear wording of questions using terms that are likely to be familiar to, and understood by, respondents can improve the validity of the questionnaire. Most types of questionnaire include a combination of open and closed questions. **Open questions**, sometimes referred to as *open-ended questions* (Dillman, 2000), allow respondents to give answers in their own way (Fink, 2003a). **Closed questions**, sometimes referred to as *closed-ended questions* (Dillman, 2000) or **forced-choice questions** (deVaus, 2002), provide a number of alternative answers from which the respondent is instructed to choose. The latter type of question is usually quicker and easier to answer, as they require minimal writing. Responses are also easier to compare as they have been predetermined. However, if these responses cannot be easily interpreted then these benefits are, to say the least, marginal (Foddy, 1994). Within this chapter we highlight six types of closed question that we discuss later:

- *list*, where the respondent is offered a list of items, any of which may be selected;
- *category*, where only one response can be selected from a given set of categories;
- *ranking*, where the respondent is asked to place something in order;
- *rating*, in which a rating device is used to record responses;
- *quantity*, to which the response is a number giving the amount;
- *grid*, where responses to two or more questions can be recorded using the same matrix.

Prior to data analysis, you will need to group and code responses to each question. Detailed coding guidance is given in Section 11.2. You are strongly advised to read the entire chapter prior to designing your questions.

## Open questions

**Open questions** are used widely in in-depth and semi-structured interviews (Section 10.5). In questionnaires they are useful if you are unsure of the response, such as in exploratory research, when you require a detailed answer or when you want to find out what is uppermost in the respondent's mind. An example of an open question (from a self-administered questionnaire) is:

**6**    Please list up to three things you like about your job:

1..............................................................................

2..............................................................................

3..............................................................................

With open questions, the precise wording of the question and the amount of space partially determine the length and fullness of response. However, if you leave too much space the question becomes off-putting. Question 6 collects data about what each respondent believes they like about their job. Thus if salary had been the reason uppermost in their mind this would probably have been recorded first. Unfortunately, for large-scale questionnaire surveys responses to open questions are extremely time consuming to code (Section 12.2). For this reason, it is usually advisable keep their use to a minimum.

## List questions

**List questions** offer the respondent a list of responses, any of which they can choose. Such questions are useful when you need to be sure that the respondent has considered all possible responses. However, the list of responses must be defined clearly and meaningfully to the respondent. For structured interviews, it is often helpful to present the respondent with a *prompt card* listing all responses. The response categories you can use vary widely and include 'yes/no', 'agree/disagree' and 'applies/does not apply' along with 'don't know' or 'not sure'. If you intend to use what you hope is a complete list, you may wish to add a catch-all category of 'other'. This has been included in question 7, which collects data on respondents' religion. However, as you can read in Box 11.5, the use of 'other' can result in unforeseen responses!

**7**    What is your religion?

Please tick ✓ the appropriate box.

| Buddhist | ☐ | None | ☐ |
| Christian | ☐ | Other | ☐ |
| Hindu | ☐ | | |
| Jewish | ☐ | (please say:)............................................. |
| Muslim | ☐ | |
| Sikh | ☐ | |

Question 7 collects data on the religion of the respondent. In this list question, the common practice of omitting negative response boxes has been adopted. Consequently, negative responses in this question not being, for example, a Christian, are inferred from each unmarked response. If you choose to do this, beware: non-response could also indicate uncertainty or, for some questions, that an item does not apply!

---

**BOX 11.5  RESEARCH IN THE NEWS**                                    **FT**

## George Lucas is a god in Britain. Literally.

According to official census figures, 390,000 Brits said their religious faith was "Jedi". Had this been an official category, it would have been the fourth largest religion in the UK, ahead of Sikhism.

Instead, the *Star Wars* fans were registered as atheists. "We have put them among the 7.7m people who said they had no religion," a census official said. "I suspect this was a decision which will not be challenged greatly."

Evidently aspirant Jedi masters were inspired by an e-mail that asked them to record the unrecognised faith in the hope that their support would force the government to put Lucas on the same level as Moses, Christ and Mohammed.

"Imagine the official statistics of your country claiming a percentage of the population as practising 'Jedi Knights'!!!" says the website *jedicensus.com*. Yes, imagine that.

*Source: Financial Times*, 14 February 2003. Copyright © 2005 The Financial Times Ltd.

---

### Category questions

In contrast, **category questions** are designed so that each respondent's answer can fit only one category. Such questions are particularly useful if you need to collect data about behaviour or attributes. The number of categories that you can include without affecting the accuracy of responses is dependent on the type of questionnaire. Self-administered questionnaires and telephone questionnaires should usually have no more than five response categories (Fink, 2003a). Structured interviews can have more categories provided that a *prompt card* is used (Box 11.6) or, as in question 8, the interviewer categorises the responses.

8   How often do you visit this shopping centre?

   *Interviewer: listen to the respondent's answer and tick ✓ as appropriate.*

   ☐ first visit                              2 or more times a week                    ☐
   ☐ once a week                             less than once a week to fortnightly  ☐
   ☐ less than fortnightly to once a month   less often                              ☐

You should arrange responses in a logical order so that it is easy to locate the response category that corresponds to each respondent's answer. Your categories should be *mutually exclusive* (should not overlap), and should cover all possible responses. The layout of your questionnaire should make it clear which boxes refer to which response category by placing them close to the appropriate text.

## BOX 11.6 WORKED EXAMPLE

### Use of a prompt card as part of a structured interview

As part of his interview schedule, Peter asked the following question:

Which of the following daily newspapers have you read during the past month?

*Show respondent card 3 with the names of the newspapers. Read out names of the newspapers one at a time. Record their response with a √ in the appropriate box.*

|  | Read | Not read | Don't know |
|---|---|---|---|
| The Daily Express | ☐ | ☐ | ☐ |
| Daily Mail | ☐ | ☐ | ☐ |
| The Daily Mirror | ☐ | ☐ | ☐ |
| Daily Star | ☐ | ☐ | ☐ |
| Financial Times | ☐ | ☐ | ☐ |
| The Guardian | ☐ | ☐ | ☐ |
| The Daily Telegraph | ☐ | ☐ | ☐ |
| The Independent | ☐ | ☐ | ☐ |
| The Sun | ☐ | ☐ | ☐ |
| The Times | ☐ | ☐ | ☐ |

Peter gave card 3 to each respondent prior to reading out newspaper names and collected the card after the question had been completed.

---

3

# THE DAILY EXPRESS

# Daily Mail

# The Daily Mirror

# Daily Star

# FINANCIAL TIMES

# *The* Guardian

# The Daily Telegraph

# THE INDEPENDENT

# The Sun

# THE TIMES

## Ranking questions

A **ranking question** asks the respondent to place things in rank order. This means that you can discover their relative importance to the respondent. In question 9, taken from a postal questionnaire, the respondents are asked their beliefs about the relative importance of a series of features when choosing a new car. The catch-all feature of 'other' is included to allow respondents to add one other feature.

9  Please number each of the factors listed below in order of importance to you in your choice of a new car. Number the most important 1, the next 2 and so on. If a factor has no importance at all, please leave blank.

| factor | importance |
|---|---|
| acceleration | [  ] |
| boot size | [  ] |
| depreciation | [  ] |
| safety features | [  ] |
| fuel economy | [  ] |
| price | [  ] |
| driving enjoyment | [  ] |
| other | [  ] |

..........................  (⇦ please describe)

With such questions, you need to ensure that the instructions are clear and will be understood by the respondent. In general, respondents find that ranking more than seven or eight items takes too much effort, so you should keep your list to this length or shorter (Kervin, 1999). Respondents can rank accurately only when they can see or remember all items. This can be overcome with face-to-face questionnaires by using prompt cards on which you list all of the features to be ranked. However, telephone questionnaires should ask respondents to rank a maximum of three or four items, as the respondent will need to rely on their memory (Kervin, 1999).

## Rating questions

**Rating questions** are often used to collect opinion data. They should not be confused with **scales** (discussed later in this section), which are a coherent set of questions or items that are regarded as indicators of a construct or concept (Corbetta, 2003). Rating questions most frequently use the **Likert-style rating scale** in which the respondent is asked how strongly she or he agrees or disagrees with a statement or series of statements, usually on a four-, five-, six- or seven-point rating scale. If you intend to use a series of statements, you should keep the same order of response categories to avoid confusing respondents (Dillman, 2000). You should, however, include both positive and negative statements so as to ensure that the respondent reads each one carefully and thinks about which box to tick.

10  For the following statement please tick ✓ the box that matches your view most closely.

| | agree | tend to agree | tend to disagree | disagree |
|---|---|---|---|---|
| I feel that employees' views have influenced the decisions taken by management. | ☐ | ☐ | ☐ | ☐ |

Question 10 has been taken from a delivery and collection questionnaire to employees in an organisation and is designed to collect opinion data. In this rating question, an even number of points (four) has been used to force the respondent to express their feelings towards an implicitly positive statement. By contrast, question 11, also from a delivery and collection questionnaire, contains an odd number (five) of points on the rating scale. This rating scale allows the respondent to 'sit on the fence' by ticking the middle 'not sure' category when considering an implicitly negative statement. The phrase 'not sure' is used here as it is less threatening to the respondent than admitting they do not know. This rating question is designed to collect data on employees' opinions of the situation now.

**11** For the following statement please tick ✓ the box that matches your view most closely.

|  | agree | tend to agree | not sure | tend to disagree | disagree |
|---|---|---|---|---|---|
| I believe there are 'them and us' barriers to communication in the company *now*. | ☐ | ☐ | ☐ | ☐ | ☐ |

You can expand this form of rating question further to record finer shades of opinion. However, respondents to telephone questionnaires find it difficult to distinguish between values on rating scales of more than five points plus 'don't know'. In addition, there is little point in collecting data for seven or nine response categories, if these are subsequently combined in your analysis (Chapter 12). Colleagues and students often ask us how many points they should have on their rating scale. This is related to the likely measurement error. If you know that your respondents can only respond accurately to a three-point rating, then it is pointless to have a finer rating scale with more points!

In question 12 the respondent's attitude is captured on a 10-point **numeric rating scale**. In such rating questions it is important that the numbers reflect the feeling of the respondent. Thus 1 reflects poor value for money and 10 good value for money. Only these end categories (and sometimes the middle) are labelled and are known as self-anchoring rating scales. As in this question, graphics may also be used to reflect the rating scale visually, thereby aiding the respondent's interpretation. An additional category of 'not sure' or 'don't know' can be added and should be separated slightly from the rating scale.

**12** For the following statement please circle O the number that matches your view most closely.

This concert was... Poor value for money    1  2  3  4  5  6  7  8  9  10  Good value for money

Another variation is the **semantic differential rating scale**. These are often used in consumer research to determine underlying attitudes. The respondent is asked to rate a single object or idea on a series of bipolar rating scales (Box 11.7). Each *bipolar scale* is described by a pair of opposite adjectives (question 13) designed to anchor respondents' attitudes towards service. For these rating scales, you should vary the position of positive and negative adjectives from left to right to reduce the tendency to read only the adjective on the left (Kervin, 1999).

**13** On each of the lines below, place a X to show how you feel about the service you received at our restaurant.

Fast     \_|\_|\_|\_|\_|\_|\_|\_|\_|\_    Slow

Unfriendly     \_|\_|\_|\_|\_|\_|\_|\_|\_|\_    Friendly

Value for money     \_|\_|\_|\_|\_|\_|\_|\_|\_|\_    Over-priced

---

## BOX 11.7 FOCUS ON MANAGEMENT RESEARCH

### Semantic differential rating scales

In their study of the perception of messages conveyed by review and audit reports published in the *Accounting, Auditing & Accountability Journal*, Gay, Schelluch and Baines (1998) reviewed the academic literature to identify the messages that these two types of report were intended to convey. Based upon this they developed a semantic differential scale consisting of 35 bipolar adjectival statements separated by a seven-point scale. These adjectival statements were worded as polar opposites and included (Gay *et al.*, 1998:480):

| | 1 | 2 | 3 | 4 | 5 | 6 | 7 | |
|---|---|---|---|---|---|---|---|---|
| The financial statements give a true and fair view | | | | | | | | The financial statements do not give a true and fair view |
| The entity is free from fraud | | | | | | | | The entity is not free from fraud |

By using the semantic differential scale, Gay *et al.* (1998) were able to measure perceived messages in relation to the reliability of financial statements, auditor/management responsibility and the usefulness of such financial statements for decision making.

---

Rating questions have been combined to measure a wide variety of concepts such as customer loyalty, service quality and job satisfaction. For each concept the resultant measure or **scale** is represented by a scale score created by combining the scores for each of the rating questions. Each question is often referred to as a *scale item*. In the case of a simple Likert scale, for example, the scale score for each case would be calculated by adding together the scores of each of the questions (items) selected (deVaus, 2002). A detailed discussion of creating scales, including those by Likert and Guttman, can be found in Corbetta (2003). However, rather than developing your own scales, it often makes sense to use or adapt existing scales. Since scaling techniques were first used in the 1930s, literally thousands of scales have been developed to measure attitudes and personality dimensions and to assess skills and abilities. Details of an individual scale can often be found by following up references in an article reporting research that uses that scale. In addition, there are a wide variety of handbooks that list these scales (for example, Miller and Salkind, 2002). However, you need to beware: they may be subject to copyright constraints. Even where there is no formal copyright, you should note where you obtained the scale and give credit to the author.

### Quantity questions

The response to a **quantity question** is a number, which gives the amount of a characteristic. For this reason, such questions tend to be used to collect behaviour or attribute data. A common quantity question, which collects attribute data, is:

**14** What is your year of birth?   | 1 | 9 |   |   |

(for example, for 1980 write:)   | 1 | 9 | 8 | 0 |

Because the data collected by this question could be entered into the computer without coding, the question can also be termed a *self-coded* question.

### Grid

A **grid** or *matrix* enables you to record the responses to two or more similar questions at the same time. Although the 1991 UK census form was designed using a matrix format, this was not continued for the 2001 census form. Questions were listed down the left-hand side of the page, and each household member was listed across the top. The response to each question for each household member was then recorded in the cell where the row and column met. Although using a grid saves space, Dillman (2000) suggests that respondents have difficulties comprehending these designs and that they are a barrier to response.

### Question wording

The wording of each question will need careful consideration to ensure that the responses are valid – that is, measure what you think they do. Your questions will need to be checked within the context for which they were written rather than in abstract to ensure they are not misread (Box 11.8). Given this, the checklist in Box 11.9 should help you to avoid the most obvious problems associated with wording that threaten the validity of responses.

## BOX 11.8 WORKED EXAMPLE

### Misreading questions

Before becoming a student Tracey worked for a UK-based market research agency and was responsible for much of their questionnaire design and analysis work. During her time at the agency she noted that certain words in questions were likely to be misread by respondents. The question 'In which county do you live?' was often answered as if the question had been 'In which country do you live?' This meant that rather than answering 'Oxfordshire', the respondent would answer either 'England' or 'UK'. Later questionnaires for which Tracey was responsible used the question 'In which town do you live?', the response being used to establish and code the county in which the respondent lived.

### Translating questions into other languages

Translating questions and associated instructions into another language requires care if your translated or target questionnaire is to be decoded and answered by respondents in the way you intended. For international research this is extremely important if the questions

BOX 11.9 CHECKLIST

## Your question wording

✓ Does your question collect data at the right level of detail to answer your investigative question as specified in your data requirements table?

✓ Will respondents have the necessary knowledge to answer your question? A question on the implications of a piece of European Union legislation would yield meaningless answers from those who were unaware of that legislation.

✓ Does your question talk down to respondents? It should not!

✓ Are the words used in your question familiar, and will all respondents understand them in the same way? In particular, you should use simple words and avoid jargon, abbreviations and colloquialisms.

✓ Are there any words that sound similar and might be confused with those used in your question? This is a particular problem with interviewer-administered questionnaires.

✓ Are there any words that look similar and might be confused if your question is read quickly? This is particularly important for self-administered questionnaires.

✓ Are there any words in your question that might cause offence? These might result in biased responses or a lower response rate.

✓ Can your question be shortened? Long questions are often difficult to understand, especially in interviewer-administered questionnaires, as the respondent needs to remember the whole question. Consequently, they often result in no response at all.

✓ Are you asking more than one question at the same time? The question 'How often do you visit your mother and father?' contains two separate questions, one about each parent, so responses would probably be impossible to interpret.

✓ Does your question include a negative or double negative? Questions that include the word 'not' are sometimes difficult to understand. The question 'Would you rather not use a non-medicated shampoo?' is far easier to understand when rephrased as: 'Would you rather use a medicated shampoo?'

✓ Is your question unambiguous? This can arise from poor sentence structure, using words with several different meanings or having an unclear investigative question. If you ask 'When did you leave school?' some respondents might state the year, others might give their age, while those still in education might give the time of day! Ambiguity can also occur in category questions. If you ask employers how many employees they have on their payroll and categorise their answers into three groups (up to 100, 100–250, 250 plus), they will not be clear which group to choose if they have 100 or 250 employees.

✓ Does your question imply that a certain answer is correct? If it does, the question is biased and will need to be reworded, such as with the question 'Many people believe that too little money is spent on our public Health Service. Do you believe this to be the case?' For this question, respondents are more likely to answer 'yes' to agree with and please the interviewer.

✓ Does your question prevent certain answers from being given? If it does, the question is biased and will need to be reworded. The question 'Is this the first time you have pretended to be sick?' implies that the respondent has pretended to be sick whether they answer yes or no!

✓ Is your question likely to embarrass the respondent? If it is then you need either to reword it or to place it towards the end of the survey when you will, it is to be hoped, have gained the respondent's confidence. Questions on income can be asked as either precise amounts (more embarrassing), using a quantity question, or income bands (less embarrassing), using a category question.

☑ Have you incorporated advice appropriate for your type of questionnaire (such as the maximum number of categories) outlined in the earlier discussion of question types?

☑ Are answers to closed questions written so that at least one will apply to every respondent and so each of the list of responses is mutually exclusive ?

☑ Are the instructions on how to record each answer clear?

are to have the same meaning to all respondents. For this reason Usunier (1998) suggests that when translating the source questionnaire attention should be paid to:

- **lexical meaning** – the precise meaning of individual words (for example, the French word *chaud* can be translated into two concepts in English and German, 'warm' and 'hot');

- **idiomatic meaning** – the meanings of a group of words that are natural to a native speaker and not deducible from those of the individual words (for example, the English expression for informal communication, 'grapevine', has a similar idiomatic meaning as the French expression *téléphone arabe,* meaning literally 'arab telephone' and the German expression *mundpropaganda,* meaning literally 'mouth propaganda');

- *grammar and syntax* – the correct use of language, including the ordering of words and phrases to create well-formed sentences (for example, in Japanese the ordering is quite different from English or Dutch, as verbs are at the end of sentences);

- **experiential meaning** – the equivalence of meanings of words and sentences for people in their everyday experiences (for example, terms that are familiar in the source questionnaire's context such as 'dual career household' may be unfamiliar in the target questionnaire's context).

Usunier (1998) outlines a number of techniques for translating your source questionnaire. These, along with their advantages and disadvantages, are summarised in Table 11.3. In this table, the **source questionnaire** is the questionnaire that is to be translated, and the **target questionnaire** is the translated questionnaire. When writing your final project report, remember to include a copy of both the source and the target questionnaire as appendices. This will allow readers familiar with both languages to check that equivalent questions in both questionnaires have the same meaning.

## Question coding

If you are planning to analyse your data by computer, they will need to be coded prior to entry. For quantity questions, actual numbers can be used as codes. For other questions, you will need to design a coding scheme. Whenever possible, you should establish the coding scheme prior to collecting data and incorporate it into your questionnaire. This should take account of relevant existing coding schemes to enable comparisons with other data sets (Section 12.2).

For most closed questions you should be able to add codes to response categories. These can be printed on the questionnaire, thereby **pre-coding** the question and removing the need to code after data collection. Two ways of doing this are illustrated by questions 15 and 16, which collect data on the respondents' opinions.

**Table 11.3** Translation techniques for questionnaires

|  | Direct translation | Back-translation | Parallel translation | Mixed techniques |
|---|---|---|---|---|
| Approach | Source questionnaire to target questionnaire | Source questionnaire to target questionnaire to source questionnaire; comparison of two new source questionnaires; creation of final version | Source questionnaire to target questionnaire by two or more independent translators; comparison of two target questionnaires; creation of final version | Back-translation undertaken by two or more independent translators; comparison of two new source questionnaires; creation of final version |
| Advantages | Easy to implement, relatively inexpensive | Likely to discover most problems | Leads to good wording of target questionnaire | Ensures best match between source and target questionnaires |
| Disadvantages | Can lead to many discrepancies (including those relating to meaning) between source and target questionnaire | Requires two translators, one a native speaker of the source language, the other a native speaker of the target language | Cannot ensure that lexical, idiomatic and experiential meanings are kept in target questionnaire | Costly, requires two or more independent translators. Implies that the source questionnaire can also be changed |

*Source*: Developed from Usunier (1998) 'Translation techniques for questionnaires' in *International and Cross-Cultural Management Research*. Copyright © 1998 Sage Publications, reprinted with permission

| **15** Is the service you receive? (please circle O the number) | Excellent<br>5 | Good<br>4 | Reasonable<br>3 | Poor<br>2 | Awful<br>1 |
|---|---|---|---|---|---|
| **16** Is the service you receive? (please tick ✓ the box) | Excellent<br>☐5 | Good<br>☐1 | Reasonable<br>☐3 | Poor<br>☐2 | Awful<br>☐4 |

The codes allocated to response categories will affect your analyses. In question 15 an ordered scale of numbers has been allocated to adjacent responses. This will make it far easier to aggregate responses using a computer (Section 12.2) to 'satisfactory' (5, 4 or 3) and 'unsatisfactory' (2 or 1) compared with the codes in question 16. We therefore recommend that you do not allocate codes as in question 16.

In contrast, if you are considering using an Internet- or intranet-mediated questionnaire you can create an **online form** (questionnaire) containing text boxes where the respondent enters information, check boxes that list the choices available to the respondent allowing them to 'check' or 'tick' one or more of them (as in the TGI Friday's questionnaire), and drop-down list boxes that restrict the respondent to selecting only one of the answers you specify. Online forms are often included as part of word-processing software such as Microsoft Word™. Alternatively, as for question 17, you can use online software tools such as SurveyMonkey to create your online form. Both allow you to create a professional questionnaire and the respondent to complete the questionnaire online and return the data electronically in a variety of formats such as Excel™, SPSS compatible or a comma-delimited file.

For open questions you will need to reserve space on your data collection form to code responses after data collection. Question 18 has been designed to collect attribute data in

*Source*: Question layout created by the online software tool SurveyMonkey (2005), reproduced with permission.

a sample survey of 5000 people. Theoretically there could be hundreds of possible responses, and so sufficient spaces are left in the 'for Office use only' box.

**18** What is your full job title?

...................................................................

for Office use only

□   □   □

Open questions, which generate lists of responses, are likely to require more complex coding using either the multiple-response or the multiple-dichotomy method. These are discussed in Section 12.2, and we recommend that you read this prior to designing your questions.

## Designing the survey form

### The order and flow of questions

When constructing your questionnaire it is a good idea to spend time considering the order and flow of your questions. These should be logical to the respondent (and interviewer) rather than follow the order in your data requirements table (Table 11.2). To assist the flow of the survey it may be necessary to include **filter questions**. These identify those respondents for whom the following question or questions are not applicable, so they can skip those questions. You should beware of using more than two or three filter questions in self-administered questionnaires, as respondents tend to find having to skip questions annoying. More complex filter questions can be programmed using Internet- and intranet-mediated questionnaires and CAPI and CATI software so that skipped questions are never displayed on the screen and as a consequence never asked (Dillman, 2000). In such situations the respondent is unlikely to be aware of the questions that have been skipped. The following example uses the answer to question 19 to determine whether questions 20 to 24 will be answered. (Questions 19 and 20 both collect data on attributes.)

**19** Are you currently registered as unemployed?   Yes   □₁
*If 'no' go to question 25*   No   □₂

**20** How long have you been registered as unemployed?   ☐☐ years   ☐☐ months

(for example, for no years and six months write:)   $\boxed{0}$ years   $\boxed{6}$ months

Where you need to introduce new topics, phrases such as 'the following questions refer to . . .' or 'I am now going to ask you about . . .' are useful. And when wording your questions, you should remember the particular population for whom your questionnaire is designed. For interviewer-administered questionnaires, you will have to include instructions for the interviewer (Box 11.10). The checklist in Box 11.11 should help you to avoid the most obvious problems associated with question order and flow. For some questionnaires the advice contained may be contradictory. Where this is the case, you need to decide what is most important for your particular population.

## BOX 11.10  WORKED EXAMPLE

### Introducing a series of rating questions in a telephone questionnaire

As part of a telephone questionnaire, Stefan needed to collect data on respondents' attitudes to motorway service stations. To do this he asked respondents to rate a series of statements using a Likert-type rating scale. Because his survey was conducted by telephone the rating scale was restricted to four categories: strongly agree, agree, disagree, strongly disagree.

In order to make the questionnaire easy for the interviewer to follow, Stefan used italic script to highlight the interviewer's instructions and the words that the interviewer needed to read in bold. An extract is given below:

**Now I'm going to read you several statements. Please tell me whether you strongly agree, agree, disagree or strongly disagree with each.**

*Interviewer: read out statements 21 to 30 one at a time and after each ask . . .*

**Do you strongly agree, agree, disagree or strongly disagree?**

*Record respondent's response with a tick ✓*

|  | strongly agree | agree | disagree | strongly disagree |
|---|---|---|---|---|
| **21**  I wish there were a greater number of service stations on motorways | ☐4 | ☐3 | ☐2 | ☐1 |

## The layout of the questionnaire

Layout is important for both self-administered and interviewer-administered question-naires. Interviewer-administered questionnaires should be designed to make reading questions and filling in responses easy. The layout of self-administered questionnaires should, in addition, be attractive to encourage the respondent to fill it in and to return it, while not appearing too long. However, where the choice is between an extra page and a cramped questionnaire the former is likely to be more acceptable to respondents (Dillman, 2000). Survey design and analysis software such as Snap and SphinxSurvey and online software tools such as SurveyMonkey contain a series of style templates for type-faces, colours and page layout, which are helpful in producing a professional-looking questionnaire more quickly (Snap Surveys, 2005; Sphinx Development, 2005; SurveyMonkey, 2005). For paper-based surveys, the use of colour will increase the printing costs. However, it is worth noting that the best way of obtaining valid responses to questions is to keep both the visual appearance of the questionnaire and the wording of each question simple (Dillman, 2000).

## BOX 11.11 CHECKLIST

### Your question order

- ✔ Are questions at the beginning of your questionnaire more straightforward and ones the respondent will enjoy answering? Questions about attributes and behaviours are usually more straightforward to answer than those collecting data on opinions.

- ✔ Are questions at the beginning of your questionnaire obviously relevant to the stated purpose of your questionnaire? For example, questions requesting contextual information may appear irrelevant.

- ✔ Are questions and topics that are more complex placed towards the middle of your questionnaire? By this stage most respondents should be completing the survey with confidence but should not yet be bored or tired.

- ✔ Are personal and sensitive questions towards the end of your questionnaire, and is their purpose clearly explained? On being asked these a respondent may refuse to answer; however, if they are at the end of an interviewer-administered questionnaire you will still have the rest of the data!

- ✔ Are filter questions and routeing instructions easy to follow so that there is a clear route through the questionnaire?

- ✔ (For interviewer-administered questionnaires) Are instructions to the interviewer easy to follow?

- ✔ Are questions grouped into obvious sections that will make sense to the respondent?

- ✔ Have you re-examined the wording of each question and ensured it is consistent with the position in the questionnaire as well as with the data you require?

Research findings on the extent to which the length of your questionnaire will affec your response rate are mixed (deVaus, 2002). There is a widespread view that longer ques tionnaires will reduce response rates relative to shorter questionnaires (Edwards *et al.* 2002). However, a very short questionnaire may suggest that your research is insignifi cant and hence not worth bothering with. Conversely, a questionnaire that takes ove two hours to complete might just be thrown away by the intended respondent. In general, we have found that a length of between four and eight A4 pages has been accept able for within-organisation self-administered questionnaires. Telephone questionnaire of up to half an hour have caused few problems, whereas the acceptable length for struc tured interviews can vary from only a few minutes in the street to over two hours in a more comfortable environment (Section 10.6). Based on these experiences, we recom mend you follow deVaus' (2002) advice:

- Do not make the questionnaire longer than is really necessary to meet your research questions and objectives.

- Do not be too obsessed with the length of your questionnaire.

One way you can reduce apparent length without reducing legibility is to recorc answers to questions with the same set of possible responses as a table. Usually you place questions in the rows and responses in the columns. Instructions on how to answer the question and column headings are given prior to the table and on each subsequent page as illustrated by questions 23 and 24. These were designed to collect data on respondents' behaviour using a delivery and collection questionnaire.

**For each of the following statements please tick the box that most closely matches your experience . . .**

|  | monthly | every 3 months | every 6 months | less often | never |
|---|---|---|---|---|---|
| 23  I receive a company site newsletter . . . | $\square_1$ | $\square_2$ | $\square_3$ | $\square_4$ | $\square_5$ |
| 24  I receive other company publications . . . | $\square_1$ | $\square_2$ | $\square_3$ | $\square_4$ | $\square_5$ |

Box 11.12 discusses the order of a questionnaire used to research the effects of total quality management and Box 11.13 summarises the most important layout issues as a checklist.

## BOX 11.12 FOCUS ON MANAGEMENT RESEARCH

### Questionnaire order

Lagrosen and Lagrosen's (2005) paper titled 'The effects of quality management – a survey of Swedish quality professionals', published in the *International Journal of Operations & Production Management*, includes as appendix a full copy of their questionnaire translated from Swedish. Their questionnaire is divided into three parts, presenting a logic flow of questions to the respondent. The first, consisting of two attribute questions, collects general data about the organisation by which the respondent was employed or, for those who were consultants, with which they were currently working. These ask for the organisation's broad sector and the approximate number of employees. The second is concerned with the respondent's opinion about the organisation's values, as well as behaviours such as the quality management standards used by the organisation and the tools used by the organisation to help manage quality. The final part focuses on the respondent's opinion regarding the effects of the quality management work undertaken. This includes two filter questions, each followed by an open question. The first of these filter questions asks (2005: 952):

Have you noticed any positive effects of your quality work?

If so, which is the most prominent effect? ....................................................

...........................................................................................................

whilst the second is concerned with negative effects. The final question asks respondents to rate the organisation's 'quality management work' on a seven-point scale using the bipolar phrases 'very badly' and 'very well'.

## Explaining the purpose of the questionnaire

### The covering letter

Most self-administered questionnaires are accompanied by a **covering letter**, which explains the purpose of the survey. This is the first part of the questionnaire that a respondent should look at. Unfortunately, some of your sample will ignore it, while others use it to decide whether to answer the accompanying questionnaire.

## BOX 11.13 CHECKLIST

### Your questionnaire layout

- ✔ (For self-administered questionnaires) Do questions appear squashed on the page? This will put the respondent off reading it and reduce the response rate. Unfortunately, a thick questionnaire is equally off-putting!

- ✔ (For self-administered questionnaires) Is the questionnaire going to be printed on good-quality paper? This will imply that the survey is important.

- ✔ (For self-administered questionnaires) Is the questionnaire going to be printed on warm-pastel-coloured paper? Warm pastel shades such as yellow and pink generate slightly more responses than white (Edwards *et al.*, 2002) or cool colours such as green or blue. White is a good neutral colour but bright or fluorescent colours should be avoided.

- ✔ (For structured interviews) Will the questions and instructions be printed on one side of the paper only? You will find it difficult to read the questions on back pages if you are using a questionnaire attached to a clipboard!

- ✔ Is your questionnaire easy to read? Questionnaires should be typed in 12 point or 10 point using a plain font. Excessively long and excessively short lines reduce legibility. Similarly, respondents find CAPITALS, *italics* and shaded backgrounds more difficult to read. However, if used consistently, they can make completing the questionnaire easier.

- ✔ Have you ensured that the use of shading, colour, font sizes, spacing and the formatting of questions is consistent throughout the questionnaire?

- ✔ Is your questionnaire laid out in a format that respondents are accustomed to reading? Research has shown that many people skim-read questionnaires (Dillman, 2000). Instructions that can be read one line at a time from left to right moving down the page are therefore more likely to be followed correctly.

Research by Dillman (2000) and others has shown that the messages contained in a self-administered questionnaire's covering letter will affect the response rate. The results of this research are summarised in the annotated letter (Figure 11.3).

For some research projects you may also send a letter prior to administering your questionnaire. This will be used by the respondent to decide whether to grant you access. Consequently, it is often the only opportunity you have to convince the respondent to participate in your research. Ways of ensuring this are discussed in Section 6.4.

### Introducing the questionnaire

At the start of your questionnaire you need to explain clearly and concisely why you want the respondent to complete the survey. Dillman (2000) argues that, to achieve as high a response rate as possible, this should be done on the first page of the questionnaire in addition to the covering letter. He suggests that in addition to a summary of the main messages in the covering letter (Figure 11.3) you include:

- a clear unbiased banner or title, which conveys the topic of the questionnaire and makes it sound interesting;

- a subtitle, which conveys the research nature of the topic (optional);

- a neutral graphic illustration or logo to add interest and to set the questionnaire apart (self-administered questionnaires).

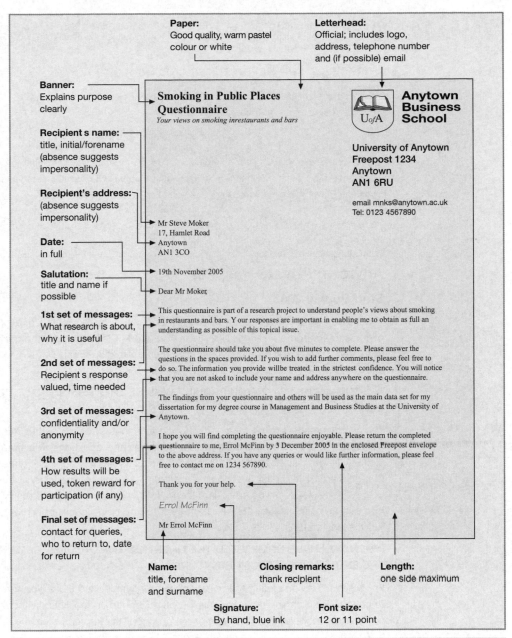

**Paper:** Good quality, warm pastel colour or white

**Letterhead:** Official; includes logo, address, telephone number and (if possible) email

**Banner:** Explains purpose clearly

**Recipient s name:** title, initial/forename (absence suggests impersonality)

**Recipient's address:** (absence suggests impersonality)

**Date:** in full

**Salutation:** title and name if possible

**1st set of messages:** What research is about, why it is useful

**2nd set of messages:** Recipient s response valued, time needed

**3rd set of messages:** confidentiality and/or anonymity

**4th set of messages:** How results will be used, token reward for participation (if any)

**Final set of messages:** contact for queries, who to return to, date for return

**Smoking in Public Places Questionnaire**
*Your views on smoking in restaurants and bars*

Anytown Business School

University of Anytown
Freepost 1234
Anytown
AN1 6RU

email mnks@anytown.ac.uk
Tel: 0123 4567890

Mr Steve Moker
17, Hamlet Road
Anytown
AN1 3CO

19th November 2005

Dear Mr Moker,

This questionnaire is part of a research project to understand people's views about smoking in restaurants and bars. Your responses are important in enabling me to obtain as full an understanding as possible of this topical issue.

The questionnaire should take you about five minutes to complete. Please answer the questions in the spaces provided. If you wish to add further comments, please feel free to do so. The information you provide will be treated in the strictest confidence. You will notice that you are not asked to include your name and address anywhere on the questionnaire.

The findings from your questionnaire and others will be used as the main data set for my dissertation for my degree course in Management and Business Studies at the University of Anytown.

I hope you will find completing the questionnaire enjoyable. Please return the completed questionnaire to me, Errol McFinn by 3 December 2005 in the enclosed Freepost envelope to the above address. If you have any queries or would like further information, please feel free to contact me on 1234 567890.

Thank you for your help.

*Errol McFinn*

Mr Errol McFinn

**Name:** title, forename and surname

**Closing remarks:** thank recipient

**Length:** one side maximum

**Signature:** By hand, blue ink

**Font size:** 12 or 11 point

**Figure 11.3  Structure of a covering letter**

Interviewer-administered questionnaires will require this information to be phrased as a short introduction, which the interviewer can read to each respondent. A template for this (developed from deVaus, 2002) is given in the next paragraph, while Box 11.14 provides an example from a self-administered questionnaire.

Good morning / afternoon / evening. My name is (your name) from (your organisation). I am doing a research project to find out (brief description of purpose of the research). Your telephone number was drawn from a random sample of (brief description of the total population). The questions I should like to ask will take about (number) minutes. If you have any queries, I shall be happy to answer them. (Pause). Before I continue please can you confirm that this is (read out the telephone number) and that I am talking to (read out name/occupation/position in organisation to check that you have the right person). Please can I ask you the questions now?

## BOX 11.14 WORKED EXAMPLE

### Introducing a self-administered questionnaire

Liz asked her project tutor to comment on what she hoped was the final draft of her questionnaire. This included the following introduction:

ANYTOWN PRIVATE HOSPITAL STAFF SURVEY

*All your responses will be treated in the strictest of confidence and only aggregated data will be available to the Hospital. All questionnaires will be shredded once the data have been extracted. The Hospital will publish a summary of the results.*

Not surprisingly, her project tutor suggested that she redraft her introduction. Her revised introduction follows:

Caring for All

### Anytown Private Hospital

### Staff Survey 2006

This survey is being carried out to find out how you feel about the Hospital's policies to support colleagues like you in your work. Please answer the questions freely. You cannot be identified from the information you provide, and no information about individuals will be given to the Hospital.

**ALL THE INFORMATION YOU PROVIDE WILL BE TREATED IN THE STRICTEST CONFIDENCE**

The questionnaire should take you about five minutes to complete. Please answer the questions in the space provided. Try to complete the questions at a time when you are unlikely to be disturbed. Also, do not spend too long on any one question. Your first thoughts are usually your best! Even if you feel the items covered may not apply directly to your working life please do not ignore them. Your answers are essential in building an accurate picture of the issues that are important to improving our support for people working for this Hospital.

**WHEN YOU HAVE COMPLETED THE QUESTIONNAIRE PLEASE RETURN IT TO US IN THE ENCLOSED FREEPOST ENVELOPE**

I hope you find completing the questionnaire enjoyable, and thank you for taking the time to help us. A summary of the findings will be published on the Hospital intranet. If you have any queries or would like further information about this project, please call me on 01234-5678910.
Thank you for your help.

*Elizabeth Petrie*

Elizabeth Petrie
Human Resources Department
Anytown Private Hospital
Anytown AN99 9HS

You will also need to have prepared answers to the more obvious questions that the respondent might ask you. These include the purpose of the survey, how you obtained the respondent's telephone number, who is conducting or sponsoring the survey, and why someone else cannot answer the questions instead (Lavrakas, 1993).

## Closing the questionnaire

At the end of your questionnaire you need to explain clearly what you want the respondent to do with their completed questionnaire. It is usual to start this section by thanking her or him for completing the questionnaire, and by providing a contact name and telephone number for any queries she or he may have (Figure 11.3). You should then give details of the date by which you would like the questionnaire returned and how and where to return it. A template for this is given in the next paragraph:

**Thank you for taking the time to complete this questionnaire. If you have any queries please do not hesitate to contact (your name) by telephoning (contact telephone number with answer machine/voice mail).**

**Please return the completed questionnaire by (date) in the envelope provided to:**

**(your name)**

**(your address)**

## Pilot testing and assessing validity

Prior to using your questionnaire to collect data it should be pilot tested. The purpose of the **pilot test** is to refine the questionnaire so that respondents will have no problems in answering the questions and there will be no problems in recording the data. In addition, it will enable you to obtain some assessment of the questions' validity and the likely reliability of the data that will be collected. Preliminary analysis using the pilot test data can be undertaken to ensure that the data collected will enable your investigative questions to be answered.

Initially you should ask an expert or group of experts to comment on the representativeness and suitability of your questions. As well as allowing suggestions to be made on the structure of your questionnaire, this will help establish content validity and enable you to make necessary amendments prior to pilot testing with a group as similar as possible to the final population in your sample. For any research project there is a temptation to skip the pilot testing. We would endorse Bell's (2005:147) advice, 'however pressed for time you are, do your best to give the questionnaire a trial run', as, without a trial run, you have no way of knowing your questionnaire will succeed.

The number of people with whom you pilot your questionnaire and the number of pilot tests you conduct are dependent on your research question(s), your objectives, the size of your research project, the time and money resources you have available, and how well you have initially designed your questionnaire. Very large questionnaire surveys such as national censuses will have numerous field trials, starting with individual questions and working up to larger and more rigorous pilots of later drafts.

For smaller-scale questionnaires you are unlikely to have sufficient financial or time resources for large-scale field trials. However, it is still important that you pilot test your questionnaire. The number of people you choose should be sufficient to include any major variations in your population that you feel are likely to affect responses. For most student questionnaires this means that the minimum number for a pilot is 10 (Fink, 2003b), although for large surveys between 100 and 200 responses is usual (Dillman, 2000). Occasionally you may be extremely pushed for time. In such instances it is better to pilot test the questionnaire using friends or family than not at all! This will provide you with at least some idea of your questionnaire's **face validity**: that is, whether the questionnaire appears to make sense.

As part of your pilot you should check each completed pilot questionnaire to ensure that respondents have had no problems understanding or answering questions and have followed all instructions correctly (Fink, 2003b). Their responses will provide you with an idea of the reliability and suitability of the questions. For self-administered questionnaires additional information about problems can be obtained by giving respondents a further short questionnaire. Bell (2005) suggests you should use this to find out:

- how long the questionnaire took to complete;
- the clarity of instructions;
- which, if any, questions were unclear or ambiguous;
- which, if any, questions the respondent felt uneasy about answering;
- whether in their opinion there were any major topic omissions;
- whether the layout was clear and attractive;
- any other comments.

Interviewer-administered questionnaires need to be tested with the respondents for all these points other than layout. One way of doing this is to form an assessment as each questionnaire progresses. Another is to interview any interviewers you are employing. However, you can also check by asking the respondent additional questions at the end of their interview. In addition, you will need to pilot test the questionnaire with interviewers to discover whether:

- there are any questions for which visual aids should have been provided;
- they have difficulty in finding their way through the questionnaire;
- they are recording answers correctly.

Once you have completed pilot testing you should write to your respondents thanking them for their help.

## 11.5 | Administering the questionnaire

Once your questionnaire is designed, pilot tested and amended and your sample selected, the questionnaire can be used to collect data. This final stage is called *administering* the questionnaire. As part of this you will need to gain access to your sample (Sections 6.2 and 6.3) and attempt to maximise the response rate. Edwards *et al.* (2002) identify 292 studies that have assessed between them the impact of 75 different strategies for increasing the response to postal questionnaires. These trials were published predominantly in marketing, business and statistical journals (42 per cent), medical and health-related journals (32 per cent) and psychological, educational and sociological journals (23 per cent). The findings of those studies that had more than 1000 participants are summarised in Table 11.4. However, such increases in response rates are dependent upon your questionnaire being clearly worded and well laid out. In addition, it must be remembered that organisations and individuals are increasingly being bombarded with requests to respond to questionnaires and so may be unwilling to answer your questionnaire (Box 11.15).

Which of these techniques you use to help to maximise responses will inevitably be dependent on the way in which your questionnaire is administered. It is the processes associated with administering each of the five types of questionnaire that we now consider.

**Table 11.4 Relative impact of strategies for raising postal questionnaire response rates**

Note: strategies in *italics* increase response rates relative to those in normal font

| Strategy | Relative impact |
|---|---|
| **Incentives** | |
| *Monetary incentive* v. no incentive | very high |
| *Incentive sent with questionnaire* v. incentive on questionnaire return | high |
| *Non-monetary incentive* v. no incentive | low |
| **Length** | |
| *Shorter questionnaire* v. longer questionnaire | very high |
| **Appearance** | |
| *Brown envelope* v. white envelope | high but variable |
| *Coloured ink* v. standard | medium |
| *Folder or booklet* v. stapled pages | low |
| *More personalised* v. less personalised | low |
| *Coloured questionnaire* v. white questionnaire | very low |
| *Identifying feature on the return* v. none | very low but variable |
| **Delivery** | |
| *Recorded delivery* v. standard delivery | very high |
| *Stamped return envelope* v. business reply or franked | medium |
| *First class post outwards* v. other class | low |
| *Sent to work address* v. sent to home address | low but variable |
| *Pre-paid return* v. not pre-paid | low but variable |
| Commemorative stamp v. *ordinary stamp* | low but variable |
| Stamped outward envelope v. franked | negligible |
| **Contact** | |
| *Pre-contact* v. no pre-contact | medium |
| *Follow-up* v. no follow-up | medium |
| *Postal follow-up including questionnaire* v. postal follow-up excluding questionnaire | medium |
| Pre-contact by telephone v. *pre-contact by post* | low |
| Mention of follow-up contact v. none | negligible |
| **Content** | |
| *More interesting* v. less interesting questionnaire | very high |
| *User friendly questionnaire* v. standard | medium |
| *Attribute and behaviour questions only* v. attribute, behaviour and attitude questions | medium |
| *More relevant questions first* v. other questions first | low |
| *Most general question first* v. last | low but variable |
| Sensitive questions included v. *sensitive questions not included* | very low |
| Demographic questions first v. other questions first | negligible |
| 'Don't know' boxes included v. not included | negligible |
| **Origin** | |
| University sponsorship as a source v. *other organisation* | medium |
| *Sent by more senior or well-known person* v. less senior or less well-known | low but variable |
| *Ethnically unidentifiable/white name* v. other name | low but variable |
| **Communication** | |
| *Explanation for not participating requested* v. not requested | medium |
| *Choice to opt out from study offered* v. not given | low |
| Instructions given v. *not given* | low but variable |
| *Benefits to respondent stressed* v. other benefits | very low |
| Benefits to sponsor stressed v. other benefits | negligible |
| Benefits to society stressed v. other benefits | negligible |
| Response deadline given v. no deadline | negligible |

*Source*: Developed from Edwards *et al*., 2002

## BOX 11.15 RESEARCH IN THE NEWS     FT

### Companies face an avalanche of questionnaires

For those seeking to hold companies to account for their behaviour, transparency has become a buzzword over the past few years. But how much transparency is enough? Have demands for ever-greater disclosure gone too far?

Take the workload created by these demands at BT, the telecommunications group. The company receives more than 200 questionnaires a year about its governance and corporate responsibility practices, says Chris Tuppen, head of sustainable development and corporate accountability. Requests for information come from big government clients, investors, academics and consultancies.

"In 1990, there were probably about five questionnaires a year. It has grown exponentially since about 2000," he says. "Some of the questionnaires have 80 to 100 questions, often with sub-questions." One person now devotes two to three days a week responding to these questionnaires, at a direct cost to the company of £25,000 ($45,000) a year.

BT is not alone. Concern about the risks posed by poor governance, ethical lapses or environmental mismanagement have swelled requests for detailed information about whether companies are meeting acceptable standards.

"There is no question that there has been a huge increase over the last couple of years," says Al Loehnis,

a director of the Investor Relations Society, a European professional body. "It genuinely has created problems at companies."

The resulting "questionnaire fatigue" afflicts investor relations officers, company secretaries and corporate responsibility managers, who face piles of paper and online forms that often cover similar ground, but each from a slightly different angle.

Bridget Walker, head of investor relations at Scottish & Newcastle, the international brewing group, says many questions are irrelevant. The concerns that S&N must address are those that can directly affect its reputation, such as responsible alcohol consumption or labour standards in its operations in emerging markets. Questions such as how much electricity it uses in each of its UK sites are a side issue. "We don't need to talk about this."

There is pressure, however, to take part in big questionnaire and ranking exercises, such as the FTSE4Good Index and the Corporate Responsibility Index run by Business in the Community, even at the risk of scoring less than brilliantly. "If we're not in it, it would look like we'd have something to hide," she says.

*Source*: Article by Alison Maitland, *Financial Times*, 26 March 2004. Copyright © The Financial Times Ltd.

### Internet- and intranet-mediated questionnaires

For Internet- and intranet-mediated questionnaires it is important to have a clear timetable that identifies the tasks that need to be done and the resources that will be needed. A good response is dependent on the recipient being motivated to answer the questionnaire and to send it back. Although the covering email (letter) (Section 11.4) and good design will help to ensure a high level of response, it must be remembered that, unlike paper questionnaires, the designer and respondent may see different images displayed on their monitors. Alternative computer operating systems, Internet browsers and display screens can all result in the image being displayed differently, emphasising the need to ensure the questionnaire design is clear (Dillman, 2000).

Internet- and intranet-mediated questionnaires are usually administered in one of two ways: via email or via a website (Hewson *et al.*, 2003). The first of these uses email to 'post' and receive questionnaires and is dependent on having a list of addresses. Although it is possible to obtain such lists from an Internet-based employment directory or via a search engine (Section 3.5), we would not recommend you obtain them this way. If you are considering using the Internet for research, you should abide by the general operating guidelines or *netiquette*. This includes (Hewson *et al.*, 2003):

- ensuring emails and postings to user groups are relevant and that you do not send junk emails (*spam*);
- remembering that invitations to participate sent to over 20 user groups at once are deemed as unacceptable by many net vigilantes and so you should not exceed this threshold;
- avoiding sending your email to multiple mailing lists as this is likely to result in individuals receiving multiple copies of your email (this is known as **cross-posting**);
- avoiding the use of email attachments as these can contain viruses.

Failure to do this is likely to result in 'few responses and a barrage of mail informing the researcher of their non-compliance' (Coomber, 1997:10). Despite this, questionnaires can be successfully administered by email within organisations provided that all of the sample have access to it and use it. However, unless an anonymous server or mailbox that removes email addresses is used for returning questionnaires, respondents will be identifiable by their email addresses (Witmer *et al.*, 1999). If you choose to use email, we suggest that you:

1 contact recipients by email and advise them to expect a questionnaire – a **pre-survey contact** (Section 6.3);
2 email the questionnaire with a covering email. Where possible, the letter and questionnaire should be part of the email message rather than an attached file to avoid viruses. You should make sure that this will arrive when recipients are likely to be receptive. For most organisations Fridays and days surrounding major public holidays have been shown to be a poor time;
3 email the *first* **follow-up** one week after emailing out the questionnaire to all recipients. This should thank early respondents and remind non-respondents to answer (a copy of the questionnaire should be included);
4 email the *second follow-up* to people who have not responded after three weeks. This should include another covering letter and a copy of the questionnaire. The covering letter should be reworded to further emphasise the importance of completing the questionnaire;
5 also use a *third follow-up* if time allows or your response rate is low.

Alternatively, the questionnaire can be advertised by email, on the Internet or on the intranet and respondents invited to access a website and to fill in an online questionnaire. Adopting this web-based approach observes netiquette and means that respondents can remain anonymous and, of equal importance, are unable to modify the questionnaire (Witmer *et al.*, 1999). The stages involved are:

1 Ensure that a website has been set up that explains the purpose of the research and how to complete the questionnaire (this takes the place of the covering letter).
2 Ensure that the questionnaire has been set up on the web and has a direct link (*hyperlink*) from the website.
3 Advertise the website widely using a range of media (for example, an email pre-survey contact or a banner advertisement on a page that is likely to be looked at by the target population), using a hyperlink to the questionnaire and highlighting the closing date.
4 When the respondent completes the questionnaire, ensure that the data file is generated and saved automatically and that the web-based software prevents multiple responses from one respondent.

5 For web-based questionnaires advertised using an email pre-survey contact, email all recipients one week after the initial email thanking early respondents and reminding others to respond.

6 For web-based questionnaires advertised using an email pre-survey contact, email a *second follow-up* to people who have not responded after three weeks. The email should be reworded to emphasise further the importance of completing the questionnaire. For anonymous questionnaires a second follow-up will not be possible, as you should not be able to tell who has responded!

Response rates from such an approach are likely to be very low, and there are considerable problems of non-response bias as the respondent has to take extra steps to locate and complete the questionnaire (Coomber, 1997). Consequently, it is likely to be very difficult to obtain a representative sample from which you might generalise. This is not to say that this approach should not be used as it can, for example, enable you to contact difficult-to-access groups. It all depends, as you would expect us to say, on your research question and objectives!

## Postal questionnaires

For postal questionnaires, it is also important to have a well-written covering letter and good design to help to ensure a high level of response. As with online questionnaires, a clear timetable and well-executed administration process are important (Box 11.16).

Our advice for postal questionnaires (developed from deVaus, 2002) can be split into six stages:

1 Ensure that questionnaires and letters are printed, and envelopes addressed.

2 Contact recipients by post, telephone or email and advise them to expect a questionnaire – a *pre-survey contact* (Section 5.3). This stage is often omitted for cost reasons.

3 Post the survey with a covering letter and a return envelope (and fax cover sheet). You should make sure that this will arrive when recipients are likely to be receptive. For most organisations Fridays and days surrounding major public holidays have been shown to be a poor time.

4 Post (or email) the *first follow-up* one week after posting out the survey to all recipients. For posted questionnaires this should take the form of a postcard designed to thank early respondents and to remind rather than to persuade non-respondents.

5 Post the *second follow-up* to people who have not responded after three weeks. This should contain another copy of the questionnaire, a new return envelope and a new covering letter. The covering letter should be reworded to emphasise further the importance of completing the questionnaire. For anonymous questionnaires a second follow-up will not be possible, as you should not be able to tell who has responded!

6 Also use a *third follow-up* if time allows or your response rate is low. For this it may be possible to use recorded delivery (post), telephone calls or even call in person to emphasise the importance of responding.

deVaus (2002) also advises placing a unique *identification number* on each questionnaire, which is recorded on your list of recipients. This makes it easy to check and follow up non-respondents and, according to Dillman (2000) and Edwards *et al.* (2002), has little, if any, effect on response rates. However, identification numbers should not be used if you have assured respondents that their replies will be anonymous!

## Questionnaire administration

Mark and Adrian undertook an attitude survey of parents of pupils at a school using a questionnaire. Prior to the survey, a pre-survey contact letter was sent to all parents, using their children to deliver the letter. The questionnaire, covering letter and postage-paid reply envelope were delivered in the same manner a week later. By the end of the first week after the questionnaire had been delivered, 52 questionnaires had been returned. This represented 16 per cent of families whose children attended the school. At the start of the next week a follow-up letter was delivered by hand to all parents. This thanked those who had already responded and encouraged those parents who had yet to return their completed questionnaire to do so. After this, the rate at which questionnaires were returned increased. By the end of the second week 126 questionnaires had been returned, representing a 38 per cent response rate. By the last day for receipt of questionnaires specified in the covering letter, 161 had been returned, increasing the response rate to 48 per cent. However, an additional 41 questionnaires were received after this deadline, resulting in an overall response rate of 60 per cent. The administration of the questionnaire had taken over four weeks from the pre-survey contact letter to the receipt of the last completed questionnaire.

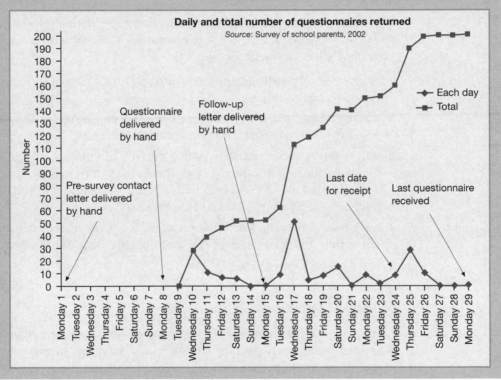

## Delivery and collection questionnaires

The administration of delivery and collection questionnaires is very similar to that of postal questionnaires. However, you or field staff will deliver and call to collect the questionnaire. It is therefore important that your covering letter states when the questionnaire is likely to be collected. As with postal questionnaires, follow-ups can be used, calling at a variety of times of day and on different days to try to catch the respondent.

A variation on this process that we have used widely in organisations allows for delivery and collection of questionnaires the same day and eliminates the need for a follow-up. The stages are:

1 Ensure that all questionnaires and covering letters are printed and a collection box is ready.

2 Contact respondents by internal post or telephone advising them to attend a meeting or one of a series of meetings to be held (preferably) in the organisation's time (Section 6.3).

3 At the meeting or meetings hand out the questionnaire with a covering letter to each respondent.

4 Introduce the questionnaire and stress its anonymous or confidential nature.

5 Ensure that respondents place their completed questionnaires in a collection box before they leave the meeting.

Although this adds to costs, as employees are completing the questionnaire in work time, response rates as high as 98 per cent are achievable!

## Telephone questionnaires

The quality of data collected using telephone questionnaires will be affected by the researcher's competence to conduct interviews. This is discussed in Section 10.5. Once your sample has been selected, you need to:

1 ensure that all questionnaires are printed or, for CATI, that the software has been programmed and tested;

2 where possible and resources allow, contact respondents by post, email or telephone advising them to expect a telephone call (Section 6.3);

3 telephone each respondent, recording the date and time of call and whether or not the questionnaire was completed. You should note any specific times that have been arranged for callbacks. For calls that were not successful you should note the reason, such as no reply or telephone disconnected;

4 for unsuccessful calls where there was no reply, try three more times, each at a different time and on a different day, and note the same information;

5 make callback calls at the time arranged.

## Structured interviews

Conducting structured interviews uses many of the skills required for in-depth and semi-structured interviews (Section 10.5). Issues such as interviewer appearance and preparedness are important and will affect the response rate (Section 10.4). However, once your sample has been selected you need to:

1 ensure that all questionnaires are printed or, for CAPI, that the software has been programmed and tested;

2 contact respondents by post, email or telephone advising them to expect an interviewer to call within the next week. This stage is often omitted for cost reasons;

3 (for large-scale surveys) divide the sample into groups that are of a manageable size (50–100) for one interviewer;

4 contact each respondent or potential respondent in person, recording the date and time of contact and whether or not the interview was completed. You should note down any specific times that have been arranged for return visits. For contacts that were not successful, you should note down the reason;

5 try unsuccessful contacts at least twice more, each at a different time and on a different day, and note down the same information;

6 visit respondents at the times arranged for return visits.

## 11.6 | Summary

■ Questionnaires collect data by asking people to respond to exactly the same set of questions. They are often used as part of a survey strategy to collect descriptive and explanatory data about opinions, behaviours and attributes. Data collected are normally coded and analysed by computer.

■ Your choice of questionnaire will be influenced by your research question(s) and objectives and the resources that you have available. The five main types are Internet- or intranet-mediated, postal, delivery and collection, telephone, and interview schedule.

■ Prior to designing a questionnaire, you must know precisely what data you need to collect to answer your research question(s) and to meet your objectives. One way of helping to ensure that you collect these data is to use a data requirements table.

■ The validity and reliability of the data you collect and the response rate you achieve depend largely on the design of your questions, the structure of your questionnaire, and the rigour of your pilot testing.

■ When designing your questionnaire you should consider the wording of individual questions prior to the order in which they appear. Questions can be divided into open and closed. The six types of closed questions are list, category, ranking, rating, quantity and grid.

■ Wherever possible, closed questions should be pre-coded on your questionnaire to facilitate analysis.

■ The order and flow of questions in the questionnaire should be logical to the respondent. This can be assisted by filter questions and linking phrases.

■ The questionnaire should be laid out so that it is easy to read and the responses are easy to fill in.

■ Questionnaires must be introduced carefully to the respondent to ensure a high response rate. For self-administered questionnaires this should take the form of a covering letter; for interviewer-administered questions it will be done by the interviewer.

■ All questionnaires should be pilot tested prior to collecting data to assess the validity and likely reliability of the questions.

■ Administration of questionnaires needs to be appropriate to the type of questionnaire.

## SELF-CHECK QUESTIONS

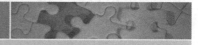

*Help with these questions is available at the end of the chapter.*

**11.1** In what circumstances would you choose to use a delivery and collection questionnaire rather than a postal questionnaire? Give reasons for your answer.

**11.2** The following questions have been taken from a questionnaire about flexibility of labour.

i    Do you agree or disagree with the use of nil hours contracts by employers?   strongly agree ☐$_4$
   (please tick appropriate box)                                                       agree ☐$_3$
                                                                 disagree ☐$_2$
                                             strongly disagree ☐$_1$

ii    Have you ever been employed on a nil hours contract?                        yes ☐$_1$
   (please tick appropriate box)                                                                  no ☐$_2$
                                                not sure ☐$_3$

iii    What is your marital status?                                          single ☐
   (please tick appropriate box)             married or living in long-term relationship ☐$_2$
                                                   widowed ☐$_3$
                                                 divorced ☐$_4$
                                                      other ☐$_5$
                           ................................ ( ⇐ please describe)

iv    Please describe what you think would be the main impact on employees of a nil hours contract.

For each question identify:
a  the sort of data that are being collected;
b  the type of question.
You should give reasons for your answers.

11.3  You are undertaking research on the use of children's book clubs by householders within mainland Europe. As part of this you have already undertaken in-depth interviews with households who belong and do not belong to children's book clubs. This, along with a literature review, has suggested a number of investigative questions from which you start to construct a table of data requirements.

| | | | |
|---|---|---|---|
| **Research question/objective:** *To establish mainland Europe's householders' opinions about children's book clubs* | | | |
| **Type of research:** *Predominantly descriptive, although wish to explain differences between householders* | | | |
| *Investigative questions* | *Variable(s) required* | *Detail in which data measured* | *Check measurement question included in questionnaire* ✔ |
| *a Do householders think that children's book clubs are a good or a bad idea?* | | | |
| *b What things do householders like most about children's book clubs?* | | | |
| *c Would householders be interested in an all-ages book club?* | | | |
| *d How much per year do households spend on children's books?* | | | |

| e Do households' responses differ depending on: i number of children? ii whether already members of a children's book club? | | | |
| --- | --- | --- | --- |

a For each investigative question listed, decide whether you will need to collect data on opinions, behaviours or attributes.

b Complete the table of data requirements for each of the investigative questions already listed. (You may embellish the scenario to help in your choice of variables required and how the data will be measured as you feel necessary.)

11.4 Design pre-coded or self-coded questions to collect data for each of the investigative questions in self-check question 11.3. Note that you will need to answer self-check question 11.3 first (or use the answer at the end of this chapter).

11.5 What issues will you need to consider when translating your questionnaire?

11.6 You work for a major consumer research bureau that has been commissioned by 11 major UK companies to design and administer a telephone questionnaire. The purpose of this questionnaire is to describe and explain relationships between adult consumers' lifestyles, opinions and purchasing intentions. Write the introduction to this telephone questionnaire, to be read by an interviewer to each respondent. You may embellish the scenario and include any other relevant information you wish.

11.7 You have been asked by a well-known national charity 'Work for All' to carry out research into the effects of long-term unemployment throughout the UK. The charity intends to use the findings of this research as part of a major campaign to highlight public awareness about the effects of long-term unemployment. The charity has drawn up a list of names and addresses of people who are or were long-term unemployed with whom they have had contact over the past six months. Write a covering letter to accompany the postal questionnaire. You may embellish the scenario and include any other relevant information you wish.

11.8 You have been asked to give a presentation to a group of managers at an oil exploration company to gain access to undertake your research. As part of the presentation you outline your methodology, which includes piloting the questionnaire. In the ensuing question and answer session one of the managers asks you to justify the need for a pilot study, arguing that 'given the time constraints the pilot can be left out'. List the arguments that you would use to convince him that pilot testing is essential to your methodology.

## REVIEW AND DISCUSSION QUESTIONS

11.9 Obtain a copy of a 'customer questionnaire' from a department store or restaurant. For each question on the questionnaire establish whether it is collecting data about opinion, behaviours or attributes. Do you consider any of the questions are potentially misleading? If yes, how do you think the question could be improved? Discuss the answer to these questions in relation to your questionnaire with a friend.

11.10 Visit the website of an online questionnaire provider. A selection of possible providers can be found by typing "online questionnaire provider" or "online survey provider" into the Google search engine. Use the online software to design a simple questionnaire. To what extent does the questionnaire you have designed meet the requirements of the checklists in Boxes 11.9, 11.10 and 11.13?

**11.11**  Visit your university library or use the Internet to view a copy of a report for a recent national government survey in which you are interested. If you are using the Internet, the national government websites listed in Table 8.3 are a good place to start. Check the appendices in the report to see if a copy of the questionnaire used to collect the data is included. Of the types of question – open, list, category, ranking, rating, quantity and grid – which is most used and which is least frequently used? Note down any that may be of use to you in your research project.

## PROGRESSING YOUR RESEARCH PROJECT

### Using questionnaires in your research

☐  Return to your research question(s) and objectives. Decide on how appropriate it would be to use questionnaires as part of your research strategy. If you do decide that this is appropriate, note down the reasons why you think it will be sensible to collect at least some of your data in this way. If you decide that using a questionnaire is not appropriate, justify your decision.

☐  If you decide that using a questionnaire is appropriate, re-read Chapter 7 on sampling and, in conjunction with this chapter, decide which of the five types of questionnaire will be most appropriate. Note down your choice of questionnaire and the reasons for this choice.

☐  Construct a data requirements table and work out precisely what data you need to answer your investigative questions. Remember that you will need to relate your investigative questions and data requirements back to the literature you have reviewed and any preliminary research you have already undertaken.

☐  Design the separate questions to collect the data specified in your data requirements table. Wherever possible, try to use closed questions and to adhere to the suggestions in the question wording checklist. If you are intending to analyse your questionnaire by computer, read Section 12.2 and pre-code questions on the questionnaire whenever possible.

☐  Order your questions to make reading the questions and filling in the responses as logical as possible to the respondent. Wherever possible, try to adhere to the checklist for layout. Remember that interviewer-administered questionnaires will need instructions for the interviewer.

☐  Write the introduction to your questionnaire and, where appropriate, a covering letter.

☐  Pilot test your questionnaire with as similar a group as possible to the final group in your sample. Pay special attention to issues of validity and reliability.

☐  Administer your questionnaire and remember to send out a follow-up survey to non-respondents whenever possible.

# References

Bell, J. (2005) *Doing Your Research Project* (4th edn), Buckingham, Open University Press.

Blumberg, B., Cooper, D.R. and Schindler, P.S. (2005) *Business Research Methods*, Maidenhead, McGraw-Hill.

Bourque, L.B. and Clark, V.A. (1994) 'Processing data: the survey example', *in* Lewis-Beck, M.S., *Research Practice*, London, Sage, pp. 1–88.

Coomber, R. (1997) 'Using the Internet for survey research', *Sociological Research Online* 2: 2 [online] (cited 27 November 2005). Available from <URL:http://www.socresonline.org.uk/2/2/coomber.htm>.

Corbetta, P. (2003) *Social Research: Theory, Methods and Techniques*, London, Sage.

deVaus, D.A. (2002) *Surveys in Social Research* (5th edn), London, Routledge.

Dillman, D.A. (2000) *Mail and Internet Surveys: The Tailored Design Method* (2nd edn), New York, Wiley.

Edwards, P., Roberts, I., Clarke, M., DiGuiseppi, C., Pratap, S., Wentz, R., and Kwan, I. (2002), 'Increasing response rates to postal questionnaires: systematic review', *British Medical Journal* 324: May, 1183–91.

Field, A. (2005) *Discovering Statistics Using SPSS* (2nd edn), London, Sage.

*Financial Times* (2003) 'George Lucas is a god in Britain. Literally', *Financial Times*, 14 February.

Fink, A. (2003a) *How to Ask Survey Questions* (2nd edn), Thousand Oaks, CA, Sage.

Fink, A. (2003b) *The Survey Handbook* (2nd edn), Thousand Oaks, CA, Sage.

Foddy, W. (1994) *Constructing Questions for Interviews and Questionnaires*, Cambridge, Cambridge University Press.

Gay, G., Schelluch, P. and Baines, A. (1998) 'Perceptions of messages conveyed by review and audit reports', *Accounting, Auditing & Accountability Journal* 11: 4, 472–94.

Ghauri, P. and Grønhaug, K. (2005) *Research Methods in Business Studies: A Practical Guide* (3rd edn), Harlow, Financial Times Prentice Hall.

Gill, J. and Johnson, P. (2002) *Research Methods for Managers* (3rd edn), London, Paul Chapman.

Hewson, C., Yule, P., Laurent, D. and Vogel, C. (2003) *Internet Research Methods: A Practical Guide for the Social and Behavioural Sciences*, London, Sage.

Jankowicz, A.D. (2005) *Business Research Projects* (4th edn), London, Thomson Learning.

Kervin, J.B. (1999) *Methods for Business Research* (2nd edn), Reading, MA, Addison-Wesley.

Lagrosen, Y. and Lagrosen, S. (2005) 'The effects of quality management – a survey of Swedish quality professionals', *International Journal of Operations & Production Management* 25: 10, 940–52.

Lavrakas, P.J. (1993) *Telephone Survey Methods: Sampling, Selection and Supervision*, Newbury Park, CA, Sage.

Maitland, A. (2004) 'Companies face an avalanche of questionnaires', *Financial Times*, 26 March.

Miller, D.C. and Salkind, N.J. (eds) (2002) *Handbook of Research Design and Social Measurement* (6th edn), Thousand Oaks, CA, Sage.

Mitchell, V. (1996) 'Assessing the reliability and validity of questionnaires: an empirical example', *Journal of Applied Management Studies* 5: 2, 199–207.

Oppenheim, A.N. (2000) *Questionnaire Design, Interviewing and Attitude Measurement* (new edn), London, Continuum International.

Robson, C. (2002) *Real World Research* (2nd edn), Oxford, Blackwell.

Rose, D. and Pevalin, D.J. (2003) 'The NS-SEC explained', *in* Rose, D. and Pevalin, D.J. (eds), *A Researcher's Guide to the National Statistics Socio-economic Classification*, London, Sage, pp. 28–43.

Snap Surveys (2005) 'Snap Surveys home page' [online] (cited 11 November 2005). Available from <URL:http://www.snapsurveys.com>

Sphinx Development (2005) 'Sphinx Development UK homepage' [online] (cited 11 November 2005). Available from <URL:http://www.sphinxdevelopment.co.uk/index.htm>

SurveyMonkey (2005) 'SurveyMonkey.com homepage' [online] (cited 20 November 2005). Available from <URL:http://www.surveymonkey.com/>

Usunier, J.-C. (1998) *International and Cross-Cultural Management Research*, London, Sage.

Witmer, D.F., Colman, R.W. and Katzman, S.L. (1999) 'From paper and pen to screen and keyboard: towards a methodology for survey research on the Internet', *in* Jones, S. (ed.), *Doing Internet Research*, Thousand Oaks, CA, Sage, pp. 145–62.

## Further reading

deVaus, D.A. (2002) *Surveys in Social Research* (5th edn), London, Routledge. Chapters 7 and 8 provide a detailed guide to constructing and administering questionnaires, respectively.

Dillman, D.A. (2000) *Mail and Internet Surveys: The Tailored Design Method* (2nd edn), New York, Wiley. The second edition of this classic text contains an extremely detailed and well-researched discussion of how to design postal and Internet-based questionnaires to maximise response rates.

Foddy, W. (1994) *Constructing Questions for Interviews and Questionnaires*, Cambridge, Cambridge University Press. This contains a wealth of information on framing questions, including the use of scaling techniques.

For WEB LINKS visit
www.pearsoned.co.uk/
saunders

Hewson, C., Yule, P., Laurent, D. and Vogel, C. (2003) *Internet Research Methods: A Practical Guide for the Social and Behavioural Sciences*, London, Sage. Chapters 3 offers a useful overview of Internet-mediated research, including a discussion of questionnaires, whilst Chapter 5 discusses design issues concerned with Internet-mediated questionnaires.

# Topic 5
# Project Management

For Saunders Chapter 2, please refer to Semester 2 Topic 1

# Introduction: Project Management

## Research Project Planning

Remember all the things that have been addressed in the session so far and that you will need to address before your project plan can be implemented. There should be enough information to make it feasible for someone else to pick up the research project and do it based on the information in the research proposal. Take a resource perspective on your project and generate something to address the timetable criterion. Remember you should be choosing one main research method and not planning to do every type.

| Session | Title | Time and Resource issues |
|---------|-------|--------------------------|
| 1 | Topic & Objectives | Add research questions – review and re-write |
| 2 | Evaluating Literature | What more literature and secondary information sources are required to be read and critically reviewed? |
| 3 | Research Methods Qualitative | a) Sampling recruiting and gaining access to respondents. Focus groups are difficult/ costly to set up. Access to key decision makers in multinationals is practically impossible<br>b) Research Time to do interviewing, focus groups: time for transcription<br>c) Analysis time for coding, (and revising coding scheme) time for interpretation (like the star case study) and time to write up and answer research questions. |
| 4 | Research methods Quantitative | a) Sampling Access to lists, designing quota, waiting for interviewees<br>b) Research Designing interviews, training interviewers, mounting web surveys emailing to lists, printing and posting to addresses, collecting data, entering and checking<br>c) Analysis Interpreting tables (like session 4 exercise) writing up and answering research questions |

Make a list of the key activities – generate at least a table if not a schedule (Cameron Figure 16.5) and a critical path diagram. (Cameron Figure 16.4). Saunders Chapter 2 section on Writing a research Proposal is very useful, with two or three pages and an example. Section 2.5 addresses writing a research proposal specifically. Cameron Chapter 16 (Managing projects) is a first level introduction to scheduling and other issues like negotiating access.

# Managing projects

Task forces and project teams are a common form of work organisation today. You are likely to spend large parts of your working life leading or working in task forces and project teams. Most courses will include a substantial project or dissertation to help you develop the relevant skills. This chapter will help you to do well in course projects, and to contribute effectively to a range of projects at work.

## Learning outcomes

By the end of this chapter you should:

- understand the specific demands of project work and how they relate to skills already covered
- be able to choose a suitable topic for a project or dissertation to meet your course and personal objectives
- be aware of the steps needed to gain access or commitment to a project within an organisation
- know how to draw up an initial research plan
- understand some of the specific requirements of project reports or dissertations.

'Project' can be used in many different ways, but normally includes the idea of some specific task that is non-routine, somewhat complex and discrete. In contrast with the continuous nature of much traditional management, there is a clear goal to *complete* the project by a specified time. This greater clarity brings into sharp focus the managerial roles described earlier. Because they relate to something specific, they are easily identified. Control, in particular, is highly visible. The chapter looks at each stage of project management from the viewpoint both of a course project and the sort of project you may well encounter at work.

## PROJECT TEAMS

A project-based form of organisation has many advantages. It allows for devolution of authority – a task force with a clearly defined remit can be left to get on with it, subject to fairly simple controls. The person responsible for the group (or the group as a whole if autonomous) can adapt rapidly to changes in the environment in order to remain on target. It is thus a more flexible structure. People organised in this way are more motivated. A clearly defined and manageable task, as consideration of expectancy theory makes apparent, should allow for closer links between performance and both intrinsic and extrinsic outcomes. In addition to the autonomy already mentioned, the job is high on task identity so feedback is likely to be more clear cut. Objectives can more easily be specified in CSMART terms.

Such project teams require their members to have virtually all the skills covered in this book:

- self-management skills to perform their part of the collaborative task effectively
- planning skills to help them contribute to designing the project and the way in which the team will share the work
- interpersonal skills for communication with other team members
- problem-solving skills to address the inevitable snags that will arise
- creativity skills to enable the unforeseen to be envisaged and difficulties which defy resolution by a merely rational approach to be overcome.

These skills will be equally relevant to any project you do as part of your course work.

## GROUP PROJECTS

You may well be required as part of your course to do a group project. This is excellent preparation for being part of a project team at work, and will allow you to reinforce the team-working skills addressed in Chapter 10. (Revisit this to check on your skills levels.)

> **Group project work will be more satisfying if:**
> - members are equally committed
> - there is a good mix of strengths
> - objectives are clarified and agreed
> - meetings are frequent
> - attention is paid to process
> - efforts are coordinated
> - progress is monitored regularly.

The success of the project, and hence your grade, will not be totally under your control. It will depend upon the efforts of others, as well as your own, so it matters who you are working with. Aim to be in a group with others who are prepared to exert the same level of effort as you are, and have a similar level of concern with success. There is nothing worse than being part of a group where you feel you are the only one who actually cares about getting the work done well. It can be fairly difficult, too, if you take a relatively relaxed approach and the others in the group want to work every hour there is in pursuit of perfection.

Managing the group process is equally important. When forming a group it is a good idea to aim for a mix of academic strengths and of preferred team roles. You will do better if at least one in the group is good at analysis, one is good at organising people's contributions, one is good at drafting and so on. This chapter is written primarily from the perspective of work on an individual project. If you are working as part of a team, you need additionally to be absolutely sure that you are all clear as to what you are trying to do and how. At each stage you need to have a clear and *shared* understanding of the group's objectives, of how responsibilities have been allocated and of how progress will be monitored. You will need frequent meetings to share progress so that you continue to move in the same direction, and to build on each other's work.

Coordination will be crucial throughout. Any conflicts need to be addressed as soon as they surface. You will not have time to repair damage later. In particular, you need to be firm about setting, and *meeting*, interim targets. While you may feel sorry for a friend's troubles, whatever they are, and feel it is mean to insist that they keep on schedule regardless, sympathy can be dangerous. So is optimism. You cannot afford to *hope* that a colleague will sort things out in time to catch up with their part of the work. You need as a group to address any such problems and work out ways of handling any slippage as soon as it occurs.

If despite your best efforts not all members play a full role, this needs to be discussed with your tutors. Your report can often usefully indicate the roles played by different group members. If you end up having to do more than your fair share, it is worth documenting this fact, together with the unsuccessful efforts you made to avoid the situation occurring.

Whether you are doing it individually or as part of a team, working on a project which appears to be under control can be highly motivating and the experience deeply satisfying, not least because you will be aware of using a wide range of skills to achieve a challenging objective and because your success or otherwise will be clearly apparent. The converse is that a project which goes less well, whether because you lack the necessary skills or because you fail to exercise them as well as you might, can be a nightmare. Figure 16.1 maps some of the necessary skills on to the stages you are likely to go through in such a project, indicating the chapter numbers where these are covered. This shows clearly the function of project work in integrating a wide range of skills. The discussion which follows looks at the different stages of such a project, expanding on the way in which the skills shown on the diagram are needed. This should help you to manage any project more successfully, whether it is academic or work related.

## PROJECT PLANNING

For projects, as with everything else, clarity of objectives is essential. In real projects there are normally three sets of project objectives which will need to be specified. These concern:

- performance
- cost
- time.

For example, a project might have the objective of designing a new IT system to a particular specification, within a specified cost, for implementation in 18 months' time.

For a student project or dissertation, there will be *learning* objectives in addition to the explicit project aims. These will influence the objectives for the project itself. It is worth understanding your tutors' likely perspectives before going further. Although these are

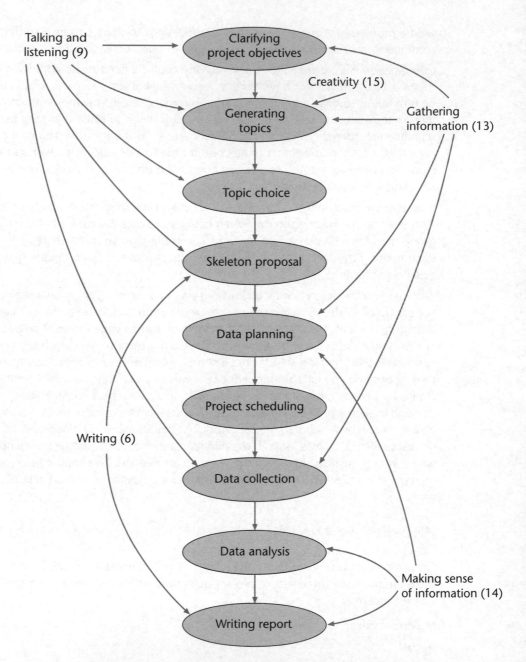

**Fig. 16.1 Skills needed for project management**
(NB for clarity, project and self-management skills, which are needed at *every* stage,
are not shown, nor are the group skills needed at every stage of a group project.)

outlined with respect to management research, you will find close parallels with social science research more generally and indeed with any research. If you are studying something other than management, it should not be too difficult to translate them into something relevant to your own area.

Management research can take a number of different forms. It may aim to:

- resolve theoretical questions
- explore a topic of general interest to managers
- evaluate some aspect of an organisation's performance
- address a practical organisational problem, culminating in a set of recommendations for action
- implement and evaluate changes, based on recommendations as above.

Where your project will lie on this theory–action scale will depend on the practical bias of your course and whether or not you have facilities to cooperate with an organisation in order to address a genuine concern. Your tutors will probably be aiming to provide you with as many of the learning opportunities listed below as practical considerations allow. Such potential learning from projects includes the ability to practise:

- liaison with 'clients', developing negotiation, communication and other interpersonal skills
- diagnostic work on complex situations, using concepts, diagramming and other techniques and talking and listening skills
- problem-formulation and data-planning skills
- evaluation of different methodologies and selection and application of appropriate methodologies
- techniques for planning and scheduling your work
- information-gathering skills including electronic literature search and collection of some form of primary data
- use of IT and other skills for data analysis
- evaluation of information and its limitations
- research skills relevant to a postgraduate degree
- written communication skills needed to integrate data and descriptions into a compelling argument.

## Setting clear objectives

Different sets of objectives were outlined above: learning objectives; general objectives which a project must meet to pass; your task objectives for your specific project; the objectives any client may have for the project. It is important to distinguish these sets when clarifying objectives. Clearly, one of your first tasks will be to clarify your tutors' requirements, highlighting the skills on the list above which are most relevant to your situation, adding any others and making sure in general that you know what requirements are specified for the project or dissertation.

If you are doing an in-company project as a student, you need to be very careful that the 'client's' objectives for the work are consistent with those of your tutors. You cannot firm up your choice of project until this has been established. If you are doing project work for real, it is equally important to check that client objectives are appropriate. They need to be capable of being met within the resources likely to be available and capable of resolving the problem situation if met.

'Define objectives' is easily said, but less easily done. Clients may be unclear about what they want. Or they may express their objectives clearly, but you may feel that these reflect a faulty diagnosis of the situation or no real diagnosis at all. You may feel that further investigation is necessary before you can be sure that the specified objectives are appropriate.

Suppose that your client is demanding a new IT system. You have a strong suspicion that the existing one could more than meet the required specification if staff were only trained to use it properly. If you are in the market for supplying such systems and the existing system was provided by a competitor, you might be tempted to go along with this (although it raises interesting ethical questions). If you are an 'internal supplier' you may do your company better service by questioning the stated objectives, showing what could be achieved by training and perhaps saving hundreds of thousands of pounds. This is just one example of the need to question given objectives. It is for this reason that the diagnostic and investigative skills covered in Chapter 12 are so important.

Diagnosis is absolutely crucial. In any complex situation, diagnosis is essential to ensure that objectives are clear, appropriate and understood by both you and your client. Talking to those likely to be affected by the project can give you valuable information. And implementation of any proposed changes is likely to be more successful, and less problematic, because of this communication. The plans themselves are likely to be far better because of the information you gained at this stage. Furthermore, people are more likely to cooperate if they feel that they have contributed to planning a change. Changes seen as imposed from above are likely to be strongly resisted.

Although in work contexts you are likely to be given a project, that does not (usually) mean that you have to accept objectives as specified. Clarification and exploration of the context which generated the idea for the project may produce agreement to a slight shift in focus at the outset. This can greatly increase the likelihood of a satisfactory outcome both for the internal or external client and for you as project manager. If your student project is one which is done in-company, and perhaps suggested by the company, your position is very similar to that of undertaking a project as part of your job. If you are doing a library-based project you will have more scope, but ensuring that the objectives are appropriate is perhaps even more of a challenge.

If you have worked, think about changes you experienced at work. Divide these into those where you were involved in planning the change and those where change was imposed. Rate your commitment to making the change work in each case and the extent to which you believed that it was aimed at the right objectives. If you have not worked, find two or three people who are currently working and ask them about *their* experience of change, again trying to distinguish between change with and without involvement in planning. Discuss your findings with others if possible.

## FINDING A TOPIC

For organisational projects once you are in employment, you will normally start by clarifying the objectives given to you by someone more senior (remembering that they will often need to be seriously modified). But for student projects there is a prior stage of generating the project topic in the first place. This may be the hardest part of the whole experience. It is also the most important. It is important to consider as wide a range of topics as possible before selecting one: your choice will never be better than the best option you come up with, so you need a good range.

Generating possible topics will depend on some of the techniques discussed in Chapters 12, 13 and 15. You may need to be able to look at a situation from a broad perspective in order to identify possible problem themes, you will need to be able to use the library to see what related research has already been done, and you will need to have an understanding of how to collect information and interpret it in order to know which possible topics are capable of being progressed within the resources available to you. You will even need talking and listening skills as covered in Chapter 9, as discussion with tutors and others will be extremely valuable at this stage.

When seeking ideas for projects use:
■ tutors
■ library
■ existing interests
■ past projects
■ discussions
■ brainstorming.

If you are one of those who find it impossible to think of a single topic, there is a strong risk that you will postpone even *thinking* of the project until dangerously late. You will probably hope that if you wait long enough inspiration will miraculously strike. Indeed it may do. But equally, all too often it does not. You may still be looking for a topic at a point when you should be almost at the end of your planning stage. There is then a risk that you will grasp at *any* suggested topic, regardless of its interest, and a further risk that this will turn out to be both difficult and tedious.

So even if you have almost no idea what sort of topic appeals to you, avoid procrastination at all costs. Start to think about it seriously at least six months before your project work is scheduled to begin, if at all possible. If this is not possible, then worry away at the issue of project choice as soon as you can and don't stop thinking about it until you have a topic that you are happy with. Use creativity techniques. Work with others who are similarly uncertain. Look at past projects to find topics that look potentially interesting and which you might explore in a slightly different way, or with a different sample. Talk to people in any organisation to which you have access about issues which are of current concern to them.

**ACTIVITY 16.2**

List titles of past projects or dissertations that interest you in some way, noting beside each the aspects of the topic which particularly strike you and why.

**ACTIVITY 16.3**

For one or more broad areas of potential interest, draw mind maps showing all possible questions concerning the area which might be part of, or lead to, a project topic. (Figure 16.2 gives an example of such a diagram.)

Make a project section in your file, and start to file all your project-directed activities and thoughts there.

## Topic choice

Once you have a range of possible areas, the process of clarifying objectives and choosing and refining a topic will be absolutely crucial. You may well need to go through an iterative process of broadening and narrowing – generate a range of possible areas and narrow them down on one. Tease apart a range of ways of approaching this or sub-topics within the wider area. Choose one and again pull this apart . . . Figure 15.1 showed this sequence diagrammatically.

Yet again there will be a need for communication – with your tutor to check that your shortlist of proposed topics meets course requirements, with those in any organisations which are hosting the project or allowing you access for research purposes, and with your tutor again (and again) as your ideas progress. You will need to use skills from Chapter 13 to generate keywords, search the literature (including projects by previous students) and refine your research question. The following factors should influence your choice.

### Interest

It is important that the topic you choose interests you (and interests your organisation if you are doing a work-based project). You are likely to be investing considerable effort

**Project topics need to:**
- be interesting
- offer suitable scope
- have symmetrical outcomes
- be feasible
- be low risk.

in your project. If you need organisational facilities for observation or interviewing or access to other data, the organisation will be investing too. If neither you nor the organisation cares overmuch about the outcomes, the labour can be soul-destroying. But if your client organisation does care about the topic, you may gain considerable support and help in your work and find that your final report is used to inform policy. If you are really concerned about the topic too, you will find project work engrossing.

If you are doing a library-based rather than on organisation-based project, then you may be able to make it more interesting by thinking of it as a potential publication. This could perhaps be in a non-academic periodical. By thinking of a potential outlet for something derived from your research, and perhaps making sure that you collect

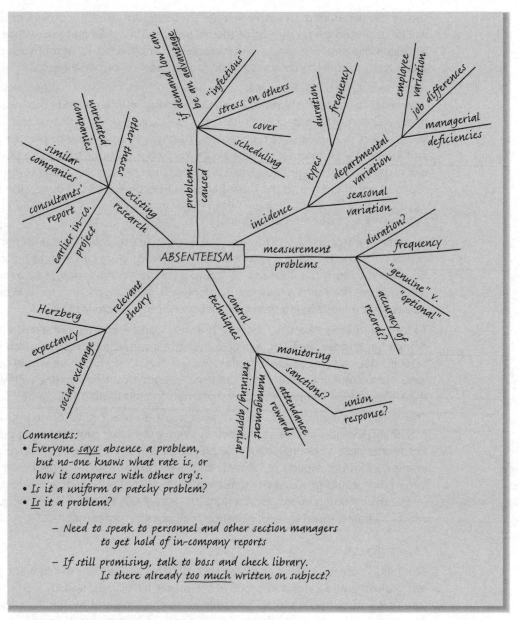

**Fig. 16.2** Student's mind map and subsequent thoughts on a possible absenteeism project

additional titbits that would make the derived article more interesting to readers, you might add to the interest value of the project for yourself.

### Scope

It is important that your chosen topic is potentially broad enough and deep enough for you to exhibit the range of skills that your tutors expect. Such expectations will vary somewhat depending on where you are studying. But usually a project or dissertation will be expected to develop generalisable investigative skills and you will be expected to evaluate possible research methodologies or approaches as part of your project, to select an appropriate one and to justify this choice in your final report.

A narrowly defined topic is unlikely to allow you to demonstrate either methodological awareness or strategic thinking. If you are working with an outside organisation and it offers you a very narrow operational topic, check with your tutor that this will allow you to meet the university's requirements. If not, you may need to practise your talking and listening skills in order to increase the organisation's understanding of what the university means by a project. Once it understands, you may be able to explore other topics of equal interest to the organisation but better suited to your course needs.

### Symmetry of research outcomes

Symmetry of research outcomes may be less familiar to you, but it is an important criterion for choice. What it means is that your research results should be of interest however they turn out. Research to 'prove a point' should therefore be avoided. If it fails to prove the point it may not be of interest. Worse, you may be so keen for your results to come out in one particular direction that bias creeps in.

To take an unlikely example, suppose you were convinced that, contrary to popular opinion (and most research), a degree does not improve job prospects. You might carefully design some research to demonstrate this. Certainly, there would be a stir if you were right. But if you were wrong, and your research came out in line with what people think they 'know' already, the general reaction to your findings might be: 'So what?'

This does not mean that you should never question received wisdom. But do it in a way that generates interesting outcomes even if the basic principle is supported. Look at whether class of degree influences prospects when A level grades are controlled for, or effects of other aspects of students and their courses. Such supplementary information could produce an interesting result even if the obvious view *is* supported by the main finding. Normally, though, it is a safer bet to pick a research question which is characterised by equal interest in all possible outcomes.

### Feasibility

Feasibility is obviously crucial. No project manager in industry would want to take on responsibility for a project doomed at the outset to failure. Similarly, you should make sure that your proposed topic is feasible given the time and resources at your disposal. To attempt the impossible shows a distinct lack of judgement. If you have little experience of project work, such judgement may be difficult. A striking feature of most student projects is the extent to which they take longer than expected. All projects have a way of expanding to use at least twice the time and energy expected at all stages from planning to writing up. To allow for this, be cautious in your aims. If ever you feel that your ideas might be even slightly ambitious, talk to your tutor and cut back your plans if so advised.

There are other warning signals that something may not be feasible. If activities will incur significant costs, or need access to data that may be commercially sensitive or require significant investment of time by others over whom you do not have control, be very wary. In general, the world is not sitting there waiting to help students with projects unless very clear advantages are apparent as a result of such cooperation.

### Scope for catastrophe

Scope for catastrophe in a project is closely related to feasibility and is just as important. It relates primarily to projects involving organisational involvement. These can be threatened by organisational changes. For example, if redundancies are planned for a group of staff you were planning to interview, you may find that you are suddenly denied access. Your project is also at risk from personnel changes. You may have one champion in the organisation, but only one. If that person leaves, you may find that cooperation is seriously reduced. Real-time projects are another area where you are at serious risk. If your project is linked to events happening in real time in the organisation and these events are put back by a few months, you may find yourself with nothing to study until after your project is due for completion! It is worth 'hazard spotting' for all suggested organisational topics in order to assess the scope for catastrophe associated with each.

Although the techniques you may use at different stages (brainstorming, literature search, discussion at the start, for example) may vary, the general approach you will need for project choice can be summarised by the algorithm shown in Figure 16.3.

### ACTIVITY 16.4

When you have settled on one or more likely topics, use the choice algorithm in Figure 16.3 to help with your decision. Note your likely topic, and your initial thoughts about it, in your file.

Once you have a likely topic, you will probably need to do a first rough literature search (unless you have already done one in the process of settling on your topic). This will enable you to check what already exists in terms of investigation of this or similar topics and the methods which have been used in such investigations. From this, you should be able to refine your topic still further.

## PROJECT PROPOSALS

Having made your choice, write as clear and detailed a draft project proposal as you can. This will assist you in planning the project and will help your tutor to know just what you have in mind. If you are doing an organisation-based project, it will also ensure that your organisation knows and is happy with the way your thoughts are developing. At this stage your thoughts will not be fully clear. Your final project proposal will need to be completed at the end of your planning stage, but a skeleton will be useful now. You can amend it as much as is necessary in the light of future thinking. At this point, simply outline your intentions under the four headings on page 363, leaving spaces if you are unsure of anything.

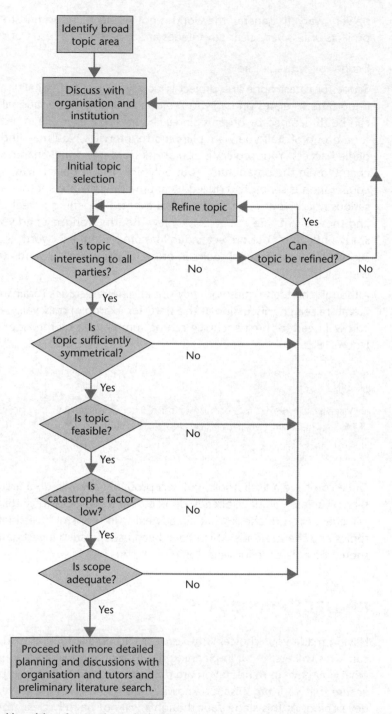

**Fig. 16.3 Algorithm for project choice**

- **Problem or topic description** – background to the project, its context and significance.
- **Value of investigation** – why would the client organisation or other reader want to know what the project aims to establish?
- **Likely project design** – possible methodology, timescale and the skills likely to be employed.
- **Data requirements** – the information needed and how data will be obtained and analysed.

## Gaining client agreement

In real-life consultancy the key skill is maintaining good relationships with the client. If you are doing a project for an organisational client, you need to pay careful attention to this. One factor which is absolutely critical is that you work out a clearly written and *agreed* research proposal. In order to obtain such agreement, it is helpful to discuss your skeleton proposal with any client. If differences of perspective emerge, it will be relatively easy to redirect the project at this early stage in order better to meet both sets of objectives. If this looks impossible, it is even more important to find this out as soon as possible, while there is still time to choose another topic. You should if at all possible obtain written agreement to this proposal and to any necessary access to information. This may seem unnecessarily legalistic, but it can provide an essential protection if your contact in the organisation moves on and is replaced by someone less committed to the project. A written agreement will not prevent all the problems such a change can cause, but can strengthen your case for continued facilities. It is also a useful protection against claims from some quarters that your research has in some way failed to meet its client's objectives. If these objectives now seem different from the agreed project objectives, the written agreement to the proposal can be very helpful.

> A clear proposal, agreed in writing with your client, is essential.

Once the skeleton has been agreed, and you have gone through the stages outlined in the following sections it is useful to develop a clear project brief that you and your client, sponsor and/or supervisor can use as a reference document. Note that this is being discussed ahead of the stage when you will be doing it, for two reasons. First, the same reasons for gaining agreement apply. Second, knowing that you need to produce this document will focus your thinking as you go through the stages that follow. Possible headings for a project brief include:

- project title
- client and researcher names
- date brief agreed
- project start and finish dates
- significant milestones
- key project objectives
- success criteria
- scope of project (including constraints)

- resources needed
- communication arrangements during project
- form of final report.

As with the skeleton proposal, the fuller brief needs to be agreed with key stakeholders.

### ACTIVITY 16.5

File your agreed project brief, together with any comments such as areas of continuing concern, or things still to be resolved. Make a plan for progressing these, and gaining agreement with key stakeholders

## DATA PLANNING

Detailed and realistic project planning is essential and should begin as soon as you are happy with your project choice, certainly well before you are due to commence any data collection. The first stage is data planning. You cannot fully assess the feasibility of your proposal until you have a detailed plan of what will be involved. This will depend on the data that you decide you need and the approach you decide on for collecting them.

No matter how carefully you have thought about possible topics and used the algorithm to test/refine them, detailed planning may highlight difficulties you had not envisaged. You need to allow time to go through further cycles of topic choice and development should such iteration be necessary. So data planning should commence as early as possible – for most projects, the bulk of your work will consist of data collection and analysis. The adequacy of any report you write and of the conclusions you present therein will depend on the evidence on which these are based. If your information is biased or inaccurate, your conclusions will be worthless.

Obviously the type of data sought will depend on your particular project. If you read Chapters 13 and 14 some time before starting your detailed project planning, re-read them with your particular topic firmly in mind. When you have done this, map out the data you will need to address your chosen problem or answer your research question.

### ACTIVITY 16.6

When you have decided on the data you will need to collect, and the approach you will take to collecting them, ask yourself the following questions:

- How accurate and reliable will the data be?
- Is the proposed sample large enough to warrant the conclusions you are likely to draw?
- Is your sample sufficiently representative of the population in which you are interested?
- Will any measures actually measure what they purport to measure?
- If they are indicators rather than direct measures, will they be the best available indicators?

Once you are satisfied that the data you propose to collect will be adequate for your purpose and the way in which you propose to collect them is an appropriate one, you are in a position to start detailed scheduling.

## PROJECT SCHEDULING

Once a project manager has clarified the performance, cost and time objectives for an organisational project, careful planning is needed to ensure that necessary resources are acquired, tasks identified and scheduled and control systems set in place. Normally completion on time will be crucial, with cost over-runs and other financial penalties if the project is not finished. For a student project or dissertation, the penalties of over-run may be at least as severe – your degree is probably at stake.

Chapter 2 introduced the ideas of charts and networks and you might find it helpful to revise these briefly before tackling the more detailed treatment which follows. You need to be clear about the use of Gantt or planning bar charts as planning and scheduling aids. For simple projects, these can simply be drawn. For more complex ones, with many interdependent activities, it would be difficult to work out how to arrange things so that everything gets done in the right order, in the minimum time and without over-straining resources at any point. Networks and critical paths were introduced in Chapter 2 as a logical approach to optimal sequencing. Your project may well be the first time that you need to construct a network 'in anger'. The following more detailed description may help.

### Critical path analysis

When you were considering charts and networks as an aid to the relatively straightforward case of managing your study, you probably did not need to draw network diagrams. However, for project management planning is crucial and often complex and constructing a network will help greatly. It is possible to construct networks by hand. Figure 16.4 is an example of such a diagram. But software is readily available for constructing network diagrams and identifying critical paths, and scheduling activities efficiently as a result of these. It is worth using this as a planning aid in any moderately complex situation. (You will be developing another IT-related skill in the process, which could add to your portfolio in this area.)

In either case, you construct the network by looking at each activity, at how long it will take and at what needs to be completed before it can start. You can see that the diagram does indeed look a bit like a net. The diagram is drawn, and read, from left to right. No activity can be started until those to the left of it are complete. There are different ways of drawing networks. (A common minor variant is to write the name of the activity on an arrow, rather than the numbers shown in the diagram.) The example described is merely one common approach. Whichever you choose, as with other diagrams, it is important to use the convention consistently. If you combine aspects of different conventions in a single diagram, you are likely to end up with a muddle. As the whole point of the exercise is clarity, avoid this!

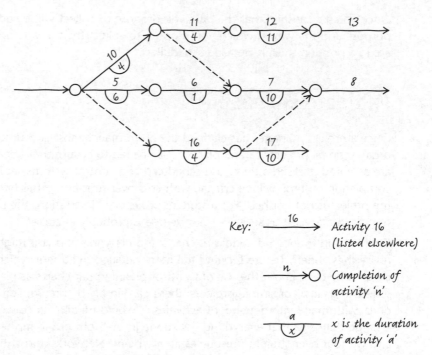

**Fig. 16.4 Part of a hand-drawn network**

In the diagram shown, activities are identified by a number (key elsewhere) on the arrow, duration of the activity is indicated not by the length of the arrow but by a number in a semicircle beneath the arrow, and 'events', that is, the completion of activities, are indicated by circles. The dotted lines on the chart represent so-called dummy activities, normally of zero duration. Such dummies are necessary to show constraints between activities – something cannot be started until several other activities have been completed. Rather than superimposing these events at the start of the next arrow, which would be hopelessly confusing and impossible to read, the dummy device is used.

Estimating how long it will take to complete various activities can be difficult. Ask advice and then (remembering the 'Topsy' nature of projects) allow some extra. Remember that there will be 'dead' time to be included, time when you are waiting for people to return telephone calls, for surveys to be posted back or for someone else (if you are lucky) to process your data. (Examples in employment might include time for an advertisement you have designed to appear in a specialist journal, or for a training course to be available for staff, or for machinery or materials that you have ordered to be delivered.) 'Dead time' means that you can schedule activities in parallel, as was shown on the bar chart in Chapter 2, as you can work on one activity when waiting for something that will allow you to progress another.

In order to do this juggling and make full use of your time despite such waits, you need the ideas (*see* Chapter 2 again) of critical paths and floats. To work out the minimum time a project can take, you need to look for the path of longest duration

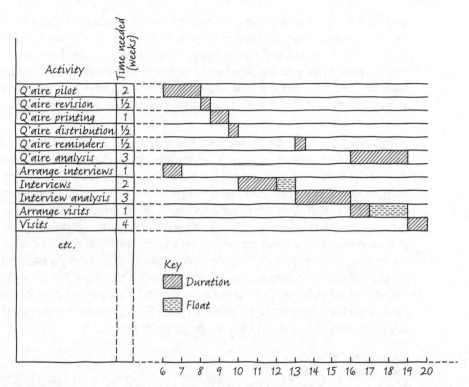

**Fig. 16.5** Part of a hand-drawn schedule for project planning

through the network. You get this by adding together the estimated activity times on the arrows forming each pathway through the net. This longest time tells you the earliest at which the end event can be reached. Any delay to any activity on this path will delay completion. Activities on this path are therefore critical, hence critical path analysis. Activities on non-critical paths *can* be delayed without affecting the completion time. This scope for delaying or slack is called 'float'.

To calculate float you work in the reverse direction, from right to left, subtracting activity durations from the time of the last event. This gives you the *latest* permissible start time for achieving each event. The difference between this and the *earliest* possible time for starting the activity is the float. In a bar chart, this can be shown by a shaded area. On a network, you could use, say, a big circle above an event enclosing the earliest event time and a square above events enclosing the latest time. (Remember, for critical events these times coincide.) Figure 16.5 shows part of a hand-drawn schedule for a project where there is some float.

## Milestones

You will remember that control needs to be exercised while there is still time to take remedial action if necessary. In planning a project it is necessary to plan for control and the idea used most frequently is that of milestones. In a complex project, with subgroups working on sets of tasks, project managers cannot monitor every activity and all the inevitable adjustments that their subordinates will make to cope with varying circumstances. It is therefore helpful for them to identify points on the critical path at which agreed and recognisable criteria need to have been met. Normally, these criteria would relate to the three sets of objectives distinguished earlier, those to do with task progress and the cost and time taken to achieve this. Your task may be somewhat simpler, but the idea can still be a useful review mechanism and help you sustain motivation.

Some milestones may be set for you. You may be required to submit a project proposal by a given date, a progress report by another and a draft report chapter by a third. But it is worth looking at your critical path and selecting other milestones that relate to completion of significant sub-tasks and highlighting these on your schedule. You will probably find that each time you approach one of these milestones you will need to put in some extra effort in order to prevent slippage. If you do this, you will find the achievement of your deadline deeply satisfying and reassuring and your motivation to do well in the project is likely to be strengthened. If no amount of effort enables you to hit the milestone on target, you know you have a problem! But provided the milestones are sufficiently frequent (say, approximately every 20% of the time allotted for completion, perhaps more often on a really long project) the problem will become apparent while there is still time to do something about it.

### ACTIVITY 16.7

Draw up a network for your project, including all the tasks necessary for completion. Identify the critical path and milestones on it. Then convert this into a schedule, drawing a bar chart to represent it and highlighting the milestones. Remember to schedule the final draft of your project proposal and gaining approval to this as either your first or a very early task.

## NEGOTIATING ACCESS

If you need to gain access to organisations in order to gather the data you need, then you need to give careful thought to how you will do this and allow considerable time for it in your plans. Some of the reasons for difficulty have already been indicated. Key reasons include:

- lack of interest in your project or failure to understand its relevance
- reluctance to commit organisational resources to anything other than normal work
- nervousness about what may be found (whether political, commercial or personal sensitivity)
- knowledge (which is still secret) about imminent change that makes research invalid or undesirable
- doubts about your competence as a researcher
- worry that research, whatever its findings, may be disruptive or generate expectations which cannot be met.

In order to gain access, you need to slant your approach in a way that best addresses whichever of these reasons are important to your potential 'client'. It will be easiest to do this if you can identify your best contact person and find their views about the topic you propose before you make your request, though this is not always possible. If you cannot, then think about their likely concerns and aim to address these. You will normally find it helpful to do the following:

- *Use existing contacts*. Here your networking skills are important. Whom can you contact through members of your current network? If existing contacts are inadequate, then develop new ones. Initial informal contact by phone or e-mail can be useful.

- *Be very clear about what you want, why and what it will involve*. Few organisations will be willing to agree to something open-ended or unclear. For example, if you want to interview some staff, you will need to say how many of which kind(s) of people you want to interview, how long the interview will take, where and when it would need to be conducted and what will happen to the results. (Confidentiality will usually be a major worry.)

- *Make equally clear the benefits of collaboration to the organisation*. If there are none, you might want to think again about the project.

- *Make a formal request in a way that reinforces your credibility*. A neatly laid-out, word-processed letter, on headed (your college or department) notepaper, giving your tutor as a reference, will help greatly. Even if you have gained informal agreement by other means, you need to confirm this via such a letter.

- *Make replying easy*. A proforma and stamped addressed envelope may seem trivial, but could increase the number of positive replies considerably. A suggestion that you will phone to discuss this after a stated period (if it may be difficult for them to phone you) may also help.

- *Keep to agreements*. If you go outside what was agreed, you may lose access. So if you have sworn not to reveal what individuals say and then tell someone's boss the views they express, you can expect (deservedly) to be denied further access. In the interests of those who may request access for future projects, you should also keep to any agreements about what you will do subsequently. If you promise a copy of the report, for example, make sure that they get one.

## MONITORING PROGRESS

Keeping control of your work is very important, given that there may be few interim deadlines imposed by your institution. Your planning chart will be an essential tool throughout your project. Display it prominently, refer to it frequently and modify it if this proves necessary. Although you should be monitoring progress all the time, find some way of ensuring a more formal progress check at each milestone. Perhaps you could schedule meetings with your tutor at these points, or at least agree to send in progress reports.

Any slippage should be treated extremely seriously. Resist the (strong!) temptation to attribute it to 'one-off' factors which will not happen again. Excusing yourself in this way, and adjusting subsequent schedules to allow for the delay that has already occurred, is likely to mean you merely have worse 'slippage' when you reach the next milestone. Instead, you should look very carefully at the possible reasons for the delay and address these causes. Above all, resist the near-universal tendency to see the final deadline as so far away that project work is not urgent. If you are to do a good project, it is urgent from the start. Time will not expand as you approach the deadline!

Unless you are absolutely sure that you *can* get back on track and avoid any similar slippage in future (and this doesn't mean that you *hope* all will magically go more smoothly), you should discuss the situation with your tutor and adjust your plans accordingly. You may need to reduce the scope of your project in some way.

If you are working on a group project, it is very important that the group sets individual as well as group milestones and that the group as a whole meets regularly to review progress against these. If one group member encounters problems, ways of adjusting workloads may need to be found and of supporting the member in difficulty, if the project is to be completed successfully.

## Writing a project log

As well as your planning chart, you should keep a detailed record of progress in the form of a project log. In this you should record all project activity, reasons for decisions, times taken, details of what happened, snags encountered and insights gained. This can be enormously helpful when you come to write up your report. It is surprising how things which seemed burned into your memory at the time can fade into oblivion before you come to describe them. Your log can be a source of observations made at the time and will be eminently quotable at appropriate points in your dissertation.

Furthermore, many institutions require students to include in, or with, their report a series of reflections on lessons learned and points where with hindsight it is realised that the project could have been approached better. This is intended to demonstrate that you have indeed learned something about the process of this kind of research and how to be critical of such investigations. (As an examiner, I find such reflections a valuable source of necessary marks for the student whose project has gone wrong for some reason.) Such a reflections section can draw heavily on your log.

Because a project draws on almost every skill covered in this book (and many more), your final report is a potential exhibit for almost any key skill or management competence you are likely to want to demonstrate. It can therefore be a valuable component of your portfolio. You would need to include a covering document with it which made explicit to your assessor the competences demonstrated and how. Again, a detailed project log would be a useful part of the 'story'.

## Keeping track of references

The importance of noting full references was mentioned earlier, but cannot be stressed too often. Either in your log, or preferably on your computer, or somewhere very safe, you should keep a full record of *all* the sources you have used, even if you are not yet sure if you will need to refer to them. It really is worth using a bibliographic software package if you can. You can waste a huge amount of time hunting for references if your notes are incomplete. And you will probably be doing it just before the project is due while you are struggling to write a substantial report to a tight deadline. The last thing you need at this point is to be distracted by a search for complete references. Avoid this by getting into good habits now!

**ACTIVITY 16.8**

Look at the references you collected while doing your initial literature search at the topic choice stage. If they are not complete (i.e. with full title, author and publication names, publishers and/or page numbers), properly organised and safely stored, sort them out *now*, either using bibliographic software or by developing a system that you can easily use throughout your project. Then use it!

## WRITING A PROJECT REPORT

If you spend some of your career as a consultant, report writing skills will be invaluable. Consultancy is a service, and largely intangible. When people are purchasing a service, they tend to be disproportionately impressed by the few tangible aspects there are, and a report is one of these. A consultant friend of mine freely admits that clients normally read only the first few pages. Yet he sees it as absolutely crucial that the report is fat, glossy and full of colour. It is the 'thwack' factor (when you thwack it down on the table) that gets him future business, he says.

You may not want to go to these lengths (though presentation will still be important). But after data collection and analysis, the most substantial task is likely to be writing your report. This activity can usefully be started much earlier than most people think. It may seem absurd to start drafting when you have scarcely started to collect your data and have little idea of what your eventual conclusions will be. But actually it can be most enlightening to write a skeleton draft based on guesses as to what the results might show. Often this will uncover a need for additional data: you may realise that, even if your results turn out as you expect, they will support only a weak argument. If you find this out at the data-collection stage, you have time to amend your plans accordingly.

Topic choice is therefore not the only time when iteration can be helpful. As with any complex problem-solving activity, a constant process of thought, experiment and refining of thoughts is necessary. This point is made explicit in many of the systems methodologies which you may be taught during your course. It also reflects the Kolb learning cycle introduced in Chapter 3. It is difficult to make sense of complexity all at once. But we can make a little sense of it, see ways in which our ideas might be improved, try these new ideas, refine them further in the light of experience and so on. Thus step by step we improve our understanding.

The other advantage of starting drafting early is that it is much less frightening to draft what you *know* is only a dummy draft. Sitting at the keyboard towards the end of your project knowing that you have to write 10 000 words or so at a single bite can, in contrast, be a prospect too awful to contemplate. If in consequence you postpone the exercise the task becomes quite impossible. You have no time left for revisions, no time even for proper thought. The resulting dissertation, despite much burning of midnight oil, is a disappointment to you, to your tutors and to any client organisation.

If you have written a skeleton draft at an early stage and are reasonably competent at word processing, writing your report can be relatively stress free. You can flesh out parts of the skeleton as you go along, revise these longer versions, incorporate your references and start analysing your data, all in parallel. Your final draft will gradually, and relatively painlessly, emerge from this process. Revisit Chapter 6 on clear writing at about the time you start to draft. There is more detail on report writing there. And most important, keep backup copies of your work somewhere absolutely safe and update these backups regularly. This is work you *cannot* afford to lose.

## Style and format

You may be given a specified format, but if not, the following is one which is widely accepted:

- Title page
- 1–2 page summary – you may be required to submit this separately, rather than binding it with your report
- Preface and acknowledgements
- List of contents – numbering should usually reflect major and minor sections, e.g. 4, 4.1, 4.2 (*see* Figure 6.4 for an example)
- List of tables, figures, etc.
- Numbered sections – these should include an initial statement of project aims, a short statement of major findings and recommendations and then detailed descriptions of relevant literature, chosen methodology with justification, data collected, analysis, conclusions and probably reflections
- List of references
- Additional bibliography, if needed
- Appendices.

Style should be clear. You will normally be expected to use academic concepts wherever appropriate, but avoid any unnecessary jargon. Equally, you need to avoid sounding over-colloquial and 'chatty'. A report should be 'considered and careful' in its expression. In particular, do not make unsupported assertions. It should always be clear how your results are derived, or upon what evidence you are basing your statements. (Where there are shortcomings in your evidence and you need to make assumptions, you should say so clearly and discuss any resulting limitations to your conclusions.)

It will be much easier for your reader to absorb your developing argument if you give a short introduction to each section. This should clarify the structure of what you are about to write, and make it easier to grasp your arguments as they are reached.

Large chunks of text can be hard to read, so it helps to include relevant diagrams and tables at appropriate points. This breaks up the text, and is easier for the reader than having to turn repeatedly between text and appendices. (Very detailed or complex diagrams, tables or other information should be included as an appendix – it would interrupt your argument if included in the main text, and only a few of your readers may want to have that level of detail.)

Errors in spelling and grammar can make your meaning unclear, and additionally will make people less likely to believe you know what you are writing about! It is important to check what you have written – use the checks on your PC, and if you are worried that this will not be enough, find a competent friend to read it through as well. Double-check that you have entered figures in tables correctly. It is very easy to make errors that can alter the whole meaning of the table.

You can further improve the impression created by your report by using good quality paper, and thinking about fonts, graphics, use of colour and binding. If a particular binding is specified, make sure that you arrange for this in good time. If there is no specification, think carefully about the best way of presenting your report. Assessments of work are subjective. While content is crucial, presentation can have a strong influence on the mark you receive.

If you do all this and allow yourself sufficient time (twice as long as you imagine you can possibly need) for drafting, your finished dissertation/report can be one of the most satisfying things you have done. It will have uses as an exhibit of your competence in a number of areas when you are seeking employment or a competence-based professional qualification and it may be a source of articles should you wish to start writing for a wider audience. The process of producing it will have developed skills that will be vital in many of the jobs for which you are likely to apply. May I wish you success in your endeavour!

## SUMMARY

This chapter has argued the following:

- Work in organisations is increasingly carried out in task or project groups.
- Project management, whether in employment or for projects you are required to do as a student, draws on almost all the skills covered in this book.
- Group projects need to be very carefully managed.
- Clarity of objectives is essential and topic choice should be approached as soon as feasible.
- Through iteration you should aim to select a topic that meets course requirements, is interesting and, if you have a client organisation, meets client needs.
- Detailed project planning is essential and cannot be undertaken until you have a clear idea of how you will proceed and the data that will be required.
- Networks, critical paths, milestones and bar charts are invaluable aids.
- Negotiating access is time-consuming and needs to be done with care, making clear what you want and why and what benefit there will be for the organisation. You need to do this in a way which reinforces your credibility.

■ Progress should be monitored carefully and corrective steps taken as soon as any delay occurs – optimism is not enough.

■ Drafting should start early, allowing time for insights from drafting to influence data collection. Ongoing redrafting will reduce the pressures of producing a final report.

■ The final report should be clear, well presented and in appropriate style, format and binding.

■ Project work presents major challenges, but can be a source of substantial learning and satisfaction.

## Further information

■ Bell, J. (1999) *Doing your Research Project*, 3rd edn, Open University Press.

■ Bryman, A. (2001) *Social Research Methods*, Oxford University Press.

■ Gill, J. and Johnson, P. (1997) *Research Methods for Manager*, 2nd edn, Paul Chapman Publishing.

■ Howard, K. and Peters, J. (1990) 'Managing management research', *Management Decision*, 28: 5. This special issue provides a clear, fairly brief coverage of different types of management research, what is involved and a short but useful bibliography.

■ Howard, K. and Sharp, J.A. (1996) *The Management of a Student Research Project*, 2nd edn, Gower. This is aimed at all types of research, not just management, and covers planning, data collection and analysis in far more detail than is possible here.

■ Jankowicz, A.D. (2000) *Business Research Projects*, 3rd edn, Business Press.

■ Saunders, M., Lewis, P. and Thornhill, A. (2003) *Research Methods for Business Students*, 3rd edn, Financial Times Pitman Publishing. This provides an excellent and more detailed treatment of the topic than is possible here, with useful material on the data-collection methods you are most likely to use in this sort of research and on analysing both quantitative and qualitative data. It also includes a number of case studies.

■ White, B. (2003) *Dissertation Skills for Business and Management Students*, Thomson Learning.

# Conclusions

# Conclusions

## Organisational change and graduate recruitment

Within the UK and globally organisations are undergoing dramatic change and re-structuring, employees are encouraged to be enterprising subjects - more self reliant, risk taking and responsible (du Gay, 1996). There may be uncertainty about future advancement or a clear career path, employees require to plan what they want and where they want to be and to have thought about their personal career motivations.

Employees and managers require to be flexible and adaptable, to be able to cope with change and new approaches to learning and development which may include CPD. In MDP2 we discussed Goleman's (1998) Emotional Intelligence (EI), as a requisite for all future managers distinguishing outstanding performers in organisations. The essential EI competencies relate to mastering the skills of self-awareness, social awareness, self-management, relationship management.

Within this changing organisational context Performance Management is central to organisational effectiveness. This process involves reviewing and reflecting on the business, team and individual competences and Personal Development Plans (PDPs). A variety of tools/ approaches may be significant in enabling a prospective employee to be successful in the workplace and critical reflection has been identified as important in the current organisational climate.

## MDP and Graduate Selection

Graduate Recruiters frequently expect graduates to have acquired a good degree and have obtained relevant work experience. In addition employers have identified competency frameworks for selection which may include communication, teamwork/ collaboration, planning and organising, analytical thinking and problem solving, personal effectiveness, research, managing information, information technology and numerical interpretation.

Students require to have identified these skills, reflected on how they have been developed, providing specific examples including behaviours used. The ability to translate what you have learnt at University into a meaningful and relevant narrative relating your r knowledge and skills to relevant personal awareness is crucial.

Selection for graduate programmes now frequently involves a more complex selection process which may involve an individual interview, panel interview, psychometric tests and assessment centre team working activities. Many organisations in all sectors now recognise the importance of person organisational fit and organisational team fit alongside individual job knowledge/ skills. Students when making career choices should consider the type of organisation they want to work in, research the organisation, reflect on their individual values and attitudes and their significance for 'organisational fit' (Johnston & Watson, 2006).

Personal Development Planning and reflection in MDP2 and 3 should have assisted you in preparing your CV and recording specific examples of competencies. Several of the examples which we used were adapted from graduate application forms.

Several examples in MDP1 include the Learning Diary, Team Working and  Presentation Skills.

In MDP2  Reflection –Entrepreneurship and leadership, role-plays  and team working.

In MDP3 you will have the opportunity to engage in a range of activities which include research, managing information, project management and team working. You should ensure that you record your reflections in your personal portfolio.

## The Careers Service and MDP

As you move into 3rd year, and so nearer the end of your degree, the concept of (your) employability becomes more and more important. In the Careers Service our contact with employers shows us how impressed they are with the Management Development Programme and we also know that what you gain from MDP will be extremely valuable in all employment sectors and in all sizes of employers. It is giving you the perfect opportunity not only to develop a package of skills which employers want but also to be able to provide the evidence of these skills on CVs, application forms and at interviews and assessment centres. If you still need to be convinced about that, have a look at Skills Employers Want (http://www.strath.ac.uk/careers/skills/) on the Careers Service website – you can see very clear matches between those skills and the ones you develop through MDP.

Equally importantly, MDP is providing you with the tools to help you manage your own career, to make decisions about what you want to do and where and how you see your career developing. Employability is defined as : 'a set of achievements – skills, understandings and personal attributes – that make graduates more likely to gain employment and be successful in their chosen occupations, which benefits themselves, the workforce, the community and the economy' (Yorke, 2004, reissued 2006). As SBS graduates, with the benefit of MDP, you will be among these employable graduates wherever your life after Strathclyde takes you!

If you would like to discuss any of the issues around your own career planning, contact the Careers Service Information Point on 0141 548 4320 to make an appointment to see one of the Careers Advisers who work with SBS students and graduates. And for further information about the Careers Service, see www.strath.ac.uk/careers .

## Psychometric assessment

Many employers use psychometrics to assess candidates' competence in the skills and qualities that are needed in the job. Sometimes employers use tests at the early stages of the process to decide who they are going to interview and sometimes tests are administered at the final stages as part of an Assessment Centre.

The Careers Service has a wide range of resources to help you prepare for these assessments. For information on the wide range of on line and paper resources available to help you prepare look at http://www.strath.ac.uk/careers/apply/

Practice is vital if you are to perform well in these tests and there are several ways in which you can gain experience including regular test sessions held in the Careers Service.  For example numerical reasoning tests usually require the use of elementary numerical skills and are not in any way related to Advanced Maths!  Brushing up on such topics as ratios. times tables etc can make a  difference to your result. Check out the web resources and visit the Careers Service

Resource Centre on Level 5, Livingstone Tower to use reference books and workbooks or to make an appointment with an adviser if you have particular concerns.

## Employers and MDP

The following employers have all been involved with MDP and the selection of statements reflect their views of the value of MDP for students especially in relation to employment opportunities. Recent graduates from Strathclyde are working in these organisations.

### Procter & Gamble

P&G's edge over competition, the advantage that's hardest to duplicate, is P&G People. When we are inspired and at our best, when we are growing as individuals, collaborating as teams or leading as owners of our business, we are unstoppable. This level of inspired performance is crucial to P&G's ability to consistently sustain growth over time and is the key reason why we strive for hiring the best, investing in talented people and developing them to their maximum potential.

It doesn't matter whether you are interested in Marketing, Sales, Finance, Information Decision Solutions or any of the other careers at P&G, the Management Development program is a great start. A chance to develop key management skills like Leadership, Decision Making and Entrepreneurship through experience and reflection. It is these skills that through P&G's promote from within policy could take you to the very top. Read about the drivers of success at P&G and how to succeed. www.pgcareers.com is the key website to use.

### Deloitte & Touche

Deloitte & Touche is one of the leading professional services firms worldwide and as part of our strategy we are constantly looking to recruit the brightest and best graduates in the UK as we understand they are the future of our practice. We believe that it's our people that make the difference to the way we work with our clients. We have a passion for commitment - we're approachable, we're straight-talking and our integrity is never compromised.

The Management Development programme serves to provide skills to students outwith the ordinary academic syllabus. It is skills such as these that we, along with other employers, look for and expect in our graduate recruits. Our day-to-day business involves interacting within teams and with other people, both colleagues and clients, and the ability of our people to work well and develop within these environments is crucial.

We support the Management Development programme because we believe it is an effective and forward-thinking initiative and look forward to meeting and working with the undergraduates during the coming years in relating the programme to working life in our firm.

### Ernst & Young

The most value we can give to our clients is our people. That's why we endorse the values of the Management Development Programme and want to re-enforce the message that your Lecturers pass on to you. Teaming, communication, decision making, integrity, commercial awareness; these are attributes that will make you stand out from your peers in the graduate recruitment market and will make you more employable. We will be involved with you throughout the semester in MDP3 and so do come and talk to us and find out more about life at Ernst & Young.

We would urge you to participate fully in the MDP3 sessions and practice your skills so that you can be as prepared as possible to get that Graduate position in one of the most successful professional services firms in the world. Develop your Employability!

## Accenture

The Management Development Programme is an innovative, informative and practical scheme offering you the chance to learn skills in key areas of management. You will also learn softer skills such as problem solving, adaptability, initiative, teamwork, effective influencing and creativity. These are all qualities we most value in our graduate recruits.

At Accenture, from the moment you join, we offer an exceptional training programme to promote the advancement and expansion of your skills, so that we can continue to deliver original solutions to our clients. The MDP programme is a great stepping stone in your development, giving you that head start - and making you much more valuable to graduate recruiters like us.

We are one of the world's leading management consulting, technology services and outsourcing companies - where we help our clients become high-performance businesses by delivering innovation

In 2006-7 500 MDP3 students participated in an Accenture case study assessment centre exercise in their group sessions: this was facilitated by SBS academic tutors and two Accenture consultants. Their feedback highlighted the strengths of our students.

'Both of us were very impressed with the quality of the presentations and the volume of creative answers put forward throughout the week. At Accenture we receive thousands of applications from graduates every year and the skills covered in the MDP will help you to set yourself above those other applicants.'

## BAE Systems

BAE Systems is a global company engaged in the development, delivery and support of advanced defence and aerospace systems in the air, on land and at sea.

Project Management, Commercial, HR and Accounts & Finance are some of the business functions that underpin our continued success and ensure that we deliver projects on time and within budget. The Management Development Programme at the University of Strathclyde provides students with key skills and awareness of these important business concepts, as well as assisting in the transition from university to working life. As an organisation BAE Systems aims to be at the forefront of the defence and aerospace industry, and as such we are looking to recruit the best graduates to maintain this position. There is a strong belief that the business awareness gained through the MDP enables graduates to fall into this category.

## References

Du Gay, P (1996) Consumption and Identity at Work, London,Sage

Goleman, D (1998) Working with emotional Intelligence. London;Bloomsbury.

Yorke, M. (2004) Employability in Higher Education:  what it is and what it is not. York: the Learning and Teaching Support Network.

Johnston, B. and Watson, A. (2006) Employability: Approaches to developing student career awareness and reflective practice in undergraduate business studies. In Higher Education and Working Life, Eds Tynjälä, P, Välimaa J, Boulton-Lewis, G. Elsevier, Oxford/Earli.

# Index